WONDER BOY

WONDER BOY

TONY HSIEH,
ZAPPOS,
and the MYTH of
HAPPINESS
in SILICON VALLEY

ANGEL AU-YEUNG and DAVID JEANS

 HENRY HOLT AND COMPANY NEW YORK

Henry Holt and Company
Publishers since 1866
120 Broadway
New York, New York 10271
www.henryholt.com

Henry Holt® and ⑪® are registered trademarks of Macmillan Publishing
Group, LLC.

Library of Congress Cataloging-in-Publication Data is available.

ISBN: 9781250829092

Our books may be purchased in bulk for promotional, educational,
or business use. Please contact your local bookseller or the Macmillan
Corporate and Premium Sales Department at (800) 221-7945,
extension 5442, or by e-mail at
MacmillanSpecialMarkets@macmillan.com.

First Edition 2023

Designed by Meryl Sussman Levavi

Map by Gene Thorp

Printed in the United States of America

1   3   5   7   9   10   8   6   4   2

For Grandad, "bula bula"
—David

For 嬤嬤
—Angel

Sure the world breeds monsters,
but kindness grows just as wild.

—Mary Karr

CONTENTS

PROLOGUE

Elizabeth Pezzello had been getting ready to leave shortly after 3 a.m. when she realized something was wrong. Dressed in sportswear, her blond ponytail swinging behind her, she and a half dozen others milled about the house, preparing to depart for an airport a few miles away on Connecticut's southern shore, where a private jet was waiting for them.

A light wind had been blowing in from the river across New London on the frigid November evening, and lines of manicured lawns had stiffened in the cold. Few clouds obscured the sky over Long Island Sound to the south, leaving the rows of homes along Pequot Avenue exposed to the night air. In just a few hours, the sun would climb above the industrial smokestacks across the river in Groton, illuminating the waterfront view afforded to the tony homes of the seashore.

Outside the home at 500 Pequot Avenue, three vehicles idled, waiting for the party to emerge. But the most important person of the group, the person paying for everyone's salaries, the private jet, and the chauffeurs, still wasn't up. A few days earlier, his dog, a fluffy white mutt named Blizzy, had died suddenly, and he had been in a depressive spiral since. For much of the evening, the man had been inhaling laughing gas from a whipped-cream canister, as if drinking from a water bottle, and after an argument with his former girlfriend, Rachael, she had ordered him out of the house until they left for the airport. He could have retreated to one of the vehicles, even a hotel nearby where other members of his staff were staying. But in his stupor, he had insisted on a storage shed attached to the home. Those in the house had relented, bowing again to his irrational demands, which had become common behavior for him. In the shed, he was exposed to the cold.

Like many people the man surrounded himself with, Elizabeth had only met him a few months before. He had spent tens of millions of dollars on mansions in the Utah ski-resort town Park City to house a growing orbit of followers, many lured by the promise of riches. Elizabeth was one of them, and had worked her way into his inner circle. As his assistant, she now controlled his schedule and much of his communication, including contact with old friends; some had tried unsuccessfully to get in touch after hearing troubling stories about the man. Elizabeth was one of the few people responsible for spending Tony's money, and had found a role for her fiancé, Brett, who had taken to doing whatever their boss told him to do in return for a handsome salary. Together, they had convinced the man to pay for the group to go on a Hawaiian getaway, starting with the private jet waiting for them this morning.

The tagalongs that evening hadn't been limited to new arrivals in the man's life. Along with Rachael, there was his brother, Andy, who had been by his side almost every day for the past few months. Two years younger, Andy was by every definition a counterweight to his brother: outgoing, fast-talking, gregarious, and with a hint of arrogance. He had worked for his brother at one point years ago, before an unsuccessful attempt to launch his own tech startup. But as the man amassed an almost billion-dollar fortune and became a best-selling author, Andy lived in his shadow, and until recently the brothers hadn't had much of a relationship.

Andy was sleeping inside the house while Brett stayed up to check on the man. They had communicated by writing messages on Post-it notes and sticking them outside the shed door. Responding to the man's demands, Brett had brought him laughing gas, marijuana, a lighter, pizza, a blanket, and candles. Lots of candles.

It had been no easy task. The man had been lying on the concrete surrounded by naked flames. At one point another assistant had found the blanket covering him starting to burn from contact with a candle, and told the man to extinguish it. The assistant had opened the shed door a short time later to see him lighting a Ziploc bag on fire. "You're going to smoke yourself out," the assistant had said. "That's poison." The man had incoherently mumbled back. At one point, the assistant had found a propane space heater and dragged it into the shed, placing it inside the door.

Now with everyone ready to leave, a more terrifying scene had begun to unfold. A carbon monoxide alarm was shrieking. Smoke was billowing from the cracks in the door frame. And the door was locked.

Elizabeth dialed 911. "What's the location of your emergency?" an operator's voice crackled over the phone.

"500 Pequot Avenue," Elizabeth responded calmly. "We need help as soon as possible, someone's locked in a room with a fire."

"There's a fire?"

"Yes."

"Where in the room are they?" the operator said. "Where in the building are they?"

"It's a house, it's a house."

"How many people are trapped?"

"Just one."

In the background, muffled shouts were becoming clearer. Elizabeth turned away from the phone and called out, "Rachael, Rachael, they really need help; is there a code to the storage room?" referring to the lock on the door. A moment later Elizabeth yelled to someone else in the house, *"Ten-fourteen!"*

"Elizabeth, has the person barricaded themself?" the operator said.

"Yes, yes, yes, yes," she replied.

The cloud of smoke was inundating the shed, growing in size with every second that passed. Elizabeth could hear repeated thudding in the distance; someone was trying to break open the door.

"Why did they barricade themself? Are they trying to harm themself?" the operator said.

Elizabeth was losing her composure. "I don't know, I don't know, I don't know."

"How old is the person?"

About forty-five years old, she said, and added, "Please hurry up, this is urgent, this is really urgent . . . this is so bad."

Fire sirens were already wailing through the streets of New London, piercing the silence over the hamlet, when another call came into the dispatch office. It was from another woman at the house.

"There's a person barricaded," the woman said into the phone. "We can't get in."

She told the operator she was a nurse who had been traveling with the trapped man, and she'd been responsible for administering an IV drip to him. She said they were supposed to leave for a flight in a few minutes.

"We are not getting a response from him," she told the operator, her words rushing out.

"Who is *he*?" the operator said.

The woman paused. "Um, his name is Tony."

■ ■ ■

More than a week would pass before the townspeople of New London—and then the world—would learn the identity of the man trapped within the shed outside a nondescript home in a Connecticut town. When fire-fighters charged into the cloud of smoke and flames engulfing the shed, they found him lying faceup on a filthy blanket with his right arm across his chest, surrounded by singed pool equipment and camping chairs, unresponsive and without a pulse.

The sight was an unrecognizable departure from the public image of Tony Hsieh. For years, Tony had been the face of Zappos, America's most popular online shoe seller, and had become the shining example of an unconventional business leader who cared more about helping others find happiness—especially his own employees—than profit margins or meeting quarterly earnings forecasts.

He wasn't a household name like Elon Musk or Jeff Bezos—arguably his equals in intellect, business acumen, and willingness to take risks—but he was one of the most consequential tech leaders of our time. The son of Taiwanese immigrants, he had graduated from Harvard in the 1990s before selling his first company to Microsoft for $265 million at the age of twenty-four. He then invested in and later took over as CEO at Zappos, where he played an integral role in writing the first rule books of e-commerce by introducing free shipping and a no-questions-asked return policy long before consumers were comfortable with buying things online. His costly, customer-focused risks were validated when Bezos himself led Amazon's charge to buy Zappos for $1.2 billion in 2009. "Zappos is a company I have long admired," Bezos said at the time. "I've seen a lot of companies and I have never seen a company with a culture like Zappos."

But being a tech leader was merely his conduit. What made Tony Hsieh a rare icon was his stated desire to advance the human condition. Countless people from Silicon Valley to New York and Las Vegas had serendipitous meetings with Tony, often over shots of his signature drink, the digestif Fernet-Branca, that led to life-changing experiences. Whether he was sporting a mohawk or a shaved head, Tony's image was plastered across magazine profiles, on documentaries, and on television during talks with Oprah and Barbara Walters. His stoic expression—sometimes broken by a cautious smile framed by dimples—was synonymous with the image of a genius focused on inspiring others.

Through a best-selling autobiography, *Delivering Happiness: A Path to Profits, Passion, and Purpose*, Tony devised a revolutionary way to run corporations—by focusing on your employees and ensuring they are happy, you'll have happy customers, and then your profits will soar. The book described his own search to understand how the science of happiness could be applied to improving the lives of employees, and how, by focusing on other people's happiness, you might just increase your own. A *New York Times* bestseller, it propelled Tony to the global speaking circuit. He toured the late-night TV shows espousing a template for achieving happiness, shared the stage with Bill Clinton, and befriended celebrities like Ashton Kutcher, Richard Branson, and the singer Jewel.

Having achieved the height of American success, Tony then plowed his fortune—almost half a billion dollars—into building a downtown Las Vegas neighborhood that he would develop into an entrepreneur's utopia, from where he envisioned more success stories like Zappos would grow. Starting in 2012, stories of his unrivaled generosity and miracle-making trickled from his new community. There was Natalie Young, a chef who had been in recovery when a chance encounter with Tony at a bar ended with him agreeing to give her the money to start a restaurant. Rehan Choudhry, a talent booker at one of the Las Vegas casinos, had always wanted to run his own music festival, a dream that became a thirty-thousand-person reality after meeting Tony. And there was Maggie Hsu, who watched Tony give a talk at Harvard Business School when she was earning her MBA, then cold-emailed him for career advice. He convinced her to come to Las Vegas and she eventually became his chief of staff. Newspapers and magazines dubbed him everything from "Mayor of Downtown Las Vegas" to tone-deaf descriptions such as "a young Buddha," with the text run alongside photos of him wearing his signature Mona Lisa smile.

His story also defied what it meant to be an Asian man in America, and he eluded stereotypes placed on him by society. From an early age, Tony wanted to be seen as something more than a quiet Asian brainiac with thick glasses. In an era when Asian men were depicted in popular culture as geeks who loved mathematics and were rarely seen in the C-suites of public companies, let alone Silicon Valley startups, Tony broke through with his life story and entered the pop culture psyche—a dynamic captured time and again through his career.

There's a photo taken at Microsoft's headquarters in Seattle, a year before Zappos was sold to Amazon. Bill Gates is standing in front of a cascade of brown boxes, flanked by six individuals, one of whom is Tony. Everyone else is white—executives and CEOs from Sears, eBay, Barnes & Noble—and wearing suits. Tony, meanwhile, appears years, even decades younger, relaxed in jeans and an untucked shirt. He looks unfazed by his company. In another photo, he is seen on a casino floor, making a face at the camera next to a grinning Jared Kushner and Ivanka Trump, who is eating a hot dog. "He wasn't just a tech entrepreneur who became cool, he was an Asian male who became cool," said Jen Louie, a former colleague of Tony's at Zappos. "He broke through the bamboo ceiling."

Renown and riches never seemed to cloud Tony's desire to be a man of the people, either. Since coming into boundless wealth at such an early age, money had empowered his brilliant ideas and let him build companies, and then an entire neighborhood, from the ground up. Rather than live in a sprawling mansion in San Francisco, in a Manhattan penthouse, or on a Caribbean island alongside other corporate leaders, Tony built a trailer park in his Las Vegas neighborhood, choosing to live alongside friends, a pet alpaca, and his dog. Just as Peter Pan had found limitless wonderment in Neverland—no rules, judgment, or fear of growing up— Tony embodied what it meant to live with unlimited freedom long into adulthood.

His childlike curiosity also illustrated how, in a world where business leaders followed bullet points and their guidance, Tony provided a model of how to throw away the corporate script to show the world that, beyond profit margins and earnings reports, companies—and communities—could thrive on happiness. He was a figure for a millennial generation in search of an alternative to the mantra of living to work.

But beneath his public message of happiness, his private search for inner peace remained out of reach, and at some point he drifted from the figurative mooring posts of the communities he had built. After a series of public relations hiccups, tragedies—including three suicides within his Las Vegas community—and internal issues with his style of management at Zappos, Tony became less visible as the face of the company and in his neighborhood. His increasing use of recreational drugs—whether fistfuls of psilocybin mushrooms at his trailer park or MDMA at the Burning Man festival—rarely alarmed those he kept close. Instead, they shrugged it off as something he did to expand his thinking, and to smooth and then deepen his connections with others. In turn, he retreated deeper into his trailer park, where those present seemed to orbit around his cult of personality.

In the months before the COVID-19 pandemic swept the United States in 2020, Tony was introduced to ketamine, the popular party drug typically used to tranquilize horses, and it uncorked long-held insecurities and breaks with reality that led him to act in ways that some saw aligned with psychosis. He started to claim that he devised an algorithm to bring about world peace, that he figured out how to cure COVID-19, and that he no longer had to urinate because his body could recycle water. After months of drug use caused his behavior to spill into his public life in Las Vegas, Tony's friends persuaded him to check into a rehab facility in Park City. It was the first of multiple failed attempts to get Tony sober, including botched interventions and attempts by his family to install a conservatorship. Each of these efforts was disrupted by a growing faction of people that were on Tony's payroll, some who enabled his continued drug use and others who indulged in his delusions.

After leaving rehab, he didn't return to Las Vegas, and instead stayed in Park City, Utah, the ritzy mountain ski town, where he invited a cast of people to join him. While they lived large in the elaborate mansions he often paid for, some of them struck multimillion-dollar deals with a man descending further toward a fatal end. By the time he arrived in Connecticut with a small contingent of these followers, Tony had cut ties with most of his old friends and members of his family until he'd wandered so far from reality that he was left surrounded only by people on his payroll.

■ ■ ■

On that cold November night, Tony's friends and family, even the firefighters who saved him, were optimistic that he would survive. After he was pulled from the shed, his body had, remarkably, not been burned in the fire, save for some damaged tissue on his shoulder. Most of the heat had been concentrated above him after the propane tank had caught fire and sent a whoosh of ignited gas through the shed.

But what they hadn't immediately considered was the extent of internal damage Tony had sustained inhaling a cloud of carbon monoxide, starving his organs and finally his brain of oxygen. Even if he had survived, he would never have been the same.

On November 27, the day after Thanksgiving, Tony's family turned off his life support at Bridgeport Hospital. News of his death flooded the internet, with thousands of messages and memories posted by people from Bill Clinton to Ivanka Trump to Jeff Bezos, offering a public mourning not seen for a business leader since the passing of Steve Jobs a decade before. The sight of his awkward smile—shared thousands of times across social media, in newspapers, and on television—crystallized his image of an uncommonly beloved tech entrepreneur, one who had changed the lives of countless people, from business leaders to workers in his call center, and strangers he'd met at the bar.

As the tributes flowed in, we were working as business reporters for *Forbes* when a number of obvious questions quickly emerged for us. Angel had covered the lives of billionaires for years, and David had a focus on investigating tech companies. We were immediately perplexed by how a certifiable tech leader—the beloved face of a beloved brand, no less—had died in a fire in a nondescript New England town, of all places. Were there suspicious circumstances surrounding the incident? Was it a suicide? Why hadn't anyone been able to help him, and what had led

Tony to this fate? It was hard to stomach the contrast of Tony's mantra of happiness with the tragedy of him dying alone, surrounded by flames.

A week after his death, we published the first article that documented in detail how Tony, a man of boundless wealth and resources, had met such an unexpected and tragic end, describing how a COVID-era spiral with drugs had untethered him from reality, and how he was surrounded by people who had done more to enable him than help him. It included a message from the singer Jewel, a close friend of Tony's who had visited him in Park City and prophesied his fate in a letter, warning him: "The people you are surrounding yourself with are either ignorant or willing to be complicit in you killing yourself."

But we kept speaking to more people who had known Tony—from Park City, from Las Vegas, and then as far back as his childhood—who led us to believe that his story was more than an oft-told rise-and-fall tale, or that of an eccentric billionaire who'd once again flown too close to the sun. For Angel, born to Chinese parents who fled the turmoil of communism and gave up everything for her and her two sisters to move to the United States and chase the elusive American dream, she understood what it meant to be on the receiving end of those sacrifices—and the pressures to succeed because of it. She also came into Tony's story with a deep understanding of the stereotypes that are often placed on Asian Americans, and what it takes—and costs—to break those assumptions. And David, who'd cut his teeth as a police reporter in Australia and had covered humanity in its best and worst forms, was immediately drawn to seek an understanding of the dynamic between Tony and those around him. He'd traveled widely before arriving in the United States and took a broader, more cynical view of Tony's effort to manufacture a world for people largely based on financial incentives. By the end of his life, Tony had fallen victim to the trappings linked to American success, leaving little room for happiness.

Together, we found that Tony's story exploited some uncomfortable truths about the opposing goals of wealth and happiness. It highlighted how one person's generosity can motivate greed in others, and how those with good intentions can stray from their moral center when the promise of riches appears. And finally, it touched on how inner peace can remain out of reach as long as there is enough money to obscure the dangers of mental health problems and addiction.

Our reporting took us first to Connecticut, then Las Vegas, New York, Park City, and then San Francisco, from where we sourced police reports, school yearbooks, court documents, photos, and financial records. Across hundreds of hours of interviews, we spoke to more than 150 people to reveal a never-before-seen look at how Tony Hsieh had changed the lives of others through every chapter of his own. Since he was a boy, we found, Tony had been running from the life that was expected of him, and searching for the life he dreamed of. "There was some prototype in his head that he desperately wanted to achieve," a childhood friend of his told us.

In the pages that follow, we've sought to document how a boy of genius intellect, born a first-generation misfit—intellectually, emotionally, and racially—searched for his place in a world where success and happiness were not supposed to be mutually exclusive goals for someone who looked like him. We've detailed the tragedy of a man who craved companionship and human connection coming into wealth that he was not equipped to handle, distorting his relationships with friends, family, and himself. And, above all else, we've tried to illustrate a cautionary tale of how a brilliant man could destroy himself over time, armed with wealth that fostered his own worst impulses and those of people around him. In the end, were those surrounding him blind to, or complicit with, his own self-destruction until it was too late?

Starting with the night of the fire, we found more questions than answers.

■ ■ ■

Andy was standing by as firefighters pulled Tony's unconscious body from the wreckage of the shed. Above him, two floodlights fixed to the roof of the house shone through the white smoke blowing around the home, illuminating the scene below. Guided by his flashlight, a firefighter walked into the house to assess the damage from the fire in the attached shed. A police officer watched as paramedics secured Tony in the stretcher.

When he was a boy, Andy had helped his brother launch one of his first entrepreneurial endeavors, selling custom-made buttons through the classified ads in a boys' magazine. When the workload had become too great, Andy recruited their younger brother, David, to help out. It wouldn't be the last time the younger brothers worked for the golden Hsieh child, but as they grew up, their relationship was distant at best. At one point, Andy had become estranged entirely from Tony. David, meanwhile, had lived modestly, eschewing any notion that his brother was a billionaire. Outside of scheduled, stage-managed events, the brothers didn't spend time together later in life.

It was a familial relationship that few understood. So when Andy had arrived in Park City months before, it came as a surprise to some who knew he hadn't had much of a relationship with Tony for years. There were murmurs that he was returning to take advantage of Tony during a low point.

But unlike David, who had largely stayed clear of Park City and Tony, here was Andy, by his brother's side. Andy repeatedly asserted that he was there on behalf of the family to make sure people weren't taking advantage of his brother. After all, it was Andy who had provided updates to family and friends like Jewel, and had discussed potentially arranging a conservatorship for his brother. At times he had told these people he was at a loss for what to do.

Privately, Andy had also negotiated for his brother to pay him a $1 million salary. He had asked for millions more in a series of proposed business deals. And like others, he quickly found himself doing what he could to stay in his brother's good graces, which, among other things, meant satisfying demands for more laughing gas.

It further muddied the dynamic between the two brothers. What had driven Andy to reenter Tony's life after nearly a decade? Why hadn't they spoken for so long? And what had brought Andy to be with his brother on that fateful night? Was it concern for his brother's well-being? Or had he assumed an obedient role alongside the countless followers chasing Tony's riches?

As fire crews hosed down the shed, Andy walked into the light, stopping a few feet from the stretcher. Wearing a backpack and a hooded puffer jacket, Andy stared for a moment at his brother's unconscious body lying before him. Then, without looking away, he slipped his hand into his pocket and pulled out a mobile phone. As paramedics pushed the stretcher away, Andy held up the phone in front of his brother's body and started filming.

■ ■ ■

WONDER BOY

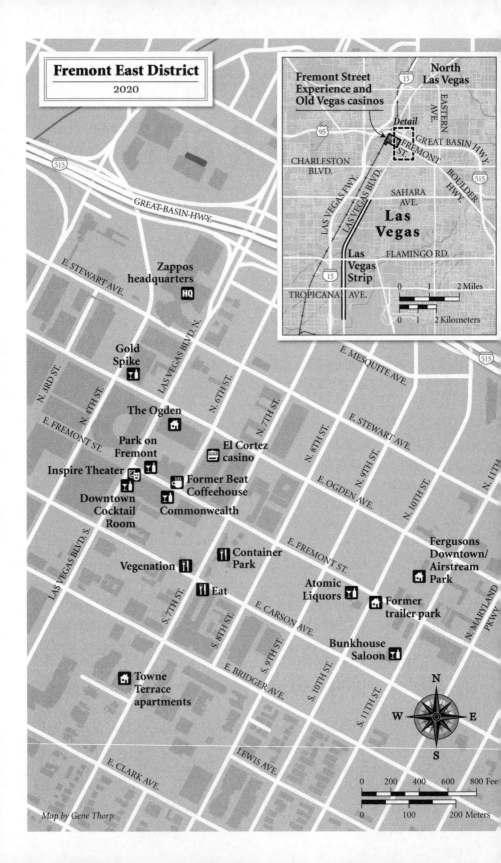

Fremont East District
2020

Fremont Street Experience and Old Vegas casinos

North Las Vegas

15

EASTERN AVE.

Detail

GREAT BASIN HWY.

95

FREMONT ST.

CHARLESTON BLVD.

LAS VEGAS FWY.

LAS VEGAS BLVD.

BOULDER HWY.

515

SAHARA AVE.

Las Vegas

FLAMINGO RD.

Las Vegas Strip

15

TROPICANA AVE.

0   1   2 Miles

0   1   2 Kilometers

GREAT-BASIN-HWY.

515

E. STEWART AVE.

Zappos headquarters

HQ

LAS VEGAS BLVD. N.

E. MESQUITE AVE.

Gold Spike

N. 3RD ST.

N. 4TH ST.

N. 6TH ST.

N. 7TH ST.

E. STEWART AVE.

N. 8TH ST.

N. 9TH ST.

N. 10TH ST.

N. 11TH ST.

515

The Ogden

E. FREMONT ST.

Park on Fremont

El Cortez casino

Inspire Theater

E. OGDEN AVE.

Former Beat Coffeehouse

Downtown Cocktail Room

Commonwealth

Vegenation

Container Park

E. FREMONT ST.

Fergusons Downtown/ Airstream Park

N. MARYLAND PKWY

Eat

Atomic Liquors

Former trailer park

LAS VEGAS BLVD. S.

S. 7TH ST.

S. 8TH ST.

S. 9TH ST.

E. CARSON AVE.

S. 10TH ST.

S. 11TH ST.

Bunkhouse Saloon

N

Towne Terrace apartments

E. BRIDGER AVE.

W   E

S

E. CLARK AVE.

LEWIS AVE.

0   200   400   600   800 Feet

0   100   200 Meters

Map by Gene Thorp

CHAPTER 1

THE GOLDEN CHILD

Tony would have been the first to admit that as a child he was obsessed with one thing: making money. Though his family was comfortably middle-class—his father, Richard, worked at Chevron, and his mother, Judy, was a psychologist—he understood early on that money equaled liberation. "To me," he later recalled of his childhood, "money meant that later on in life I would have the freedom to do whatever I wanted."

In his early years, this took form as a mildly successful string of garage sales, and then some failed ventures—including the sale of Christmas cards to neighbors one year—before he joined the workforce as a newspaper boy. His route would begin and end at the same address: 28 Coast Oak Way, Mont Marin, the two-story house where Tony and his two younger brothers grew up. About twenty miles north of the Golden Gate Bridge, the sliver of brick and weatherboard homes of Mont Marin were within the sunny enclave of the city of San Rafael, an eternal snapshot of Americana. The Hsiehs, one of the few Asian families in the suburb, lived in a house toward the bottom of the sloping street, surrounded by the rolling greenery of Marinwood and Lucas Valley. Two palm trees stood to one side of the black driveway, swaying tall above the home's terracotta-tiled roof.

Tony—a slight boy with aviator-framed glasses that seemed more suited for a geriatric and took up a third of his tiny face—would pedal through the quiet, winding streets of Mont Marin, past well-groomed front lawns. As he hurled copies of the local newspaper, his haphazard fencing of bangs would flutter in the wind.

It was the mid-1980s, and across the headlines was talk of the burgeoning technology industry that was slowly but surely stretching across the region, from the hills of San Francisco down to the Peninsula and across the expanse of the South Bay. The semiconductor industry had already laid down its roots in the region a decade before, while soon-to-be tech giants like Apple and Oracle were just in their infancy. As one historian put it, the area was encountering its "Big Bang" moment, the fateful turn of events that gave rise to the personal computer and video gaming industries. Venture capital started percolating from the gold mines that those industries became, and that started to lay the very foundations that would cause the explosion of Big Tech.

The types of people who were finding success in Silicon Valley were by definition optimistic and thought outside the box. As it turned out, the boy riding around the streets just north of the Valley was unwittingly learning on his paper route that he already had the DNA for the type of success the headlines wrote about. After adding up his pay, he realized that he was making about $2 an hour. As Tony pedaled around the neighborhood, he realized that he could make the job more favorable. Then he had an epiphany. What if, he thought, he started his own newspaper? That way, he would be the sole beneficiary of the venture, as opposed to what he reasoned was child labor exploitation by the local paper.

He quit the paper route, and the first major phase of his entrepreneurial streak began. He created The Gobbler, twenty pages of stories, word puzzles, and jokes that Tony drew and wrote out himself. Priced at $5 each, Tony had expected that his friends would become his first subscribers. "P.S.: Subscribe to the GOBBLER!" Tony wrote in a middle school classmate's yearbook, viewing a sentimental tradition as an opportunity to conduct business. His parents seemed mildly amused by their son's claim that the newsletter would sell a hundred copies. They were probably even more surprised when, after his first issue, he secured his first advertisement sale from his barber, who agreed to pay $20 for a full-page ad in the second issue.

But he managed to only sell two copies of the second issue, bringing The Gobbler's total circulation to six copies. After failing to recoup costs and find more ad buyers, Tony ended the business. Even so, with one failure behind him, he realized that he had made his *own* money through an idea that *he* had formed, so his curiosity sent him back to the drawing board.

With his younger brother Andy, who was a little less shy but equally small-framed, Tony would spend much of his time poring over *Boys' Life*, a monthly magazine (an offshoot of the Boy Scouts of America) focused on the great outdoors. Though the boys in the pages didn't look like him, it provided a perfect escape. In one issue from 1984, a headline on the cover read, "How Computers Opened a Window on a New World for One Eagle Scout." His favorite part of the magazine was always the classified ads section, which he saw as a catalog of all the "fantastic things that I never even knew existed but knew I had to have one day," he later wrote.

One day, he saw an item that struck the money-obsessed chord in him: a button-making kit for $50. Seeing the promise of profits flash before his eyes, he convinced his parents to "loan" him money to buy the machine, which could convert any photo or piece of paper into a pin-on button. Then he took out an ad himself in another book called *Free Stuff for Kids*. In his advertisement, he offered to make buttons for customers for $1 plus a self-addressed stamped envelope. After doing the math, he calculated he would earn 75 cents on every button sold.

To his parents' surprise, he paid them back within a month and was soon working four to five hours during the weekend to keep up with the orders. Eventually he bought a more automated button-making machine for $300. Through middle school, he made $200 a month—a hefty sum for a teenager in the eighties. The success spawned a tradition of Tony inviting his two younger brothers to be part of his businesses. When Tony graduated, he passed the button-making business to Andy, who then passed it on to their younger brother, Dave. It also seeded another element of his future. "I learned," he wrote later, "that it was possible to run a successful business by mail order, without any face-to-face interaction."

■ ■ ■

Thinking up ways to make money often had more to do with Tony trying to think his way out of the limitations of childhood than it did with becoming an entrepreneur. His parents fostered his efforts, sometimes unintentionally. For his ninth birthday, Tony asked for a crate of earth-worms, with the ambition of becoming the world's largest worm seller. The idea—born out of a book that Tony had read about how, when cut in two, both halves of a worm will regenerate, thereby doubling the number of worms at hand—was light on economic modeling, like whether demand would meet supply. Still, Richard and Judy were encouraging, and drove him to Sonoma to what claimed to be America's biggest worm farm. There they bought a box of mud that was guaranteed to have at least a hundred earthworms squirming within. If he cut them all in half, his product inventory would double. But operating under the ill-conceived notion that feeding the worms raw egg would make them stronger, Tony drowned the dirt in yolk, provided to him by his mother. That attracted birds to the box—a worm's worst nightmare. The next day, when he went to check on the box, not a single worm remained.

Richard and Judy were also there to indulge Tony's garage sales, which only ended when their cache of house junk was exhausted, prompting their boy to convince other friends to hold garage sales at their homes. His parents also listened to his plan to go door-to-door selling Christmas cards to his neighbors after seeing an advertisement in *Boys' Life* during summer vacation. Given that it was August, his next-door neighbor—and first potential customer—told him to come back later in the year.

Richard Hsieh, tall, lanky, and soft-spoken, was a chemical engineer at Chevron who had secured a reputation in his predominantly white neighborhood in Marin County as friendly and welcoming. Kathy Barrass, one of the Hsiehs' neighbors who lived across the street, recalled a conversation with Richard outside her home on Coast Oak Way in which she shared with him that she and her husband had always wanted to visit China. "Richard told me to stay right where I was, and he ran back inside their house," she said. Richard came back out with a travel brochure for China and instructed Kathy to call the number on the flyer. Three weeks later, Kathy and her husband were off on a seven-city tour across China, traveling by boat and plane from Shanghai to Beijing.

Judy Hsieh, a child psychologist, was the kind of mother who would make breakfast and pack lunch bags for Tony and his two younger brothers every morning. The lunches were "insanely healthy," one childhood friend recalled, adding that Tony apparently didn't like them much either—he would often try to trade his lunches for one of his friends' chocolate-frosted Ho Hos. She could also be strict at times, like many mothers, and Tony's childhood friends often found themselves intimidated by Judy's presence, despite her petite stature. "I got the feeling that she always thought I was never quite good enough for Tony," the friend said.

Of the two, Richard was the more gregarious and social parent, and many of Tony's friends later on in life found themselves on the receiving end of his FaceTime calls. But while they may have differed in communication styles, Richard and Judy, both immigrants from Taiwan, had one core goal in common: they had high expectations for their sons. They were "your typical Asian American parents," Tony later said, a title that came with a demanding curriculum and strict confines, both in school and at home. They expected their sons to strive for immense intellect and to have a disciplined work ethic, the kind of progeny who would either become a doctor or get a PhD. The latter was an endeavor they both understood well: Richard earned his PhD in chemical engineering from the University of Illinois Urbana-Champaign, and Judy waited until after the birth of their third and last son, David, to get her PhD in psychology from the California School of Professional Psychology.

Their demands on their children stemmed from a much larger phenomenon affecting a new generation of Asian American children. Richard and Judy had been two among millions of people who arrived in America as part of a massive brain drain from China, prompted by the events that followed World War II. Shortly after Japan surrendered to the Allied powers, General Tsai Lee and Peggy Lee gave birth to Judy, born Shiao-Ling Lee, on December 10, 1945, on the southern coast of China in what is today known as Guangdong Province. Two years later, on December 7, 1947, Chuan-Kang Hsieh, or Richard, was born. Richard and Judy entered a world emerging from the horrors of global warfare, only to grow up in a country where national trepidation would continue. Two opposing factions within China—the Chinese Communist Party and the nationalist Kuomintang— had resumed the final phase of their own decades-long civil war, and the Communists took over mainland China in 1949 to establish the People's Republic of China. The Kuomintang leadership and its loyalists, meanwhile, retreated to the island of Taiwan and built their own government.

In their teens, Richard and Judy independently found their way to

Taiwan, where they would both end up at National Taiwan University (NTU), a prestigious institution in Taipei from which they had an arm's-length view of the tragedies occurring on the mainland. While China endured famine, censorship, violence, and death under Chairman Mao Zedong, the citizens of Taiwan escaped the consequences of the Great Leap Forward and the Cultural Revolution. America, meanwhile, recognized Taiwan as a legitimate government, as that meshed with the U.S. agenda to hinder the communists' growing power.

As the tension between the two Chinese factions continued, Taiwanese intellectuals who wanted to explore and advance their livelihoods felt there was only one place to turn to: Mei Guo, the Mandarin name for America, which translates literally to "beautiful country." Such an opportunity was typically afforded to the best and brightest students from National Taiwan University who were accepted to graduate degree programs in the United States. That journey from NTU figured in the life stories of prominent Taiwanese like Ang Lee, the famed film director, and Min Kao, the co-founder of Garmin. Many graduates went to the University of Illinois Urbana-Champaign, which had a robust program for international Chinese students dating back to the early 1900s. When Richard and Judy arrived in the Urbana-Champaign region at the end of the 1960s, there were three Chinese restaurants, one Asian supermarket, and not much else to welcome the Chinese students. But what the town lacked in accommodations for its Chinese arrivals, it made up for in its role as a gateway toward the American dream of purported success and freedom—an image as ubiquitous here as at other elite schools like Harvard or Yale.

Richard immigrated in 1969, a year after graduating from NTU with a degree in chemical engineering, to pursue his master's and PhD in the same field. Judy, meanwhile, had graduated from NTU a year earlier but would also end up at UIUC, enrolling in the master's program for social work. It was a lonely endeavor for each of them, crossing an ocean and leaving family, friends, and everything else behind. But once at UIUC, the reality of their experience was a country and society reeling from the civil rights movement and the Vietnam War. Race relations were still tense. More often than not, Asian students found themselves striving to fade into the background, to draw less attention to themselves.

Like attracts like, and at UIUC Richard and Judy crossed paths and then fell in love. They both received their master's degrees in 1971 in their respective fields, but Richard continued to pursue his PhD at the university. He became a member of Phi Lambda Upsilon, a chemistry honor society, as well as the American Chemical Society and the American Institute of Chemical Engineers. In 1973, after Richard and Judy married, Richard published his dissertation with the esteemed Charles Eckert as his thesis advisor. Titled "Molecular Thermodynamics and High Pressure Kinetics of Polar Reactions in Solutions," his research received funding from the National Science Foundation and from the U.S. Army Research Office in Durham, North Carolina.

"No man works alone," Richard wrote in the acknowledgments section of his dissertation. "The deepest thanks are due to Dr. C. A. Eckert, not only for his encouragement, advice and assistance, but also for the corrections of poor English, bad grammar, false reasoning and obscurity in the manuscript." He continued, "I must recognize my debt and gratitude to my parents who encouraged and supported their dearest son to pursue his higher education across the Pacific Ocean, and my wife Judy, whose patience and endurance made this work possible."

A few months later, on December 12, 1973, the young couple welcomed Anthony Chia-Hua Hsieh to the world in Urbana, Illinois. With the seeds of their family sown, they were determined to make something of themselves in the foreign but free, generous though sometimes unforgiving, land of America. And just as Richard's parents pushed him to leave his home and his family behind in order to make what was then a fifty-hour flight halfway around the world to pursue his education, he and Judy would push their children to be the best they could be. Their new home was a place of opportunity and prosperity, and as long as you worked hard, seemingly anything could be accomplished.

Two years later, Tony's brother Andrew Chia-Pei Hsieh was born. Their younger brother, David, would arrive seven years later. One of Tony's only memories of Illinois was catching fireflies in jars. "In my mind, I had invented it and no one else had done it before," he later said. When Tony turned five, Richard got a job as an engineer at Chevron on the other side of the country, in Marin County, California. Richard and Judy packed up once more and moved the family out West.

■ ■ ■

Given everything they had endured, Richard and Judy shared a prescription for their children's lives: nothing short of excellence. In practice, this meant an unusual amount of pressure and work, both in school and outside of it. Tony consistently wrestled with these constraints, and made frequent attempts to control his childhood on his own terms.

Among the expectations outlined for him was a requirement for musical excellence, in the name of being well-rounded. Each weekday, if school was in session, he was expected to practice playing his instruments for two hours—thirty minutes each for the piano, violin, trumpet, and French horn. On weekends and during the summer months, Tony was required to practice each instrument for an hour. With four hours supposed to be dedicated to musical progress, this drastically cut into his summer vacation. So Tony came up with a risky scheme that would disappoint his parents and bring punishment if they ever found out. But on the slim chance that the plan succeeded, Tony would have more precious time to enjoy the kind of summer vacation he wanted. He decided to take the chance.

One summer day during middle school, Tony sat in his room and recorded himself playing his instruments. He played hour-long sessions for each instrument, hitting "stop" on the tape recorder once he was done. Then the next morning, as the sun was rising, Tony climbed out of bed and tiptoed down the staircase, mindful not to wake his parents.

Entering the sitting room clutching the tape recorder, he walked over to the piano, placed the recorder above the keys, and hit "play." The sound of his own keystrokes lilted throughout the house. Perhaps the recording would stir his parents awake ever so slightly, only for them to fall back asleep with the warm satisfaction that their son was downstairs, practicing like they had instructed, like he'd said he would. Once the hour-long piano recording finished, Tony trudged back upstairs to his room and, behind a locked door, proceeded to play the recording of his own violin playing. Instead of spending those hours improving a skill that he knew would never become his life's work, Tony instead spent the time reading issues of *Boys' Life*. The ruse was a gamble, and it paid off.

Kathy Barrass remembered hearing the bright notes of the violin and piano floating out into the street from the Hsiehs' home during her daily strolls around the neighborhood. In retrospect, perhaps she had been an early, and unwitting, observer of Tony's ingenuity. It was yet another discovery: that besides having money, thinking outside the box—which meant defying his parents' instructions, in this instance—could also allow him to define himself.

CHAPTER 2

WIDE AWAKE

Dixie Elementary School was a public school sandwiched between the fields of Lucas Valley Preserve and Sleepy Hollow. Renamed Miller Creek Elementary School District decades later due to the former name's ties to the old South and Confederate states, the school was just a five-minute drive from the Hsiehs' home on Coast Oak Way. Every morning at the school started with a Pledge of Allegiance to the American flag. From Tony's first day, it was clear he was unlike the others in his classroom.

"There was all this buzz about the new kid, the wunderkind," said Spencer Garfinkel, a former classmate of Tony's. On the first day of school that Monday, he was a first grader. By Tuesday, Tony had jumped to the second grade, putting him in the same year as Spencer. "Literally, it wasn't a week. It took a day," Spencer said. Years later, Tony would say how skipping this grade made him feel different and singled out, even more so than he may have already felt, being one of very few Asians in the neighborhood. Tony's last name was foreign enough that his elementary school soccer coach had trouble spelling out his name in writing when going over plays on a chalkboard. After a few failed tries, he quickly became "Tony H."

Richard and Judy very quickly identified the other few Chinese families in the neighborhood. "Somehow my parents managed to find all ten of them," Tony later wrote. The families built a community within a community, coming together often in comfort and familiarity. Speaking with one another in fast and expressive Mandarin, the families would make a point of celebrating traditional holidays like Chinese New Year together, taking turns hosting potluck lunches and dinners at their homes. The kids would play and watch television in one room, while the parents, in another room, gossiped and bragged about their children's accomplishments.

Tables and counters would groan under the weight of platters and bowls filled with fried and sticky rice, long noodles, and glistening braised pork. Kumquats and oranges would dot the house, the bright orange colors a symbol for gold and prosperity. The kids, Tony included, would have to bow to the parents in order to receive red envelopes, filled with $1 bills, $5 bills, even $20 bills at times. For dessert, sometimes there would be *xing ren tofu*, a traditional Chinese soft almond tofu. "But it was the Betty Crocker version, which was just Jell-O, flavored with almond extract, I think," recalled one childhood friend of Tony's. "It had canned fruit with it." The gatherings were never anything fancy, but they were significant in other ways, particularly for the children. "It was cool to get together because it was one of the few times where we would see so many Asian people together in the same place."

Richard and Judy made sure that Tony, and later on his two younger brothers, Andy and Dave, attended Chinese school in the late afternoons on weekdays and on weekends so they could keep in touch with their native language and roots. The brothers were only allowed to watch television one hour a week and had to get straight As—anything less would be a badge of shame. One friend of Tony's recalled watching him cry in elementary school because he received less than an A on a paper in French class. "He was inconsolable," he said. "I don't think it was necessarily even obvious to me how seriously he took academics because sometimes he could come off as somewhat cavalier about it."

Around the time that Tony entered Miller Creek Middle School, Judy would drive Tony and another one of his friends, Eric Liu, to the local library in the summertime for reading clubs. Aside from *Boys' Life*, Tony also devoured a book series called *The Three Investigators*, which followed three teenage boys as they solved crimes and mysteries. In the series, the headquarters for the three boys was a damaged thirty-foot trailer in a junkyard. The idea that a trailer could have everything that the boys needed to solve their investigations—a small laboratory, an office and a desk, a typewriter, books—became a concept that Tony replicated later on in his life.

In sixth grade, his first year of middle school, Tony was voted "Most Likely to Succeed." The yearbook page that commemorated this superlative pictured Tony in his thick glasses with a messy bowl haircut, a zip-up sweater, and an awkward smile—most likely the forced response to a photographer's command. He was never athletic and, as Tony H., never grew into soccer. "But he could kick your ass in ping-pong," said David Padover, another childhood friend of Tony's who, despite remembering his lack of athletic prowess, also remembered his sense of adventure very early on. "One of the things I remember doing with Tony was exploring in the hills up on Lucas Valley and the waters of Miller Creek," said Padover, who lived about two miles away from the Hsiehs. They would bike to each other's house and ride up and down the streets, sometimes going all the way to the base of the valley to hike up the hill. They stopped by creeks and used nets to catch small fish. "We would take all sorts of stuff up there so we could spend as much time hiking as we wanted," he recalled. "One time, we found an alligator lizard and a bunch of field mice. We decided to take the mice home and raise them and sell them as pets."

Peers knew Tony as the child prodigy of Lucas Valley. But there were glimpses early on that he was more than just a studious and bookish boy wonder. The tape recording of him practicing instruments was just the beginning of a pattern of behavior. One of his friends recalled that as Tony entered the first stages of puberty, he secretly borrowed The "What's Happening to My Body?" Book for Boys from the local library, a book that would have been considered contraband in his household. "I don't know how he managed to do it, but it was like a big score for us," recalled one of Tony's childhood friends. "We were going through it half horrified and half fascinated."

For Halloween one year in middle school, Tony showed up to school as Sherlock Holmes in an outfit so elaborate that it surprised his classmates, who more or less knew him as the Asian brainiac. "I remember thinking, wow, his family went all out for this. With the cape, the shawl, and the eyeglasses. He was Sherlock Holmes, literally out of England," said Spencer Garfinkel. His parents' involvement in the costume was also noticeable to Garfinkel. "I'm not sure if that was the Chinese immigrant family wanting to come and fit in," he said. Another year, Tony went a step further and dressed up as a girl. The outfit was so convincing that one of the teachers did not realize it was a costume. "It was unbelievable," Spencer recalled. "We were all lined up as contestants for the costume contest, and Ms. Troy, who was one of the judges, pointed at Tony and said, 'But what's that girl dressed up as?'" He added, "You don't expect it from the computer whiz or math geek, but he had that goofy side. You'd never assume it, and then all of a sudden he'd come up with a costume or something and it's like wow, where did that come from?"

Few were able to glimpse the inner workings of Tony's adolescent mind, but those spurts of expression indicated Tony's curiosity for creativity and desire to break from tradition and conformity. This would come out in his writing as well, in a few poems he penned during middle school. In one called "Teeth," he gave the reader vivid metaphors to chew on:

```
28 white men
standing nice
and straight,
4 more to be
hatched, but
many years to
wait.
                Some might become
                knights, and wear a
                silver suit.  Others
                might wear a gold
                outfit, recover their
                stolen loot.
    But                        rich.
      the                      very
        silver                 are
          and        all
          gold people
Only because an enemy came and dug a little

            DITCH!
The people crash against each other,
    crushing everything in between --
They often get awfully dirty, so it's
    best to keep them clean.
Every half a year, they should
    visit a friendly man,
Sometimes one is removed, and thrown
    in a garbage can
They neither walk nor drive a car,
Now try to guess who these people are.

            TEETH

            Tony Hsieh
```

In another poem, aptly called "TOOMUCHTODONESS," he writes with exasperation about his messy room and all the tasks at hand:

```
TOOMUCHTODONESS

        Dark Gray
       My Messy Room
       Ants, Beatles
     Students, Teachers
  Staring Out My Window Into A
    Cloudy Sun-Chilling Day
          5:00 p.m.
  Books, Pens, Pencils, Paper, Piano,
       Trumpet, Violin.


                    Tony Hsieh
```

But one poem seemed particularly haunted. Written about a nightmare in which Tony is running away from a menacing octopus, it's typed inside a drawing of the eight-limbed mollusk with large, soulless eyes.

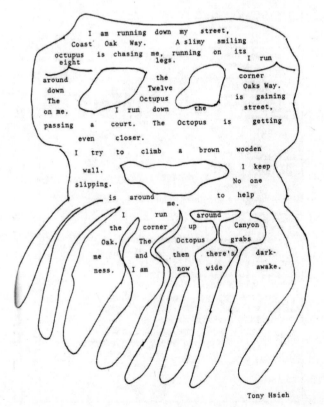

Tony Hsieh

Though Tony was barely a teenager when he wrote it, the poem was more telling than he could have known.

■ ■ ■

Nestled in a neighborhood of gated houses with long driveways, and hidden behind an imposing and carefully manicured hedge, is the Branson School, a prestigious private college preparatory school in Marin County. Once called "an enclave within an enclave within an enclave," it is a high school unlike most, in which its $50,000-a-year tuition marks it as one of the most expensive high schools in the country. Today, the student parking lot is dotted with sports cars, and the school's students are the daughters and sons of California royalty, often going on to become part of that group themselves. One alum is Jennifer Siebel Newsom, the wife of Gavin Newsom, the former mayor of San Francisco turned governor of California. Just next door is the Lagunitas Country Club, the oldest private tennis and swim club in the county, which is also well known for its exclusivity. If an invitation is extended, one enters through the two pillared Branson Gates into a sprawling campus nestled within a lush valley, complete with a small creek that runs through the school grounds.

Branson has always had a reputation for being a school that is strictly for the privileged elite. It is situated in the small town of Ross, where the median household income for the 2,300 residents is over $220,000 and the median home value is around $2 million as of 2019. It is one of the wealthiest suburbs in the Bay Area. But Tony didn't live in Ross—he lived in Mont Marin, a thirty-minute drive away, where the households earn a third of what they do in Ross and the median home value is less than half. Most of his peers at Miller Creek Middle School went on to Terra Linda High School, a public school in the neighborhood. But for some parents—certainly for Richard and Judy—Terra Linda wasn't enough. So, after a series of tests and interviews, Tony became one of four students in his class at Miller Creek who were admitted to Branson in 1987, earning seats among the eighty coveted spots. Tony got in not because of any favors from the family name but because he was academically competitive. And to Richard and Judy, Branson was the best of the best—100 percent of its students went to college after graduating. It was a feeder to the American dream.

So, every morning starting in August 1987, Tony made the trek to the other side of town, into another world. He would either be driven by his parents or carpool with Eric Liu, his longtime friend who often attended the Chinese family gatherings and who had also been admitted to Branson. They would hop on the 101 freeway for just over three miles, then exit into central San Rafael, driving past the Jack in the Box on Second Street and the McDonald's on Fourth. After winding through a series of turns, as the roads became better paved and the trees leafier, they would pass the nearly century-old St. Anselm Church. For another half mile on Fernhill Avenue, the journey took them past grand estates—homes with American flags waving on poles outside and gardeners out front. Finally, they would get to the Branson gates, which were easy to miss unless you knew to look for them. Driving through the grounds, they'd pass students playing Frisbee on the lawn, or plotting which Grateful Dead shows they were going to go to next. As they pulled up in their modest family vehicles, Tony and Eric would get out of the car, take a glance at the rows of Volkswagen Beetle convertibles and red BMWs in the parking lot, and be reminded daily that they were from somewhere else.

At a new school in a new neighborhood where none of the other students knew him as the whiz kid who skipped a grade, this could have been an opportunity for Tony to reinvent himself—but that didn't happen. "I remember thinking that the first day of high school really didn't feel that different from the last day of middle school," Tony wrote. "I guess in my head, I had thought that suddenly I would feel older and more mature, that somehow life would suddenly be different now that I was in high school."

The same factors that isolated him from most of the other kids remained at Branson, only now they were exacerbated by an immense wealth gap, textured with teenage insecurities. While many other students went to Europe for the summer or Lake Tahoe every weekend in the winter, Tony worked multiple jobs during high school. He became a video tester for Lucasfilm for $6 an hour and started a computer programming gig that paid $15 per hour. He was still one of very few Asians in a very white school. At lunch, according to a former teacher at the Branson School who taught there during this time, it was not unusual for students of minority ethnicities to sit together at the same table, though Asian students were more integrated than Black students. Tony was still physically smaller than his peers, still a full year behind in growth spurts.

His intelligence continued to burst through. In geometry his first year at Branson, he picked up concepts at such a breakneck pace that his teacher created a different set of problems specifically tailored for Tony. He still excelled. "I don't often use the word brilliant, but he was brilliant," his teacher later said. She also observed a level of restraint from Tony that she surmised was a direct response to a deep, innate desire to fit in. Though he knew the answers to every question and problem she posed to the class, he rarely volunteered his hand. "I just really got the feeling from Tony that he wanted the respect and admiration and to be accepted by his classmates," she recalled. "He didn't want to do anything that would make them go, 'Oh, there's that brilliant kid. What is he even doing in our class?'"

Tony spent his lunch hours and oftentimes his after-school hours in the computer lab, hidden in the library. He picked up the programming language Pascal and eventually became so adept at it that he taught it for a summer course. It was clear to those who paid attention, though, that Tony was not immune to the usual mischievous teenage antics. In fact, he sometimes led them. With a few other regulars at the lab, Tony figured out that the computer lab phone could make long-distance calls and they wouldn't have to pay. So he had an idea—to call 976-SEXY, which ended up being a phone sex operator. The first time he called, the woman on the other line quickly caught on and asked what year he was born. "Twenty-one years ago!" Tony cried, before hanging up. He and his friends continued making calls to the number for the next few weeks for their amusement—before the teacher inquired about a phone bill that listed three hundred calls in the past month to that number.

David Padover, who had also gotten into Branson, found himself in the computer lab as well during his freshman year, but it was not to pick up Pascal. Due to his social anxiety, he had found the cafeteria too intimidating a place to eat lunch. Instead, he preferred the quiet of the computer lab. He and Tony remained friends for the first year at Branson as one of four students from Miller Creek Middle School. But during their sophomore year, drama that had occurred during middle school followed them into high school. While at Miller Creek, a group of teenage boys used to bully

David and call him names. While Tony didn't take part, he did witness it. One day years later at Branson, when the two of them were in the school office together, David saw that Tony had drawn a comic about him. "I was stupid and dumb in this comic," David later recalled of the caricature. "And everything I did didn't work out." There were striking similarities between the comic and what David endured in middle school. Though Tony tried to downplay the comic, he couldn't explain why he had drawn it, and David ended the friendship. They never saw much of each other again at Branson or for the rest of their lives, even though both of their families remained in Northern California. Despite how hurt he remembered feeling after the incident, David later regretted ending their friendship over the comic. "I knew a Tony that many people never met," he later recalled. "But I never got to meet and experience the Tony that so many people got to know."

Tony continued thinking outside the box, which occasionally afforded him a different set of rules. Some of his teachers allowed him to not attend classes as long as he continued to ace tests. "As for homework, I tried my best to find creative ways around actually doing any hard work," he later wrote. But even the hard work was too easy for him, so he invented ways to further challenge himself. One time, for an assignment that involved writing a Shakespearean sonnet, Tony submitted his paper in Morse code. "Depending on the teacher's mood, I knew I was either going to get an A or an F. Luckily, my teacher decided to give me an 'A+++++++++++++.'"

He was on the fencing team and joined the chess club and electronics club. He was voted into the Cum Laude Society, a group that honored "excellence in classroom achievement and other pursuits." He also participated in mock trial, spending a few hours every Friday from January to March his junior year practicing debating with the rest of the team. Eric Liu was on the team as well—his last name misspelled in the yearbook photo of the mock trial club. "Branson's prosecution was represented by Tony Hsieh, Eric Lui, and Mike Michaud and was able to convict Terra Linda's Pat Haines of manslaughter," reads the caption. His teammates are wearing blazers and collared shirts in the photograph. Tony is wearing a white T-shirt that reads "Dick's Island."

Once, during his junior year, Tony drove by himself for two days from San Rafael to Mexico and back just to catch an eclipse. "I remember he came back with a Señor Frog's T-shirt," laughed one of his childhood friends, in reference to the Mexican-themed restaurant chain. "I can't believe somehow his parents let him. But that's just an amazing thing for a high schooler to do at the time."

Very rarely did Tony get in trouble, but he was suspended for one day after he was found with another student's lunch card, a debit card for the school cafeteria, in his pocket. Summoned before a disciplinary committee, Tony provided what seemed like an unsatisfactory answer: it must have been an accident. Years later, Tony would claim this to be another important moment of his teenage years. "I walked away from that experience with the lesson that sometimes the truth alone isn't enough," he said. "And that presentation of the truth was just as important as the truth."

As tradition goes, every senior is given their own page in the yearbook. Most students picked a series of photographs that represented the highlights of their eighteen or so years of life, such as photos of themselves as kids, shots of their pets, or pictures with friends at parties or pep rallies. Tony's, however, was filled with mysterious-looking doodles, drawings, quotes, and inside jokes. It looked more like an invitation to an Acid Test party from the Merry Pranksters than a yearbook page. "It was very unusual," said David. Tony wrote out his Chinese name in bold. There were references to fictional characters, including Indiana Jones and Angus "Mac" MacGyver, the dashing American TV hero who eschewed violence and instead used unconventional methods to solve conflicts and problems. Rather than a gun, MacGyver carried a Swiss Army knife. Tony drew a self-portrait of him doing a magic trick. And amid all the doodles and scrawls, he wrote a quote from the *Calvin and Hobbes* comic strip: "Sometimes I think the surest sign that intelligent life exists elsewhere in the universe is that none of it has tried to contact us."

"He had this pretty intense energy about him," said his former geometry teacher. "Like he had deep thoughts in his head and he was grasping things at a really high level even back then."

■ ■ ■

Perhaps Tony's most impactful extracurricular at Branson was theater tech, a role that required him to toil behind the scenes to ensure a successful production for plays and musicals. The job entailed being in the

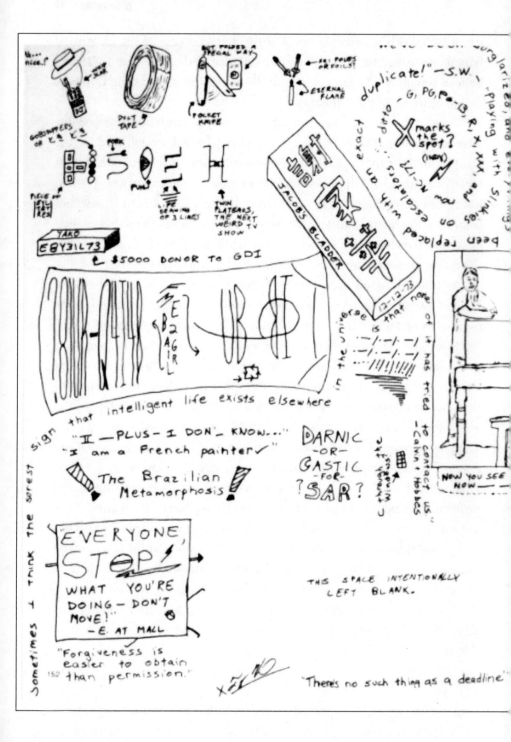

theater auditorium after school and during lunch hours, fiddling with lights, tinkering with props, and finding camaraderie with other similarly onstage-averse students. Through theater tech, Tony met Janice Lopez, a Filipino girl with wide-set eyes who was on financial aid at Branson. Like Tony, she got into the school on intelligence and wits alone, and could also be painfully shy.

Together they took theater tech jobs operating the spotlight, which meant ensuring that the audience was focusing on the right character at the right time, whether that was at the student playing Danny Zuko in *Grease* or the one playing Emily Webb in *Our Town*. Though the audience could not see Tony, they were being commanded by his light. "There was something alluring about being involved in something where the sole purpose was to create an experience and emotional journey for people," he later wrote about his time in theater production. "Then to have nothing but memories left afterward to hold onto."

Sometimes he and Janice would sit shoulder to shoulder for hours in a cramped, six-by-twelve-foot control booth, watching the stories play out in front of them. Together they became comfortable in each other's silence. It was a comfort they would find again twenty years later.

CHAPTER 3

THE BET

On a fall day in 1991, Jon Greenman was among hundreds of new students arriving for the first time at Harvard to start life among a new class of high-achieving, and often wealthy, young minds. With a thick mat of brown hair and a nervous grin, Jon led his parents to the third floor of Canaday Hall A, one of a cluster of buildings that formed a giant question mark when seen from up above, where he'd be staying for freshman year.

It was immediately clear that going to Harvard didn't mean you were signing up for prestigious living quarters. Unlike other Harvard buildings, identified by Neoclassical trim and colonial-style columns, the Canaday buildings are boxy brick structures reminiscent of drab government housing built in the 1970s. Directly across the street, the booming toll of the Memorial Church bells shook Jon's bedroom window at the stroke of every hour. Jon's bedroom, part of a four-bedroom suite, barely had enough space for his belongings. Among his roommates were Sanjay Madan, a quiet boy with deep-set eyes and thick brows, and Jose Soto, a chatty young kid who grew up in Hartford, Connecticut.

Amid the throng of students leading their wide-eyed parents around the campus, Jon ran into a tall, stick-thin Asian boy who was moving into the room across the hall. He introduced himself as Tony, and he, like Jon, was awkward and shy. They'd make fast friends, Jon figured. Tony, it turned out, had a room to himself. Jon decided he'd be spending most of his time there because Tony had two things that no one else did: a TV and video games. As residents of the third floor of Canaday A, Jose,

Sanjay, Jon, and Tony became good friends. They also ventured upstairs and befriended some of the girls who lived on the fourth floor, including Jill Wheeler and Kami Hayashi, and a few other guys below them on the second floor.

Going to Harvard had not been Tony's first choice. He had been accepted into every elite university he applied to: Brown; the University of California, Berkeley; Stanford; MIT; Princeton; Cornell; Yale; and Harvard. His original plan was to go to Brown because it had an advertising major, which Tony thought seemed more relevant to the business world than any of the majors offered by the other colleges.

But Tony's parents, Richard and Judy, had a plan for their son's future that did not involve the liberal arts bent of Brown. While they had hoped he would become a medical doctor, they could settle for a computer science degree at Harvard, the global symbol of prestige and success. Over four centuries, the university had educated eight U.S. presidents, over a hundred Olympians, and nearly eighty Nobel laureates, which "yielded the most prestigious bragging rights" for Asian American parents, Tony later wrote. After everything Richard and Judy had sacrificed to achieve the American dream, sending their son to Harvard guaranteed a life of wealth and success, they thought.

Choosing Harvard over Brown, however, would be one of the final times Tony capitulated to his parents' demands. The TV was the first thing Tony bought when he moved into Canaday. No longer did he have to adhere to the one-hour-per-week rule of his childhood; in his new space he could watch his favorite shows whenever he wanted, for hours on end. It was the first in a long line of small freedoms that allowed him to make his own rules and shape his own environment. In addition to the desk, chair, and twin-sized bed that took up most of the space, he decked out his room with a hot pot, a computer, and a printer—all prized items for freshmen at the time. He owned a video game collection unmatched in the dorm; working as an intern at Lucasfilm had provided him with consoles and games that weren't even available in stores. For dorm mates like Jon, it was these things that first drew people into Tony's orbit. Then, organically, his room became the center of the universe for their group of friends.

The main feature of his bedroom wall was a poster of Tony's favorite

idol, Angus "Mac" MacGyver, played on TV by Richard Dean Anderson. With a clean-cut face framed by a blond mullet, MacGyver had a
genius-level intellect and could speak five languages, in addition to being
proficient in sign language and having mastered Morse code. With an
extraordinary grasp of applied physics and engineering, he could defuse a
bomb using a paper clip. In one episode, he made a magnifying glass out
of a hairpin and wine to read the names of spies.

The poster was the first image Tony's friends saw as they walked into
his broom-cupboard-sized room. Soon, photos of Tony with his friends
adorned the walls. His room was right near one of the staircases that
served as the only access to the dorm's upper floors, and his door was
always open, unless he was asleep, which seemed to rarely be the case—
his friends knew they could find him awake and up for a chat deep into
the night. Between marathon evenings of Bomberman—the Japanese
strategic maze game on his Nintendo console—they crammed into his
tiny room, sometimes a dozen at a time, and stayed up all night watching
television or attempting to study. The longer they debated philosophy or
each other's romances, the higher the pizza boxes piled alongside buckets
of buffalo wings. No matter what was going on in the lives of this group of
friends, Tony and his room became the place to connect with one another.
He was always there, listening, taking it all in. "There was a core group of
about fifteen of us, and we were inseparable," Tony wrote later.

Like Tony, who was studying computer science, and Jon, who majored
in astrophysics, the circle of friends in Canaday A had come to Harvard
as the highest-graded students in their schools, achievements they had
not reached by going to high school parties or rummaging through their
parents' alcohol cabinets. With Harvard's enormous tuition fees, pressure from their families to succeed, and the crushing workload, alcohol did not meaningfully factor into the social equation of Tony's group,
nor did they express much curiosity about its ability to lubricate their
experiences. In one candid photograph Tony is sitting on the ground,
his arms around his knees, surrounded by friends. Cans of Coca-Cola,
Sprite, Pepsi, and Canada Dry ginger ale line the window sills behind
them—no alcohol in sight. There may have been a few beers at the events
they did attend, though none recall stumbling home from a PBR-soaked
college party.

But even without the excuse of a hangover, the near-constant stream of people coming in and out of Tony's room provided ample distractions from actually going to class. He arranged his schedule so that he had classes from 9 a.m. to 1 p.m. on Mondays, Wednesdays, and Fridays, leaving open Tuesdays and Thursdays. This was problematic because he preferred to stay up late and sleep in, meaning that he would choose to stay awake for thirty-two hours in a row and then sleep for sixteen hours straight. Sometimes he would cut class and instead watch reruns of the soap opera *Days of Our Lives* in his room.

While Tony did have a small circle of friends at the Branson School, he confided in Jon that there were times he had felt excluded from the popular crowd there. "He did feel some desire for inclusion," Jon said. "And he was very eager to have people happy when they were with him."

By the end of the first semester, Tony realized that he had created something special. Just before Harvard broke for the winter holidays, when everyone was preparing to go home to see their families, Tony wrote a card and distributed a scanned copy to each of his friends. In jagged handwriting, Tony scribbled on the front: "Yes, it's a xerox. Yes it's cheap. Yes, it's a form letter. But it's something I want to say to all of you so . . ."

Inside, his message continued:

A little over three months ago, we hadn't even met. Call it luck, call it fate . . . Whatever brought us together, I feel very lucky to have you all as such good friends. Quite simply, you guys light up my life. Without you guys, I wouldn't be anywhere near as happy with college as I am now (although my grades would probably be a bit better).

Because of you guys, I haven't even really felt homesick yet. Amazing what 90 or so days can do, huh?

In any case, I just wanted to say thanks to all of you, Merry Christmas, Happy New Year, and all that jazz.

Oh, and one last thing . . . I hope that each of you invites me to your wedding, because I want to be there when the people dearest to me are having one of the happiest days of their lives.

Alright, enough of this sentimental stuff . . . on with the presents!
Tony

■ ■ ■

It took all of one semester for Tony to realize that what he really wanted to do was spend more time with his friends and less time doing work, while still getting good grades. Instead of using his intellect to study hard, he invested more time in trying to figure out how to hack his Ivy League education. Like in high school, he enrolled in subjects that were the most flexible in terms of the work required: linguistics, sign language, and Mandarin (which he already spoke fluently with his parents).

During his senior year, he took a course called The Bible and Its Interpretation that met all his needs: there wasn't any homework to be graded on, so he never had to go to class. "The bad news was that my grade in the class was going to be based on what I got on the final exam, which I was completely unprepared for, since I had never opened up any of the textbooks we were supposed to have been reading throughout the semester," he wrote later. Two weeks before the final exam, the professor announced to the class that they would have to write a few paragraphs about five topics selected at random from a list of ninety possible topics discussed during the semester.

Realizing that it was humanly impossible to do all the readings in two weeks, Tony posted a message on one of the electronic news groups on the Harvard network to see if any of the several hundred students enrolled in the class wanted to do a virtual study group—a revolutionary idea at the time, given that nothing was done virtually and the internet was still an infant concept. For those who wanted to participate, Tony would assign them three topics to research and they would have to email their findings to him. Once collected, he would compile the responses in a binder, and those who contributed could purchase the study materials for $20. "If we get enough people on the 'Net together, then each person will only have to do a few identifications," he wrote on the harvard.general message board.

Tony's idea garnered enough attention to warrant a story in *The Crimson*, the student-run newspaper at Harvard. "Senior Forms 'Bible' Study Group On 'Net," the headline read. Only forty people had responded to Tony's message, according to the story, but it was enough to cover all the topics. Some students opted out of joining the group "out of concern that participating might somehow violate Harvard's rules of academic honesty." But a teaching fellow quoted in the story said, "I wouldn't see anything different between this and students getting together in a room and working together." Another student quoted said, "I think some people who use harvard.general might learn from this in the future." By slacking off, Tony had invented a new means of learning. "They say that necessity is the mother of invention," he wrote later. "Without ever opening up a book or doing any writing myself, I ended up with the most comprehensive study guide that had ever been created."

In his memoir, published almost two decades later, Tony was intent on driving the idea that he aced Harvard by barely trying. But it was clear to his college friends that he put in more effort than he let on. During his sophomore year, he was one of three people on Harvard's computer programming team that won first place in the Association for Computing Machinery International Collegiate Programming Contest, beating 600 teams from around the world. "Programmers Win Contest," a story from *The Crimson* read. "It was a really close contest," Tony told the reporter. "We were pretty much neck-and-neck with Stanford. If we hadn't got the last problem we would have lost."

A photo taken at the contest shows Tony standing between his two teammates, Craig Silverstein and Derrick Bass. They had just won $10,000. Having gone through a series of growth spurts, he towered over his companions, wearing a gray Harvard sweater, his eyes lit above a huge smile. He is gripping a trophy emblazoned with "1993 World Champions." Seeing the photo years later, Craig was struck by Tony's height; he had forgotten that Tony was taller than him. He recalled that they had barely slept in the weeks leading up to the competition. But the extraordinary achievement proved to be an early indication of the futures awaiting both men. After he graduated from Harvard, Craig was accepted to a PhD program at Stanford, where he worked alongside two other doctoral students named Larry Page and Sergey Brin. The students were working on a concept called a "search engine," which sought to find a way to connect the millions of documents on the internet to a central hub that could be searched. When they dropped out of Stanford to start their company, Google, Craig followed them and was their first hire, a career move that would make him hundreds of millions of dollars.

■ ■ ■

What Tony omitted from his memoir was his connection to New York during this time. He makes no mention of his regular trips to Manhattan, which initially began as visits to see Alex Hsu, a friend from Branson who was studying information technology at New York University. One of the first things that drew him to the city was how different Alex's college experience was from his own. Unlike Harvard's campus, which is largely siloed in Cambridge away from the bustle of Boston, NYU blended seamlessly into the urban jungle of Manhattan, which fascinated Tony. There seemed to be no clear end to the campus and the beginning of the outside world. Instead, its student housing, libraries, and classrooms were interconnected with the world they existed within, sharing bars, parks, restaurants, offices, and apartment buildings with the citizens of New York. Such a connection provided a two-way laboratory that allowed NYU students to integrate and apply their experience to the surrounding metropolis, while the city could pull from the pipeline of educated individuals and the business and innovation they brought with them. It was a phenomenon that would stick with him for years.

Tony's visits to New York became so frequent that he found himself part of an entirely new circle of friends. Much of his time was spent hanging at Alex's apartment at Zeckendorf Towers, which loomed above Union Square. The apartment served as a gathering place for Alex's friends, including his girlfriend, Mei Lawn, and another young woman named Ying Liu, who was also a student at NYU. Ying had befriended Alex after they realized they were both Taiwanese. The four of them would stay up all night playing the card game Spades, surrounded by Chinese takeout boxes of chicken or shrimp and broccoli with hot chili sauce on the side. Other nights, they went to Broadway shows or the NYU students took Tony to dorm parties across the campus. Like at Harvard, this group of friends was similarly studious and uninterested in alcohol and getting drunk.

Ying, who didn't drink, noticed Tony took pains to reveal little about himself when he met strangers at the gatherings. When asked where he was visiting from, Tony's response rarely changed. "I'm from a small school in Boston," he would say. He seemed adamant about leading people to believe he was an unexceptional wallflower. "Without Harvard, he became like everybody else," Ying said. "In fact, he was probably more invisible."

Doe-eyed with a heart-shaped face that belied her commanding demeanor, Ying initially had found Tony to be painfully shy and quiet. But as they spent more time together, his introversion transformed into an intense curiosity, and during their moments alone he peppered her incessantly with questions. Ying had a nurturing and protective personality and found herself mothering Tony. *Pour the noodles here,* she would say, or *Don't throw that on the counter, put it in the trash.* "I always felt like I had to take care of him," she later recalled.

They also shared a mutual curiosity about intimacy, as well as a lack of experience. Tony had yet to kiss a girl, and Ying had spent much of her teenage years changing schools between Taiwan, Indonesia, and Pennsylvania and New York, never staying anywhere long enough to start a relationship. She hadn't even held a boy's hand at that point, let alone kissed one, so she had few answers for Tony when he asked what girls like to do.

One night, Ying, Tony, Alex, and his girlfriend were talking about sex, and out of curiosity, the group decided to watch a pornographic video. After a few minutes, Ying announced she was afraid of having sex in the future because of how painful it looked for the woman. The others burst out laughing at her naïveté.

Ying recalled mostly assuming a big-sister role to Tony. She felt like they were on the same level and were both interested in trying to figure out why people behave in the ways they do. Sometimes she noticed how he would fixate on the smallest observations in wonderment. Other times she would accuse him of being childish—she often found his pranks immature. But as Tony's visits to New York became more frequent, their mutual friends wondered whether Tony's interest in Ying was perhaps driven by something else, maybe romance.

While Tony was at Harvard, Richard took a job in Hong Kong and moved there with Judy and Dave, so Tony used summer break to visit them. Upon learning that Tony was heading to Hong Kong, Ying mentioned that she too was planning on going to Asia during the summer to see her father, though she would be going to Taiwan. She was somewhat surprised when he promptly invited himself to come and see her. It wasn't too much trouble, he insisted, as Taipei is only a two-hour flight from Hong Kong. Ying gently pushed back: she had nowhere for him to stay. Her father lived with few means in a minuscule apartment in a run-down part of the city. There was only enough room for a tiny bathroom and a double bed, which Ying shared with her father when she visited.

Tony did not seem to care, so Ying relented and asked her father to book Tony a hotel near his apartment. The morning after Tony arrived, he met Ying at her father's apartment building. The elevator violently shook on the way up. The stench of urine filled the cabin—someone had relieved themselves in the corner. "He was okay with it," Ying said. "So I was okay with it."

Standing in the studio apartment with Ying, her father, and her brother, Tony mentioned that his first night in Taipei had been quite an experience. Ying asked him what happened. At around midnight, he explained, there was a knock at the door. A woman was standing there, offering a massage. When he declined, she clarified, saying that what she was really offering was a "happy service."

Ying turned to her father. "What did you do?"

"Oh my God," her father said. "I think I booked a love hotel."

As they laughed, Ying realized that the initial embarrassment that had made her hesitant about inviting Tony to her hometown was unnecessary. Tony, unlike many of her other NYU friends, did not come from wealth. Ying felt a quiet comfort knowing that Tony did not seem to be bothered by her family's living quarters. "I wasn't ashamed," Ying said.

But Tony's ability to put Ying at ease was overshadowed by his reluctance to communicate his own feelings, and she was never quite able to truly understand him. While she didn't press him, or even really ask, she sensed there was a disconnect between Tony and his own family. Even when they became closer, he never spoke about his parents. She only learned years later that Tony had two younger brothers.

One day on a bus during their trip in Taipei, Ying noticed Tony looking at her with his wide eyes. "Why are you suddenly speaking English to me?" he said. In New York, Tony and Ying always spoke in Mandarin with their friends, in a way that felt almost like a secret code. In Taiwan, she had switched. Tony's fascination with human behavior applied to her too, she realized.

Ying never asked Tony how he felt about her, but some, including Alex, always thought that Tony had romantic feelings for her. Sometime after the Taipei trip, Ying got a boyfriend, and Tony's visits to New York became less frequent. "When I was single, he was very close to me," she later said. "When I got a boyfriend, he drifted away."

■ ■ ■

Tony's jaunt in Taipei was one of many experiences that opened him up to the realities of the world, far from his sheltered suburban childhood. At Harvard he threw himself into opportunities outside of school. He earned a certificate in mixology at the Harvard Bartending School and started bartending at weddings and other catered events. He visited a friend's farm and learned how to milk cows. He held several computer programming internships as a student, working at Harvard Student Agencies, Spinnaker Software, and Microsoft. For another internship at BBN, a subsidiary of the military contractor Raytheon, which developed technology that eventually became the backbone of the internet, Tony had to undergo a background check to earn a security clearance with the federal government.

One summer he joined the Guardian Angels, a nonprofit organization of volunteers who patrolled the streets of Boston wearing red berets and making citizen's arrests. Initially founded in New York City in the 1970s to combat rising crime in the subway system, the organization had more than a hundred chapters in cities across the world. He spent a summer patrolling the Boston train system and sidewalks, and was given the code name "Secret," he wrote later. "I learned later that one of the other gang members had originally wanted to name me 'Ancient Chinese Secret.'"

One of his most formative experiences occurred during a trip to the hospital. David Camacho, who lived in his dorm, had cut his finger, and Tony and Jose volunteered to take him to the emergency room. As the boys sat in the waiting room, a mentally unstable patient was shouting and making a commotion. The patient approached and began flicking them with blood from a festering wound. Tony was traumatized, not least by the fear of contracting AIDS or other bloodborne diseases.

He took the experience to his creative writing class, where he wrote about the episode for an assignment. Jon recalled that Tony's essay went into vivid detail about his encounter. "We were living in a bit of a cocoon," Jon said later. "He just wanted to highlight that there was another world out there."

■ ■ ■

Tony may have been breaking loose from the shackles of childhood and beginning to understand the ways of the world, but he also missed being an entrepreneur. So in his junior year he came up with an ambitious plan: he would take over the late-night food joint in his dormitory, Quincy House, a student enterprise traditionally run by seniors. Unlike his past endeavors, such as button-making or newspaper delivery, which were motivated by Tony's desire to make money, with the Quincy House Grille Tony had a different aim. With its foosball table, pinball machines, and proximity to their rooms, the Grille could be another hub for Tony to orchestrate connections between his friends. He discussed the idea with Sanjay, who agreed to partner with Tony. Later, at a dorm party, Tony met another student named Alfred Lin and told him about his idea. While Alfred would come to devise his own way to contribute to the business, it would be the first of several money-making ideas that Tony would share with the two young men.

In order to manage the Quincy House Grille, potential student owners had to bid for ownership. Tony figured that since he was a junior and all the other bidders were seniors, he could afford to outbid all of them, as he had two years to cover the cost and even run up potential profits. So his plan was to top the highest bid by $1. It worked, and Tony and Sanjay took over the restaurant, meaning they did everything from deciding the menu and getting the ingredients to setting prices and cooking the food. For the first few months Tony took the subway to the nearest McDonald's every day, where he negotiated with the manager there to sell him one hundred frozen McDonald's hamburger patties and buns for a dollar each. Tony and Sanjay would then sell them at Quincy for $3.

But the real money was in pizzas, which could be made at a cost of $2 and sold for $10 before toppings. So they spent $2,000 on a pizza oven and reopened the Grille as a pizza shop. Considering other ways to attract customers, Tony thought about why his dorm room was most often the preferred gathering spot for his friends. He called Alex in New York and asked whether his mother, a successful television producer in Taiwan, might want to invest a couple of thousand dollars into the business. She said yes, and Tony spent the money on a new television. He then spent nights recording music videos on MTV and episodes of *Melrose Place*, the popular soap opera set in West Hollywood. Whenever commercials came on, he paused the recording, ensuring that his customers could enjoy uninterrupted viewing the next day (this was three years before TiVo was invented).

Since their conversation at the dorm party, Alfred Lin had been thinking about his own plans for the Quincy House Grille. Each night, almost without fail, Alfred arrived at the cash register with an order for a large pizza, something that didn't strike Tony as odd—Alfred had a voracious appetite, and Tony had given him the nicknames "Trash Compactor" and "Monster" due to his habit of finishing his friends' leftovers at the local late-night Chinese restaurant. But some nights Alfred would return to Tony for a second pizza. Tony soon learned that Alfred—the future chief finance and operating officer of one of his companies—had started a pizza arbitrage business, selling pies by the slice to his roommates upstairs for a profit.

The new pizza menu combined with nonstop music videos and TV shows made the Quincy House Grille into a real business venture with healthy profits; they paid off the pizza oven in three months. Had Harvard kept subsidizing employee wages at student-run enterprises, and had burglars not broken in and stolen more than $2,000 from the registers, Tony and Sanjay could have made some real money from it, and Alex's mother could have recouped her investment. But it wouldn't be the last time she invested in one of the boys' half-baked ideas.

■ ■ ■

On graduation day in the spring of 1995, Tony and his friends gathered on the lawn, dressed in black commencement caps and gowns. Tony and Sanjay had graduated summa cum laude, among the group with the highest grades in their class. Jon Greenman, who had completed an internship with NASA during his studies, graduated magna cum laude. A photograph taken on that day shows Tony with ten of his friends. Half of Sanjay's face is obscured by Jill Wheeler's graduation cap, while Tony is standing tall above his friends, staring unsmiling into the lens. The lack of expression on his face belied the overwhelming excitement he felt for an unknown future.

That excitement was evident to his classmates, who saw through his introversion to a young man who was full of adventure and curiosity and was destined for greater things, even among a class of Harvard graduates. They agreed that it would be Tony who bound them together in the years ahead. "At the time, we were surrounded by all these people who we expected to go on and do great things," Jill, who would go on to work in government in Washington, D.C., later told friends. "We were so worried that we would lose each other as life went on."

So they made a bet: If Tony became a millionaire within ten years of graduation, they would all go on a cruise and Tony would pay for everyone's trip. If a decade passed and Tony still hadn't become a millionaire, they would still go on a cruise, but everyone else would pool money to pay for it.

Tony had already done the calculations. "To me, it seemed like a win-win situation," he wrote later. "Either I would be a millionaire or I would get a free cruise. Either way, I would be happy."

CHAPTER 4

LINKEXCHANGE

It was a weekday, and Tony and Sanjay were again lounging by the pool during a very long lunch break at their new condo in San Mateo, California. They had landed jobs right after college as software engineers at Oracle, the high-flying enterprise software behemoth at the heart of Silicon Valley. Led by the brash Bronx-born contrarian and playboy billionaire Larry Ellison, Oracle, which at the time was the world's largest maker of data management software, was a keystone in Silicon Valley. Comparing their $40,000 salaries to what their other Harvard classmates would be earning, Tony and Sanjay learned they would be making a lot more money than the rest of them. "I felt that I'd succeeded," Tony said.

Aside from the pizzazz of working at a flashy company, the job checked Tony's only requirements: it paid well and required very little effort. Tony was assigned to test software for bugs and ensure that it worked after updates, a process known as regression testing. Each day it took him five minutes to set up a test and three hours to wait for it to finish. Then he would repeat the process two more times and his day would end. But instead of waiting for the tests to end, Tony walked the few blocks back to his apartment, took a long lunch, napped, and then went to the pool with Sanjay if he was home. It did not take long for Tony to realize that his initial requirements did not equal fulfillment. He also became acutely aware of how the languor he was experiencing starkly contrasted with what was happening outside Oracle.

The year 1995, business magazine *Fast Company* declared, was "The

Year Everything Changed." Silicon Valley was brimming with innovation. The World Wide Web was still in its infancy, and those who understood its potential were finding multimillion-dollar ideas everywhere they looked. In January, a young Stanford graduate called Jerry Yang had registered the website domain Yahoo.com for a database he'd been building that sorted internet pages in a hierarchical order, making them easier to find, and thus launching the first popular search engine. Two months later, as Tony was finishing his last semester at Harvard, a man named Craig Newmark started an email distribution list to his friends to highlight local events happening in the San Francisco Bay Area. This grew into Craigslist—a national online classified-advertising website that would one day strip newspapers and magazines of a vital revenue stream and change the media business model forever. Then in April, the online dating website Match.com launched, opening introductions for millions of people to meet virtually, shifting the millennia-old method of courtship online. And by July, as Tony was toiling away at Oracle, a young investment banker named Jeff Bezos launched a small online bookstore called Amazon.com out of his garage in Seattle.

Companies that were preparing society for the twenty-first century and that would one day change the world—the way we learn, meet, buy, sell—were popping up left and right, many within a few miles of where Tony lived. And because California prohibited—and continues to prohibit—companies from baking noncompete clauses into contracts, any employee could quit and immediately create a rival startup. And yet here were Tony and Sanjay—who graduated at the top of their class at Harvard—completely disengaged and bored, languishing around the pool. Making easy money at a big-name company, it turned out, didn't align with Tony's vision of being in control of his own destiny and creating his own rules.

To combat their ennui, Tony and Sanjay began toying with ideas for a side business. They landed on a website design project. Sanjay was a gifted graphic designer and programmer but was even more introverted than Tony, so he focused on designing and coding the sites. Tony, despite all his fears and insecurities when it came to talking to strangers, assumed the role of salesman.

To the surprise of both, their new venture, which they named Internet

Market Solutions, seemed to take off. After the local chamber of commerce agreed to let them design its website for free, other small businesses signed up. A local mall paid them $2,000. Tony's lunch breaks got longer. So did Sanjay's nights, as he stayed up coding once his workday was done. After five months the two had realized they weren't going to build this company from their cubicles at Oracle, and something had to give.

Tony walked past his manager's office three times before he mustered the courage to quit. "Wow! You must be joining another startup," his manager said to him. "How exciting for you." Tony thought of his two-man operation working from the living room.

Within a week, however, they learned a crucial lesson: neither of them was actually interested in web design. Tony wondered whether quitting Oracle had been a good idea; his father, Richard, made it clear that he did not think Internet Marketing Solutions would ever be a success.

So they went back to the drawing board and on a weekend in March 1996 came up with the idea of LinkExchange. By building websites for local businesses, Tony and Sanjay learned that the only option for advertising online was to buy ads from tech behemoths like Yahoo or Netscape, which at a cost of as much as $10,000 a month was cost prohibitive. Just as Tony had crowdsourced study materials for his virtual Bible study group and then packaged the information into neat binders and sold it, LinkExchange enlisted small businesses to display banner ads for other companies on their websites for free. With hundreds of small business websites, LinkExchange could then sell packages of banner ads across these sites to larger companies that would pay to advertise within the LinkExchange-enlisted websites. This was achieved with a credit system: every time a visitor viewed a small business website and viewed the banner ad, the small business owner would earn half a credit that could be exchanged to display their own ad across the LinkExchange network. So if a business had a thousand views on its website, it could display an ad five hundred times across the network of other websites. LinkExchange would keep the other half of each credit to build out its own advertising inventory to sell to large clients.

LinkExchange rapidly developed traction, and Tony and Sanjay soon found that their workload had become overwhelming. So they started calling up their friends.

Among their first hires were Tony's childhood friends Alex Hsu, who had just finished at NYU, and Eric Liu, who had just graduated from UC Berkeley. Anytime a Harvard friend visited San Francisco, Tony would try to convince them to stay and work at LinkExchange. When Hadi Partovi, a Harvard friend Tony knew through the computer programming team, was offered a role, he declined because he was already working at Microsoft. But he offered up his twin brother, Ali, who he claimed was so similar to him that they sometimes switched places for job interviews. Ali was hired as the third partner for LinkExchange in August.

Tony and Sanjay needed money to pay their new employees, so Tony turned to the only investor who knew his track record—Alex Hsu's mother. Despite losing $2,000 in his pizza business at Harvard, she was open to hearing another pitch from him. This time she agreed to provide a $200,000 seed investment.

Five months after they started in Tony and Sanjay's living room, LinkExchange had grown into an office on Second Street, in San Francisco's South of Market district, with fifteen employees. Looking around, Tony could see that with every new hire, he was recreating the magic of his Harvard dorm room. LinkExchange was becoming a hub for all his friends to be in one place. If everyone got along and had fun, he figured, they would work hard, play hard, and succeed. And like at Harvard, they often slept where they worked; employees recall Tony and Sanjay sleeping on a cot set up in the conference room.

Outsiders were starting to notice that the formula was paying off. "Any time of the day or night, somebody would pick up the phone," said Ariel Poler, a Silicon Valley veteran who had founded an internet company and served on several boards for other tech startups. Ali had reached out to Ariel, and after a meeting the three partners—Tony, Sanjay, and Ali—they asked him to be a part of LinkExchange. "I remember being blown away by how active and energetic, how smart they were," Ariel said. He soon became chairman of LinkExchange.

■ ■ ■

Other Silicon Valley moneymakers were taking notice, too. Shortly before Poler signed on as chairman, Tony and Sanjay received a call from a man named Lenny Barshack. A former Wall Street executive, Barshack had spent ten years working for Salomon Brothers and New York billionaire Michael Bloomberg before deciding to leave finance for a chance to capitalize on the dot-com boom in the mid-1990s. He started an email directory company called Bigfoot, which eventually became a holding company for several internet companies. Barshack wanted a meeting, so they went to a steakhouse in San Francisco. The pair of twenty-two-year-olds listened as Lenny, sipping a Kahlúa cocktail, made his offer: $1 million in cash to acquire LinkExchange and add it to Bigfoot's portfolio. Tony, with his mop of hair, and Sanjay, with his dark bushy eyebrows, tried not to flinch. It was a life-changing amount of money. They told Lenny they needed a few days to think about it.

Within twenty-four hours, Tony and Sanjay replied with a counteroffer of $2 million, so they could each walk away with $1 million. "I have read somewhere that you're in your best negotiating position if you don't care what the outcome is and you're not afraid to walk away," Tony said. "I've made a lot of money in my lifetime," Lenny responded, declining to meet their price. "But I've also lost a lot of money when I decided to bet the farm instead of taking money off the table. I wish you the best of luck."

Four months after Barshack's offer, Ariel introduced Tony, Sanjay, and Ali to Jerry Yang, the co-founder of Yahoo. Jerry's company had become the embodiment of the dot-com boom, its logo emblazoned on the homepage of millions of internet surfers, pre-Google. Yang had just led Yahoo through an initial public offering in April 1996, at a whopping $1 billion valuation—an extraordinary size at the time. Yang also had more in common with Hsieh than most other Silicon Valley founders at the time: they were both Taiwanese and at the helm of tech companies in an industry where the majority of C-suite-level executives were white.

The three LinkExchange partners assumed Jerry wanted to broker an advertising deal between Yahoo and LinkExchange. But Yang didn't want to negotiate a contract; he wanted to buy LinkExchange, for $20 million (the figure Tony cited in his memoir; according to Ali, it was actually $25 million). For the second time, Tony was doing everything he could not to flinch. The three founders informed their employees, still a tight-knit group of friends, of the offer, and for several nerve-racking days they considered their options. Tony understood that if they said yes to the deal, he would never have to work another day of his life. He then made a list of all the things he would buy with the money: a condo in San Francisco, a big-screen TV, a computer. Maybe some long weekends in Miami or Las Vegas. But ultimately, he realized, he would likely use the money to start another company because he loved the process of building and growing a venture. Why sell a company he was already excited about, only to start another company to be excited about?

In the end, he and the other founders turned down Yahoo's offer. It was a seminal decision he would cite over and over again to underpin his assertion that chasing profits had never been his game, that it was always about passion and purpose. "There will never be another 1997," Tony said during a company meeting, announcing that the Yahoo deal was not happening. His voice trembled as he looked around at the familiar faces of his homegrown company and realized he saw relief. This was not a moment of failure. It was time to continue building.

Yang, meanwhile, was dismayed by the failed acquisition and complained about it during a Yahoo board meeting, which caught the attention of one of his board members, Michael Moritz, a famed investor at the storied venture firm Sequoia Capital. Moritz, a British former journalist whose short-cropped hair and frameless glasses made him look more like a professor of capitalist theory than a venture capitalist, was known for being introspective and proper. Days after meeting the three founders at the LinkExchange office on Second Street, Sequoia invested $2.75 million in LinkExchange, bringing invaluable cachet and credibility to the company. Before this point, the only outside investor they had was Alex's mother.

Shortly after, Tony approached Alfred Lin, his Harvard classmate, who after graduating had decided to get a PhD in statistics at Stanford University in nearby Palo Alto. Tony had wanted to work with Alfred on a business ever since they graduated and had pitched to Alfred everything from a joint Subway sandwich franchise to LinkExchange when he and Sanjay first thought of the idea in March 1996. But Alfred was cautious as well as obedient—he did not want to anger his parents and drop out of grad school to go into what seemed like a very nascent idea with Tony. He had been intrigued enough, however, to join LinkExchange part-time while he was enrolled in his PhD program. Now with backing from Moritz, he was entirely onboard and joined the company full-time as vice president of finance.

■ ■ ■

Over the next year and a half, the company spun into overdrive. They opened sales offices in New York and Chicago, and expanded to additional floors in their building on Second Street. The three founders ensured that they were accessible to the workers, eschewing corner offices and choosing instead to sit in the pit with the rest of the rank-and-file employees. All three had a computer science background, but they played slightly different roles. None was officially given the chief executive officer title. "We didn't really have a CEO," said Poler. "We just had the three guys splitting things. They were always a group to me." Ali took charge of business development strategy, while Sanjay, still painfully introverted, remained behind the scenes as head of product. Tony, described by early LinkExchangers as genuine and authentic in more intimate settings, was not necessarily a natural choice for a leader, and he was uncomfortable with public speaking. Kevin Ascher, an early employee, recalled seeing one of Tony's speeches during a company meeting. "He was shuffling his feet. Not making eye contact and staring at the ground," he said. "He had his hands in his pockets the whole time."

But while Tony lacked presence in the spotlight, he went out of his way to ensure that everyone felt included. "Tony instantly made me feel welcomed and comfortable," said Susan Cooney, one of LinkExchange's first female employees. "It was all those small interactions. They would all be walking out the door and it would be all guys and Tony would say to me, 'Hey, Susan, come join us, we're going to grab a bite to eat.'"

Tony's words were few, which made anything he said seem more important. "Tony was the most visible founder," said Skye Pillsbury, a public relations employee at LinkExchange. "People just had a respect for Tony. He was a kind person, he always seemed fair, and when he spoke you wanted to hear what he had to say." Public speaking and building out the story around himself and the company was a skill that he wanted to improve, Skye recalled. "After we met with a journalist, he would always ask me, 'How did I do? Was it a good meeting?' He really wanted to parse it out afterwards, and he was very open to any advice and guidance that I had for him." So while there was no official CEO, to Sequoia and the rest of the board, "Tony was their darling," Susan Cooney said.

This was particularly evident from his ability to humanize LinkExchange's corporate entrants. Moritz, who had joined the board, was not necessarily an ideal culture fit—buttoned-up and twenty years older than the majority of employees—but he understood founders and also knew when to crack a smile. Shortly after Michael joined the board, the company asked him to come to the offices for the "initiation meeting," a monthly event at LinkExchange where new employees would be tricked into wearing suits and ties for what they thought was a formal event, when in reality it was a practical joke—an idea of Tony's. During this meeting, Moritz and the new hires stood at the front of the room. Then, under Tony's direction, someone broke out a boom box and started blasting Los Del Rio's "Macarena." Everyone in the room started clapping and cheering as Michael Moritz was forced to cross his arms and sway his hips in front of the entire company. Tony looked around at all the laughing faces in the room with feelings of contentment and happiness. *I can't believe this is real*, Tony thought.

Outside of hazing new hires, LinkExchange started other traditions like happy hours at the local Irish dive bar, called Kate O'Brien's. Another staple event was DrinkExchange, a monthly party hosted at different venues for tech employees from all over Silicon Valley, who were required to buy two drinks and give one away—a play on the credit system at LinkExchange. "Where Wuppies Gather: DrinkExchange Draws Hundreds Every Month," read a 1997 headline from the *San Francisco Chronicle*. A play on "yuppie," the word "wuppie" was reserved for flashy young professionals who made their fortunes on the web. "Last month, 400 revelers—mostly people in their 20s who work for Internet startups—congregated at Backflip in the Tenderloin," the *Chronicle* article stated. "A line snaked out into the street and the wait at the bar was so long that people snuck in beers from the outside." Many of those who worked at LinkExchange during this time recalled a fast-paced and exciting culture. "It still goes down as my favorite work experience for my whole career," said Kevin Ascher. "It was magical, and it was just fun. Everyone liked each other, and it was as much a social life as it was a work life."

Tony started to drink more at LinkExchange. Having lived mostly a life of sobriety, he was now twenty-three years old and willing to embrace libations. Michael Bayle, one of the employees who organized Drink-Exchange, remembered Tony being one of the biggest supporters of the event, even with his "Asian flush"—a reaction to alcohol that typically affects people of Asian descent (because of a missing enzyme that processes alcohol in the body) and which turns people's faces red while speeding up their heart rate and inducing headaches and nausea. "He would turn super red within seconds of any beer," Bayle said. Skye Pillsbury also recalled Tony's enthusiasm during one press tour trip, when he bought everyone tequila shots. "I actually remembered being really surprised because I didn't picture him as a guy who would stay up until 1 a.m. drinking tequila shots," she said. She recalled him being giggly and funny that night. "I remember feeling that he was more himself, like he came out of his shell after drinking."

■ ■ ■

To those who saw and worked with Tony during this time, he seemed like a natural leader who was still learning but had all the potential to be great. To former Harvard classmates whom Tony had hired to help out at LinkExchange, he remained the mischievous and curious friend with wild ideas. In the summer of 1998, Tony organized an impromptu trip to Yosemite, and went to the camping store near the LinkExchange office to buy everyone tents. In addition to Sanjay and Alex Hsu, other college friends including Jill Wheeler and Kami Hayashi joined them. Packed into Tony's mother's minivan, they left after work and arrived at Yosemite after dark, complicating the process of setting up the tents. No one remembered to bring flashlights, but of course Tony kept night-vision goggles in his mother's minivan. Once they finished setting up one of the newly purchased tents, they realized yet another mistake: they would not be able to fit inside because Tony had bought ones meant for kids. The party ended up sleeping in the van.

Tony was also in charge of groceries for the trip, which to him meant a bag of potatoes, hot dogs, and beer. The plan was to cut open the beer cans and cook the potatoes inside. But cooking potatoes on a campfire took longer than expected, so they ended up eating cold hot dogs. Just as the group thought not much else could go wrong, the minivan's brakes over-heated on the drive home and stopped working as they wound through Yosemite Valley. Counting the mishaps and hijinks, the trip made for yet another typical adventure with Tony. It was the fairy tale that Tony had envisioned for himself and his friends all along.

But even fairy tales have an ending. Tony's time at LinkExchange was soon marred by internal politics and drama that led to lessons learned. In 1997, as the dot-com era was in full swing, Ali had started discussions with Viaweb, a newer startup led by Paul Graham (who would later launch the storied startup accelerator Y Combinator), about merging their busi-nesses. Just as the discussions were starting to finalize, Jerry Yang came knocking again. He offered $125 million for Yahoo to buy LinkExchange.

It was a lot of money, and enough to do away with any previous hes-itations Tony, Ali, and Sanjay might have had. They said yes to Yahoo, signed a term sheet, and agreed to cut off talks with Viaweb. Days before signing the final agreement, Ali met Jerry Yang—the "undisputed king of internet at the time," Ali later recalled—for drinks. In Ali's excitement, he suggested to Yang that Yahoo should also think about acquiring Viaweb to make Yahoo's search engine a powerhouse. "Our guys looked at them," Yang responded. "We weren't that impressed with their people."

Ali, an excitable twenty-five-year-old, his confidence boosted by alcohol as well as the looming prospect of more wealth than he had ever imagined, challenged Yang. "Jerry, your guys are wrong," he said. "The Viaweb team is amazing. Their engineers are probably better than yours." Then Ali added, "They are hands down better than us."

"Interesting," Yang replied.

A few days later, after news of the Yahoo acquisition had already filtered through the LinkExchange halls, exciting employees of every rank, the founders received a devastating call. The $125 million deal was off. LinkExchange chairman Poler, who knew Jerry Yang personally, remembered that Yahoo had claimed there was "an issue with a pooling of interest or accounting problems," he said. But in fact, with the help of Ali, Yang realized there was a better deal out there. A few weeks later, a new headline blared through the press and across the internet: Yahoo was buying Viaweb for $49 million.

LinkExchange soon realized that they needed a backup cash reserve, in case their revenue suddenly disappeared. An initial public offering (IPO), which could generate much-needed cash while paying out to investors like Sequoia that were seeking high-yield returns, seemed the most obvious resolution. That was until the Russian financial crisis hit in August 1998, creating a cascading effect on economies worldwide that suddenly erased the possibility of an IPO. The other solution would be to seek an emergency round of funding or an acquisition. To prepare the company for a big exit, LinkExchange's board decided to bring in a new chief executive officer named Mark Bozzini. At the time, it wasn't unusual for a board to bring in a more seasoned CEO to a company in which the founders were very inexperienced business-wise. But according to several former LinkExchangers, hiring Mark—who was the chief executive at Pete's Brewing Company before joining and did not have relevant experience in tech—was not a good move from the beginning. "Things did not go well with the CEO," said Ariel Poler. "Not a happy thing. I don't think it was a good cultural fit."

"I would not describe him as someone who was beloved," Skye said. It felt like "outsiders coming in to make us look ready for the next step. Tony didn't sound like a talking-points founder. Mark was the opposite." Meanwhile, according to one former LinkExchanger, there were employees who wanted to invest in the company ahead of the acquisition so they could make money by selling shares when the company was worth more. Tony and Sanjay were pushing for this plan, but other leaders shot the idea down. "Tony and Sanjay were doing their darndest to keep the culture together, and I believe they both struggled," according to the employee.

Now in three cities with hundreds of employees, Tony started seeing unfamiliar faces in the office. "At the time, I didn't think it was necessarily a bad thing. If anything, not recognizing people due to our hypergrowth made things even more exciting," he later said. "But looking back, it should have been a huge warning sign for what was to come." Tony never said whether there were specific employees who were hired or certain events that happened that led to his feelings of ill will toward the LinkExchange culture. Instead, he described it as a death by a thousand cuts. "Drop by drop, day by day, any single drop or bad hire was bearable and not that big a deal," Tony said. "But in the aggregate, it was torture." Somehow along the way, Tony felt he had lost control of the culture and direction of LinkExchange.

Toward the end of 1998, Tony became disengaged. One morning he found himself pressing the snooze button on the alarm clock six times before coming to a harsh realization: the last time he'd pressed the snooze button that many times was when he was running software tests at Oracle. His detachment was felt throughout the company. "When Mark came in, you just saw less of Tony," Pillsbury recalled. Despite Tony's personal withdrawal, the board was still searching for funding that could help it survive a potential economic crisis but realized that LinkExchange remained an attractive asset with solid financials. In the end, Microsoft came to LinkExchange with the highest offer. Hadi, the twin brother of Ali, who worked at Microsoft, sent a message to Microsoft's chief executive at the time, Steve Ballmer, vouching for LinkExchange. As part of the deal, Microsoft wanted all three founding partners—Tony, Sanjay, and Ali—to stay at LinkExchange for another twelve months. In most acquisitions, the board of directors has a say in such requests. But in this instance, in another vote of confidence, Michael Moritz turned to the three founders during a board meeting and said, "Look, guys, it's your company. Whatever you want to do."

After some deliberation, they decided to go through with the sale, which garnered mixed feelings. At the time, Microsoft was seen as "the evil empire" by many in Silicon Valley. The company was in the midst of major antitrust investigations launched by the U.S. government and was largely viewed as a bully to competitors. There was also a sense that Yahoo could have been a better fit as a parent company. "Yahoo was more our culture," said Skye. "Being acquired by Microsoft felt like being acquired by corporate America. It wasn't the acquisition or exit that a lot of us pictured."

The exit negotiations left a deep impact on Tony. It was his first experience in true corporate America—the dog-eat-dog kind of dealmaking that was unforgiving toward empathetic leaders who cared more about changing the world and helping employees and small business owners than just a big, cash-positive heavy exit strategy. "Without getting into too much detail (and to protect the guilty), it was an education to me in human behavior and character," he later wrote. "Large amounts of money have a strange way of getting people's true colors to come out. I observed the greed of certain people who had joined the company right before the acquisition trying to negotiate side contracts for themselves at the risk and expense of everyone else in the company. There was a lot of drama as people started fighting and trying to maximize the financial outcome only for themselves."

According to Steve Valenzuela, the chief financial officer of Link-Exchange who was brought in right before the acquisition to work with Alfred Lin and prepare the company for an IPO, the negotiations started at noon on a Sunday in Redmond, Washington, at Microsoft's head-quarters. Microsoft first punted over a price tag of $120 million, which Valenzuela said was "totally unacceptable." After six hours of back-and-forth in the board room, Valenzuela finally got Microsoft to $250 million. He then negotiated an additional $15 million to go toward key employees of the company for retention purposes—which Tony and Sanjay then took to the LinkExchange board for approval.

Tony also encouraged executives to give up some of their equity to give back to employees who did not have as much stock, including some lower-level employees. This was not well received by all the executives at LinkExchange. "It was pretty unusual at the time," Valenzuela said, who gave up some of his own equity, per Tony's suggestion.

As for the financial outcome for Tony, he would be set for life. If he agreed to stay for the full year after the acquisition, his take-home would be $40 million in Microsoft stock. If he didn't, he would still take home roughly $32 million.

A few weeks later, in early November 1998, Tony and Sanjay found themselves at lunch together at a restaurant close to LinkExchange. As they were about to finish eating, Tony got a call. It was Alfred. He had just heard from Steve, who was closing the deal at Microsoft's headquar-ters. "Well, I guess the deal closed," Tony said to Sanjay. They stared at each other—Tony with the same mop of hair, Sanjay with the same thick brows. Except this time they weren't staring at each other in shock, as they had after Lenny Barshack made his offer. It was in apathy and relief—relief that this was finally over. "I guess we should probably walk back to the office then," Tony said to Sanjay. "Okay," he replied.

Shortly after, Tony found himself making a list similar to the one he'd made when they got the first offer from Jerry Yang. This time, however, the list was not about all the things he would buy with his newfound wealth. It was a list of the happiest periods in his life. He realized that none of those moments involved money. All of them included building businesses and experiences. "Being creative and inventive made me happy," he said. "Connecting with a friend and talking through the entire night until the sun rose made me happy. Trick-or-treating in middle school with a group of my closest friends made me happy."

Tony left LinkExchange before a year passed. Though he left about $8 million behind, his stake was still worth $32 million—an eye-watering sum for a twenty-five-year-old. Shortly after, he took his friends from Harvard and a few others on a cruise. A bet is a bet, and Tony had become a millionaire within three years of graduating. But while surrounded by friends in the Bahamas as a newly minted millionaire, Tony felt a sense of melancholy. *What's next? What is happiness? What am I working toward?* he wondered.

Such questions guide the lives of many, only now Tony had more money than most would ever see in a lifetime. "If you hate someone, give them a winning lottery ticket and announce it to the world," his childhood friend Alex Hsu later said. "Having so much financial success in your twenties and early thirties comes with a different set of challenges that most people will never have to face."

CHAPTER 5

RAVING

Their heads swayed in unison, their minds and bodies seemingly connected by the bass line thundering through the warehouse, as green laser beams cut through the darkness. Black light illuminated the neon-hued objects and artworks that soared above their heads and decorated the walls, while the acrid smell of fog machines and sweat filled their nostrils. Thousands of faces looked forward, as if possessed by a higher power, their eyes transfixed on the DJ commanding the space at the end of the room.

With every tweak of the track, every bass drop, every brush with the person next to him, Tony was experiencing an epiphany. For the first time, his body and mind were connected to a group of unknown people through techno. "The steady wordless electronic beats were the unifying heartbeats that synchronized the crowd," Tony later wrote of the night in early 1999. "It was as if the existence of individual consciousness had disappeared and been replaced by a single unifying group consciousness, the same way a flock of birds might seem like a single entity instead of a collection of individual birds. Everyone in the warehouse had a shared purpose. We were all contributors to the collective rave experience."

In what seemed like a single moment in time at a run-down warehouse somewhere on the outskirts of the Bay Area, Tony let go of all the logic and rationale that had guided his life to that point and instead found himself being swept by a sense of spirituality. Not a religious feeling, but a connection to those around him. The experience would prove life changing, like an undiscovered power had been unlocked in his mind. "I had awakened," he wrote later. "I had been transformed."

The rave scene in San Francisco had been sparked in the early 1990s, partly driven by self-professed computer geeks who arrived in San Francisco as open-minded, sexually liberated, optimistic young people. "They not only created Internet communities around rave culture; they nurtured and participated in the dot-com boom itself," wrote one journalist. Fueled by acid and MDMA (Ecstasy), the Bay Area was awash in party drugs, with raves popping up in abandoned warehouses all over. To avoid authorities trying to shut the events down in a game of Whac-A-Mole, organizers used clandestine methods to issue times, dates, and locations to attendees by handing out rave flyers at company events or college campuses. One reveler recounted that for one such rave, known as Eon, attendees were told to call the number on a flyer. A voice on the other end of the line provided the next step: *Go to the donut shop on San Pablo Avenue in Berkeley and find the two men sitting in a corner with a cash box and hand over five dollars.* Then the men would write instructions and an address on a piece of paper, revealing the secret location. "Some rave club owners and promoters sell specialty items to dancers in a way that arguably promotes MDMA use," read a notice from the National Drug Intelligence Center at the time. "They provide bottled water and sports drinks to manage hyperthermia and dehydration; pacifiers to prevent involuntary teeth clenching; and menthol nasal inhalers, and chemical lights, and neon glow sticks, necklaces, and bracelets to enhance the effects of MDMA."

Tony tried MDMA for the first time in 1999, the same year he went to his first warehouse rave, and not long after he became a millionaire at twenty-five years of age. "The drug was transformative for us to a certain degree," said a close friend of Tony's who had known him for years and was present when Tony first tried the drug. "It kind of consumed our lives for a little bit." The experience of taking MDMA can be cathartic, and by coupling that with raving, Tony was connecting to a side of himself he hadn't tapped into previously. The most common effects of the substance are to give users a heightened sense of awareness, well-being, empathy, and transcendence. The chemicals release a rush of neurotransmitters such as serotonin, dopamine, and norepinephrine that medical practitioners say provide "optimal conditions for engaging in processing of difficult or traumatic material." Later in life, he'd deflect reporters' questions about potential drug use, but acknowledged that it was part of the scene. Unlike the Tony of yesteryear, who'd remained quiet around strangers and stuck close to his circle, during the warehouse raves he found himself opening up and meeting strangers in a euphoric state and felt his walls come down. "At raves, it was part of the culture and considered perfectly normal to approach strangers and strike up a conversation," he later said. This was a practice that he took beyond the warehouse raves. "I learned to feel comfortable starting conversations with complete strangers no matter where I was or who they were." Tony also began to experiment with acid. After he tried it, "he would just try to do it himself just to explore who he was," a friend said.

■ ■ ■

While the raves were a defining feature of Tony's newfound freedom after his LinkExchange windfall, he and his friends were building their next idea. One day during the winter, Tony had been driving around San Francisco in his modest Acura Integra when he saw that AMC Theaters was opening a new complex at 1000 Van Ness Avenue, an ornate building in the center of town. Upon closer inspection he learned that the building, which had formerly been a Cadillac showroom, had just been converted into a flashy mixed-use residential and retail space. Tony saw what it could become, with its high ceilings, tall windows, and architecture that mixed Renaissance Italy with idealized Spanish colonial style, and he convinced Alfred, Sanjay, Eric Liu, and Alex Hsu to buy residential condos in the building alongside him. He also bought a handful of other apartments to convince other friends to move in.

He and Alfred started an investment firm called Venture Frogs—a name chosen after one of their friends dared them to name the firm after her pet frog—with a mandate to invest in companies with great founders and great ideas. They convinced Sanjay, Alex Hsu, Ali and Hadi Partovi, Ariel Poler, and other former LinkExchangers to back the firm. Together, they raised $27 million. Venture Frogs would be headquartered in one of the loft apartments at 1000 Van Ness, and they took over two retail spaces adjacent to the lobby. In one of the spaces would be the Venture Frogs Incubator—an office space their portfolio companies could work from, with the hope that the companies' teams would collide and germinate new ideas. Eric, who founded a web design company that Venture Frogs invested in, worked in the incubator. There were days when they never left the building because there simply was no need—the commute from home to work was a short elevator ride.

The other retail space would be the Venture Frogs Restaurant, which Tony gave to his parents, Richard and Judy, to manage with the goal of feeding the founders and other employees working out of the incubator. It would go through several iterations, including noodle dishes and boba. At one point its menu had a tech industry theme, with cocktails named after venture funds on Sand Hill Road, the famous street in Palo Alto where all the biggest firms like Kleiner Perkins and Accel were located. The dishes, meanwhile, were named after tech companies, like SoftBank Chicken Satay and Cisco Chinese Chicken Salad.

More than a decade before Adam Neumann, the Israeli entrepreneur and marketing spin doctor who blurred the lines between work, play, and other parts of life with the ethos of the co-working venture WeWork and its residential arm WeLive, Tony fused those elements together at 1000 Van Ness, just as he had done at Harvard. Once they moved into the building, Tony and his friends owned 20 percent of its apartments— technically registered to a separate address, 151 Alice B. Toklas Place, because the complex was so large—and had 40 percent of the seats on the board of the building's homeowners' association. "We could create our own adult version of a college dorm and build our own community," he wrote later. "It was an opportunity for us to create our own world. It was perfect."

But at Harvard, he and his friends had been connected by an under-lying thread: they were all naturally gifted intellectuals. They would stay up all night together, to be sure, but it was not to party—it was to watch movies, play cards or video games, and order takeout. Until now, he had spent his life on a strict path first laid out by his parents and then guided by his own intelligence and ambition, and there hadn't been time or the environment for him to truly let loose. The adventurous and experience-creating side of him that dared to take out *The "What's Happening to My Body?" Book for Boys* from the local library or drive all the way to Mexico by himself to watch an eclipse was about to enter a new phase. "I think all the growing up that we all did, in high school and college and post-college, a lot of that was delayed for him," said a close childhood friend.

While he already lived in a 1,400-square-foot loft on the seventh floor, there was a sprawling 3,500-square-foot penthouse on the floor above: unit 810. Seeing the open space in his new figurative dorm, Tony knew exactly what to do with it. He purchased the loft and decided that the space would be used to "architect our parties and gatherings," as he later said. It quickly became the central hub for socializing, partying, and after-hours debauchery. With two bedrooms, a contraband indoor hot tub, a setup for a deejay to spin, and a living room so large that it would look empty even if a hundred people were in there, it became an epic party spot for his growing circle of friends (much to the chagrin of his neighbors).

Club BIO, as it became known because the unit number looked like the letters B-I-O, was part of Tony's grand vision to re-create elements of the TV shows *Friends* and *Melrose Place*: all of his friends living, working, and partying in close proximity. Tony was enamored with the idea of creating an enclosed world for him and his friends within a single city block. "I wanted 810 to become our tribe's own private version of Central Perk," he later wrote, referring to the famous coffee shop in *Friends*. "I envisioned our friends gathering in 810 on Sundays for champagne brunches. I envisioned 810 as being the afterparty meet-up spot after a night out at a club, bar, or rave."

Victoria Recano first met Tony and Alfred when she arrived at 1000 Van Ness to interview them for a piece on ZDTV, a cable channel that focused on computers, technology, and the internet. She'd been skimming news stories looking for a lead and had come across an article that detailed how Tony and Alfred, after the success of LinkExchange, had launched a new startup incubator in the former Cadillac building. It was Tony's first on-camera interview, and he appeared terribly nervous. She thought it was intriguing that his parents were managing the restaurant in the building, and interviewed them, too. Once the cameras were off, Tony mentioned they were having a party at their place at 1000 Van Ness and that Victoria should come. In her early twenties, Victoria, who had grown up in St. Louis, Missouri, still considered herself both conservative and pretty innocent—she hadn't ever been drunk—but she had arrived in San Francisco only recently and didn't know many people.

So she agreed, and brought along a friend of hers named Tom. When they walked into the party in Club BIO, the first thing they noticed was the hot tub in the living room. Tom thought it was awesome. Victoria thought it was gross. Walking farther into the space, Tony showed her over to a table, where there was a gigantic bowl of punch and other drinks. "Let me make you something and you can try it," he said to her, adding that if she didn't like it, she didn't have to drink it. "I had a couple of sips and that was that," Victoria recalled. Looking around at the party, she saw a group of people having fun. She and Tom attended a few other parties at Club BIO, but often left early enough to avoid the wildness of the wee hours.

Another new entrant to Tony's life during this era was a man named James Henrikson. The two met on a camping trip in 1998 when Tony's childhood friend Eric Liu brought along James, whom he knew from UC Berkeley, where they had been fraternity brothers. "It was not what you thought of when you think of Greek life," said James. "It was more a bunch of guys with no money going on ski trips with no girls." James studied biology, physics, and chemistry at Berkeley, then moved to Hawaii with his girlfriend for a year to study for the MCAT with the intention to go to medical school. After a year in the Aloha State, he decided he did not want ten more years of school. So he went back to San Francisco and, after a year of little income, started working three jobs: options trading for a brokerage firm, lab work at UC San Francisco, and retail management at the clothing store Abercrombie & Fitch. After getting back in touch with Eric, who was still at LinkExchange right around the time of the acquisition, James found himself making s'mores around a campfire next to Tony.

"When I got there, I didn't know who Tony was," James said. "When I left, we were best friends." The two connected over a love for meeting new people. But while Tony was initially shy around strangers, James was extroverted in comparison, which made him a perfect companion for Tony. The two started hanging out together and soon became inseparable. Though James lived only a few blocks away, Tony asked him to move to 1000 Van Ness. "You need to move in with me," Tony said to him. "I'm tired of walking back and forth." James moved into the building shortly thereafter.

San Francisco was the bedrock of two social undercurrents that peaked in 1999: the lavish dot-com era and rave culture. The dot-com bubble had been frothing for a few years by now, and startup companies that had zero track record and no path to profitability were still somehow either getting venture funding or going public in the markets. Whether the companies were celebrating an IPO or a new product, tech startups became notorious for spending excessively on massive soirees. "Dot-Com Party Madness" was one headline from the online publication *Salon*. "Forget about return on investment. Bay Area tech companies spend $1 million a month on food, drink and music in exchange for 'buzz.' . . . In any given week, technology companies throw 15 to 20 parties in the San Francisco Bay Area." Tony and James became regulars on the circuit. Shortly after Marc Benioff launched Salesforce.com in 1999, a company that would propel him into the billionaire ranks and make him the self-appointed benefactor-in-chief of San Francisco in decades to come, he threw a party to commemorate the company's founding. "The company had 200 customers by then but still minuscule revenues and no profits," read a CNN story at the time. "That didn't stop Benioff from wanting to throw the best launch party ever." Benioff rented the entire Regency Theater in San Francisco for a 2,000-person event headlined by the B-52s, whose hit "Love Shack" could send even the most introverted software engineers into a hip sway. "It's simply become part of the way we do business," Craigslist's Craig Newmark told a reporter at the time.

Tony dove deep into his new social life and picked up new interests. He found a group of people to start playing poker with, and another set of friends who partied much more than his Harvard and LinkExchange friends. He reconnected with high school friends who since their time at Branson had met new people, who were now brought into the sphere. Tony relished it. "As our group grew, I realized that forming new friendships and deepening the connections within our burgeoning tribe was bringing both a sense of stability and a sense of excitement about the future for all of us," he wrote later. "The connectedness we felt was making all of us happier, and we realized it was something that we had all missed from our college days."

On nights at Club BIO, friends recalled as much as $10,000 being spent on alcohol, only to have it run out before midnight. DJ Solomon, the local deejay for the Golden State Warriors, the Bay Area's NBA team, would occasionally be seen spinning a record in a corner, amid enough fog machines to cause a fire hazard. At one point, one of the rooms in the penthouse earned the nickname "the penalty box"; it was a room full of mattresses. "Let's just say they kind of liked to explore the boundaries," said the friend.

On a weekly basis, Tony and his group were attending warehouse raves or going to nightclubs. Some friends recalled what felt like endless nights at 1015 Folsom, a nondescript building in a then-seedy part of San Francisco's South of Market. On any given Friday, two chaotic dance floors were illuminated with strobe lights and lasers flickering around the windowless club, piercing the faux fog. The floor would be covered with sweat, spilled drinks, and empty beer cans. As bouncers bottlenecked the line snaking from the entrance doors out on the sidewalk, Tony and his friends were getting lost in the rhythm of techno inside. Their nights ultimately continued with a thirty-minute pilgrimage back to Club BIO, where the party would live on.

But as the partying intensified and the spontaneous afterparties ultimately wound up at 1000 Van Ness, college friends like Alfred and Sanjay often skipped the Club BIO nights, preferring to go back to their own apartments instead. Some were in serious relationships; most were simply disinterested in this new lifestyle. Where they left holes, Tony found people to fill in the gaps. Tony would think, "'I like partying with this person, and I shall absorb her into the orbit,'" said a close childhood friend. "Which is just really different from what kind of drove the earlier groups."

■ ■ ■

By day, away from the raves and drug experimentation, Tony was still reserved, shy, and thoughtful. He often slept in one of the rooms at Club BIO, but when he needed quiet or solitude, particularly when he wanted to read, he'd hang out in the lobby of the building or go to Unit 706, where his younger brother, Andy Hsieh, had moved. That unit "was a more controlled environment," said James. "[Unit] 706 was basically Andy, and quiet. It was kind of like Tony's bat cave."

One night in 1999, Tony met a woman named Eva Lee during a group dinner. Small and slight, she was similarly introverted and kept to herself.

For a while, their friendship was platonic—but it was clear Tony took a liking to her. After learning that she was a huge fan of *Star Trek*, Tony took her to see Star Trek: The Experience, a themed attraction at the Las Vegas Hilton, despite his having a fever.

Tony finally worked up the courage to ask Eva out around nine months after they met, and even then, he found a roundabout way to do it. Instead of outright asking her, Tony gave her a CD for the single "Sometimes" by Britney Spears, who had just released her debut album in January.

Sometimes I run, Sometimes I hide.

Sometimes I'm scared of you. But all I wanna do is to hold you tight.

Britney's sweet and gentle croon, it seemed, was enough to sway Eva. They started dating shortly after, and Tony saw in her someone he could connect with. He took her to her first rave. Eva went with Tony and his family back to Branson to attend his younger brother Dave's high school graduation. Eventually Eva moved into 1000 Van Ness with Tony and started working for the Venture Frogs Restaurant as the assistant manager.

One event they attended together as a couple was the wedding of Victoria, the news reporter, and her friend-turned-husband Tom. There's a photo of the just-married couple with a group of friends, including Tony and Eva. Tony, looking like another version of himself—out of character in a black suit, tie, and a crisp white shirt—has a slight smile on his face. Tucked behind him is Eva, wearing a black dress, her head tilted toward the lens. At first glance, they look like they could have been the next couple in the group to tie the knot.

■ ■ ■

Amid the parties, raves, and relationships, Tony was still running a $27 million fund with Alfred at the height of the dot-com bubble in 1999. Though Alfred was rarely seen at the afterparties or clubs, he was the one being photographed next to Tony in news clippings about Venture Frogs. In one photograph for the *San Francisco Chronicle*, the two are smiling and looking at each other—Alfred in thick glasses and a blue button-down tucked into khakis, and Tony in a black-and-white checkered collared shirt, unbuttoned and untucked.

Their investment philosophy was to make small angel investments—anywhere from $100,000 to $3 million—in a lot of internet companies. Then after a few months, during which the companies would ideally be working out of the Venture Frogs Incubator and eating from the Venture Frogs Restaurant, they would get the bigger venture firms like Sequoia and Accel to invest as well. In their first year, they invested in twenty-seven companies, including AskJeeves, OpenTable, Tellme Networks, Entango, NeoPlanet, and Fusion.

But it quickly turned out that they were better at leading companies than investing in them, and not all of their investments were well thought-out. In 1999 there was a frenzy to buy internet website addresses when people realized that often-used words generated vast internet traffic. Many of the domain names, as they are known, were sold through auctions. For example, www.business.com was sold for $7.5 million to a company called eCompanies, while Bank of America paid $3 million to own the domain www.loans.com. Tony decided he wanted to buy www.drugs.com, and won with a bid for $823,456, a number he chose because it was Alex Hsu's cellphone number. "We hope to be partnering with Drugstore.com and PlanetRx and other online pharmacies," Tony said at the time, though the mischievous side of him simply enjoyed the idea of owning drugs.com. They never got around to it, and sold the domain within two years. Tony also decided to purchase www.bbq.com and asked Alex to repurpose it to sell grills, along with two other former Harvard classmates who were now working at Venture Frogs. "I was coming to work every morning being like, wait, what am I doing with my life?" Alex said.

One day, as Tony and Alfred walked into their Venture Frogs office—which was still in the one-bedroom loft—Tony saw a blinking red light on his voice message machine. The voicemail was from a man named Nick Swinmurn. He had recently bought the domain name www.shoesite.com and set up a website, he said, and wanted to create the largest online shoe store in the world. Tony's immediate thought was that it made for a ridiculous premise for an internet company: *There's no way people would be willing to buy shoes online without trying them on first.* Then the disembodied voice started citing data points, which piqued Tony's interest. *Footwear is a $40* *billion industry in the United States. Catalog sales make up $2 billion. It is likely that e-commerce will continue to grow. And it is likely that people will continue to wear shoes in the foreseeable future.* Soon after, Tony invited Nick to an informal meeting at the Venture Frogs office. Nick, who had just graduated from college a few years earlier, showed up wearing shorts and a T-shirt, which made Tony like him even more.

The idea behind ShoeSite, Nick told Tony, had grown out of his frustration with buying footwear in stores. What if there was a single place online where people could search for exactly the shoe they want, in exactly the right size, and have it show up on their doorstep in a few days? Repeating his voicemail pitch, Nick told Tony that 5 percent of sales in the $40 billion footwear industry were already conducted through paper mail-order catalogs. The numbers not only disproved Tony's initial reaction that people wouldn't buy shoes without trying them on but also made him realize the opportunity was massive.

Though Nick's pitch hyped ShoeSite as a tech-driven company, its origins were laughably archaic. Nick would go to a nearby shoe store, take photos of their inventory, and put it up on the website. When a customer purchased shoes from shoesite.com, Nick would go back to the store, buy it, and ship it out himself. And he'd started getting customers. The theory worked—people *were* willing to buy shoes online. Now he just had to refine it and make it scalable and profitable. At the moment, he'd only raised $150,000 from friends and family, and Nick wanted Venture Frogs to be his first outside investor.

Hearing Nick's pitch and story, they were intrigued. But on a call later, Alfred asked a simple question: "Do you have any experience in the footwear industry?"

CHAPTER 6

THE SHOE GUY

Fred Mossler was surrounded by boxes in a stockroom when he noticed the light on his desk phone blinking. Probably another voicemail from a vendor, he figured. As the regional men's shoe buyer for Nordstrom, he had spent the last eight years working his way up through the ranks of the retailer. He was good at what he did, and until that moment before he picked up the phone to listen to the message, he had what he figured was a pretty easygoing, well-to-do life. After graduating from Southern Oregon University in 1990 with a business degree, Fred had headed north to Seattle for a job at Nordstrom's headquarters. It was still an old-school shop nearing its centennial at that point, and the retailer still required all of its employees—including the fourth-generation Nordstrom family members—to work the shop floor before moving into corporate roles. From selling shoes, Fred had since moved with the company from Seattle to Sacramento, then to Hawaii—where he met his second wife—and now back to the San Francisco Bay Area, where he'd grown up in the 1960s and 1970s.

At six foot four, with the look of a Northern California surfer and a thick shock of hair that framed a face some would say resembled the movie star Nicolas Cage's, he had recently become a father to a baby boy, and he and his wife were planning out their future; they had just put a deposit down on a house in San Francisco. It had taken him hard work to get to this point, but now, in his early thirties, life's promises were opening up before him.

The voice on the other end of the line introduced himself as Nick Swinmurn. He was a recruiter for a new internet startup that was selling shoes online, and he was looking for someone with experience in shoes. He did not immediately offer that he was also the CEO and primary employee of this company, ShoeSite. What he did say was that his startup was going to be revolutionary: *the* destination for online shoe shopping.

Nick couldn't have known he was leaving a message for someone who also harbored a sense of entrepreneurialism, something that hadn't been satisfied by dealing with vendors for Nordstrom. Back at Southern Oregon University, Fred had come up with a range of ways to make money and create things, like hosting a baseball card show, or hiring a dance instructor to put on lessons for students. So while he now had a mortgage and a family to support, there seemed no harm in calling Nick back.

A few days later, in June 1999, Fred met with Nick at Fourth Street Bar and Grill to hear his pitch. The concept had already been proven, Nick told him; people were buying shoes unseen from his website. He began reeling off the metrics about the size of the current retail market, customers' willingness to buy shoes through catalogs, and so on. He had interested investors, but the problem was they wouldn't commit until Nick had hired someone with retail buying experience—a "shoe guy." Fred told him that it sounded like an interesting prospect, but he was hesitant: his life commitments were currently supported by a well-paying and stable job at Nordstrom. Nick suggested another meeting, this time with investors. *What the heck,* Fred figured, and agreed.

■ ■ ■

When Nick had last spoken to Tony and Alfred, they had given him some advice. First, he should consider renaming the company. ShoeSite was too generic and too limiting, Tony had said. What if he wanted to expand to selling other categories of merchandise?

After some thinking, Nick came back to them with a new name: Zapos, from *zapatos,* the Spanish word for shoes. Tony said he should put an extra "p" in it, to avoid people mispronouncing it as "ZAY-poes." Thus in July 1999 was born a name that would stick with them forever.

Nick also had found a solution to their other piece of advice. By cold-calling Nordstrom he'd found a potential "shoe guy." On an afternoon in July, Nick, Fred, Tony, and Alfred met over lunch at Mel's, a casual diner chain a block away from Venture Frogs. Sitting down over turkey sandwiches and chicken noodle soup, they began to talk business. Since Nick had last seen Tony and Alfred, Zappos had more than proven that people were willing to buy shoes online. They were averaging about $2,000 worth of orders weekly, and the numbers were increasing, fast. If Fred decided to join, they felt they could convince shoe brands to start shipping from their own warehouses directly to customers, meaning they wouldn't have to worry about running a warehouse on their own. At the end of the meal, they found themselves in a stalemate: Fred would join only if Venture Frogs invested, and Tony and Alfred would invest only if Fred was in.

"Nick and Fred were exactly the type of people we were looking to invest in," Tony later wrote. "We didn't know if the shoe idea would work or not, but they were clearly passionate and willing to place big bets." They invested $500,000 in seed capital into Zappos. Fred quit his Nordstrom job a week later.

For the next few months, Nick and Fred hustled, traveling to as many shoe conferences as possible to sign footwear brands to Zappos.com. At their first conference in Las Vegas, they approached eighty brands. Only three agreed to do business with them. Because this was a nascent business in the still-nascent industry of e-commerce, no question they received was too trivial for them to address—*Who is your shipping carrier? How do you plan to handle returns? What is an email? How do I make an email for myself?*

Every two weeks, Tony and Alfred checked in on Zappos, as they did with every other company in their portfolio. But Tony found himself checking in with Zappos more and more, offering as much technical advice as he could. And despite his nonstop social calendar and two dozen other companies to think about, he was starting to miss the grind, the highs and lows of being part of a burgeoning startup. He wanted to start building again.

■ ■ ■

Anticipation hung in the air in December 1999. It was the last month of the millennium, and the invisible threat of Y2K—the shorthand term for the year 2000—was upon humankind. It was also the holidays, and Tony's birthday was coming up. For months, Tony had been planning two massive parties at Club BIO—one for his twenty-sixth birthday on December 12, and another party for New Year's Eve.

These were potentially the last parties that Club BIO would host. The week before his birthday party, Sequoia told Tony and Alfred that they were not willing to invest in Zappos. Tony and Alfred had wrongly assumed it was a no-brainer—after all, they had turned Sequoia's $2.7 million investment in LinkExchange into a $68.3 million exit (once the firm sold the Microsoft shares it received in the acquisition). But there were now even more signs that the economy was going to turn, so venture firms were less bullish than before, and they wanted to see more progress and growth before investing. Sequoia suggested they reach out again in several months. But this was problematic: Zappos was days away from running out of cash.

Tony and Alfred had a decision to make. Providing a second round of capital to Zappos was technically against their investment philosophy. It would also prevent them from investing in another company. But they liked the team's passion and drive—and they believed in Nick and Fred. So they decided to invest in another round, under the condition that Zappos move into the Venture Frogs Incubator. This would save Zappos money on rent, and it would also allow Tony to be more involved, as he lived right upstairs. However, the incubator space was under construction at the time. "I have my birthday party this weekend, and a New Year's party in two weeks," Tony said to Alfred. "Let's have them move into my loft right after New Year's. We'll convert it into an office until the incubator offices are ready downstairs."

"Sounds good," Alfred replied.

Tony then called Fred to deliver the news—they were going to provide three to four months' worth of funding. However, Tony was going to be much more involved, and they would have to move into his loft. They accepted his terms.

The parties were a resounding success. Tony planned for them to have an underground warehouse feel to them, which meant thumping electronic music, dancing, fog machines, and a huge amount of alcohol. At the New Year's Eve party, after most of the partygoers had left by 3 a.m., Tony decided to turn on all the fog machines at full blast to fill the entire Club BIO with fog. Then an alarm started shrieking—he had set off the smoke alarms for the entire building. Firefighters showed up and, after realizing it was all a fluke and the person who was responsible was a shy, goofy young Asian man, they laughed it off and wished Tony a happy new year. A chance encounter with an anonymous blond woman shortly after that episode had an impact on Tony that night:

"Isn't this amazing? You created all of this," Tony later recalled the woman saying in his memoir.

> *I looked over to see who it was, but it was someone I didn't recognize. She had blonde hair and blue eyes, and was also leaning out the window to marvel at the flashing lights of the fire trucks below.*
>
> *"Yeah, they were pretty nice about it. I was worried that they would be mad at me, especially since it's New Year's," I said.*
>
> *"That's not what I meant. I mean all of this," she said. She turned and gestured toward the rest of the people that were still at the party. "You could have done anything you wanted and you chose to create an experience that people will remember forever."*
>
> *She gazed into my eyes. I could still hear the music in the background, but the rest of the world seemed to disappear. I had no idea who this girl was, but somehow the universe had brought us together for a single moment in time that I would remember forever.*
>
> *"Envision, create, and believe in your own universe and the universe will form around you," she said softly. "Just like what you did tonight."*

Her words convinced Tony he no longer wanted to just be a passive investor in Zappos. He wanted to be deeply involved in creating something again. And while the parties he was architecting were great, he found himself yearning for something more. He was addicted to the art of building a company from the ground up. So Tony decided that with the new year, he was going to go all in on Zappos.

■ ■ ■

A long, hard road lay ahead. The new millennium brought forth a dose of skepticism and higher interest rates that prompted the market to crash.

All the optimism and hope that had been building behind tech companies imploded in April 2000 as the stock market cratered. Capital immediately dried up, and many tech startups whose entire business models depended on external funding for free services—including some of Venture Frogs' portfolio companies—soon went bankrupt. Though a few Venture Frogs companies moved into the incubator office, and others had presented small exits when they were sold or went public, most of them failed to secure additional funding from the bigger venture firms. With Zappos becoming the primary bright spot in their portfolio—and even that was relatively dim—Tony and Alfred decided to use what was left in the fund to invest again in Zappos. "Our decision to focus on (Zappos.com) is that it seemed like a much bigger opportunity," he later said.

They tried to raise a second fund from new and existing investors, but no one wanted to park their money in a tech-focused fund. They continued calling Sequoia to invest in Zappos, but the larger venture capital firm remained disinterested. Tony had already begun to personally fund Zappos, but as the year dragged on, he became chief executive officer of Zappos. Nick and Fred were still intimately involved in steering the ship, but it was clear they were now depending on Tony to see the company through. "Right now, because we are unprofitable with very limited cash, we are in a race against time," Tony wrote in an email to the company in October 2000. "Once we get to profitability, then we will be able to think longer-term and bigger picture, and fantasize more about how to rule the world."

The path to profitability for Zappos, first and foremost, meant cutting expenses wherever possible. They laid off nearly half of their forty employees, and those remaining had to take pay cuts. Zappos's headquarters moved from Club BIO to the Venture Frogs Incubator in the lobby of 1000 Van Ness, and Tony put five beds into Unit 810 to start housing Zapponians for free, including Nick. The other three condos that Tony owned in the building also started to house Zappos employees for free. Less than three years before, he'd been a newly minted multimillionaire. Now, with four condos, the retail space in 1000 Van Ness, other property investments, his dabbling in day trading and poker, and his lavish spending at parties and bars (where he most often paid the tab for others), on top of his personally funding Zappos every three to four months, he watched the numbers in his bank account dwindle.

In one of his last-ditch attempts to raise money, he tried to get Alex Hsu and his mother to invest in Zappos. "Listen, I know everything's going belly-up," Tony said. "But there's one company I want you to invest in. I'm sure it will do well."

"Tony, there's just no way," Alex said.

There seemed to be no other way out for Zappos, so Tony sold nearly all his properties in the Bay Area for less than what he'd paid for them. Eventually, all that remained were two properties, including Unit 810. Tony and Alfred also sold all the domains that Venture Frogs had bought, including drugs.com, to fund Zappos. "That's right, Venture Frogs, a startup incubator run by Tony Hsieh and Alfred Lin, is in the process of selling its domain name drugs.com to an undisclosed buyer," *Wired* reported in 2001 about the sale. "Instead, the company will focus on building out Zappos.com, its e-commerce site that sells more than 100 brands of shoes."

It became clear to Tony that the company needed a deus ex machina—an unexpected miracle in a hopeless situation. They had tightened the company's belt as far as possible in order to cut costs. Tony, meanwhile, had more or less poured his entire net worth into the company. If they did not come up with another solution quickly, everything they built would be lost. "The situation was dire," Tony recalled later. "Everything I was involved in was running out of money. The restaurant, the incubator, Zappos and myself personally."

One weekday afternoon, Tony and Fred were having a drink at the bar in Venture Frogs Restaurant. They were feeling downtrodden and rudderless. Over a beer (Fred's) and a Grey Goose and soda (Tony's), Fred helped Tony realize that their initial business plan of not having their own inventory of shoes to sell from was not going to work. If they were going to make it through, they needed their own warehouse. They also needed to somehow convince shoe brands to sell to them; at the time, brands like Skechers or Nike only sold their shoes to third-party vendors that had brick-and-mortar stores. Zappos was supposed to be purely online.

So they devised a plan. They would hire more employees who had experience managing and buying shoe inventory. Their headquarters at 1000 Van Ness would become a hybrid office space and warehouse to store inventory. They would buy a small, cheap brick-and-mortar shoe store to create the illusion of having a physical location for shoe brands. In the meantime, they would use their office address and hope that shoe brands would not ask to tour their "store." They would also need to update the Zappos software for these changes. Doing the math, they calculated that their new plan would cost about $2 million.

"Where are we going to get the money?" Fred asked.

"I'll worry about that part," Tony replied. "Just assume that if you can convince a brand to sell to us, then we'll have the money to pay for the inventory for that brand."

Fred had recently been thinking about the leap he'd taken leaving Nordstrom. Seated behind Tony in the apartment/office space at 1000 Van Ness, Fred had been awestruck by him on a daily basis, and had come to trust him. One afternoon, Tony had swiveled around in his chair and asked, "What would make Zappos better?" Fred had been drowning in the monotony of trying to manually register Zappos's hundred-plus vendors into the online portal and uploading their products to the website, and he told Tony that if there was some kind of portal where these vendors could log in and submit their products themselves, then Fred could focus on actually running the business. Tony had swiveled back without a word. "Three hours later, he turned around and said, 'Something like this?'" Fred recalled. Lo and behold, the Zappos extranet had been born—a portal that would come to define the company's success and be used by thousands of vendors.

While they had been talking at the Venture Frogs bar, Tony had come to another decision. He was going to sell everything in his name at firesale prices, including Unit 810, and put all the money back into Zappos. He did not want to give up on his dream of a Central Perk for him and his tribe, but right now he had a more important dream to achieve. *Friends* would have to wait.

■ ■ ■

Tony would sell a total of eleven properties and pour almost $6 million of his own money into the business before the plan worked. In 2000, Zappos's gross sales were $1.6 million. By the end of 2001, sales had quadrupled to $8.6 million. To get there, they first turned the reception area of their office into a small shoe store in lieu of an actual separate brick-and-mortar location. Soon after, Fred found a small shoe store in a town two hours north of San Francisco that was looking for a buyer, and by chance there was an abandoned building across the street. They bought both, and turned the latter into Zappos's first official warehouse. Tony worked side by side with the engineers to rewrite the website code so that it could handle the new business model of selling both inventoried products as well as products that could be shipped directly by shoe brands. Fred, meanwhile, also delivered, signing on more and more shoe brands to Zappos.

But the company was still not profitable. As much as they were making, they were spending just as much to buy the inventory and cover the added costs. Eventually, Tony decided they needed a warehouse located somewhere in the middle of the country; shipping times from California to the East Coast were simply too long. They settled on Kentucky, near a distribution center with close proximity to carriers. But the process of setting up the new warehouse was fraught with problems. While driving inventory from California to Kentucky, one of the semitrailer trucks got into a major accident and flipped over. Around $500,000 worth of shoes, or 20 percent of their inventory, was now scattered on the side of a highway. Separately, it came to light that the warehouse logistics company they were working with to get the Kentucky warehouse up and running had oversold its capabilities—they had never worked with products that had as much variance as shoes did (colors, sizes, widths, brands). Entire swaths of Zappos's inventory languished outside of the warehouse, unsorted and uncataloged—which meant it couldn't be sold because it hadn't been logged into the system.

■ ■ ■

By the middle of 2002, Zappos was once again strapped for cash. The company had about two months left of funds before it would go out of business. Tony was also nearly out of cash, too. The future of Zappos and Tony's fiscal health now depended on the sale of Unit 810, which Tony had overpaid for and was now proving to be impossible to sell without taking a huge loss in a down market.

The efforts to sell the property had coincided with a long-scheduled trip to Tanzania, where Tony planned to scale Mount Kilimanjaro, the tallest peak in Africa. For the three-week journey, he would be joined by a young woman named Jenn Lim, whom he had met at his twenty-sixth-birthday bash in the apartment he was now trying to sell. They'd become fast friends, and after Jenn was laid off from her internet consulting job, she and Tony thought the adventure would be a great chance to get away.

Though the trip couldn't have come at a worse time, considering the logistics mishaps and the cash drain, Tony had figured there was nothing he could do to help solve either of those issues by staying. But ten thousand miles from San Francisco, he found those problems weighing on him. Neither Tony nor Jenn was all that athletic, and neither took great pleasure from physical activity. On their first day of the hike they found themselves walking through a rainforest downpour only to then head up into a cooler climate that left them shivering in their drenched clothes. Collapsing in his tent, Tony struggled to stay both awake and asleep.

In the darkness, his phone was ringing, which was weird: there wasn't supposed to be reception on the mountain. His real estate agent was on the end of the line giving him the news he wanted to hear: they had found a buyer and Unit 810 had sold. "Zappos was saved," Tony recalled later. But it turned out to be no more than a vivid dream, and when he awoke, there were still four more days of hiking ahead.

When he and Jenn returned to San Francisco, Tony's real estate agent told him there had in fact been an offer on the unit, but the buyer backed out because their fortune teller had told them the apartment had bad feng shui. Tony instructed the agent to drop the price to 40 percent below what he had paid for the condo. Shortly after, he found a buyer.

"As your friend and financial adviser, I'm advising you not to do it," said Alfred. He had since left Tony's immediate orbit and started working for Tellme Networks, a telephone tech company that Venture Frogs had invested in, as vice president of business development. But Alfred still looked out for Tony's blind spots. "It may pay off in the long run, but it's not worth the risk." Tony and Alfred were two very different people, however. Alfred had always been more careful and deliberate. Tony, meanwhile, had always been willing to risk it all for an idea. He accepted the offer on the apartment.

Now the company had at least half a year of runway. Tony rolled up his sleeves and got to work at the warehouse. It had been his idea to open up a warehouse in Kentucky, so he felt it was his problem to solve. Tony ended up spending five months there, cleaning up the mess as well as building an entirely new warehouse system that they decided to call WHISKY, an acronym for Warehouse Inventory System in Kentucky. They stopped working with their previous warehouse logistics partner and, despite not having any background in warehouse operations, somehow built a system within a fifty-thousand-square-foot space that could work for Zappos.

By the end of 2002, the company had nearly quadrupled its revenue to $32 million. Tony's bets had paid off. "Everyone could feel it," Tony later said. "We were at a turning point for the company."

■ ■ ■

By now, Tony and Fred were inseparable. Both were obsessed with the company and its potential, and they talked about its future and prospects at every opportunity, whether it was at the Venture Frogs Restaurant or Mel's Diner, the spot where it had all started. After a series of lunches, they decided that they didn't want Zappos to be just about selling shoes. It needed to have a bigger purpose than taking as much market share in the shoe category as possible. Reflecting on their journey over the last few years, there was an underlying theme beneath it all—they had always chosen the route that would improve the experience for the customer, even if it was hard or incurred short-term losses. If they followed that edict for all of their operating decisions, could it keep customers coming back, and pay back tenfold? They decided that Zappos as a brand would be about providing the very best customer service. Full stop.

The first decision they made was to remove Zappos's practice of allowing shoe brands to send products directly to customers. They realized that the best customer service came when all the inventory was processed in their own warehouse systems. Though this would wipe out about 25 percent of sales on Zappos.com, they bet that it would improve the Zappos experience in the long term.

And they were right: in 2003, the company ended with $70 million in gross sales. The next year, in keeping with Zappos's newfound purpose, Tony and Fred discussed their own customer service department. It was hard to find competent workers in this industry in San Francisco—the workforce in the Bay Area catered more to Silicon Valley tech companies. The majority of workers were trained as engineers, sales representatives, or marketing consultants; working at a call center was not what the average San Franciscan saw as a promising career trajectory. They needed to move the company to a place where hospitality and customer service were priorities. They also decided that instead of building out a satellite call center, they needed to move the whole company. Customer service was not going to be an afterthought for Zappos. It was its entire business model.

So, after weeks of deliberating between various cities, from Phoenix to Portland to Des Moines, they landed on Henderson, a suburban town just south of the city limits of Las Vegas. Though it wasn't the cheapest place to build a company, it was more affordable than San Francisco. There was no state income tax in Nevada. And its proximity to Vegas—a city built on nightlife and hospitality—meant that employees in the area typically worked for one of two industries that hinged on the experiences of their customers. Above all, Tony believed that Las Vegas would be the happiest option for his employees. So in 2004, Tony sent out an email to the ninety Zapponians that the company was moving to Sin City. Seventy employees agreed to make the move. Tony had made yet another decision that would change the course of the company. This time it would change the course of Tony's life, too.

CHAPTER 7

THE TRIFECTA

Mark Guadagnoli was one of the first parents to arrive at the elementary school math competition that afternoon in 2006. His six-year-old son had a knack for numbers, and Mark was quietly confident that he might even win. Scanning the auditorium, Mark saw a tall lanky man sitting on his own, and decided to go over and introduce himself. Looking up with a genial smile, the man said his name was Fred, then pointed at his own son, the tall half–Pacific Islander boy towering above all the other students.

In his early forties, with a Mediterranean face and a subtle Texan twang, Mark exchanged pleasantries with Fred as they watched the number of child contestants onstage dwindle. By the end of the competition, it was just their sons left standing. The final problem was an impossible equation, and Mark was sure there was no chance either boy knew the answer. Fred's son, Kalei, passed on the question. Mark's son, Max, was up by one point; because he wouldn't lose any points if he too passed on the question, all he had to do was pass, and he'd win the competition. Mark sighed heavily as Max attempted the problem, provided the wrong answer, and lost his lead. Then, to Fred and Mark's bewilderment, the two boys looked at each other and embraced in a bear hug, Max disappearing into Kalei's arms. "What Max knew was that if he answered the question wrong, he would be deducted points, and he and Kalei would tie," Mark said. "So they both won."

Mark invited Fred and his family over for dinner to celebrate a few days later. Over homemade pizza, Fred became fascinated by Mark's backstory.

Mark was a tenured kinesiology professor at the University of Nevada, Las Vegas, and recently he had been helping struggling athletes reinvent their game through a type of talk therapy he had created. He explained that he had been working with a kicker on UNLV's football team who'd had a stellar freshman year but was now a train wreck, making only half of his field goals, and the coaches were at a loss for what to do. Aware of Mark's work, they asked if he could try and turn this young man's future around. When Mark arrived at training, the kicker set up the ball on a small stand and repeatedly nailed the shot between the posts from forty yards out. But when Mark simulated a real game by holding the ball in place for the kicker, the ball went spinning far away. Mark began working with the player and after two months the kicker was making 85 percent of the goals.

"Hey, I've got a friend," Fred said. "I think he'd be really interested in talking to you."

■ ■ ■

The year before, Mark had emerged as a minor celebrity in academic circles after co-authoring a study on the science of learning. Under an unmemorable title, the Challenge Point Framework, his paper claimed to have discovered a revolutionary hack: by undertaking a customized challenge, an individual could change their thinking to learn a task three to four times quicker than if they followed a conventional curriculum. The root cause of failure in elite athletes, for example, often lay in training regimes that either didn't challenge them enough or pushed them too far beyond their limits. In essence, Mark's research provided a scientific backbone to a philosophical conundrum: How much is too little, or too much, and where is the sweet spot?

In the case of the UNLV kicker, Mark found that the kicker did no mental preparation before taking a shot, and the presence of Mark holding the ball in place made him so nervous that it became overwhelming. After several weeks, the kicker became comfortable with Mark standing nearby and then ultimately holding the ball. He later broke the career goal record for the regional conference and ended his senior year on the list of top potential draft picks in the nation, signing a free-agent contract with the St. Louis Rams.

In the years after Mark's paper was released, more than a hundred subsequent studies cited his research, testing the framework out on overworked surgeons, burned-out PhD students, and more struggling athletes, each of whom saw astounding results. Mark had since been hired to consult for USA Track and Field and for the PGA Tour.

Seated at an American-style restaurant a few minutes' walk from the Zappos headquarters, Tony was listening with intense curiosity as Mark retold his story. Alfred was also there, having joined Zappos in 2005 as chairman and chief operating officer, and he had questions too. Fred sat back and watched his introduction unfold. At Zappos, Tony explained, he was trying to figure out ways to improve the orientation program for new hires. Could the Challenge Point Framework be applied to corporate executives, employees, and entire companies, creating a workforce that learned and then performed multiple times faster, better, more effectively?

It hadn't been done before, Mark said, but he couldn't see why not. When the group stood up to leave, Tony suggested Mark join them back at the Zappos office for a tour. At the front entrance, Fred opened the glass door for Mark, and Tony walked in alongside him. Looking up at Mark, Tony said, "Would you come work for Zappos?"

Beyond being a tech company, Mark had little idea what Zappos did, nor what roles the three men in front of him held. But after spending an hour at lunch with these guys, he felt a synergy between them that he'd never encountered, and whatever they had in mind, he was sure it would be worth the risk. "I'd love to join," Mark replied.

■ ■ ■

On his first day, Mark was shown his seat in a row of cubicles shared with Fred, Alfred, and Tony. His first task would be to build on the orientation program for new employees using elements of his Challenge Point Framework. They had been looking for a way to get new hires engaged that didn't involve sitting through hours of lectures. The end result was a program that focused on employees' motivations. For instance, an offer to pay employees to leave the company during orientation tested whether they were committed. The program also required that everyone from new executives to entry-level employees spend time working in the call center before they started their official roles—a practice that had proven success-ful for Fred during his time at Nordstrom.

But Mark's work quickly expanded beyond its initial purview. Tony often complained that their cubicle was referred to as "executive row," so Mark took to calling it "monkey row" and decorated the space to illustrate the point with a series of nets to the ceiling from which stuffed animals and plants hung. Once Tony added some more plants to make it feel like a jungle, the ceiling was barely visible.

Multiple times a day, Tony would spin around in his chair and toss out an idea that Mark would frantically scribble down and then try to figure out how to execute. One day, Tony told Mark he wanted a Zap-pos University. When Mark asked what that was, Tony replied, "We don't know; we'd like for you to tell us." Building on the orientation program, and the company's existing curriculum around customer service, culture, and warehouse operations, Mark launched Zappos University by expand-ing it to an in-house professional development program that could teach employees new skills—regardless of whether they applied that skill to their job—from yoga classes to playing golf. It also involved other initia-tives that would pay employees to do community service, or volunteer at a local soup kitchen during work hours. Another pillar of Zappos Univer-sity was Zappos Insights, which provided consultations to other compa-nies on how to improve their corporate culture. Over three-day "camps," executives from other companies would learn how Zappos managed HR, how to give their employees more impetus to focus on customer service, and how to achieve a "wow" factor. On the final day, attendees went to Zappos's legendary quarterly all-hands meetings, led by musicians and rousing speeches—years before concert-style corporate gatherings were made famous by WeWork and its enigmatic CEO, Adam Neumann.

To try to keep up with Tony's cascade of ideas, Mark devised a system in which he wrote all of Tony's suggestions on a whiteboard and asked Tony to rank them by urgency. But no matter how hard he tried, he could never remain as calm as Fred, who seemed to have an intuitive system for mentally sifting through Tony's ideas and deciding whether it was possible to execute them. Alfred, meanwhile, would punch away at his computer, ensuring that execution lay within the bounds of fiscal responsibility. "[Tony] comes up with ideas, brilliant ideas, sometimes crazy ideas, sometimes crazy, brilliant, all different variations," Mark said later. "But his ideas were much more interesting to him than execution. I mean, he wanted the execution to happen; he just didn't want to have to be the guy who made it happen."

Watching Fred, Alfred, and Tony, Mark realized that the three men together were a trifecta—each parlaying their skills into a Venn diagram of effective leadership—unlike any other he'd encountered. Within the company, the trio were known as "FAT," and each played integral roles to support the others. Without one of them, the Zappos flywheel could stop spinning. "If you take anyone out of that mix," Mark said, "it's nothing like it is."

■ ■ ■

Zappos had clearly proven that buying shoes online without first trying them on was something that customers could embrace—and its success was helping to build the foundation blocks of a nascent e-commerce industry. By 2004, the year Zappos moved to Henderson, eBay was operating in dozens of countries and making $800 million a quarter while shaping the world of online auctions for new and used goods. It had expanded into car sales and even sold a private jet on its platform. It was also building an arsenal of tools and features to offer the ideal online marketplace. It acquired the payment processing company PayPal for $1.5 billion, and bought Rent.com, America's largest real estate leasing site, for $415 million. It even took a 25 percent stake in Craigslist, which had since expanded its online classifieds far beyond San Francisco.

The other e-commerce giant fighting for ground was Amazon, which had moved beyond just selling books and established a vast portfolio of music, videos, and consumer electronics. By the end of 2004, Amazon's largest sales category was no longer books but electronic gadgets. Amazon also started allowing third parties to sell on its site, which vastly expanded the number of products it offered, pushing Amazon further in the direction of becoming an "everything store" and changing the instruments of consumerism. Buyers were becoming more and more comfortable with the idea of shopping online rather than in malls. But selling clothing through computers was more of a challenge for Amazon because customers weren't ready to abandon storefront changing rooms. Zappos, which had generated $70 million in sales the previous year, would make a fine crown jewel to propel Amazon's clothing venture.

But when Jeff Bezos flew to see Tony in 2005, meeting him in a conference room at a DoubleTree hotel a few blocks from the Henderson headquarters to discuss buying Zappos, the answer was a hard no. "I realized that to Amazon, we were just a leading shoe company," Tony wrote later. "That was why we told Jeff that we weren't interested in selling at any price. I felt like we were just getting started."

In an era when the drab offices of the 1990s were standard, business attire was limited to crisp shirts and blazers, and co-working companies like WeWork had not yet ushered in the beautification of office spaces with plants, open-plan offices, and free coffee and beer, Zappos was different. As opposed to the top-down management that guided corporate giants of the previous century, Tony turned to egalitarianism to devise Zappos's core values by sending a company-wide email asking employees to submit what they thought should guide the company and represent its culture. After a year of workshopping the submissions, Zappos's company policies looked more like the list of rules for a summer camp than a corporate policy: "Create fun and a little weirdness"; "Build a positive team and family spirit"; "Be adventurous, creative, and open-minded"; "Be humble"; and, finally, its number one policy, "Deliver WOW through service."

Zappos was first a customer service-oriented company, a shoe seller second—an ethos its new values set in stone. Rather than marketing a product heavily to drive sales, Tony believed that extraordinary customer service would lead to a critical mass of return customers, lowering marketing costs and widening profit margins. Workers in the Zappos call center were encouraged to spend more time, not less, talking to customers and getting to know them, while going far beyond what any customer could expect from a company help line; the record for the longest customer service call was ten and a half hours. During one weekend in Los Angeles when Tony and a few of his friends got back to their hotel after a night out, they tried to order pizza through room service and found that the kitchen had closed. As a joke, one of his friends decided to call the Zappos customer service line to see if the rep could help in this situation. Incredibly, the Zappos rep found the five closest pizza shops to their hotel that were still open at that time.

To double down on the customer service emphasis, Tony became obsessed with the happiness of his own employees, which he believed would translate to happy customers. So he vowed to make Zappos among the best places to work in the world. It paid 100 percent of its employees' health insurance premiums and invested in professional development courses. Individuality was treasured and encouraged: employees brought their home and personal lives with them to the office, filling every inch of their cubicle walls with personal photos, notes, cards, Silly String, or whatever else most represented them. Beyond monkey row, plants hung from the ceiling throughout the office like a greenhouse, a style of which Tony was the architect.

The company was also growing at such a pace that Tony and Fred could no longer interview new hires for culture fits, and so they devised a secondary interview process for new hires, who would be judged against the company's core values. To weed out those who made it through but still weren't in it for passion, the company built on Mark's orientation program and went from offering new hires $100 to quit Zappos within their first few weeks to as much as $5,000.

Growing sales coupled with the move to Henderson, for which seventy employees and their families uprooted their lives from San Francisco, validated that Tony's model was working. For Chris Peake, one of the Zapponians who agreed to move to Henderson, it was an easy decision. He had worked at Lombardi Sports, an athletic apparel company, in San Francisco just down the street from Zappos's previous office at 1000 Van Ness for over a decade before quitting to join Tony and Fred as an assistant buyer in 2003. He was thirty years old at the time with a newborn, and it had been surprisingly easy to convince his wife to move the family to Henderson. The prospect of Nevada excited the Peakes, and his new role invigorated him in a way that Lombardi had not.

In his first year, Chris received an assignment from Fred, his new manager, that made him realize he was working for a unique company. During one of their regular check-ins, Fred reached into a box full of books that was lying on the floor inside the office, picked up one, and handed it to Chris. "Read this by Wednesday," he said curtly. The book was called *The Fred Factor*—which made Chris think that Fred was having him read his autobiography. The book was in fact written by motivational speaker Mark Sanborn, who retold the true story of a postman named Fred who saw real purpose and passion in his job. "Where others see delivering mail as monotonous drudgery, Fred sees an opportunity to make a difference in the lives of those he serves," the book's cover summarized. Through Fred's story, Sanborn teaches readers four principles that will bring creativity and inspiration to life and work: make a difference every day, no matter how small; build strong relationships for more success; create value for others without spending money; and constantly reinvent the self.

The following Wednesday, the book was discussed at the weekly Zappos roundtable meeting, which consisted of all the Zappos managers and buyers. "I just get goosebumps thinking about it," Chris later recalled. "When was the last time I read a book? When was the last time someone told me to learn a job besides the job?" That's when Chris realized Zappos was not just focused on him as an employee but "also focused on me becoming the best version of myself," he said later.

Tony and Fred were intent on making sure that employees bought into the customer-service-centric ethos of Zappos. Having their employees read the same books they were reading, like *The Fred Factor*, was one method of cultivating this idea. If the company was sold to Amazon, Zappos would become just another brand of the growing conglomerate, and everything Tony had worked for in this company would be lost. Besides, Zappos had big plans: it saw itself as more of a company like Virgin, which owned music labels, airlines, and a spaceflight venture. Zappos was already considering an airline. By Tony's calculation, Zappos was going to do just fine on its own: it was on track to generate $1 billion in revenue by 2010.

■ ■ ■

It may have seemed, to those looking in, that Tony had it pretty good. His company was soaring; it was influencing other tech companies with its maniacal focus on corporate culture, and it was being sought out as an acquisition target by the bigger players. He had happy employees like Chris Peake, and customers who were leaving rave reviews on Zappos's website. And he was surrounded by longtime friends every day, Fred and Alfred among them, who knew his every whim and ambition—people who could sense when to indulge him and when to say no. But Tony had been searching for something more than good business mantras and lessons. Something deeper, perhaps closer to the meaning of life, or inner peace. Something that would give everything he did purpose. Something he had been searching for since he was a boy.

What he found was the science of happiness. Psychological treatment for mental health had largely focused on healing people with mental health issues by abating anxiety, depression, and other symptoms. But Tony was intrigued by an emerging concept called positive psychology, with the stated goal of reinforcing sustained happiness. Among his required readings was the 2006 book *The Happiness Hypothesis: Finding Modern Truth in Ancient Wisdom* by social scientist Jonathan Haidt, who drew on ancient teachings from India, China, and the Mediterranean and reinterpreted readings from the Bible, the Koran, and Confucius to establish a series of philosophies and questions that could lead one to sustained happiness. At its climax, the book answers what Haidt sees as the meaning of life, and therefore happiness.

> *I don't believe there is an inspiring answer to the question, "What is the purpose of life?" Yet by drawing on ancient wisdom and modern science, we can find compelling answers to the question of purpose within life. The final version of the happiness hypothesis is that happiness comes from between. Happiness is not something that you can find, acquire, or achieve directly. You have to get the conditions right and then wait. Some of those conditions are within you, such as coherence among the parts and levels of your personality. Other conditions require relationships to things beyond you: Just as plants need sun, water, and good soil to thrive, people need love, work, and a connection to something larger. It is worth striving to get the right relationships between yourself and others, between yourself and your work, and between yourself and something larger than yourself. If you get these relationships right, a sense of purpose and meaning will emerge.*

Tony went further and studied the story of Tal Ben-Shahar, who wrote a book called *Happier: Learn the Secrets to Daily Joy and Lasting*

Fulfillment. Ben-Shahar was a lecturer at Harvard who had launched a class on positive psychology in 2002. It was a nascent concept, and only eight students signed up; two dropped out. In the class Ben-Shahar sought to answer what he "believed to be the question of questions: how can we help ourselves and others—individuals, communities, and society—become happier?" Two years after he started the course, it became the most popular class at Harvard when 855 students enrolled. The popularity of his curriculum led Ben-Shahar to believe that he was tapping into a deep desire within the American psyche for happiness. Americans, citizens of the richest and most powerful country on earth, had earned great material prosperity as the decades went on. But in the meantime, rates of depression had soared: in the early 2000s they were ten times higher than they had been in the 1960s. Quoting Mihaly Csikszentmihalyi, a leading scholar in the field of positive psychology, Ben-Shahar posed this question: "If we are so rich, why aren't we happy?"

In *Happier*, Ben-Shahar laid out a series of findings that conclude with meditations, asking the reader to consider things like balancing self-interest and benevolence, temporary highs, and patience, before concluding:

> *One of the common barriers to happiness is the false expectation that one thing—a book or a teacher, a princess or a knight, an accomplishment, a prize, or a revelation—will bring us eternal bliss. While all these things can contribute to our well-being, at best they form a small part of the mosaic of a happy life. The fairytale notion of happiness— the belief that something would carry us to the happily ever after— inevitably leads to disappointment. A happy—or happier—life is rarely shaped by some extraordinary life-changing event; rather, it is shaped incrementally, experience by experience, moment by moment.*
>
> *To realize, to make real, life's potential for the ultimate currency, we must first accept that "this is it"—that all there is to life is the day-to-day, the ordinary, the details of the mosaic. We are living a happy life when we derive pleasure and meaning while spending time with our loved ones, or learning something new, or engaging in a project at work. The more our days are filled with these experiences, the happier we become. This is all there is to it.*

What Tony came to see through his research was that, for most people, "achieving their goal in life, whatever it was—whether it was making money, getting married, or running faster—would not actually bring them sustained happiness," he wrote later. He pointed to research on lottery winners, whose happiness levels may have spiked with the new wealth but a year later had reverted to where they had been before. "And yet, many people have spent their entire lives pursuing what they thought would make them happy."

He drew on concepts like Maslow's hierarchy of needs, which determines that once the requirements of survival—things like water and food—are met, humans can achieve happiness by first pursuing security and safety, then family and a sense of belonging, a sense of self-esteem and respect within a community, until self-actualization is reached, meaning the display of creativity, acceptance of facts, self-sufficiency, and morality.

A more distilled version of happiness could be attributed to three experiences: pleasure, a sense experienced for short periods of time; passion, when peak performance meets peak engagement, and sense of time is lost; and finally, a higher purpose, or the sense of being a part of something bigger than oneself. Taking it a step further Tony realized that there were parallels between happiness achieved by oneself—pleasure, passion, and purpose—that could be applied to Zappos, and every company in the world: profits, passion, and purpose.

Tony ultimately concluded that happiness was about four things: perceived control, perceived progress, connectedness to others, and being part of something bigger than yourself. Using these four principles, Tony surmised that they all applied to leading his company. He could give perceived control to Zappos call-center workers by offering pay bumps every time they learned a new skill offered by Zappos, giving them the impression they were in control of their own pay. Previously, entry-level employees in the merchandising department could only be promoted after eighteen months, but to give a sense of perceived progress, he implemented a rule that gave three mini-promotions over the same time period, even though at the end they would reach the same level of seniority in the company. He believed that Zappos's emphasis on company culture met the requirements of a sense of connectedness, and that Zappos's vision— which was changed in 2009 to "delivering happiness in the world"—met the conditions of his fourth principle of happiness: being part of a higher purpose.

He wrote later: "Whether it's the happiness that customers feel when they receive the perfect pair of shoes or the perfect outfit . . . or the happiness that employees feel from being part of a culture whose values match their own personal values—the thing that ties all of these things together is happiness." Not until later would these philosophies define him to the world. But when Tony's obsession with happiness began, few had the foresight to ask: What was he looking for?

■ ■ ■

If Tony was building his own mantra, he was going to live and lead by it too. It was something that Mark saw time and again. Zappos off-site meetings were known to get rowdy, and libations were a staple of the events. On the final evening of a seminar held at a small hotel in Mesquite, at the edge of Nevada's border with Utah, Zappos employees were milling about a lounge in the lobby. Whoever had booked the accommodation appeared to have found one of the only hotels in the state that didn't have a bar. But no matter—someone had fetched a few cases of Bud Light to appease the group.

As the night was nearing its end, Mark was sitting on a couch opposite Tony watching the group mingle and talk. One employee staggered over and paused to inspect a case of beer before fishing out a bottle. As they watched the employee weave diagonally through the lobby, Tony noticed a grand piano standing silently across the room. Without saying a word, he stood up and walked over to it, then sat down in front of the keys.

Mark had by now become accustomed to Tony's ability to surprise. One time during a presentation to Zappos employees, Mark had told a joke and then laughed as he delivered the punchline. At the end of the presentation, Tony approached him and, looking directly at him without expression, said, "Next time when you tell the joke, it would be funnier if you didn't laugh," and then walked off without saying a word. Mark burst out laughing. He later learned that Tony had been studying the art of comedy to work on his own public speaking. Another time in the Zappos office, Mark had told Tony he was trying to figure out a way to change Zappos's external messaging to reflect how its customers talk about the company.

Tony, typing away, appeared to ignore him. Mark continued, saying that perhaps there was a way to go through the company's customer emails and find out what they were saying about the company. Turning to face Mark, Tony said, "Here's the frequency of the top ten words that people are saying." In the time Mark had been talking, Tony had written a programming script to scan through thousands of emails.

Now, though, watching Tony's fingers glide up and down the piano keyboard was something else. "He started playing some of the most beautiful music I've ever heard," Mark said. The space hummed with a warm timbre, as the keystrokes flowed seamlessly from Tony's memory. Against the backdrop of the lobby's bland decor, it was as if someone were filling the room with color.

Tony had been so absorbed that by the time he stopped and looked up, the group had thinned out until it was just Mark and another executive. The employee who'd fished out another Bud Light had long called it a night and disappeared into the elevator.

After cleaning up, Mark was standing shoulder to shoulder with Tony when the elevator chimed and the doors opened. As they walked in, they looked down to see shards of a smashed Bud Light bottle strewn across the floor. Beer was everywhere. They were quiet while the elevator shuttled them upstairs; when it came to a halt, Mark stepped off. He returned to the elevator a minute later with a trashcan and towel he'd fetched from his suite. But when the doors opened again, he was surprised to see Tony, on his hands and knees, scrubbing the floor. Mark knelt down beside him, and the two men cleaned in silence.

■ ■ ■

While Tony was doing everything he could to upend corporate culture and build Zappos into an anti-corporate establishment, the corporate shadow of Amazon continued to grow. In 2007, it launched its own online shoe and handbag site, Endless.com, selling brands like Ben Sherman and Bruno Magli. Under images of shoes and notices of promotions, within an information box titled "Our Promise to You," the website shouted what amounted to a direct challenge to Zappos: free overnight shipping, free return shipping, 365-day returns, and a 110 percent price protection guarantee—phrases it mirrored from the Zappos website.

"For Bezos and Amazon, the irresistible temptation was Zappos.com," wrote Brad Stone, a journalist who profiled Jeff Bezos in his book, *The Everything Store*. "In many ways, Zappos was the Bizarro World version of Amazon; everything was slightly similar but completely different. Hsieh, like Bezos, nurtured a quirky internal culture and frequently talked about it in public to reinforce the Zappos brand in customers' minds. But he took it even further."

Despite Amazon's efforts, Zappos kept jumping from success to success. After almost a decade of Zappos trying to get Nike, the athletic apparel giant finally agreed to sell on the company's platform, bringing huge credibility. New Balance also signed on as a footwear partner. Revenue soared, and Zappos made $100 million in sales in a single month. Despite increasing revenue in recent years, Zappos had still been losing money as marketing, logistics, and sales costs rose alongside the company's growth. But by the end of 2007, it had $840 million revenue for the year and, for the first time, a profit. The next year, it was on track to hit $1 billion in annual sales, two years before its initial timeline.

Tony saw this as further validation that his bet on culture and customer service had trumped concerns of generating sales by traditional means. Still, the bean counters on his board weren't convinced, and viewed such endeavors as Tony's "social experiments." Venture capitalists look for returns of many multiples of their initial investment, and typically achieve this by pushing startups to focus on maximizing sales and then go for an initial public offering, at which point the VCs can sell their shares in the company at a higher price. Things like company culture are secondary to making money.

When the 2008 financial crisis hit in September, every bank—and investor—in the country was looking for ways to tighten their belts. A few weeks after Lehman Brothers collapsed, Sequoia held a meeting with its portfolio companies to convey a straightforward message: cut expenses and get to profitability as soon as possible. While Zappos was profitable, it was still growing and had to cut expenses, which meant that it would need to fire employees.

On November 6, Tony sent a company-wide email announcing that Zappos was laying off 8 percent of its workforce, about 100 employees. While such a move seemed to fly in the face of Zappos values like "Build a Positive Team and Family Spirit," Tony took pains to point out that they would take care of the departing employees with exceptional benefits— costs that would drive the company's expenses *higher* for the year, rather than lower. "Because we are being proactive instead of reactive about it, we are able to take care of our employees and offer them more than the standard 2 weeks' severance (or no severance) that most other companies are giving. We are offering to pay each laid-off employee through the end of the year (about 2 months)." Long-term employees would be given a little more, and health care benefits would be paid for another six months.

While the move garnered some positive media attention—"Zappos became a model of how to nurture employees in good times and bad," read one article in *Fortune*—the company was facing an even greater threat. At the time, Zappos had a revolving $100 million asset-backed line of credit that it used to purchase its thousands of shoes and apparel items. But the loan was contingent on the company meeting revenue and profit targets, and if any of those targets were missed, the lender could theoretically recall the loan and cork Zappos's access to more inventory. Considering the credit crisis, there weren't lenders lining up to give the company another $100 million. In other words, the company needed a more stable source of money, and the current board was unwilling to give it.

If he didn't act, Tony would likely be replaced as CEO and his "social experiments" would all but be abandoned. With Zappos facing a dwindling number of bad options, one solution would be to find new investors to buy out Sequoia and existing shareholders, which would cost about $200 million. When word got out that Zappos was looking for new investors, Jeff Bezos came calling again.

Tony flew to Seattle in April 2009 and met with Bezos at Amazon's headquarters. Tony stuck to his typical presentation notes, focusing on Zappos's corporate culture and how that translated to good customer service and therefore sales. As he concluded the presentation, Tony turned to the science of happiness and its role at Zappos.

Jeff interrupted. "Did you know that people are very bad at predicting what will make them happy?" he said. Tony clicked to the next slide, and the very words Jeff had just uttered appeared on the screen. "Yes," Tony said, "but apparently you are very good at predicting PowerPoint slides."

While Tony had reservations about the gulf between Amazon's approach to customer service—providing the lowest prices—and the Zappos mantra of making personal connections with customers using old-school phone calls, he left Seattle convinced that it was the best option. With the money from selling itself to Amazon, Zappos would be able to buy out its board and install a new group of believers.

Part of Bezos's pitch to Tony had been that Zappos was onto something with its focus on employee culture and customer happiness. Amazon had already started mirroring Zappos's overnight shipping and free returns at Endless.com. But Amazon was about twenty-five times Zappos's size. What if some of Zappos's teachings were implemented at Amazon? They would have twenty-five times more impact there. Tony was seemingly more than aware of this opportunity. But he was thinking bigger. What if, by infecting Amazon with Zappos's policies, those precepts could then be adopted by other conglomerates, and then change the lives of millions of workers?

On July 22, Tony sent an email to his employees, announcing that Zappos was being bought by Amazon. With Amazon as a partner, Tony said, Zappos would remain unchanged, its culture untouched, but it would achieve its goal of delivering happiness to customers, employees, and vendors faster.

> *It's definitely an emotional day for me. The feelings I'm experiencing are similar to what I felt in college on graduation day: excitement about the future mixed with fond memories of the past. The last 10 years were an incredible ride, and I'm excited about what we will accomplish together over the next 10 years as we continue to grow Zappos!*

He included a message from Michael Moritz that sounded more like a dismissal: "You are now free to let your imagination roam—and to contemplate initiatives and undertakings that today, in our more constrained setting, we could not take on." (Tony later took a parting shot in his book: "Unlike our former board of directors, our new management committee seems to understand the importance of our culture—the 'social experiments'—to our long-term success.")

In addition to assuring employees that their jobs would be unaffected, Tony also stressed that neither he, Fred, nor Alfred would leave the company. "We believe that we are at the very beginning of what's possible for Zappos and are very excited about the future."

The deal ultimately closed in October 2009, at a value of $1.2 billion, making it Amazon's largest acquisition at the time. Once again, Zappos had hung on by the skin of its teeth by doubling down on an unhinged commitment to disrupting corporate culture. As if to prove that it would keep to its core culture and values, the company threw a wedding-themed company holiday party to commemorate the "marriage" between Zappos and Amazon. "Most people came dressed as either brides or grooms," read a descriptor for a video from the holiday party uploaded by Zappos. "There were bachelorette and bachelor parties (complete with semi-clothed strippers) and Elvises marrying people. You HAD to be there!"

But just as Mark Guadagnoli and Chris Peake had noticed, as had other employees, old friends, and any entrepreneur who had visited the Henderson office, the implementation of Tony's vision was by no means a single person's achievement. Rather, it was a joint effort that involved the other two men who sat beside him in monkey row. Alfred, in particular, had been keeping Tony's chaos under control since college. "Tony didn't mind throwing a thousand plates in the air and juggling a ton of balls," Chris Peake said later. "Alfred was then really good at saying, okay, cool, let's take away all those plates except for this one or that one, and you focus on this stuff."

Jeff Bezos noticed it too. "You're in such great hands with Fred, Alfred, and Tony," Bezos said in a video to Zappos employees to announce the acquisition. "That's a really big deal. I've seen a lot of leaders of companies too, and I haven't seen people better than those three."

CHAPTER 8

DELIVERING HAPPINESS

One afternoon in the fall of 2009, Tony was gliding around a kitchen island on a scooter, trying his best to avoid the dozen people milling about his mansion in the Southern Highlands neighborhood of Las Vegas. Papers were scattered across the floors and counters, like in a crazed academic's office. He looked up as a woman named Holly McNamara, blond with the affect of someone who was quick to laugh, ambled into the kitchen. It was her birthday, and she had plans to go out for dinner with Tony and some friends. She watched with bewilderment as he zoomed past. "What are you doing?" she asked. "And who are all these people?"

"I'm writing a book!" Tony yelled, like a kid during recess.

Holly had been introduced to Tony by one of his poker friends a few years before, and he had since opened his world to her. Though she lived in San Diego, her job as a structural engineer often brought her to Vegas during the housing boom, and he would invite her to group dinners at Yellowtail in the Bellagio or to Korean barbecue joints off the Strip with confidants like Fred and Alfred. If there was someone that Holly didn't know at the dinner table, Tony always took the time to introduce her. "This is my friend Holly," Tony would say. "She's friends with us now." Holly had become such a part of this new community that Vegas started to feel like a second home, and she would often stay at Tony's mansion.

"We're putting the chapters together," Tony said. He pointed to a woman with shoulder-length hair, who looked up and smiled. "This is Jenn. She's my editor," he said. It was Jenn Lim, who had grown so close to Tony since they hiked Mount Kilimanjaro seven years before that some referred to her as his girlfriend. To each other, they were partners. "Holly, why don't you write a passage for the book?" Tony said.

He was pretty famous now. After Amazon announced it was buying Zappos, curiosity around the wunderkind chief executive—who had introduced the world to free shipping and zany corporate culture—had become unmanageable. There were no longer enough hours in the day to answer the thousands of emails from fans, admirers, customers, and entrepreneurs seeking his advice or direction. The days of obsessively answering every inquiry at LinkExchange were long gone.

With his newfound popularity, Tony realized that a book would provide a single channel to share the lessons he'd learned and his philosophies. Called *Delivering Happiness: A Path to Profits, Passion, and Purpose*, the book would become a gospel of his accomplishments and failures, from his backyard worm farm to Zappos. An autobiographical self-help memoir and corporate handbook rolled into one, the story would start with his childhood in Marin County, discuss his pizza business at Harvard University, show how he built LinkExchange, and then provide a riveting account of saving Zappos—success he'd achieved by believing in himself and his team.

Beyond his life story, Tony would also use the book to espouse his study of the science of happiness. It would outline the four core principles that he believed underpinned the road to happiness: perceived control of one's destiny, perceived perception of progress, connectedness with others, and being a part of something bigger than yourself. It was a template he believed could make people, companies, and the world happier. The treatise would conclude with the most important lesson he'd learned during his thirty-six years: that "by concentrating on the happiness of those around you, you can dramatically increase your own."

With help from Jenn, he had already written most of the book. The two had hunkered down in a cabin at Northern California's Lake Tahoe and written the manuscript in two weeks, fueled by coffee beans soaked in vodka and Excedrin, an over-the-counter migraine medicine. "I found the most effective technique was taking Excedrin when I didn't have a headache because there's actually a lot of caffeine in Excedrin," he told a reporter.

Now Tony's confidants, friends, and advisors had been arriving at the mansion to push the draft of the memoir through a round of edits. What

Holly was witnessing was the final effort to get the book done. But despite the chaos and looming deadline, Tony was still going to make time to celebrate Holly's birthday that weekend. She felt buoyant being at the center of his world.

■ ■ ■

A few months later, Holly and Tony were getting into the back of a car in front of the Palms Casino Resort. It was the end of a long evening. An Amazon executive had been in town to meet Tony for dinner, and Tony had invited Holly and her friend along to join them for drinks once business had been discussed. For Holly, the night had been a distraction from the fact that she was now unemployed. She'd long contemplated a move away from engineering before finally following through on it, and Tony was now encouraging her to chase her newfound passion for being a nightlife concierge in Las Vegas. But after days of meetings and networking, she was growing increasingly frustrated with an industry that felt so different from construction and engineering.

As the car pulled away from the Palms, Holly was curious to know the outcome of Tony's discussion with the Amazon executive, Peter Krawiec, the vice president of worldwide corporate development. But before she could ask, Tony turned to her in his seat and began peppering her with questions: "So, your new business, you're moving to Vegas? Where are you going to live? What do you actually want for your future? How much money do you need to live every month? Are you worried?"

As the car rolled through the shimmering lights of Las Vegas, Holly struggled to come up with answers. *Where is this going?* she thought. *Is this an interview?* Before long, they were pulling up to Tony's home. As they stepped out, Tony turned to her again.

"I have a proposition for you," he said. He was getting ready to embark on a press tour to drum up interest in his book, and he needed help managing his calendar, answering emails, and handling booking arrangements as well as managing the distribution and press campaign for *Delivering Happiness*. Jenn was leading the team, but they needed more assistance. Most importantly, he needed someone he could trust. This person would have access to everything from his address book to his American Express Black Card. Why not help me out, while you get your concierge business off the ground? Tony suggested. He offered her $3,000 a month, less than she was used to making, but the offer came with a free room in his mansion and a front-row seat to his whirlwind life.

He technically already had two personal assistants, one at Zappos, and another named Mimi Pham, who managed his affairs outside of the company. But the Zappos assistant was about to go on maternity leave. And Mimi, petite, sharp-chinned, with a huge grin, was "never around," he said.

Holly had met Mimi a few years earlier during a pool party on Memorial Day weekend at the Southern Highlands house. Holly remembered Mimi being a friendly and bubbly presence. She also recalled thinking she must be close to Tony, because her clothes, purses, shoes, and other belongings were scattered around Tony's house. Though she seemed to be an infrequent presence in Vegas, Mimi had a permanent room there. She likely worked for him, Holly thought, but what she did exactly was a mystery.

The two women had become friendly enough that Mimi invited Holly and her friend to crash at her apartment in Los Angeles one weekend. During the stay, Holly asked Mimi what exactly she did for Tony. Mimi explained she did "whatever Tony needed," from planning trips to house chores.

As if as an afterthought, she added, "Don't tell Tony that I have this apartment in LA."

Why? Holly asked.

"Tony just doesn't need to know that I have this apartment," Mimi said.

"How does he not know? Don't you live in his house?" Holly asked.

"Well, yeah. But he just doesn't need to know."

"What does Tony think you're doing in LA, then?"

"He thinks I'm sleeping at friends' places."

It struck Holly and her friend Kimberly Schleifer as odd. Why would Mimi want to hide from Tony the fact that she lived in a humble unit off Santa Monica Boulevard? After all, most of her belongings were in Tony's mansion. "She was always so mysterious and secretive," Kimberly recalled.

Unbeknownst to Holly and Kimberly, Mimi's role in Tony's life was undefined by design, much like the role of a consigliere. People often cycled in and out of Tony's life, but Mimi had remained a constant presence from the moment she met him at a shoe conference years before. They had initially bonded over a common feeling of being misunderstood by their Asian parents. But Tony came to rely on her to *manage* his life.

She proved efficient at juggling tasks ranging from mundane to the seemingly impossible—from organizing housework and buying his meals to booking itineraries and screening people for meetings. Ahead of music festivals and parties, Tony and his friends knew that Mimi was the go-to person to arrange recreational drugs. (She had previously had a brush with the law after a drug-related incident: in 2001, she was arrested in Northern California when her boyfriend sold MDMA to an undercover police officer. She was a passenger in the car during the transaction and pleaded guilty to possession of a controlled substance. The conviction was expunged in 2016.) "I think the reason why Tony trusted her a lot and that she stayed around for so long is because she played her cards right," Joey Vanas, an ex-boyfriend of Mimi's who would also join Holly on the book's press tour, said later.

When Tony had bad news to give, it was Mimi who most often delivered the message—distancing him from decisions that would upset those around him. Most importantly, Mimi had maintained her role in Tony's life by guarding her territory. She was possessive of her tasks and her access to Tony's world, which included his schedule, his house (they shared an address on their driver's licenses at one point), and his bank accounts. "She has a very direct manner," said Joey. "A lot of people's impressions were that Mimi was always trying to leverage to have more power."

While Tony's offer to Holly seemed like a genuine effort to help her during a tough time, her role as personal assistant on the book's press tour would directly conflict with Mimi's responsibilities, something that was sure to complicate her relationship with Mimi.

When Holly arrived at the Southern Highlands house at the start of 2010 and moved into a room filled with Mimi's things, she asked Tony whether they could make some more room for her own belongings. "Just ask her to clean it up," Tony said.

With those few words, Holly's collision course with Mimi was charted. When Holly called to ask if Mimi could move her stuff out of the room, Mimi stated adamantly that her belongings were there to stay, and accused Holly of trying to replace her. As the conversation derailed, Mimi said something to Holly that gave her a sense of what she was walking into: "Tony is all I have."

A day later, Mimi flew to Vegas. When she entered the house, she briefly met Patricia McHale, who had recently become Tony's other assistant at Holly's suggestion. That day, as Patricia tended to the hummingbird feeders and misters in the backyard, Tony and Mimi walked outside. Mimi was crying, and Tony looked guilty. "She was telling him something that made him feel bad," Patricia said later. "She wouldn't stop crying."

■ ■ ■

The press tour started in March 2010, three months before the book was to be released, with Tony crisscrossing the country to meet with reporters. One of those stops included South by Southwest (SXSW), the annual film, technology, and arts festival in Austin, Texas, that had earned a spot on the event calendars of the tech glitterati.

"I'm outside South by Southwest with Tony Hsieh from Zappos, and he's got a new book coming out in June," said tech journalist Frank Gruber during a video interview in front of the Delivering Happiness coach, an old school bus painted gray with the words DELIVERING HAPPINESS in bold. A large yellow smiley face was plastered on the side. Inside, it looked like a typical party bus—no rows of seats, just benches lining the perimeter around a central dance floor. With blacked-out windows and green LED lights dangling from the ceiling, the school bus could become a mobile nightclub at the flick of a switch.

"It's empty now 'cause it's in the middle of the day, and we don't really start drinking until what—3 p.m., 4 p.m.?" Tony said to the journalist, grinning. As Gruber and the camera crew followed Tony into the bus, they found Jenn Lim tidying up. "Last night we had about fifty people on this bus, so it was pretty crazy."

A rolling thunderclap of events and interviews ensued across the country. The bus appeared at some events, but Tony was most often flying to interviews. Despite being a certified multimillionaire, he made a point of flying Southwest Airlines, the low-cost airline that only offered economy-class seats. During one flight, as Tony and Holly were boarding the plane, another passenger looked up from his seat, saw Tony in his Zappos T-shirt, and said, "Hey, my daughter works at Zappos!"

Tony smiled. "Oh, really? That's great," he said.

"Do you work at Zappos?" the man asked, not realizing he was talking to its chief executive.

"Yeah, I do!" Tony replied with a grin.

The press tour culminated in three book launch events in June, held in Las Vegas, Los Angeles, and New York City—each an opportunity for Tony to hold court and hobnob with other celebrities. There were sponsors at the launch parties such as cancer support nonprofit Livestrong as well as vodka brand Grey Goose, Coors Light beer, and Red Bull energy drinks. Among the stars at the New York event was Ivanka Trump. The year before, Tony had appeared as a guest judge on *The Apprentice*, the reality show hosted by Ivanka's real estate mogul father, Donald Trump, and their friendship had since grown. The New York event was only the latest photo opportunity for the pair: shortly before his *Apprentice* appearance, Ivanka and Tony had been photographed in front of the White House, where Tony had been invited to meet Barack Obama for a meeting about rebuilding the recession-devastated economy along with other young entrepreneurs, including Twitter co-founder Evan Williams. Standing next to a broadly grinning Ivanka, Tony looks unrecognizable at first glance: it was one of the few times he had been photographed wearing a suit and tie. It was Tony, Ivanka later said, who showed her the power of social media, and how it could be used "to push your company's core values and core beliefs in a personal way." Years later, in 2017, after her father had been elected U.S. president, Tony provided an editorial review for her 2017 self-help book, *Women Who Work: Rewriting the Rules for Success*. "The advice is spot-on for everyone, not just women," he wrote.

At the New York book party, Tony was holding a drink while trying to shuffle into position for a photo alongside Ivanka and Jenn Lim at the book party, when his new publicist, Christine Peake (no relation to Chris Peake), ran over to interrupt.

She had met Tony a few weeks prior at an event in Vegas, after being introduced by a mutual friend who thought Tony could use her public relations services. In one of their first conversations, Christine confided in Tony that she had brought her teenage son as her plus-one to the event in hopes that he might spot Tony Hawk, the pro skateboarder, who was also in attendance. Moments later, Christine spotted the two Tonys chatting. Unexpectedly, Tony Hsieh waved Christine and her son over to them and introduced her son to the skateboarder. Touched by this unusual show of kindness from a celebrity, Christine offered her public relations services to Tony—and he accepted.

She had been watching him at the New York event to ensure that he and those around him looked good; pictures are forever, especially on the red carpet, so no lipstick on teeth, no holding handbags, no smoking, and no alcohol. To style the photo, Christine quickly took Ivanka's jacket. She then went to grab Tony's drink and was met with slight resistance before he gave it up. "It was a bit of tug-of-war," she later recalled.

Once the camera flashed, a member of Tony's team approached Christine and scolded her. "You don't take away his drink, ever," the person yelled. Tony was one of the most humble clients Christine had ever worked with, but as a new entrant to his world, she had just learned the cardinal rule: never separate him from alcohol, his social lubricant. "At that moment, well, we've established we've got a drinking problem," Christine later said.

■ ■ ■

At one point, Tony and Holly had mailed out advance copies of *Delivering Happiness* to friends and celebrities. Among them was the rapper Curtis Jackson, better known as 50 Cent. Tony wrote a note on 50 Cent's copy and used two quarters to draw smiley faces. As Holly started laughing, Tony giggled, "Do you think he's going to find this funny?"

His media tour had been going well—so well that by the end of June, buzz around *Delivering Happiness* had driven the book to the top of the *New York Times* bestseller list.

In July, Tony briefly left the media tour to attend a political fundraiser for Nevada senator Harry Reid in Las Vegas. President Barack Obama was also in attendance. Photos from the event show the three men in blazers, deep in conversation. Tony, true to form, was the only one without a tie. At the event, Tony gave a copy of his book to Reggie Love, President Obama's aide, in hopes that he would pass it along to the president. Ten days later, Reggie wrote to Tony, "I was unable to get the President to read your book, b/c I've been glued to it." He continued, "If you ever have time to connect or chat, my phone is always on and my door is always open." He ended with a PS: "I'll now also be sure to pass along your book."

With accolades coming from everywhere, Tony thought that perhaps it was time to take the promotion of his book to the next level. He decided to take an entourage on another tour. This one would be a three-month, twenty-three-city bus tour across the country to promote the book. This time the vehicle would be a new and improved Delivering Happiness bus. They would hold events and book readings in universities, at company offices, and with charitable organizations. It could deliver Tony's template of happiness to the masses. As if to drive the rock star theme home, he purchased a tour bus from the Dave Matthews Band and wrapped it with his Delivering Happiness sign and yellow winky faces—a logo that had become synonymous with his brand.

A tour on the scale Tony was thinking would typically take months, even a year, to plan. But he wanted to launch by the end of the summer. So he turned to Joey Vanas, Mimi's ex-boyfriend and an event producer who had overseen Zappos's corporate events for years—including the vendor parties and the wedding-themed party celebrating the Amazon acquisition—and had most recently helped Tony pull off the whirlwind of press events around the book. Joey had two and a half months to figure out the logistics of a massive nationwide bus tour.

During the first meeting to organize the tour, Joey could see the nervous excitement of those around him. Tony addressed the members of his new entourage in the living room of his Southern Highlands home— Jenn, Mimi, Holly, and several others, each keen to prove themselves to *the* Tony Hsieh—then gave the floor to those gathered. Tony listened as people came up with ideas on where to visit and what to do in each location. Some proposals made a lot of sense, and others had great intentions. But by Joey's account, there were too many ideas being thrown out and not enough decision-making from Tony. "I just had a sinking feeling. We're going to end up way overcommitted, underprepared, with a hodgepodge team," Joey said. The only way to continue, Joey thought, would be to temper his own expectations for the tour, realizing that it was likely going to be chaotic; if so, it was better to run with it instead of fighting against it. In other words, Joey later said, "I remember thinking we're fucked."

■ ■ ■

Angela Morabito was among the younger members of the bus tour group. An impressionable college graduate from Arizona State University, she had recently been hired by a small marketing firm called Digital Royalty, which Tony had invested in and had hired to do marketing for the book tour. Angela had already worked on some earlier Delivering Happiness events, but she was eager to impress Tony. Her boss had told her that Tony thought she was not talkative enough, and Angela took that to mean that her boss valued partying stamina over work ethic, especially if the client was Tony. She wasn't much of a partier, but the last thing Angela wanted to be labeled was "the not-fun one" while working for one of the world's most successful business figures.

One night in August, the Delivering Happiness team gathered for a group dinner at Pink Taco at the Hard Rock Hotel. After many drinks, Tony asked everyone to huddle in one of the private rooms inside the casino. Sitting around a purple velvet gambling table, what was supposed to be a kickoff meeting quickly devolved into something more bizarre. It started when Tony abandoned formalities and dared someone in the meeting to fit themselves inside a Delivering Happiness sports bag. Eleen Hsu, whose title on the team was "Project Specialist Supreme," got in the bag, and the group started carrying her down the hall.

The group headed outside to the Delivering Happiness tour bus and went inside. Next came Tony's second idea: What if we passed a vodka shot from mouth to mouth in a row? In theory, the shot would have gone from Tony to Jenn to Angela and down the line. The idea sounded gross, but Angela felt that keeping up with these antics was part of the job, so she tried to catch the shot in her mouth as it dribbled from Jenn's. She failed, as the vodka shot was mostly saliva. Right after, Angela turned to her boss, Amy Jo Martin, who was also on the bus. "I remember looking at Amy's face," Angela later recalled. "I didn't know if it was disappointment, anger, or jealousy." The bus tour hadn't even started, but Angela figured it was time to look for another job.

The Delivering Happiness bus departed Vegas in August. At each stop, Tony was typically committed to several engagements. "We were over-committed and always playing catch-up when we would get somewhere that we didn't have proper time to prep for," Joey recalled. While the purpose of the bus tour was to promote Tony's book, Tony did not actually travel with the bus for the majority of the tour. For the most part, he and Jenn would fly into a city, meet up with the bus, attend the speaking engagements, and then party hard with the crew. Tony and Jenn would then head back to the airport, either to return to Vegas or to go to some other non-book-related engagement. "And then it was just a bunch of hungover people rushing to get from here to there after all the disorganization and stress from the weekend," Joey recalled. If Joey asked why they'd drunk so much the previous night, they would often remind him that it had been Tony feeding them shots.

To add to the growing headaches, they had to find a new bus driver, twice. The first driver kept stopping for smoke breaks, while the second driver was a wild card. "He was a tough Aussie who you would want on your Armageddon team," Joey said later. "He was running people off the road, flipping people off. And he was driving what was supposed to be the happiest bus!"

With Tony's missing leadership creating a vacuum, petty arguments snowballed into seemingly insurmountable conflicts. During the first weeks of the tour, the crew would eat meals together and hang out during breaks. But as the bus journeyed on, the Delivering Happiness workers kept to themselves whenever they could. Mimi, who was also flying in and out of some cities and held the title "Little Miss Sunshine," was helping to program the tour. She was central to the complaints of several people on the bus, Joey said later, who took issue with her demands. "Everybody complained about Mimi," he said.

No one was more bitter about Mimi's presence than Holly. The tension between the two women was palpable. Mimi had assumed many of the duties that Holly, whose title was "Life Managing Director," believed she was responsible for, and Holly was increasingly incensed about the minimization of her role. She had raised complaints to Tony and Jenn at the beginning of the bus tour, but they were mostly ignored. Her breaking point came during their fourth stop, in Chicago. Normally Holly would meet the public relations team prior to interviews, conduct sound checks, and make sure Tony had his outfit sorted. But when they arrived in Chicago and Holly went to speak with Tony to prepare him for an interview, Tony dismissed her: "Mimi has it, it's done."

It might have been a subtle comment, but Holly felt slighted. She had left a stable career and had been giving her new concierge venture a red-hot go in Las Vegas. Tony had made what seemed a goodwill offer to help her during a hard time, but now this tour was consuming her life, and she felt not only ostracized from Tony's world and without a clear purpose on the bus but isolated from him too. In tears, Holly called Patricia, the friend she had convinced Tony to hire as an assistant. "I was told Tony would take time to talk with me, which never happened," Holly said. Patricia, who was back at Tony's Southern Highlands mansion to look after his affairs while he was on tour, was alarmed, fearing that Holly was on the edge of slipping into depression, and sent Jenn an email:

> *It's human nature to want to help people whenever we can . . . and we're supposed to be delivering happiness. This is a confusing time for Holly and she really needs support right now . . . she's not feeling part of this team, for more than one reason. I'm sure at this point it's an accumulation of more than one thing. I hope you might help her move through this difficult time on the three month journey you are all on.*

Jenn quickly responded and checked in on Holly, to little avail. The fight between Mimi and Holly was an issue that could only be resolved by one person: Tony. After all, the two women were jockeying for his support. They were also fighting for their livelihoods. Both women's entire worlds revolved around him, from their jobs to their rooms at his mansion. But he refused to enter the fray, seemingly hoping that they would resolve the conflict on their own, which only made it worse. "He was off-loading the conflict, effectively," Joey said later. Their fight was just one episode from the Delivering Happiness bus tour, Joey later concluded, that highlighted the downside of Tony's hands-off management style, and how it could bring out people's worst instincts. It was also something that would have far greater consequences one day in the future, when Tony would oversee an entire neighborhood underpinned by his mantra of happiness. "The bus tour for me was the microcosm for pretty much all that happened later on in downtown Vegas," said Joey.

■ ■ ■

At one point, Tony finally made an effort to resolve the conflicts. In October, around the halfway point of the bus tour, the crew was staying in

Miami for a few days. He noticed the team's energy was low. As he prepared to leave the bus again with Jenn, he sent an email, reminding those on the bus tour that they were promoting a book that focused on the importance of culture. "This email is meant as a Step 1 for our core values exercise to do over the next few days while Jenn and I are away from the bus," he started. His email, sent to everyone on the tour, instructed everyone to make four lists.

The first list would be names of people "that you enjoy connecting with," Tony wrote, while the second would be "a list of people or types of people that annoy you." From these two lists, Tony instructed, the writer should try to understand what values they had in common with people in the first list, and what was missing in the second list.

The third was a list of the happiest moments in the writer's life, and the fourth the least happiest. "The happiness usually comes from one or more of your values being expressed," he explained. "Write down what those values are next to each moment" on the third list, he instructed.

"Get ready for step 2!" he wrote at the end of the email.

Tony never sent the second part of the exercise. It seemed he moved on to something else, and the crew continued to fend for themselves. At the last stop in Seattle in November, just before the Thanksgiving holiday, Holly brought up the battle against Mimi with Tony once more.

"I've been mustering up the energy to talk to you about this, but what's going on? One day I'm doing everything," she said. "Then all of a sudden I'm doing nothing. Did I do something wrong?"

"No, no, you did nothing wrong," Tony said.

"Well, what's going on?"

"I don't want to talk about it," Tony replied.

To outsiders, the Delivering Happiness bus tour looked like the embodiment of joy. The bus crew had filmed a rap music video, which received coverage from TechCrunch. At the center of the video is an enigmatic young woman, Laura Lombardi, whose title was "The Happiness Fairy." Her lyrics are catchy and the video *looks* happy, with clips showing children lunging forward in potato-sack races, or the crew riding bikes around Times Square brandishing signs with the yellow winky face logo. And by quantifiable measures, the book and the bus tour were a success. Tony had given his presentation espousing his life story and the science of happiness to packed rooms and auditoriums across the coun-try. The book remained on the *New York Times* bestseller list for twenty-seven weeks straight. It reached the *USA Today* bestseller list, staying there for nine weeks, and was among the top ten Amazon bestsellers for June and July 2010.

But the Delivering Happiness rap video presented a misleading image of a group of young, energetic crew members having the time of their lives, when they were actually miserable.

The book's presence on the bestseller lists was also phony. Tony used ResultSource, a company that helps authors buy their way to the top of these lists by taking bulk buys and breaking them up to look like individ-ual purchases, circumventing safeguards used by the lists to prevent this. Asked by a reporter later about his work with ResultSource, Tony gave a written response, polished with spin: "At many of those events, people paid to come watch me speak and receive an autographed copy of my book. ResultSource managed the speaking, book ordering, and distribu-tion of the books for us during the tour. We're excited that the book has continued to do well over the years since the launch, and are also excited that the paperback version of the book will be coming out next month!"

Most of the bus crew members came on tour with lofty expectations—reinforced by the literal message of "Delivering Happiness"—only to have them unfulfilled. Angela, the young college graduate from Digital Roy-alty, quit after they stopped in Chicago. Laura Lombardi had hopes of hosting Zappos.TV—a series of Zappos videos uploaded onto YouTube—after her role in making the rap video, but it never happened.

Holly's role, meanwhile, dissipated as soon as the tour ended. Tony introduced Holly to several of his lieutenants in Las Vegas and Zappos to try and find a new position for her, but nothing came to fruition. A few months later, Tony told Holly he needed all the rooms at the Southern Highlands mansion for Zappos and other events, and gave her two weeks to move out of the mansion.

While she remained an acquaintance of Tony's, their friendship never recovered. She eventually moved back to her hometown in Massachusetts and got into local politics. Over the years, her experience on the tour often came to mind. "Tony would invite people into his world and give someone the earth, moon, and stars and sun without realizing how the other person might perceive it," Holly later mused. "It might have been my bad for having certain expectations, but the lack of structure, the lack of confrontation and communication—it became very negative. It was almost like the opposite of Delivering Happiness." Holly was given access to Tony's world but couldn't get what she—and many others after her—would want and come to expect: access to Tony himself.

There was one other thing that she sometimes thought about, and discussed with her friend Patricia, as she watched Tony's world from afar. After Patricia had seen Mimi crying in the backyard in the summer of 2010, Mimi kept coming and going from the Southern Highlands mansion. One day before the start of the bus tour, Mimi called Patricia and asked her to go into one of the spare rooms in the house to throw some documents away. The room, decorated in a rock-and-roll theme with a guitar on display, was technically a guest room, though Mimi had taken over the closet. As Patricia walked into the room, she noticed a trash bag that already had some papers in it. Mimi asked her to put the rest of the documents scattered on the floor of the closet into the same trash bag and discard them.

As Patricia put the papers in the trash bag, she noticed they were Tony's bank statements, bills, and other financial records. With the bag in hand, she went to find Holly, who was working in Tony's library, a room with fifteen-foot ceilings, walls lined with book-filled shelves, and a scattering of empty Grey Goose vodka bottles. Patricia told Holly what Mimi had asked her to do and said that something felt off. So the two women sat on the ground and started looking through the documents. Mimi had full access to Tony's accounts, so it was not unusual for her to sign documents or checks for Tony. However, Holly recalled seeing duplicates of certain transactions. For example, there would be a check to a landscaper for several thousand dollars. Below that, there would be a check of the same amount written out to Mimi, and the memo line for that check would say "landscaping"—as if she were reimbursing herself for a service that had already been paid directly to the vendor. By her estimate, there were hundreds of thousand-dollar checks written to Mimi. They never threw away the documents. Instead, they hid them in a corner of the library.

CHAPTER 9

THE NEW PROJECT

Tyler Williams was at a crossroads. It was the spring of 2011 and he had moved to Las Vegas three years before, with a dream of making it big in the music industry—only to have it taken away when his band's label became victim to a corporate takeover. He had been on the move around the West Coast for nearly a decade, working one construction job to the next to support his passion. He'd also been working to pay his wife's medical bills. After years of life on the road, Tyler was ready for some semblance of stability.

The son of a Pentecostal Christian youth pastor, Tyler had grown up in an idyllic town in southern Oregon, before moving with his family to Anchorage, Alaska, when he was twelve. The outdoors had afforded him a life of creation and wonderment, and he had watched his father build water balloon catapults as an activity director for a Bible camp.

Tyler had learned early on about the power of empathy when his mother started a foster home for Alaska Native youths, and the family adopted four children and became the legal guardian of four others. As a singer in the church band, his mother also ensured that music was a major pillar of their lives, and Tyler found himself more focused on his high school band than his studies. He also found himself focused on a girl named Elissa, whom he started dating. After graduating, the couple traveled south, got married at the age of twenty-one, and moved to Seattle.

But their honeymoon period hadn't lasted. Elissa started experiencing intense symptoms of rheumatoid arthritis, and she struggled to get out of bed in the mornings, her joints too stiff to move. Some days, Tyler would draw her a hot bath, then carry her into the tub to bend her legs and arms as she cried in pain.

Saddled with medical bills, the couple were just getting by when Tyler got a call in 2007 that had the potential to change their fortunes: his friend was looking for a drummer to join a Las Vegas–based band. A place where Elton John or the Grateful Dead's Bob Weir could be playing on any given night, Vegas was the place where Tyler might finally turn his music dream into reality. Plus, the warm climate might help Elissa's condition.

While the band had gained some recognition and toured the country, it was dropped by its label within a year. But the couple was determined to stay in their newfound city; Elissa's symptoms had improved immensely. Tyler was looking for other jobs when Elissa started working as a Monster Energy girl, passing out samples of the energy drink along the Strip, at conferences, and in offices, including those belonging to a tech company called Zappos.

She was amazed. It was unlike any office she had seen before: employees were parading around the office in costumes amid a tangle of plants hung from the ceiling. It was all a bit weird—just like Tyler. Upon Elissa's urging, Tyler found himself Googling the search terms "Zappos" and "Tony Hsieh." None of the web pages that he found had anything to do with selling shoes.

What he found instead was that Tony and Zappos were well on their way to becoming part of tech industry folklore. Though still soft-spoken and slightly awkward, Tony had become the perfect host for the onslaught of visitors and camera crews coming to Henderson to capture the nontraditional corporate culture of Zappos. While other tech companies like Google and Facebook were developing the "golden handcuffs" of Silicon Valley—above-market salaries and extraordinary employee benefits like on-site gyms, yoga classes, dry cleaners, and free food, making it impossible for workers to leave—Zappos already had most of these things, and it also offered a different benefit: a place for misfits to find purpose and a home.

"When you have the little Z's on people's cheeks, you can understand why people would say, 'Oh, it feels a little cult-like,'" commented a journalist who visited the company with a camera crew in 2010 on Bald and Blue

Day, an annual event where Zapponians shaved their heads, dyed their hair blue, or had "Zappos" or "Z" painted in blue on their bodies to show company spirit. "You mean, that's not normal?" Tony had answered with a smile.

From costume parades to Superhero Week, it was not unusual to see a Zapponian walking around the office in a full-body Spider-Man suit or a male employee in a barmaid outfit. Loud cheers erupted in the middle of the day as employees gathered around a set of cubicles to watch two toy cars race down a miniature track. Employees recited legendary stories from the Fourth of July barbecues and New Year's Eve parties that Tony would host at his home in Southern Highlands every year. There were workout rooms and areas where employees could go lie down and take a nap. There was an open bar with whiskey, vodka, and beer. Balloons, streamers, and Silly String hung from the ceiling year-round, giving the sense of a perpetual, never-ending office party. "It was pure happiness," said Carolyn Goodman, the mayor of Las Vegas.

Tony, meanwhile, rarely strayed from his uniform: a black Zappos T-shirt or a Zappos hoodie, jeans, and black Donald J. Pliner slip-ons. Journalists would come to Henderson, follow Tony around, and leave perplexed by his idiosyncrasies. "At times, Mr. Hsieh came across as an alien who has studied human beings in order to live among them," wrote a reporter for the *New York Times*. "That can intimidate those who are not accustomed to his watchful style."

Antonia Dodge, who was working at Zappos as a personality assessor, told the reporter that Tony had a form of social phobia. "But he gallantly walks over it by not letting it stop him and always pursues social situations," she said. "And second, he lubricates with tons of vodka." Tony's romantic life was a quandary as well. "For all of Mr. Hsieh's emphasis on the importance of relationships, his romantic life remains a mystery," the reporter wrote.

"I don't usually define dating or not dating, together or not together," Tony told the *New York Times*. "I prefer to use the term 'hang out.' And I hang out with a lot of people, guys and girls. I don't really have this one person I am dating right now. I am hanging out with multiple people, and some people I hang out with more than others."

While Tony may have seemed out of place, the company he built was even more so. The Zappos culture—fun, weird, and referred to by Barbara Walters as Tony's "social experiment"—was also off-putting for some, especially for buttoned-up corporate America. But in a post-recession world in which tech companies seemed to have all the answers to society's problems, a new generation of young workers without technical coding skills looked away from big tech firms in Silicon Valley and instead to Zappos, with its lack of formality and an emphasis on hiring around culture, not resumes.

Its core business was selling shoes online, but that seemed to be the last thing that came to mind when people thought of Zappos and Tony Hsieh. The news segments and talk show interviews—from Tony explaining Zappos's core values of staying humble and embracing weirdness to B-roll of pranks being pulled in the office—mythologized Tony and his stated purpose of creating happiness for customers and employees. They also became recruiting tools for the company: Tony was sending out smoke signals to people looking for *more* in their lives. Tony could show them the way.

The more Tyler learned about Zappos, the more he became intrigued by Tony's way of talking about his business, as if his workforce were a true community of like-minded individuals, bonded and built upon a core set of values.

Then he saw one statistic that caught his eye: at the time, the company claimed that Zappos was harder to get into than Harvard. Tyler, who never went to college, felt compelled to apply.

■ ■ ■

Tyler didn't know it yet, but he was about to enter Tony's world as it entered a new chapter that would expand far beyond Zappos. For all the hullabaloo about the successful leadership synergy at the top of Zappos between Tony, Fred, and Alfred Lin, it didn't last long after Amazon bought the company. A year after the sale, Alfred departed and took a role at Sequoia alongside his mentor Michael Moritz, where he would end up steering investments into companies like DoorDash, Instacart, and Reddit. (In 2012, he joined the board of Airbnb.) With Alfred gone, there were rumblings that Tony and Fred were working on something massive. "They were actually very, very explicit about the fact that they had this secret project," recalled Chris Peake, the Zappos employee who reported to Fred.

Tony and Fred had been inspired by an economist named Edward Glaeser, whose book *Triumph of the City* unpacked how urban metropolises like Athens, London, Tokyo, and Singapore have historically fostered humans' leaps forward. Cities "spur innovation by facilitating face-to-face interaction, they attract talent and sharpen it through competition, they encourage entrepreneurship and they allow for social and economic mobility," read a *New York Times* review of the book. Glaeser's theory posits that when cities increase in size, the productivity and innovation of each resident increase. But when companies increase in size, the opposite happens—with more bureaucracy and red tape, each employee actually becomes less productive and creative. With this in mind, Tony and Fred had embarked on a new kind of project, one that would be centered around making Las Vegas a hotbed for innovation. Perhaps Sin City could become the next Silicon Valley.

An opportunity had emerged in 2009, when Tony was introduced to Oscar Goodman, the infamous mob-lawyer-turned-mayor of Las Vegas, who had preceded his wife, Carolyn, before she was elected in 2011. Decades earlier, Oscar had been a fixture of downtown Las Vegas, north of the modern Strip, when it was a glitzy playground for Hollywood royalty, vagabonds, and the mafia alike, an escape from the rigidity of the nation's metropolises. But the area had become a forgotten corner of America and fallen to crime and poverty once the corporate mega-casinos started emerging from the desert floor along Las Vegas Boulevard in the 1990s.

Some efforts had been made to bring the downtown area back to its former glory, including the construction of a gigantic canopy made of 50 million LED lights that featured mesmerizing visual displays over the neighborhood's main vein, Fremont Street. Under Oscar's tenure, the city had doubled down and embarked on a head-spinning number of projects, acquiring sixty acres of land west and south of Fremont Street. The famed architect Frank Gehry was hired to design a world-class brain disease research center, a crumpled metal structure that looked as though it had been crushed by a giant fist. Plans were drafted for a performing arts center, and construction began on the area's first green space, Symphony Park. A cluster of antiques stores and furniture wholesalers south of Fremont Street became known as the Arts District, attracting hip locals to new bars. By 2008, construction on the five-million-square-foot showroom complex World Market was completed, attracting hospitality conventions. Finally, Oscar vowed to build a new City Hall to anchor his newly modern neighborhood.

But the one thing missing was a large company to bring jobs to the area. So when a shrewd local real estate dealmaker named Andrew Donner told Oscar about a tech company called Zappos that was interested in moving to the area, he realized the company could move into the old City Hall building—a semicircular structure built in the 1970s that had recently undergone renovations—and complete his downtown puzzle. His hunch was confirmed when he toured Zappos's Henderson office soon after. "It was unlike any business I had ever seen," Oscar later recalled. "I didn't know what they did. Apparently, they were selling shoes over the telephone."

In 2010, Zappos announced that it would be moving to downtown Las Vegas and would take over the old City Hall building when the council moved out in 2012. (After lengthy negotiations, Andrew Donner's company, Resort Gaming Group, closed on the acquisition of the property in the summer of 2012, ultimately paying $18 million, and Zappos's parent Amazon committed to a fifteen-year lease.)

It came as a surprise to some. Why move hundreds of employees out of suburbia to a rough part of town? Despite the development over the past decade, the neighborhood was still pockmarked by boarded-up properties, run-down motels, and empty lots. Although it explained why Tony and Fred had been spending less time on Zappos affairs recently— they had been making trips downtown to take clandestine meetings at a bar and there were rumors of plans for employee housing and charter schools for the children of Zapponians—but it still wasn't clear what was behind the announcement.

What Zapponians could assume, however, was that Tony and Fred thought big, and whatever secret project they were working on was going to be a whole lot more than simply moving the company headquarters again.

Away from Vegas, Tony and Fred had been touring the famed campuses of Google, Nike, and Apple. Tony found them beautiful. At Nike's headquarters in Portland, he loved the running track that bordered one of its buildings, as well as an on-site pub in another building. "We need one of those," Tony said. But he also found the campuses incredibly insular, and with "golden handcuff" perks, there was little reason for employees to leave; these companies had essentially built fortresses. At the Googleplex in San Mateo, there was no need for a Google employee to buy lunch at a local restaurant—thereby contributing to the local economy—or to integrate with the community when everything was provided.

Instead of looking at company campuses, Tony had been thinking about his visits to New York University when he was at college. What he liked most about NYU was that there were no clear lines for where the campus ended and city life began. "The more we thought about it, the more we thought maybe we should actually turn this whole idea inside-out," Tony later said during a presentation at a tech sustainability conference. "What if instead of just investing in ourselves, we invested in the community and the ecosystem?"

■ ■ ■

Whatever they were planning, it was going to be people like Tyler Williams who would one day ensure its reality. Though he could not have foreseen what awaited him after entering Tony's world.

Applying for a role at Zappos seemed a long shot, Tyler thought, but he had tried, succeeded, and failed more than once in life. He saw an option to apply with a video cover letter—so he got to work, creating a catchy beat that spelled out Zappos's ten core cultural values. To perform the song in the video, he cloned himself seven times, creating a full band of Tylers with mohawks. Five versions of him played instruments, from the drums to maracas, while the other two fiddled with a Rubik's cube and snapped to the rhythm. The Tyler with the guitar crooned:

It's a family that loves to play.
It's a place that I'd like to go someday.
Throw all my insecurities away and be honest in the things I'd say.
You can be a little weird if you're humble.
Grow and learn while having fun.
Creating open-minded sense of adventure.

Train for a marathon. Determined to run.
Yes it's true. Yes it's true.
Za-a-a-ppos. Where they embrace the change with a click.
Za-a-a-ppos. They create a masterpiece,
Out of only a wish.

The music video not only secured him the job but became a Zappos legend. He started at the call center, as most other Zappos employees had before him. Even though he applied for the position of events and audio-visual technician, he was happy to work his way up in the company. A few months after his start date, the company hosted its annual costume contest on Halloween. Tyler made a centaur costume so elaborate that his managers told him to take the day off the phones to walk around the office and make people laugh. At one point, he made his way past a glass-walled conference room in which Tony was filming a video interview. The interviewer and Tony laughed as the centaur ambled through the camera frame, emphasizing Tony's point that Zappos embraced fun and weird-ness in the office.

Later that day, when Tyler was on his way back to his desk, Tony caught up with him. "What are you doing tonight?" Tony said to Tyler. There was a Halloween parade that night in downtown Las Vegas, and Zappos had submitted a float for it. "Would you like to come?"

Tyler, who had never spoken to the CEO before, stumbled through an explanation that he too would be downtown that evening, but he couldn't accept the invitation because he had a show to play that night with the Beau Hodges Band, a new part country, part rock, part blues band that Tyler had joined. Tony, who didn't have a costume on, asked where they were playing. Tyler told him that it would be at an outdoor stage far removed from the main street and well after the Halloween parade ended. Tony nodded with a smile and walked off. Tyler wondered whether he had just missed the opportunity of a lifetime.

That night, the Beau Hodges Band started playing to about five people on an empty street. Tyler and his four bandmates treated the show as a rehearsal. But thirty minutes into their set, they heard some honks and saw a caravan of large vehicles driving toward the stage. A red double-decker, a school bus painted in an Alice in Wonderland theme, the Delivering

Happiness tour bus, and a Zappos parade float pulled up, and close to sixty people poured out of the vehicles to dance to the Beau Hodges Band. Tyler saw Tony watching from the top of the open double-decker bus, smiling down at the Zapponians swaying to the music. As Tyler watched Tony and the scene before him, he started to understand the magic behind his boss. "Tony instilled in me that night what 'wow' really means," Tyler later remarked. "It's about making someone feel really special."

■ ■ ■

Such enchantment was about to take hold in downtown Las Vegas. At the start of 2012, Tony and Fred announced during a company all-hands meeting that they were finally moving the Zappos headquarters into the former Las Vegas City Hall building in the Fremont East district. The move would happen in phases, with the first task at hand being to convert the jail cells on the second floor into either conference rooms or a speakeasy. But they saved the biggest announcement for last. They would be embarking on an entirely new venture: a $350 million investment, most of which would be privately funded by Tony, to revitalize Fremont East, a long-decaying corner of Las Vegas, and turn it into a mecca for technology, culture, and community.

Tony called it "the city as a startup"—as if it were possible to apply the "move fast and break things" ideology of Facebook and other high-flying tech startups to an entire metropolis. His fourteen hundred employees weren't just moving offices. They were going to rebuild their own slice of Las Vegas. "How many opportunities in a lifetime do you have to help shape the future of a major city?" he stated during one of his talks.

The project, led by Tony and ten of his most trusted lieutenants, including Fred, Tony's cousin Connie Yeh, and her husband, Don Welch, would be named the Downtown Project, with the new Zappos headquarters serving as an anchor to the community. The $350 million would be distributed across four categories: $50 million to attract small business owners to open up restaurants, coffee shops, grocery stores, and more in Fremont East; another $50 million on art and cultural projects, including an art museum and new live music venues; $50 million to invest in tech startups, on the condition they move to downtown Vegas, just as Tony had required his portfolio companies to move into the Venture Frogs incubator in San Francisco; and finally, $200 million to buy up land and buildings downtown and build residential high-rises to house the entire vision.

Underpinning the Downtown Project were three central goals. The first was to make downtown Vegas the most community-focused city in the world. The second was to provide everything one of its citizens would need to live, work, and play within walking distance. Third, Tony wanted to make downtown Vegas the co-learning and co-working capital of the world. These goals were not only lofty; some were simply unquantifiable. How do you measure whether a city is focused on its community? And how do you define and determine what makes a co-learning capital of the world?

To address this, Tony invented new metrics to decide which companies and ventures the Downtown Project would invest in. Instead of maximizing return on investment (ROI)—a common measure in business to assess profitability—he said he would only invest in businesses and projects that focused on maximizing long-term return on community (ROC). Like Zappos's reputation for hiring employees based on whether they aligned with its culture, the logic was now being applied to entire companies: the definition of the Downtown Project "community" seemed largely dependent on whether a company would simply fit in with the neighborhood Tony was creating. Another metric he would use to determine where his capital went was return on luck (ROL), a phrase borrowed from Jim Collins in his book *Great by Choice*, which meant he would invest based on whether a business or project would encourage more serendipitous collisions among strangers, bringing new ideas to light. All this meant that even if a business could make Tony and the Downtown Project a lot of money, but it was not good for the community, then he wouldn't invest. "This is part of the reason why we don't have outside investors and we're not working with traditional building developers or land developers," Tony quipped later. No outside investors also meant another consequence (or perhaps an advantage, in Tony's eyes): despite the overwhelming emphasis on giving back and focusing on the community, Tony would ultimately have full control of the entire venture.

Zapponians were sold. "This was way bigger than just the campus," recalled Chris Peake. "We felt like this could go down in history books as something that Tony Hsieh, Fred Mossler, and Zappos did to recharge cities."

Since Tony had so much of his personal money on the line, onlookers wondered what motivated him to do this. "Some speculate it's ego, a desire to remake downtown in his image—his personal Hsiehville," wrote the *Las Vegas Sun* in 2012. "But others say Hsieh looks like a young Buddha, hinting that some Eastern religious ethic accounts for what can be viewed as a selfless endeavor. Still, others say he can't pass on a once-in-a-lifetime opportunity to help remake the urban center of a city known around the world."

CHAPTER 10

THE DESERT TECH UTOPIA

Like other locals of downtown Las Vegas, Natalie Young had heard that there was a rich guy walking around the neighborhood. Rumor had it he was going to spend millions of dollars to transform the area. But she was wary of this new arrival, Tony Hsieh. He was always surrounded by an entourage, like some hotshot. The last thing downtown needed was a mon-eyed tech bro to gentrify the neighborhood and break open the tight-knit group of locals who spent their nights at the Downtown Cocktail Room.

But on a fall night in 2011, Natalie's life changed. She had been reluctant to go out that evening. Actually, she wasn't much of a night owl at all. She'd been in recovery for more than a decade, and going to bars with friends wasn't her idea of a good time. But after months of unemployment, she'd relented and agreed to go check out the new Thai restaurant downtown. After one thing led to another, she was now seated in a booth with her girlfriends in the dim light of the Downtown Cocktail Room.

She had been a cook since she could remember, a career she pursued at the insistence of her father. When she was younger, she had gone astray with the wrong crowd in her hometown, Aurora, Colorado, but after multiple stints in rehab she got sober in her late thirties, and landed a job as a broiler cook at Eiffel Tower Restaurant in the Paris Hotel. Standing in front of a superheated cooker preparing rib-eye, rabbit, veal, and Dover sole for ten hours a day was grueling, adding to the pressures of working for a fine-dining establishment on the Strip. But the discipline held her life in place, and she channeled her energy into her work. After being promoted to sous-chef, she was recruited by the Hard Rock Casino to work as a room chef at one of its restaurants.

After a decade in Las Vegas, though, she was beginning to feel that it was time to move on. She was thinking of moving to Santa Fe, New Mexico, where the pace was slow and the food was good. Whether Natalie was in the kitchen or outside, rarely was she in anything but Dickies trousers and Chuck Taylors. She had a round face with a full-bodied grin, but her expression could darken in an instant, with the seriousness of someone who knows what happens when a line is crossed. Her last job in Vegas leading a kitchen had ended acrimoniously and left a bad taste in her mouth, marring a successful run as a chef in the Strip's casinos: after being lured with a big paycheck to open a new restaurant, she had set up the business only to be replaced by someone being paid less. Had she done some due diligence, she would have learned that the employer had a history of shady business practices. "I was going to either commit suicide or homicide . . . seriously," she said later.

While plotting her exit from Vegas, she spent most days at the downtown neighborhood's only cafe, the Beat Coffeehouse, a beloved spot on the corner of Fremont and Sixth Street where customers were encouraged to bring in their own vinyls to play on the store's record player. That, and dogs were allowed; it was Natalie's idea of a perfect place to pass the time in an otherwise run-down part of town.

She was close with the owners of the Beat, married couple Michael and Jennifer Cornthwaite, the latter of whom she'd gotten to know when she was working in the casinos. The couple also owned the Downtown Cocktail Room. It had been Michael's dream to build a bar downtown for years, one that didn't rely on slot machines or cable TV to draw patrons, and in 2007 he'd made it a reality. Housed at the bottom of a windowless brick building on Las Vegas Boulevard, a few steps south of Fremont Street, it had the feel of a Prohibition-era speakeasy, with an inconspicuous entrance in an alleyway several feet from the boulevard. After ringing the doorbell, patrons passed through heavy curtains that concealed the intimate space within. A long polished-concrete bar extended away from the entrance, opening up to a low-slung room dotted with candlelit tables. Beyond the main floor space an even smaller room was filled with booths, where Natalie was now sitting, sipping on a Coke.

Michael slid into the booth and sat next to her. "Are you set on Santa Fe?" he said.

"Yeah, I'm pretty set," she responded.

"Is there anything that can change your mind?"

"I don't really, you know, see what's next here."

"Well, what if you could have your own restaurant?"

"You're stupid," she said. "I don't have any money."

"What if you don't need any?"

Someone approached the table. "Hey, Michael, Tony's here." Before leaving to greet his new arrival, Michael turned to Natalie and looked at her seriously. "Don't leave."

She hung around for a little while longer before going to find Michael to say goodbye. When she found him, he asked her to follow him to a table where Tony was sitting with his party.

"Hey, Tony, how's it going?" she said. "I'm Natalie."

"I know who you are," Tony responded. "What size restaurant do you want?"

▪ ▪ ▪

Understanding how blighted corners of cities transform into "cool" neighborhoods—the study of gentrification—has been the focus of urban planners for decades. Williamsburg, a former manufacturing neighborhood in Brooklyn, was once a cluster of run-down warehouses and home to an insular sect of Orthodox Jews and Italian immigrants. Over a decade, the neighborhood became unrecognizable. Now countless high-rise towers line the East River and offer residences with panoramic views of Manhattan; at street level are boutique stores and overpriced coffee shops. Despite scarce parkland, it is the kind of neighborhood where new one-bedroom apartments often start at $4,000 per month and young New York elites go to be seen.

Most who study these urban transformations agree that they typically occur as a series of clear and predictable events. In 1979, an MIT professor named Phillip Clay published one of the first comprehensive studies of gentrification called *Neighborhood Renewal: Middle-class Resettlement and Incumbent Upgrading in American Neighborhoods*, which laid out four stages in which neighborhoods transform from poor, run-down areas into enclaves for the upper class. While some modern factors can affect how gentrification occurs, the study remains true for many cities. According to Clay, who became the chancellor of MIT, the first indication that change is afoot is the arrival of artists in search of cheaper housing or members of LGBTQ communities seeking safe spaces to move into. These people begin renovating individual spaces. A music and arts scene inevitably builds around them, breathing fresh air into local bars or developing new ones. Street art will begin to mask blighted buildings and add light to dark alleyways.

Next, vacancies drop and foot traffic spikes with the arrival of more residents, attracting middle-income earners, who begin buying up more properties from the original residents and pricing them out of the neighborhood. With more money, the properties are renovated and the allure of the neighborhood improves.

As eyesores start to disappear behind new facades and trees are planted in front of trendy cafes, corporate and public money begins to flow in, growing the demand for boutique storefronts, Starbucks, and hotel chains. Roads and streets are improved, and new parks are built. Public institutions like universities and hospitals are built. A modern twist on Clay's model would include the arrival of hipsters and moneyed millennials.

By stage four, the artists that catalyzed the change in the area have themselves been priced out of the neighborhood, to make way for a solid upper class who move into flashy new condo buildings that fill the remaining vacant lots or are built on land where the old homes once stood. The original residents have long been forgotten, pushed farther away as surrounding neighborhoods have similarly been boosted, in a continuous cycle.

In March 2010, as Tony basked in the success of the Amazon sale and prepared to promote his memoir, the downtown neighborhood of Las Vegas was very much on the cusp of Clay's first stage. Tony had loved the urban vibe of San Francisco with its sense of "cool." Living and working in Henderson amid the banality of suburbia had left him wondering if there was any place that felt anything like San Francisco in Las Vegas. He was told that there was one bar north of the city called the Downtown Cocktail Room. Walking into the sultry space, Tony felt it was exactly what he'd been looking for.

But it was in Michael Cornthwaite, the bar's owner, that Tony found an enthusiastic guide to lay out an idea for downtown that he'd been dreaming about for years. Michael's vision had been shared by Mayor Oscar Goodman, who had vowed to invest in the area, promising to improve the roads and streets. The city had plans for an arts center nearby, and construction on a park had begun. And a newer, younger, cooler crowd had started coming to the area as new bars—Beauty Bar, Vanguard, and the Griffin—opened along Fremont Street. While those watering holes supported a blooming nightlife on the block, they did little to brighten Fremont Street during the day, which was still pockmarked with run-down storefronts. A pawn shop stood at one end and a sex shop at the other. In the middle of the block was a take-out spot that sold Philly cheesesteaks, which occasionally came with a viewing of cockroaches.

Other establishments did little to attract the type of crowd that Michael's bar did. Just north was the Gold Spike casino, which advertised "sexy blackjack" and "$1 shots." Its gaming floor was filled with cigarette smoke and penny slot machines, and attracted a tough clientele; gang members had once robbed the place at gunpoint. Another time a woman was shot by her husband in the parking lot. East along the next block, opposite the Beat, on the corner of Sixth Street and Fremont, was the El Cortez casino, a place where one might see someone being kicked out of the venue instead of enjoying a pleasant evening of roulette. For another five blocks, the only respite from empty car lots and run-down motels was an old dive bar on the corner of Tenth Street called Atomic Liquors—a name it earned during the 1950s, when its patrons could stand on its roof and watch the nuclear bomb tests to the north send mushroom clouds bulging above the desert.

But if there was one more reason to see the neighborhood as a diamond in the rough, a burgeoning grunge rock music scene was what stitched the place together. Just a block from Atomic Liquors was one more venue, called the Bunkhouse, a saloon-style bar that, locals declared, was where one could experience the "real Vegas." The bar looked like it was falling apart, adding to its allure. Inside the peach stucco walls was an open floor space soaked with years' worth of beer, with a foot-high stage at one end and a long bar at the other. On the walls hung aged posters of Roy Rogers and John Wayne, and a stuffed stag head. When the bar was full and a band was playing, there would often be headbangers down at the front.

"Downtown is a happening scene, there's a revolution down there and it's great to be a part of it," Tony DiVincenzo, a bass guitar player with the local band Lazy Stars, told a reporter after a gig at the Bunkhouse. "You know, musically, artistically, spiritually, man. It's awesome."

Among the scene's most die-hard fans was James Woodbridge, a philosophy professor at the University of Nevada, Las Vegas, who had realized that the energy of the Bunkhouse could be expanded to a festival that signed bands like the Lazy Stars to play at the downtown bars and showcase the neighborhood. Realizing this vision, he co-founded the Neon Reverb festival in 2008, mostly by using his own savings. The festival only drew around fifty people in its first year, but by the time Michael took Tony to see the festival in the fall of 2010, there was a Red Bull–branded party bus shuttling hundreds of fans from the Bunkhouse to Beauty Bar to the Downtown Cocktail Room. "Here we had this amazing thing where the whole area was activated," Woodbridge said.

Save for the El Cortez and Michael's businesses, Tony and the Downtown Project would eventually own all of these properties and businesses. They would also pour money into the Neon Reverb festival. As Tony came and went from downtown, he learned that his own Zappos staff had been frequenting the bars independently of him. Tony saw that downtown Las Vegas was ripe for reinvention, like the Sixth Street district in Austin, Texas. The artists were already here, and so were the bars. And with so many vacant lots, there was plenty of space to create. Fred introduced Tony to Andrew Donner, the real estate developer who owned some properties in the neighborhood and knew who owned what. On tours around the area, ideas were flowing for Tony as he walked from block to block. One day, as they approached the corner of Stewart Street and Sixth Street, in front of the old City Hall building, Tony turned to Andrew and pointed at a dusty lot. "Can we build a ski slope right here?"

By Clay's reckoning, the process of gentrification can take years, often more than a decade. By the time Zappos announced in December 2010 that it was moving into the former City Hall building, Tony's vision for the neighborhood was unfurling by the day. And if Tony was going to be the primary catalyst behind the transformation of Downtown, he wasn't going to wait decades to see how his investment would pay off.

In 2011 Tony went to the Burning Man festival for the first time and had seen how a vibrant community could be built seemingly in an instant. The festival, held every September in the Nevada desert, draws almost a hundred thousand revelers, who essentially build a self-sustaining city with its own neighborhoods and infrastructure that exist for a week before disappearing overnight again. People sleep in elaborate "camps," complete with arts projects, musical performances, and fire-breathing sculptures that distract from the intermittent dust storms and heat waves. "Citizens," as attendees of the event are known, exchange items rather than pay for goods in currency.

To convince people to move to a neighborhood in Las Vegas, away from the Strip, Tony would first need to attract artists, creatives, and small business owners to make the neighborhood cool. Then he envisioned building an element of Silicon Valley in the neighborhood, where innovators and technologists could come, create, and invent, without fear of failure. To sweeten the arrival—and supercharge the development—new citizens would have a place to stay, sometimes for months at a time, for free.

At the time, there was only one residential building that could seem appealing to young millennials and tech workers arriving in the run-down neighborhood. The Ogden was a 248-unit luxury condominium building that towered above the corner of Las Vegas Boulevard and Ogden Avenue, virtually a halfway point between the former City Hall building to the north and Fremont Street to the south. From a distance, the white facade of the building stood as one of the most visible markers of downtown. The building had recently been pulled out of bankruptcy, which it had endured thanks to poor sales following the Great Recession, and when Tony moved there in May 2011, it was only 20 percent occupied. Tony's condo, twenty-three stories above the street, was in fact several apartments connected together, with views looking south toward the Strip and north toward the valley. Walking through closets or obscure doors could lead to another apartment, where surprises abounded; one room was designed to look like a dark jungle, with plants covering the walls and hanging from the ceiling, illuminated by purple light. Fred moved into a neighboring apartment, in an arrangement not dissimilar to Tony's fiefdom at 1000 Van Ness in San Francisco, where all his work colleagues and friends had moved in while he oversaw Venture Frogs. Only Tony would scale the experience of living at 1000 Van Ness exponentially: within a year, the Downtown Project had leased eighty units in the building.

Beyond the Ogden, part of the Downtown Project's plan was to buy as many of the surrounding apartment blocks as possible, freshen them up with renovations, and then install new residents who belonged to the growing community. When the Downtown Project was announced in January 2012, Andrew Donner had by then been leading a real estate acquisition campaign that would grow to forty-five acres of land and buildings mostly surrounding Fremont Street. Once the buildings were acquired, the Downtown Project contractors would move in and renovate the properties. They purchased the single-story motels that lined Fremont Street—formerly places that charged by the hour and served as locations for prostitution and shelter for drug addicts—and boarded them up. In front they installed new neon signage, illuminating the names of hotels and motels along Fremont Street that had last seen their glory days in the 1960s: the Western, the Ambassador, Fergusons, the Star View Motel, the Las Vegas Motel, and the Fremont Motel. The Downtown Project would eventually oversee a residential real estate portfolio of almost a thousand apartments.

The process of beautifying a neighborhood may sound like a positive thing, but mention "gentrification" in a local bar, and it's sure to divide a crowd. While the new facades looked nice, Tony's organization was moving into a place that had existing residents. He and other Downtown Project lieutenants had repeatedly referred to the area as a series of empty lots—an ignorant assertion considering the dozens of low-income apartment blocks, which were in turn surrounded by homeless encampments. Referring to it that way also ignored the reason the city's vulnerable had been drawn to the area in the first place: there were several social service agencies based in the area, along with soup kitchens operating out of the area's churches.

When the Downtown Project began trying to insert new residents, they were met with immediate hurdles. After a $1.5 million donation to Teach for America, Tony convinced the organization to move its Las Vegas office to the neighborhood. With more than a hundred teachers set to arrive in the neighborhood, the Downtown Project bought a boxy fifty-unit apartment block known as Towne Terrace to house them.

The only problem was that people already lived in the building. After waiting anxiously to learn if they would be evicted from their homes, the residents met with Andrew Donner, who—clearly underestimating the hurdles to evicting tenants—told them that the Downtown Project would extend their leases for another twelve months, and promised to be transparent if anything changed. Tony later told a reporter from the *New York Times* that he would do better: "We made some bad assumptions. Next time, we'll dig deeper."

■ ■ ■

While Natalie had led her own kitchen several times, she'd never *owned* a restaurant. After her encounter with Tony at the Downtown Cocktail Room in late 2011, she'd been asked to submit a business proposal to Don Welch, a task that quickly became overwhelming. She had to learn how to set up small business insurance. In fact, she'd need more than one type of insurance: she'd have to obtain general liability, professional liability, business income coverage, and workers' compensation. She'd need to learn how to balance books and install a phone line. She submitted her proposal seven times, and each time was told to try again. Michael spent days with her at the Beat coaching her on how to refine the plan. On the seventh attempt, she had herself a deal.

What Natalie didn't know was that Tony had a lot riding on her: her restaurant would be his new neighborhood's first small business investment. Tony agreed to provide $150,000, and a further $75,000 would be contributed by Fred Mossler, Don Welch, Andrew Donner, and Donner's partner Todd Kessler. The money came with some conditions, which would become the standard offer for other small businesses in the Downtown Project, from tech startups to bars. The capital would be interest-free, and there was the unusual caveat that if the restaurant failed or shuttered, Natalie could walk away from it with no questions asked, nor any obligation to pay back the money. But in exchange, the investors would be entitled to 50 percent of all future profits of the business. Essentially, they were taking a huge chunk of the potential upside to offset the risk of the downside.

Even though Natalie knew little about running a business, the future profits clause seemed like a burden. When she spoke to a business-savvy friend, though, he pointed out that "fifty percent of something is better than one hundred percent of nothing," Natalie recalled the friend saying. And after being burned by her previous employer, Natalie was intent on doing her research on Tony. "I went as far back as I could, and I couldn't find a negative thing about the guy," she said.

The next challenge was finding a location. She didn't expect to generate enough revenue to be able to afford any of the high rents on Fremont Street, next to the other bars and restaurants. Prices had begun to shoot up amid the buzz that Tony was preparing to splash $200 million buying property in the neighborhood. One searing hot day, Natalie was cooling down in the Beat and lamenting to Michael that there was no way she could start a restaurant nearby on her budget. There was a place she might be able to afford, he told her, but it was a couple of blocks away.

Standing on the corner of Seventh Street and East Carson, a block south of Fremont Street, Michael showed her a boarded-up storefront that occupied the corner of a run-down duplex apartment building. The space had been closed for years, and in her time living in the area, she'd never noticed it. Looking around, she saw a Motel 6 directly across the street that charged $30 a night, and not much else. But at $2,000 per month, she could afford it, and so she began work on the neighborhood's newest restaurant, Eat.

A restaurant like Eat, with an eclectic brunch menu and good coffee, was one among dozens of ideas spread out on a wall in Tony's apartment in the Ogden. Tony and a Zappos employee named Zach Ware, who was helping to organize the transition of the company's headquarters, began leading tours of downtown that started in Tony's apartment. Those on the tours were encouraged to scribble their business ideas on multicolored Post-it notes that were added to the wall and sorted in a grid. Ideas ranged from an outdoor chess board to a vintage music store, artist/music development, a doughnut shop, a dry cleaner, a beauty salon, a thrift shop, and a restaurant serving raw vegan cuisine.

New arrivals to downtown Vegas came together at a block party organized by Joey Vanas called First Friday, held the first week of every month at a rotating slate of bars, which allowed people to see what the buzz was about. Paul Carr, a journalist with TechCrunch and a contributor to the *Huffington Post*, agreed to go on a tour around the downtown neighborhood, at Tony's invitation. "This will be a completely different area in the next five years," Tony said. "We're bringing food, live music, an entertainment scene; we've even talked about opening a charter school." Developing the neighborhood was sort of like playing a real-life game of Sim City, Tony added. "From Sin City to Sim City." He paused. "You know, like adding another little hump on the 'n.'"

During another visit months later, Carr met with Tony at the Downtown Cocktail Room. Carr had just quit his job, and with a glass of Fernet-Branca in hand, Tony asked Carr what he wanted to do: "Like, if you could do anything in the world, professionally, what would it be?" Carr said he'd start a wildly unprofitable print magazine, like *The Economist*, but with jokes. On the condition that Carr start the business downtown, Tony said, he would fund him. Tony would end up investing around half a million dollars in Carr's news website, NSFWCorp.

Some people even traveled halfway across the world to join Tony's world. Mark Rowland, a British retail executive who lived in Sydney, first heard of Tony in 2010 when he was researching how to improve the corporate culture of Wagamama restaurant chains, for which he was CEO of the Australian licensee. When he came across Zappos, he'd been so amazed that he decided he was going to start his own company, StyleTread, to essentially be a carbon copy of Zappos, but in Australia. Before he went ahead, he wrote to Tony to inform him of his plan and that he meant no ill will. Tony had responded fifteen minutes later, saying that it was he who was sorry: after eating at Wagamama in the United Kingdom, he'd stolen the idea for his restaurant at 1000 Van Ness that his parents had managed a decade earlier.

Now, at the start of 2013, Mark had just sold StyleTread and was looking for his next challenge. Tony suggested he come to Las Vegas and start a mentoring business that could help guide members of the community. The result: a coaching company called ROCeteer—a name that played on the Downtown Project's "return on community" metric. Neither man could have imagined that Mark's venture would become a literal lifeline to some of the neighborhood's new citizens.

■ ■ ■

From the start of 2012 until the end of 2013, it felt like businesses were sprouting out of vacant lots or glossing over eyesores every week. Old office buildings were being refurbished to house arriving tech companies and organizations, most of which were funded through an arm of the Downtown Project called the Vegas Tech Fund. Whether at bars or offices, entrepreneurs would go through several rounds of pitching before facing Fred Mossler. Sometimes Tony would sit in the corner, typing away at his computer, seemingly not listening.

Among their first investments was a company led by a young entrepreneur named Keller Rinaudo, a recent Harvard graduate who'd been part of a team that developed a tiny, implantable biological computer made of human DNA and RNA, a breakthrough technology that could one day be used to direct therapies to diseased cells or tissues. Rinaudo was lured to downtown Las Vegas to work on his new startup called Romotive, which made toy robots that could be controlled by iPhones. Rinaudo was given $500,000 to build the company, growing it from three to fifteen employees, all of whom lived in the Ogden. Keller said he chose downtown Las Vegas over San Francisco because it was a place where he could truly build his company culture from scratch. "I don't think there's a chance there [in San Francisco] of building a tribe of people who love each other, and that's what we've built here," he told a reporter.

Jody Sherman, a frizzy-haired surfer from Santa Monica who'd known Tony for years through the tech industry, had come in late 2011 to see what Tony was building. Standing in Tony's penthouse apartment in the Ogden, he stared at the Post-it wall of ideas, and then looked out the window overlooking Tony's neighborhood. "Downtown basically sells itself," Jody told a reporter about the view from the Ogden. With a $600,000 investment from the Downtown Project, Sherman agreed to move his e-commerce company Ecomom to Vegas in 2012. Jody himself moved into the Ogden, four floors below Tony.

To house companies like Ecomom and Romotive, the Downtown Project acquired three- and four-story office buildings dotted around the area. Most were located several blocks from the central Fremont Street vein, so Tony introduced rules that would force people to intermingle with the community. "Even though there's plenty of parking inside those office buildings, we're actually requiring new tenants to park a couple of blocks away, so they have to crisscross the city," Tony said during a talk at SXSW in 2013. "So we prioritize collisions over convenience." His host was bewildered. "That's fascinating," she said. "You're playing like, not God, [but] in some way, orchestrating interesting situations."

On the ground, fervor surrounded the Downtown Project's leader. At any one time, Tony could be followed by an entourage of five or even up to a dozen people. "They'd be talking passionately and trying to pitch their idea to him," Mike Henry, a former stage manager for SXSW who was hired to manage the Downtown Project's music events booking, said later. "They'd come closer and then come closer and you'd be like, 'Oh, fuck, oh, fuck, it's gonna happen again.'" Ultimately Tony would introduce his gaggle to Mike and suggest they all talk to him; perhaps there might be some synergies, or things they could work on together. "And then Tony would bolt and you would just inherit these fucking people," Mike recalled. (After such interactions, Mike typically walked the group to a bar, where he made his own exit.)

Just as Tony had envisioned, a tech community was emerging from the desert floor. To ensure that it lasted, he would need a pool of talent to pull from. Silicon Valley had Stanford, the University of California, Berkeley, and Cal Poly students, who were ripe for picking for the tech workforce. The University of Nevada, Las Vegas, meanwhile, did not have the same strengths in innovation or science, so Tony struck an agreement with an organization called Venture for America and donated $1 million to the organization. The brainchild of entrepreneur Andrew Yang, who would later run unsuccessful bids for U.S. president and mayor of New York City, the organization was similar to the concept behind Teach for America by pairing college students and recent graduates with startup businesses based in lower-tier cities around the country, like Detroit, New Orleans, Cleveland, and Baltimore—and now downtown Las Vegas.

Among the first class of students who arrived in 2012 was a bright-eyed twenty-three-year-old named Ovik Banerjee, who had just graduated at the top of his class from the University of North Carolina at Chapel Hill. Ovik had studied environmental science and biology, but he was also tugged by an entrepreneurial streak. Weeks before his arrival he wrote with measured enthusiasm about joining a societal experiment unlike any other. "The path will not be easy. Urban revitalization is not a formula that can always be solved with money, endorsement and enthusiasm," he said in a blog post. "Cities are complex, and the Downtown Project may leave Vegas where it started, or even worse. But it is an incredible experiment in urbanism, and I for one am excited to be a part of it."

■ ■ ■

Last, to bind the neighborhood together, Tony would need art, and lots of it. Mimi, who had been managing some of the Downtown Project's rollout, was assigned to strike an agreement with the Burning Man festival to import art sculptures and the iconic "mutant vehicles"—ranging from alien spaceships to beat-up cars on which were poised frightening creatures—to be displayed around the neighborhood like an outdoor gallery. It would also be an opportunity to intertwine some of the philosophies behind the festival with the neighborhood, like radical self-expression and civic responsibility. "Tony asked them to submit anything from small projects to large projects," Mimi told a reporter. "But he likes fire." Perhaps the most impressive arrival was a rusted praying mantis with bulging eyes that glowed a neon green at night and could shoot jets of fire from its antennae. "It is not about, 'Let's try to make downtown Vegas a mini Burning Man,'" Hsieh said at the time. "It is really about combining all these different perspectives . . . that can help build a unique community for downtown Las Vegas."

As more citizens flooded in, buildings that were once to be avoided at all costs were now go-to spots. No longer was the Gold Spike a place to drive past and ignore. After buying the Gold Spike, the Downtown Project bought a neighboring business, the Oasis Motel, and combined the buildings into a single place connected around a swimming pool. Tony wanted to make the building one of the main nerve centers of the Downtown Project—a place where people could get work done and then stay for drinks as the day turned into night. They tore out the slot machines, banned smoking, and upgraded the Wi-Fi. Now oversized games like chess and Jenga filled the former gaming floor.

And if the Downtown Project was going to be a place where big ideas were driving its mission, then it would need to host a perpetual roster of big-thinking speakers—in essence, a place to hold TED Talk–style events. So they partnered with Michael Cornthwaite and purchased a shuttered convenience store next to the Downtown Cocktail Room, which they turned into a three-story building that housed a 150-seat theater complex, complete with a rooftop bar, a cocktail lounge, and a cafe. It would be called the Inspire Theater.

When Natalie opened her restaurant in May 2012, a few months after Tony and Fred had announced the launch of the Downtown Project, she was all too cognizant of the opportunity that Tony's generosity had afforded her. No one had ever invested in her like this before, let alone a stranger, and she was determined to show that she was deserving of the opportunity. She paid herself $66 per day, which she calculated was enough to cover her rent, food for herself, and food for her dogs. She forwent everything she deemed nonessential: car insurance, health insurance, cable TV. "It was very important for me to get his money back," she said later. She paid back her loan in a year and three months.

Almost immediately she saw that her hard work was going to pay dividends. Her restaurant was becoming a central place drawing people into a previously darkened corner of Las Vegas, and it was only getting brighter. Two months before she opened, the Downtown Project announced that it had bought the Motel 6 across the street and planned to demolish it. In its place would be an open-air shopping center built with shipping containers, with boutique retail shops, funky restaurants and bars, and a children's playground. Welcoming people to the Container Park, as it would be called, would be the giant praying mantis, shooting flames fifty feet above the ground from its antennae.

CHAPTER 11

LIFE IS BEAUTIFUL

Opening a Las Vegas casino in the twenty-first century requires a lot of money, but arguably less creativity than it did decades before. Unlike the elaborate themed resorts built in the 1990s, like the Luxor or Paris, which lured visitors with a sense of wonderment, newer casinos sought to create buzz by rolling out a calendar full of live events and performances with the biggest artists in the world. When the Cosmopolitan opened in December 2010, with its two glass towers that would look at home in Manhattan, its talent schedule was unrivaled in Las Vegas, perhaps even the world. In its first eighteen months, dozens of headliners, most of whom were used to selling out stadiums—Jay-Z, Coldplay, Florence + The Machine, Adele, and Mumford and Sons—played in the resort's various bars and clubs. Deadmau5 played his first Las Vegas concerts there.

With the Cosmopolitan's checkbook, Rehan Choudhry had perhaps one of the most envied talent booking roles in America. Most of his nights would end with strobe lights and the thumping bass line of another musician he had booked. His life in Vegas felt far removed from his childhood in Virginia, which had in some ways been limiting: the son of Pakistani parents, he often dealt with the tensions of growing up in a first-generation immigrant family. After college, and a few other roles, he landed at Caesars Entertainment in Atlantic City, booking celebrity chefs for its casinos there. Shortly after, the Cosmopolitan had poached him to lead their opening. The thirty-year-old was now a regular fixture at most big Las Vegas events, with what felt like the keys to Sin City.

But amid the glitz of being the go-to guy at the Strip's clubs, there was one thing Rehan dreamed about: his own music festival. So in early 2012, when the Cosmopolitan decided it had spent enough, Rehan decided it was time to strike out on his own. What he had in mind was a small festival somewhere in Vegas that would combine music, keynote speakers, and high-end food offerings.

Rehan was always throwing ideas around with Ryan Doherty, a close friend who co-owned a media and publishing company in Las Vegas. Ryan, a creative with an extraordinary attention to detail, had seen opportunity in the Tony Hsieh buzz happening downtown and was currently opening a couple of bars in the area, Commonwealth and Park on Fremont, independent of the Downtown Project.

Rehan had first met Ryan and his business partner, Justin Weniger, when they were working with the Cosmopolitan to help promote its launch, and they featured him in one of their magazines, *Vegas Seven*. Ryan and Justin had started a flyer printing business in the days before social media and had since built a company called Wendoh Media, a play on their last names, which included a video production unit, multiple magazines and websites, and a marketing agency. While Justin was more of a friendly acquaintance, Rehan and Ryan were often seen together around town. "I was very new to the city, so Ryan became a friend early on," Rehan said later. "We just became buddies. We went to shows together, we went to dinner together."

As Ryan listened to Rehan's festival idea, he thought the best person for Rehan to speak to was the new neighborhood patriarch, Tony Hsieh.

As it happened, Rehan had been trying to broker a meeting with Tony. Like some who entered Tony's orbit, Rehan didn't know much about him, but he was aware that Tony was the rich guy throwing money around downtown. Through a mutual contact, Rehan was told to come to the Zappos all-hands meeting in June 2012, which was being held at the recently opened Smith Center for the Performing Arts. Outside, Rehan was introduced to Tony, and he stammered his way through a thirty-second elevator pitch: to bring a music festival to the Downtown area that "celebrates the beauty and love and hope in the world." Tony stared ahead and made no eye contact, nodding a couple of times. It reminded Rehan of the times he'd spoken to disinterested celebrity musicians—"like talking to a wall that wanted nothing to do with me."

But as Rehan mulled his insecurities, Tony was absorbing the pitch like a sponge. A music festival was exactly what he'd been looking for. Though he'd spent plenty of time with reporters, talking about his zany ideas about how collisions could transform a neighborhood, no amount of press coverage could draw tens of thousands of people to the downtown area like a music festival. Just as he had seen the several hundred people being shuttled from venue to venue in the Red Bull party bus during Neon Reverb, he could fill the city blocks with people and music and lights and art.

During several meetings with Fred Mossler and Don Welch at the Downtown Cocktail Room, which had since become the de facto headquarters of the Downtown Project, Rehan laid out his idea to take over six city blocks of downtown. Joey Vanas, who had been running the monthly block party First Friday, was brought in to provide further feedback. Rehan envisioned a stage for live performances, alongside keynote speakers like Bill Clinton and Jay-Z. There would be an area to screen art-house films, and a "village" where some of the best chefs in the world would be flown in to provide fine dining. Poets would read their work on the street, as surprise fashion shows popped up seemingly out of nowhere. All this would come together under the festival name: Life Is Beautiful.

In the kitchen of Tony's sprawling Ogden apartment, Rehan made his final pitch to Tony, Fred, Joey, Don, and Michael Cornthwaite. As a best-case scenario, he calculated that after ticket sales and expenses, the festival would lose around $600,000 in its first year, and become profitable the following year. His presentation concluded with a touch of high-mindedness: "The downtown Las Vegas community has the opportunity to achieve whatever their minds can dream for the future." Tony didn't say much. Rehan was then asked to leave.

Sitting in a pizza shop at the Plaza Hotel an hour later, Rehan got a call from Don, saying he and Fred were looking for him. When they arrived, Fred informed him that the festival had been greenlit. He'd be given $1.5 million; in a structure similar to Natalie's restaurant agreement, Tony and the Downtown Project would put up 100 percent of the cash for 50 percent equity in the company. It would also be entitled to 50 percent of future profits, and any other future investors would first need to be approved by Tony and the Downtown Project. In addition, Joey Vanas would come on as a co-founder, and be given a minority stake in the company. As the co-founder and CEO of the festival, Rehan's salary would start modestly, at $60,000 a year. And if it all failed, Rehan could walk away, no questions asked.

While he digested the terms of the agreement, he considered the fact that he was, after all, being given an opportunity beyond his wildest dreams. He had booked big names for events, and done concerts, but never led his own festival. Fred told Rehan that there was an all-hands meeting happening for the Downtown Project, at the Plaza Hotel, right now, and Tony wanted him to announce the festival in a few minutes. "I just became a part of the family," Rehan recalled.

Minutes after his speech in front of the Downtown Project employees, Joey grabbed him and led him to a table to meet more people. One of them, Joey commented on the way over, was Mimi, who, Joey warned, would not like him: Rehan was yet another person to enter Tony's orbit without her approval. This warning was confusing to Rehan. Once he sat down with her, he found that "she was polite, but clearly not enthusiastic about meeting me."

When the festival was announced in November 2012, the *Las Vegas Review-Journal* ran a front-page story quoting Rehan, and from then on he became the face of the festival. He was talking to reporters from *Entrepreneur* and NBC. Ryan and Justin put him on the front cover of *Vegas Seven*. "I had the mayor on speed dial. I could get permits approved, deals done with 48 hours' notice," he said. "I was invited to every major charity gala, every major event . . . There's a lot of social clout that came with it."

To put it subtly, Rehan's ego had become enlarged. Mike Henry recalled that during his job interview to do music booking for Downtown Project events, Tony was showing him around the neighborhood when they bumped into Rehan, and Tony suggested the two men chat over their mutual interests in bringing shows to town. As Rehan looked at him with what felt to Mike like contempt, Mike thought, "I will never fucking hear from this guy. Not once. No way. And I didn't either."

During one press interview, Rehan had talked about the marvel of the existing music scene in the neighborhood—namely, the Neon Reverb festival. But when James Woodbridge's team contacted Rehan with an idea to launch a stage for local bands under the Neon Reverb name, or program some shows at local bars, they were met with radio silence. Several more requests were made, and none of them got any response. "A reply of some sort would have been nice to prevent the impression of just being completely blown off," James said later. Another slighted Neon Reverb musician put it more bluntly: "I took it very personally that the work that had been done organically by locals to build the Neon Reverb festival was ignored in favor of, you know, giving millions and millions of dollars to a douchebag like Rehan Choudhry to basically do a terrible, awful version."

Little of the naysaying mattered to Rehan: he'd made one pitch, one time, to one organization and, just like that, had been given more than a million dollars to launch a multiday music festival with the biggest musicians in the world. He could not help but feel awestruck by the power Tony had granted him. Rehan found himself among a swirling group of people who were enamored of Tony's presence. He was spending time with celebrities as Tony pushed further into the realm of pop culture icon. The model Amber Valletta came by one day to meet Tony. Ashton Kutcher stopped by another time. Richard Branson did multiple tours of the neighborhood. One time, Rehan was standing in a VIP section at Coachella with Tony and Kimbal Musk, when Elon Musk walked over and put his arms around them, grinning. Anything felt possible. "We drank the Kool-Aid. We changed all of our social media feeds to promote our relationship with him," Rehan said later. "We had gained press associated with him, we gained awareness associated with him, we were meeting people through him that we would never have met before."

Rather quickly, Rehan was wielding significant social capital within the community as the head of the Downtown Project's biggest marketing exercise. He soon learned that holding such a role meant that his responsibilities extended far beyond just spearheading Life Is Beautiful. He was being thrust into situations in which he had no experience, like weighing in on business ideas or helping with recruiting. "All of a sudden, I was in meetings for things that I had nothing to do with," he said. "I was being asked to vet people that I had no business vetting, or didn't really understand the context for."

One day, a young woman named Aimee Groth showed up at his door.

FLIRT   MOST LIKELY TO SUCCEED

Teresa Weiss   Damian Berst   Barbara Gibb   Tony Hsieh

ALL-AROUND   DRESSED

Caroline Muir   Chad Wong   Robin Jacobs   Spencer Garfinkel

Even at a young age, his peers recognized his unusual intellect. In the sixth grade, Tony won the "Most Likely to Succeed" superlative.

Eric Liu
Andrew Atherton

Anthony Hsieh
David Padover
Jonathan Sheer

Alex Hsu

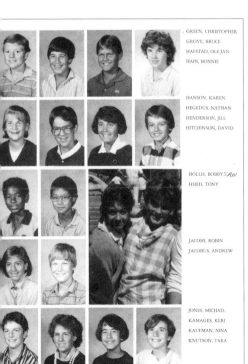

GREEN, CHRISTOPHER
GROVE, BRUCE
HAFSTAD, OLE-JAN
HAIN, BONNIE

HANSON, KAREN
HEGEDUS, NATHAN
HENDERSON, JILL
HITCHINSON, DAVID

HOLLIS, BOBBY SAN
HSIEH, TONY

JACOBS, ROBIN
JACOBUS, ANDREW

JONES, MICHAEL
KAMAGES, KERI
KAUFMAN, NINA
KNUTSON, TARA

25

3

(Above, center photo) Tony (left) in his first year at the Branson School with friend David Padover (center). Tony and David were two out of four students from Miller Creek Middle School who were admitted to the prestigious private college prep. Despite growing up together, Tony and David's friendship ended at Branson due to a disagreement.

A school portrait of Tony in the seventh grade at Miller Creek Middle School.

(Right, bottom left photo) Tony (left) in his sophomore year at Branson with friends, including Alex Hsu (center). They were two of very few Asians at the elite college prep. Tony and Alex would maintain a friendship, long after high school.

Amy Collins, Jenny Simonds
Dariah Winter, Laura Belmont

Julie Clarke, Erica Goldman
Amy Mannila, Amy Hillerstrom

Eric Liu, Jonathan Sheer

MOCK TRIAL

from left to right: Tony Hsieh, Carrie Esler, John Prato, Julie Clark, Ben Schwartz, Rebecca Hutchinson, Hadley Mullin, Ashley Wells, Chris Panzton.

Thirteen students from the debate club were selected by Ms. Ayres as a panel of six lawyers to participate in the 1990 second annual Mock Trial Competition. From January to March the group met every Friday for a few hours, preparing the case and honing their debate skills. Ben Schwartz, John Prato, and Julie Clarke represented the defendant, Pat Haines played by Hadley Mullin, accused of manslaughter by Marin Catholic's prosecution. Branson's prosecution was represented by Tony Hsieh, Eric Lui, and Mike Michaud and was able to convict Terra Linda's Pat Haines of manslaughter. The trial was so realistic that Ben Schwartz and Cristi Wong made pretrial arguments for the prosecution and the defense, arguing the constitutional right of citizens to bear arms.

With the coaching of history teacher Jennifer Ayres and Deputy Maria Osterloh, the defense placed second, and the prosecution came in third, earning Branson third place overall. Witnesses Hadley Mullin, Amy Hillerstrom, Chris Panzton, Ashley Wells, and bailiff Carine Carrie Esler contributed greatly to the team's success. Having experienced the duties of an attorney, the students in the debate club felt that they learned and benefited tremendously from participating in the Mock Trial Competition.

Bailiff Carrie Esler swears in witness Rebecca Hutchinson.

Defendant Pat Haines, alias Hadley Mullin, stands trial for manslaughter. She was later convicted and 'cuffed and stuffed.

56 Academics

(Above, top photo) Tony (left) in Branson's mock trial club. He was on the prosecution team with childhood friend Eric Liu (not pictured), and successfully convicted the opposing team for manslaughter. While his teammates are wearing blazers, collared shirts, and long skirts, Tony is dressed much more casually.

Tony Hsieh, George Petersen
Alex Hsu, John Prato

Marikka Hopkins

Electronics Club

Tony Hsieh and Chris Gewald at the electronics booth at the Ho Festival.

In the last year, a new Branson club has been formed, called the Electronics Club, quite possibly one of the most active clubs known to Branson. The club's activities center around amateur radio communication. Activities include local communication on small, handheld 2-meter radios (of which 15 to 20 of Branson students own and long distance communication including Alaska, Japan and Italy) on the popular 10-meter radio using donated school equipment. The club also builds electronic circuits and amplifiers to allow a greater radio range. Roger McGehee organizes the group and publishes a regular newsletter to keep the members informed of current events, equipment, and bulletins. The club hopes to continue its operations and expand in the future with money raised or donated by outside sources.

Seth Friedman, Tony Hsieh, and Ethan Bodle demonstrates principles of electronics using school equipment.

August Jaenicke operates the school long-distance (DX) radio equipment.

Alexander Price puts in long hours building his new antenna.

(Above, center left photo) Tony (center) in the electronics club during his senior year at Branson. He was also on the fencing team and in chess club.

Tony at graduation at Harvard University, surrounded by several friends who later became employees at LinkExchange. Included in the group photographs are Jose Santos, Jon Greenman, Sanjay Madan, Jill Wheeler and others.

Zappos's San Francisco office, circa 2000.

Tony and Ying Liu in front of the Theater Museum in Taipei, Taiwan, during the summer of 1993.

Nick Swinmurn and Fred Mossler, circa 2004.

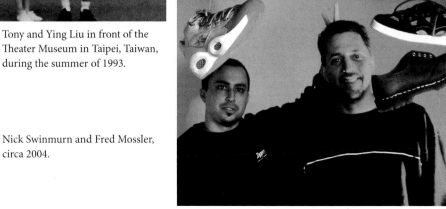

Tony with his book, *Delivering Happiness*.

11

In July 2010, Tony briefly left the media tour for *Delivering Happiness* in order to attend a political fundraiser for Senator Harry Reid (left). President Barack Obama (right) was also in attendance. Tony gave a copy of his book to Reggie Love, President Obama's aide, at this event, in hopes he would pass it along to the president. Ten days later, Reggie wrote in an email to Tony, "I was unable to get the President to read your book, b/c I've been glued to it. . . . I'll now also be sure to pass along your book."

12

Tony Hsieh judges contestants during the annual Las Vegas Halloween Parade in 2013.

13

Tony with Mimi Pham in 2014 at the
Vanity Fair New Establishment Summit
Cocktail Party in San Francisco.

Tony with Michelle D'Attilio.

14

15

16

July 4 holiday break in Bigfork, Montana, 2017.

From left to right: Justin Weniger, Ryan Doherty, Tyler Williams, and Tony.

Tony (center) with Fred Mossler (far right).

Tony cooking in Park City.

20

Andy Hsieh and a friend with Brett Gorman and Elizabeth Pezzello (right couple).

21

The shed where Tony was pulled from the fire in November 2020.
Courtesy of New London Fire Department.

View of the backyard
of 500 Pequot Avenue.
The shed that caught
fire is attached to
the right side of the
home. *Courtesy of
New London Fire
Department.*

22

Tony Hsieh
American Entrepreneur
&
Downtown Las Vegas Visionary
...73 - 2020 (46 yrs)

"Whatever you are thinking, think bigger."

Memorial of Tony at Fremont Street Experience.

Tony had sent her there to learn from him, but Rehan took that to mean she was there to be vetted. She had just moved to Downtown to launch her own project: a book that was to document life in the Downtown Project. She'd been convinced to move into the neighborhood after a chance meeting with Tony in 2012. Aimee had been a senior editor at Business Insider when she met Tony at a Venture for America gala in New York. Later at a Manhattan nightclub, he turned to her and asked, "If you could do anything in the world, what would you do?"

■ ■ ■

The Life Is Beautiful festival would also help to reinforce another message about Tony's social experiment: it was a constant party. Part of what bonded the neighborhood together was the seemingly never-ending cycle of social events and the blurred lines between work and the rest of life. The common denominator was the presence of alcohol, and as the man at the center of the village, Tony's alcohol intake rose alongside his increasing fame.

Tony had recently expanded his Delivering Happiness brand and launched a company of the same name with Jenn Lim, with the goal of providing Zappos-style human resources and leadership training to other corporations and businesses looking to improve employee satisfaction. In one video interview, done in London in 2012 to discuss the new venture, Tony deferred to Jenn whenever the interviewer asked questions. While she answered, Tony took hold of a bottle of vodka and poured generously into three glasses. "An actual video of Tony Hsieh pouring me a vodka," the interviewer says. "This is quite gangster, I've got to say."

In the first years of the Downtown Project, the company had no corporate office. Instead workers were encouraged to meet and work at the various bars in the neighborhood, like the Gold Spike or Michael's Downtown Cocktail Room. Another venue that became a fixture was Parlour Bar, an unappealing black-walled space on the gaming floor of the El Cortez. Kenny Epstein, a longtime Vegas casino figure who owned the El Cortez, recalled how Tony would come into his casino, almost without fail, around 3 p.m. Tuesdays through Fridays and slump down in a bench seat in a corner of the bar. A half hour later, another half dozen people would come in, either groups from Zappos and the Downtown Project or new arrivals pitching business, and slide into the bench seats around two knee-high tables. It was hardly a suitable work space, but with a constant stream of liquor, the group would sit around, their faces illuminated by the screens of their MacBooks, while the *ring-ding* of the gaming floor floated in. After three or four hours, they would leave and their evening would begin.

Unlike many of his newer colleagues, Tony's older friends noticed the increasing role of alcohol in his life. Jon Greenman, his former Harvard roommate, came to see Tony multiple times in Las Vegas. Whether at the Bellagio for dinner or at a house party, Tony would order round after round of shots. It was certainly a different Tony from his days in Harvard, but it also didn't seem problematic to Jon. Tony's drinking never became a cause for alarm for Jon because, by all appearances, Tony simply held his alcohol well, and his day-to-day output never seemed to be impaired. He didn't become belligerent, violent, or overly happy.

Ying Liu also noticed a difference from their days at NYU. It had been nearly two decades since she and Tony explored New York as college students, when she'd been touched by Tony's curiosity about her. They had been in and out of contact over the years, and she visited him in Las Vegas on two occasions. On the first visit, she was initially put off by the fact that she needed to schedule time with him through an assistant. When she and her family showed up for their appointment, what she thought would be a catch-up breakfast with Tony ended up being a group tour of the Downtown Project. "I'm sorry," he said to Ying after he finished leading the tour. "I just couldn't find the time. Are you guys going to stay longer?" They chatted for a few minutes, but he seemed preoccupied. Ying complained about his new attitude to Alex Hsu, the fellow NYU classmate and childhood friend of Tony's who was also visiting Las Vegas that weekend. "He is not the same Tony anymore," Alex reasoned. "He's an influential leader now. What did you expect?"

On her second visit, however, she decided to leave the family at home, and instead she came to Las Vegas with her girlfriends. On this visit, Tony made time for her. Per an itinerary sent by his assistant, she was instructed to meet Tony in the afternoon at a bar in downtown Vegas. "The schedule said, 'Drink with Tony,'" she recalled. Tony had already been at the bar for hours when she and her girlfriends arrived, and he was surrounded by people. "I still don't drink," she said. "And he was already heavy with alcohol." Tony then took Ying and her girlfriends to his favorite Chinese restaurant in downtown Vegas. He asked Ying if she might serve him a chicken drumstick—*just like college*, she thought. It was a glimpse of the old Tony, the one she would mother and serve food to from Chinese take-out boxes during her NYU days.

Later that evening, Tony invited Ying and her girlfriends to an out-door event space where members of the Downtown Project often gathered around a fire. At one point, Tony turned to Ying with a playful look. "Do you still think women screaming during sex is because they are in pain?" Ying rolled her eyes.

But the fond reminiscence didn't last long. Ying watched as Tony offered each person sitting around a campfire a tiny bottle of Fernet-Branca—one of the defining factors of every visit to the Downtown neighborhood. An Italian herbaceous digestif typically consumed in small amounts after a meal, Tony had adopted the drink as his signature. Visitors like Ivanka Trump would recall drinking Fernet with Tony. While he provided sev-eral explanations for his love of the obscure drink, another reason he gave to a friend was that it allowed him to create a new experience for everyone who did it with him. "He said that you could have a lot of it and you won't have that hangover effect," Ying recalled.

As the night continued, Tony was surrounded by others, and Ying again found it difficult to have a conversation of substance. As the evening slowed down, Tony came over, put his arm around Ying, and asked her how she was doing. It was one of few moments Tony and Ying had been alone, and it could have been a good time to chat—but she didn't quite know where to start. She mumbled a response and they stood in silence, staring at the campfire. "I just felt guarded because he was not Tony any-more," she later said. "He wasn't the same."

Drug use also factored into the routine of events, festivals, and nights out. In her book *The Kingdom of Happiness: Inside Tony Hsieh's Zapponian Uto-pia*, published years later, Aimee Groth recalled taking MDMA at several events alongside friends and people in Tony's orbit. Tony himself refused to discuss his relationship to drugs publicly—he told Aimee, "I stay away from talking about religion, politics, or drugs in general because those topics are very polarizing, and people have already made up their minds on what side of the issues they want to be on." In an interview with *Playboy* magazine, he said, "My hesitation in answering questions like these is that there's a perception that you need to do drugs in order to have certain experiences. People have a visceral reaction to that idea, so I don't like to state a preference one way or the other."

The constant drinking and partying was something that Rehan, who had been around the club scene for years, had recognized as an element of the culture of the Downtown Project: alcohol would factor into almost every situation. He could remember meetings ending at 11 a.m. with Tony offering everyone a round of Fernet. Because of the flow of people and meetings, Tony was rarely surrounded by the same group of people for more than a couple of hours. "Nobody could ever really get a sense of how much he was drinking at any given moment," Rehan said. One morning after an event to announce the lineup for the Life Is Beautiful festival, Rehan was supremely hung over and went for a walk with Tony. He turned to Tony and asked how he kept up with drinking so much. "At some point along the way, I stopped getting hangovers, so I wake up in the morning feeling fine," Tony replied. "I think that that may be the first sign of being an alcoholic."

■ ■ ■

As the party of the Downtown Project rolled on, the neighborhood's inaugural festival was approaching. Rehan had managed to secure hometown superstars the Killers to headline Life Is Beautiful. Other international acts included the Kings of Leon, Beck, and Imagine Dragons. Fine-dining restaurants were slated to open pop-up stalls at the festival, providing a culinary experience that departed far from the fast food offered at most events.

But the contracts were still being negotiated with musicians when several other festivals across the country announced that they were being canceled, citing financial issues. As a result, talent agencies like William Morris Endeavor, which represented the Killers, began demanding 50 percent up-front payments, as opposed to the typical 10 percent deposit, according to Rehan. Life Is Beautiful would also need to guarantee that 100 percent of the money would be paid, even if the festival did not go ahead. What this meant was that Tony and the Downtown Project would need to pour in an additional $2 million.

Rehan's request for money immediately ricocheted around the Downtown Project. Several people wondered whether they had made the wrong decision by choosing him to lead the festival. Tony, looking around his leadership, decided that he needed someone who could inspect the finances, so he appointed Andrew Donner to consult for the business before joining as a partner. Andrew offered Rehan $1 million to buy out his equity in the festival and to step down from his management role. "I was still very much good friends with Tony," Rehan said. "I was very much one of the leaders of Downtown Project's social structure, and had a good amount of influence in the organization." Rehan turned down the offer and felt reassured about his decision when Fred pulled him aside during a trip to New York. He and Tony valued people who didn't try to make a quick buck, Fred said. "It shows that you're with us and shows your faith in us." (Fred said he didn't recall the conversation.)

On October 26, around thirty thousand people descended on the festival grounds. The two parking lots that separated the Ogden and the Zappos headquarters were now the main stage. The festival spanned more than a dozen blocks along Fremont Street; one section was covered in grass. Pop-up art installations lined the streets, new street art was covering the walls of old buildings, and fine-dining restaurants like Nobu had their own storefronts.

Now that the streets were filled with festivalgoers, it was exactly what Tony had imagined his neighborhood would look like at its most vibrant. "Tony was really excited," Joey recalled. "It was something that was really important to him." The greatest power of the event, Joey realized, was that it exhibited the neighborhood to its highest and best potential. For the first time in half a century, downtown Las Vegas was teeming with life again.

Unlike the megafestivals Coachella and Electric Daisy Carnival, where more than a hundred thousand people would squirm through jam-packed mosh pits or wait an hour in line for the bathroom, the first year of Life Is Beautiful felt like revelers were being offered all the perks of a music and arts festival without any of the usual downsides. There were barely lines for food, drinks, and bathrooms, and because it was held in an urban center, there was plenty of space for car parking. "It was magic," Joey said later. "You're eating Nobu, watching Kings of Leon . . . As you're laying out in the grass, you have five feet around you of space."

On the second and final day of the festival, strong winds swept through the grounds. The day before, a beam at the main entrance gate had fallen down. The organizers lowered the stage towers and shut down a Ferris wheel. But the bands and DJs played on.

Not long after the Killers finished their closing set and the last revelers trickled out, Joey walked around the festival grounds. The winds were still blowing trash around. On his walk home, he sent Tony a text: "On a scale of one to 10 how happy are you right now?"

Tony replied: "11."

CHAPTER 12

THE DARWINIAN PERSPECTIVE

Much as new business partners like Rehan felt like they were on cloud nine once they'd entered Tony's inner orbit, the experience for the women in his life was similarly intoxicating. But Michelle D'Attilio was going to learn that loving Tony came with a big caveat.

At thirty-nine, with two preteen kids from a previous marriage, she was around the same age as Tony when they met in April 2013. He was visiting Milwaukee for a speaking engagement at an entrepreneurship event. At the time, she ran a social media marketing firm called Sosh and was also in a committed relationship. When her company was hired to promote the entrepreneurship event, Michelle offered to do it for free as long as she could get time with the Zappos leadership team in exchange. She had been shopping on Zappos for years, and she wanted to land them as a client.

Michelle soon got a text from one of the organizers of the event. "The Zappos crew is here," he said, "it's Friday night, and they are getting drinks at the Iron Horse Hotel before going out." So Michelle, wearing a cock-tail dress that complemented her jet-black hair and piercing green eyes, joined the Milwaukee welcoming committee and met Tony, Fred Mossler, and Andrew Donner. Initially, the plan was to go to a posh lounge at the top of a twenty-three-story building that had panoramic views of the city and Lake Michigan. "I took one look at these guys and said, 'No. This is a group of people who have been all around the world. They've already been to all of the nicest bars.'" Instead of taking them to the best and fanciest that

Milwaukee had to offer, Michelle announced she would be taking them to Victor's, a bar with a dance floor that was all neon and leather. En route in a party bus, the group was bopping to classics when a song came on and someone asked who the artist was. Tony immediately answered that it was Kylie Minogue, and Michelle laughed and poked fun at him for knowing who she was. At the bar, the group danced all night to songs from the nineties. Hours later at closing time, the bar served frozen pizzas.

Michelle sensed Tony's comfort with her. He texted her after he gave his talk, asking where she was. During a dinner that weekend, Michelle had to leave early as she had told her kids she would be home by ten that night, and Tony offered to walk her out, suggesting he wanted a cigarette, anyway.

They exchanged emails over the next few months. Michelle was growing her business and was eager for advice from *the* Tony Hsieh. He invited her to a conference in August in downtown Vegas. Known as Catalyst Week, and billed as "more affordable and less exclusive than TED Conferences," the four-day event series included talks, tours of Zappos and the Downtown Project, and networking events for entrepreneurs. As Tony's guest, she stayed at a unit in the Ogden.

Shortly after she arrived, she met Tony at his penthouse apartment on the top floor of the Ogden. After a few pleasantries they walked out of the apartment and waited for the elevator. "I'm a small-town Wisconsin girl, standing here with this extremely successful human, and I'm feeling nervous," she said. But as she darted a glance at Tony, she saw that he was keeping his eyes on his phone. He started pacing sheepishly around the elevator bank. Eventually, at the mercy of a slow elevator, he started walking in circles around her. She realized he was nervous too. "It was really endearing to see this human who had so much success still be nervous or anxious," she later recalled. That day, he took her on a tour around downtown, showing her his favorite Vegas haunts. They talked about their shared love for junk food. They agreed that chicken tenders with light breading were superior; she preferred a thicker patty in a cheeseburger, while he liked it thinner. They also realized that they both had social anxiety and needed solitude to recharge. Years later, when they were together and needed to get away from crowds or noise, they took long walks without saying a single word. Afterward, Tony would say to her, "Nice talk."

The morning after their tour around downtown, Michelle woke up early to go for a run around the neighborhood. She had mentioned to Tony the day before that it was part of her routine to go on a jog and wake herself up. When she entered the lobby downstairs, a security guard was waiting to join her on the run. Though Downtown Project–powered gentrification was crawling across the neighborhood, parts of it were still unsafe, and Tony wanted her to run with a security detail.

They stayed in touch over the next year. She attended several more Catalyst Weeks, and their friendship grew. But had she ever considered romance? Well, there was *one* thing that made her pause.

■ ■ ■

One of Tony's favorite books was *The Game: Penetrating the Secret Society of Pickup Artists*. Published in 2005 by journalist Neil Strauss, the book describes a series of social techniques used by so-called pickup artists to seduce women. With chapter titles such as "Select a Target," "Isolate the Target," and "Blast Last-Minute Resistance," the book lays out a miso-. gynistic road map for supposedly training awkward, insecure men to seduce beautiful women, while also pushing the idea that women are simply inconsequential compared to the whims of men. Despite Strauss's later conclusion that a life solely focused on chasing women was "empty" and "for losers," the book was a bestseller and became a bible for men in need of a confidence boost.

For someone who often felt challenged by social engagements and would sometimes make those around him uncomfortable with his shyness, Tony saw techniques in the book that could offer instruction on how to manipulate social settings for certain outcomes, not unlike the enchanting question he had posed to Aimee Groth—"If you could do anything in the world, what would you do?"—that ultimately convinced her to move to the downtown neighborhood. Aimee, who spent five years coming and going from the neighborhood, staying on couches or renting one of the Downtown Project's apartments, concluded in her book that by issuing invitations that contained lofty ideals, Tony had used techniques from *The Game* and the pickup artist community to convince her and others to come to the neighborhood.

In an interview with *Playboy*, Tony acknowledged as much, and said that his interest in the theories generated by the pickup community had partly inspired his thinking about how the Downtown Project was created. "I remember hearing that if you're going on a date with a girl, the best thing to do is change locations every half hour or hour and do something different," he explained. "Basically, at the end, if you've gone to seven different locations, it will have the same effect on memory as going on seven dates in single locations."

The whole point of compressing memory, and seemingly time, in this way is to seduce a girl faster. "But that technique has other applications as well," he said. "It's part of what I'm trying to do with Downtown Project. When people come visit us we basically hop from location to location to location, so even though they've been here only two or three nights, it will seem as though they've been here two weeks. It'll have a big impact on their memory. Humans remember things in terms of geography and number of stories. I want a city where all this stuff is within walking distance so you can have a bunch of different experiences."

But given how literally he interpreted the social engineering tools in Strauss's *The Game*, surely he had used them in his sex life. The *Playboy* reporter pointed out that he was forty and single. What were his thoughts about monogamy? Well, from a Darwinian perspective, Tony responded, a monogamous guy would have fewer copies of his genes in the next generation than a guy who wasn't. "I think it's pretty hard to find one partner and call it a day," he went on. "Using the analogy of friends, why not find just one friend and call it a day? The answer is because you get a different type of connection, different conversations, different experiences with different friends. I would say the same thing is true on the dating side."

It was something Tony had no qualms talking about both publicly and privately. Sometimes at events—it could be a Zappos holiday party or a conference—there would be two, three, four women who were there as his dates. Sometimes women would arrive and Tony would introduce them to the other women.

Often it seemed like Tony was engaged in some type of game, and as young women flooded into the neighborhood, many of them tried to get close to him. He dated people from Zappos, people from the Downtown Project, and others who orbited the community. One girlfriend was

Rachael Brown, who had joined Zappos in 2004 as a temporary worker in the call center before she was promoted to train new customer service hires. At some point Tony had taken a liking to her and promoted her to teach Zappos culture to all new hires, and by 2010 she was overseeing production of the company's famous quarterly all-hands meetings. It was also around this time that she and Tony started dating. While they eventually went their separate ways, and Rachael ended up leaving Zappos to turn her attention to her new career as a cellist in Las Vegas, she would reenter Tony's life years later.

To outsiders, it may have raised eyebrows for the CEO of a company to engage in a relationship with a subordinate. Certainly, as cultural views on workplace behavior sharpened in the wake of the #MeToo movement, such relationships might have attracted further scrutiny years later. But to those inside the community at the time, the fact that Tony dated employees and was expressly open about being polyamorous seemed to allow most to overlook any questions they had. This arrangement also existed in a community he was building where the traditional boundaries of work, life, and play were essentially nonexistent; people worked in the same offices, lived in the same apartment buildings, and drank at the same bars.

While polyamory was a consistent thread in Tony's romantic life, the outcomes often differed. Suzie Baleson, a former high school cheerleader who grew up in a bayside town on the outskirts of Houston, Texas, was in her late twenties when she met Tony in 2012. She had spent the better part of a decade working as a tax consultant for Deloitte and the global professional services firm Alvarez & Marsal when a mutual friend introduced her to Andrew Donner, who was looking to hire someone to help on the financial side of his real estate company, Resort Gaming Group. Andrew, who now oversaw most of the Downtown Project's real estate deals, was joined by Tony for a trip to New York where they met with Suzie for an interview. She joined Andrew's firm, then moved into the Ogden and was sucked into the local community. She also spent more time with Tony, and before long she was hopping on airplanes, visiting places around the country with him, and going to Las Vegas Knights games. "When you are his plus-one to something, people literally felt like they were the chosen one," Suzie recalled. "He made me feel special all the time." Like Rachael, she also maintained a friendship with Tony over the years before playing a significant role in his life later on.

The setup worked for some women, but not for others. Antonia Dodge, the Zappos contractor who had been quoted by the *New York Times* discussing Tony's social phobias, first met Tony in the summer of 2010 when she was hired by Zappos to assess the personalities of a small team within the company. As part of Zappos Insights, the team held in-person workshops for C-suite-level executives from other companies who wanted to learn more about how Zappos built its culture. Antonia was brought in to understand what every team member's blind spots were in order to effectively train the high-ranking executives who were coming through their workshops. While she acted as a consultant for Zappos, she was also asked to assess Tony. Though it was unclear to her whom that directive came from, one thing *was* clear—it was not something that he had requested for himself.

"He barely answered" her questions, Antonia later recalled. "He could not have been more uncomfortable about being personality-profiled by a stranger." As she started asking her usual round of questions—*What is your relationship to alone time? What is your relationship to deadlines or schedules?*—she watched as Tony slowly started to physically turn into himself like a roly-poly bug as he pulled his knees to his chest and cradled his head with his own arms. Eventually she cut the session short. "I think he might have been one of the top five most uncomfortable people in a profiling session."

The next week, Antonia was at a party with other Zapponians at Tony's house in Southern Highlands. When she approached Tony, bracing herself for yet another awkward conversation, she found a man entirely different from the one she had profiled during her evaluation. Instead she met Tony the host. He started giving her a tour of the house and introduced her to other guests. It was a different side of Tony, and one that she was drawn to when they became friends shortly after. As she got deeper into the Zappos circle, she understood that Tony had at least two girlfriends at the time, one of whom was Rachael Brown.

A few months after her work with Zappos had ended, Tony asked Antonia if she would join him at a Halloween golf tournament that the company hosted every year for vendors. Still in her early thirties, and having had friends who were in polyamorous communities, she found herself intrigued. When she arrived, she quickly realized that she was not his only date to the event. There were five other, much younger women surrounding him, dressed in Halloween costumes. "I showed up as part of a little harem," she said. "It was essentially as many women as you could fit into a golf cart." Antonia, with a set of serious green-yellow eyes and signature streaks of white hair, found herself the odd woman out. "All the other girls were dressed up as the sexy version of whatever they were dressed up as. And I never dress up as the sexy version of anything. So I think he wanted eye candy, and then he wanted conversation. I suspect I was the conversation." As the golf tournament progressed, Tony and Antonia got into a heated discussion about romantic relationships. She shared with him and the rest of the women that in order for her to be in a relationship with a partner, she needed him to be an equal in terms of success and ambition.

"I don't agree with that," quipped one of the younger women in the group.

"I don't agree with it either," Tony said. *Of course you don't,* Antonia thought as she glanced at the swarm around Tony.

By the end of the tournament, Antonia found herself laughing about the absurdity of the day. But Tony texted again a few weeks later, this time inviting her to a Zappos holiday party. *Why not?* she thought. When she arrived at Tony's house in Southern Highlands, in jeans and a shirt, she expected to be greeted by yet another group of women. But it was just Tony. As they rode in the car together, Antonia found him disengaged, choosing to pay attention to his BlackBerry instead of conversing with her. She ended up chatting with the driver in order to pass the time. When they arrived at the location, she realized it was a house. In fact, it was an intimate, swanky party of senior-level Zappos employees at Fred Mossler's home. *Oh, okay,* she thought. *I guess this is a date.* As she tried to make conversation with Tony throughout the night, however, he continued to either ignore her or feign disinterest.

Antonia thought about Tony's study of the pickup artist community. "That night, I couldn't tell whether he legitimately found me incredibly boring or if he was running [The Game]," she said. "But either way, I was being strategically ignored." According to the rules of pickup artists, ignoring a person was supposed to enhance attraction. Later on that night, Tony suggested that Antonia should date another party attendee she had just met. Again, Antonia wondered, *Is The Game being run?* "It was a weird night," Antonia later recalled. "It was probably the last time I really ever hung out with him."

■ ■ ■

In September 2014, Michelle's long-term boyfriend broke up with her on her birthday. "He basically walked out on me," she said. After hearing what happened, Tony had an idea.

"Come to Hawaii with me," he said to Michelle.

"What are you talking about?" she laughed.

The plan was to go to Honolulu to celebrate a friend's fiftieth-birthday party for a few days, and then go to Atlanta for the electronic dance music festival TomorrowWorld. Along with Fred, they were going to do some research for Life Is Beautiful. Michelle was eager to take her mind off her breakup, and Tony said he'd cover the costs—so she said yes.

From the start of the trip, Tony's antics were on full display, endearing him more and more to Michelle. On the flight over, Tony started pulling several power cords out of his backpack. He shared that he always brought them traveling because it was the best way to strike up a conversation with strangers at an airport, where people were often looking for an outlet. In the process of pulling out the cords to show her, he dropped his phone, which led to a chaotic scene of Tony pulling off all the cushions in search of his mobile while Michelle watched, laughing.

As they sat in first class—Tony had since abandoned his habit of flying budget airline Southwest—they shared headphones connected to an iPod and danced in their seats for most of the six-hour flight. She remembered how she could not stop laughing. "This silly, magical, fun side of Tony was the reason that people fell in love with him," she said. "Not necessarily romantic love. I mean the human who could create fun out of any little thing."

Soon after, Tony invited Michelle again to Hawaii. Until this point, their relationship had been platonic. Michelle had never felt pressure from Tony, but she wondered whether his feelings were warming. Maybe he had been courting her since they met eighteen months before. All these thoughts, she realized, were emerging because she was starting to develop romantic feelings for Tony. "It was a gradual build," she said. "When you have two people who have social anxiety, putting yourself out there is a little frightening."

They discussed what they looked for in a partner, and their futures. Tony was steadfast in his views around polyamory. Michelle craved the stability and comfort of monogamy. But, she found comfort in Tony, and she was having *fun*. The only pressure she felt from Tony was whether she had the bandwidth to jet-set with him around the world. There was one element of Tony's polyamory that suited her: radical honesty and transparency. For example, if Tony was spending time with another woman, he would never hide it. Though Michelle knew that at the end of the day she wanted a partner who was committed only to her, she found herself opening up to the idea of dating Tony. She understood they would most likely never marry. But if she could date Tony while continuing to date others, she saw no harm in adding herself to his growing group of lovers.

The next month, ahead of his birthday, Tony flew Michelle to Las Vegas. She was known for her meatball recipe, and that night it was on the menu for the few dozen people gathered for Tony's birthday dinner. Looking around, she found herself welcome in Tony's community with open arms. "I have always struggled with the feeling of home," Michelle said. Later that night, Tony and Michelle kissed.

Seemingly overnight, Michelle found a part of her life revolving around Tony. They came up with a system where Tony would email her a list of engagements he had coming up in the next few weeks—from weddings to conferences to birthday parties—and she would respond with the events she would attend. For those that she couldn't come to, Tony would usually then invite another woman. Unless it was an international trip, she rarely liked to leave Wisconsin for longer than three days at a time because of her kids. Throughout 2015, they crisscrossed the globe, from New York and Florida to South Africa and Dubai. Though Michelle never asked, Tony always paid. He visited her in Milwaukee a handful of times. Sometimes, Michelle would bring her kids with her to Vegas, and she enjoyed watching him interact with her kids. In turn, she met Tony's parents. During Life Is Beautiful one year, his mom, Judy, took a photo of

Michelle with her kids. Looking up at her, Judy remarked how nice it was that she had such a close relationship with her children.

At times Michelle felt conflicted, but she reminded herself that blurred lines were part of the deal. "We were never in a fully committed relationship," she said. "He dated other women, and I dated other men. But he was basically *my person*. He always came first, and I was comfortable in that situation. In fact, I met some of the most amazing women I've ever met in my life through him."

It went well—until it didn't. During a trip to New York in October 2015, Michelle was with Tony at a group dinner at the Ace Hotel in Manhattan when she took notice of his interest in two other women at the table. It was a bit much. "He turned it on a little more when they were around," she recalled, seeing him tell more jokes or become more animated in telling stories. After the dinner, she decided to bring it up with him. "I know we're not monogamous," she started. "But when we're together, you are *with me*." Tony didn't understand why she was upset. As they argued, Tony applied his logic to the situation: Michelle knew what she was signing up for, he said, and he hadn't done anything to break their rules of engagement. The discussion reached an impasse, but in the weeks after, Michelle started having doubts about their relationship. She soon visited Tony in Vegas again, but left feeling uncertain once more about where they stood. Some weeks later, after yet another whirlwind trip, she texted him from an airport, expressing as much. With hopes of comforting her, Tony responded, "This too shall pass."

Over the holidays, Michelle found herself at a crossroads. A friend had reentered her life and he wanted to be in a committed, monogamous relationship with her. Given her feelings of doubt about Tony, Michelle realized it was time to end the romance with him. "Hey, we need to be friends for a little bit," she told Tony on a FaceTime call that December. "That means no physical relationship."

"Why?" he asked.

She'd met someone, she said. She'd bent her own rules to be with Tony, but regardless of her love for him and the comfort she found within his world, she knew that being true to herself ultimately meant being in a monogamous relationship.

Tony never called Michelle his girlfriend while they were dating, but after they broke up, he would tell people she was his ex-girlfriend. Michelle, meanwhile, maintained her friendship with him. He eventually hired her to manage all of his social media accounts. "You're the only one that understands how to communicate in a way that I would," he said to Michelle.

To outsiders, it may have appeared Tony was capitalizing on the women in his sphere. For some of the women who took his arm at events or jetted with him to foreign corners, Tony was exciting to be around. For Michelle, he was someone to spend time with until she found a lifelong monogamous partner, and Tony never indicated that it bothered him. But even as the rotating cast of women ensured that Tony was never alone, they also allowed him to spread himself a mile wide, across relationships often an inch deep, and avoid the struggles and rewards of committing to a single person.

CHAPTER 13

ANDY

If Tony's dalliances with women were unconventional, his relationships with his two younger brothers were just as ill-defined. The three Hsiehs were by no means a close set of brothers. Over the years, Tony had rarely mentioned Andy and Dave in public or to friends. As for Andy and Dave, it was rare *not* to have Tony mentioned in conversation, whether they wanted to talk about him or not.

Even so, Tony had made room for Andy and Dave in his various business ventures. Starting with his newspaper route and button-making enterprises in Marin, when he passed the roles down to his brothers, he then went on to hire them at Zappos. Sometimes they would even share clothes.

"So is it true, I heard that you don't even have a business suit?" Oprah Winfrey asked Tony during a 2008 interview on her talk show. That day's episode was called "Young Millionaire Moguls" and Tony, who was thirty-four at the time, was featured in a segment that followed an interview with Mary-Kate and Ashley Olsen, the twenty-two-year-old actress twins who had a combined estimated net worth of $100 million from their films. Though the twins appeared on-set for the interview with Oprah, Tony opted to call in through a video conference. As Oprah and the audience shifted their attention to the large screen, Tony's face filled the camera view. Behind him, a thicket of ferns hung from the roof above his desk in the old Henderson office of Zappos.

"I'm not much for dressing up, so my brother and I actually share a suit," Tony answered. The studio audience roared with laughter. "But it's a little awkward when my brother and I have to go to the same wedding. Usually, I just end up wearing a collared shirt instead."

Tony had never been selfish nor boastful about his fortunes, but it inevitably forced Andy and Dave to live under the very large shadow of their big brother. For Dave, the dynamic seemed to instill in him a deep desire to avoid the fact that his brother was almost a billionaire. While Tony referred to him as David in *Delivering Happiness*, he was known to most as Dave. Dave was soft-spoken and awkward, and people were often shocked by his resemblance to Tony. But while Tony lived in a penthouse in the Ogden, in addition to his mansion in Southern Highlands, Dave lived in a modest home with his girlfriend. "He was sweet and quiet," said Jen Louie, who met the Hsieh brothers when she was an event producer in Las Vegas in the early 2000s. "Dave is not a man of many words." Rarely was he seen around Tony outside of family events.

Friends who knew Andy, though, observed a spark of jealousy within the middle Hsieh brother that generated a constant desire to prove himself. And as the years wore on, some saw the beginnings of a Shakespearean tale of fratricidal strife. "[Andy] didn't have the golden touch that Tony did, but not very many people do," recalled one friend who worked with Andy at Zappos. "I never saw any warmth between them."

■ ■ ■

When Tony left for Harvard in the early 1990s, Andy was already following in his big brother's footsteps by attending the Branson School, the elite college preparatory school in Ross, California. He assumed the role as head of the button-making business and proved to be a gifted piano player, even more skilled than Tony. After graduating from Branson, Andy was admitted to an industrial engineering program at Stanford University in 1994. Dave, meanwhile, went with Richard and Judy to Hong Kong for a brief stint during this time, after Richard got a promotion at Chevron.

Like the hundreds of freshmen arriving at the storied Stanford campus, Andy took part in Rush Week, an orientation where first-year students tour the campus meeting with fraternities and sororities to vie for an invitation. By the end of the week, Andy was welcomed into Lambda Phi Epsilon, an Asian American fraternity.

As one Lambda Phi Epsilon alum put it, their fraternity was "less gross" and slightly more academic than the other fraternities that weren't exclusively Asian. But still, it wasn't without the traditional hazing. One of Andy's former fraternity brothers remembered the new members being forced to do push-ups on command at random moments of the day. Other times they were ordered to run laps of the football field. Once they were instructed to run naked around the Stanford Quad, the university's central courtyard.

Andy was a popular kid within Lambda Phi Epsilon. He was easy to talk to and immediately personable, especially among his fraternity brothers, who came from Japanese, Korean, and Taiwanese families. He was not overly gregarious, one fraternity brother recalled, nor did he run for any leadership positions in the fraternity, but he was open and friendly.

The hazing went on for six months before Andy graduated from pledge to brother. By this time, Tony had gone from Harvard grad to the millionaire tech founder of LinkExchange, and any hope that Andy would match his brother's achievements grew further out of reach. His brother's success was evidently weighing on his own vision for the future. One evening during the fraternity induction process, brothers had to share something that made them vulnerable. When Andy's turn came, he told those gathered that he felt immense pressure living his entire life in the shadow of his brother.

■ ■ ■

Andy graduated from Stanford in 1999 with a bachelor's and master's degree in industrial engineering, seemingly with a world of opportunity before him. But within three years he was working for Tony at Zappos. He worked briefly as a consultant for a specialty food marketing company after graduating, but he remained well within his older brother's orbit—he moved into one of Tony's units in 1000 Van Ness during the heydays of LinkExchange and Venture Frogs. Andy's apartment was a two-bedroom unit on the seventh floor directly below the infamous Club BIO, which was dubbed "Tony's batcave." While Club BIO was for socializing, Tony sought peace and quiet in his younger brother's apartment.

"No one went into 706 except for me, Andy, and Tony," recalled James Henrikson, Tony's old friend who lived in 1000 Van Ness.

When Zappos moved to Las Vegas, Andy followed Tony there and took a job with the company, landing on the merchandising team. For the most part, there was little acknowledgment at the company that Andy and Tony were brothers, and Tony purposely kept an arm's-length distance from Andy. "If there was a problem with Andy or even if it was a win for Andy, Tony had nothing to do with it," recalled Chris Peake, who worked alongside Andy under Fred. Dave also eventually joined Zappos, working in the human resources department.

Andy had shown a desire to prove himself at Zappos, but he was less enthusiastic about his role on the merchandising team, which was to secure vendors for kids' shoes. To combat his ennui, he had been assigned to work with Mark Guadagnoli in a team internally called Black Ops, which was tasked with finding new—sometimes abstract—revenue streams for Zappos. Andy combined pep talks with an entrepreneurial drive and streams of ideas during BlackOps meetings. Mark said he often talked about "hitting home runs."

Andy had found a confidant in Mark, and some of their work was earning nods from Zappos brass. They launched the Zappos yearbook, a collection of photos and memories from employees—hot-dog-eating contests and office parades—and sold advertisements to vendors for a quarter million dollars a year. Another venture included designing a limited-edition Zappos Monopoly. Instead of train stations, different models of Clarks shoes were for sale. Rather than Boardwalk, Lacoste went for $400, or to the highest bidder.

Their projects together also meant the two men would work late at Zappos's headquarters. During some of these evenings, there were moments when Andy confided in Mark about his relationship with Tony. First and foremost, Mark recalled, Andy admired Tony. Andy saw his brother as someone who had achieved everything he had been taught to value as a child: vast wealth, success, and admiration.

Mark also sensed sibling rivalry during some of these conversations. Not resentment, but a wanting within Andy for what his brother had amounted to. Andy believed that if he too could catch a lucky break, then he could achieve what his brother had.

■ ■ ■

By the time Tony became known to the world, the younger Hsieh brothers' tenures at Zappos had come to abrupt ends. Dave was let go during the 2008 financial crisis when Zappos announced it was firing 8 percent of its workforce and around 100 employees were let go. Getting laid off had hit Dave particularly hard, according to Holly McNamara, who had been acquainted with all the Hsieh brothers but was yet to work for Tony on the Delivering Happiness tour. Dave confided in Holly at the time that it was not just being let go from Zappos that hurt—it was that Tony never talked to him about it afterward.

Andy's departure, meanwhile, was less straightforward, with conflicting accounts about why he left Zappos. In the recollection of one Zapponian who worked on the same team as Andy, it was a mutual decision that boiled down to Andy being a poor cultural fit. "We had different ideals of what Zappos was and different ideals of work ethic and leadership," the person said. In short, Andy did not seem as hardworking as his older brother, and he used his familial status to skate by.

But Andy's departure from Zappos presented him with an opportunity to chase a lifelong pursuit: creating a company just as successful as his older brother's. As Andy mused on what he hoped would be his billion-dollar idea, he thought about his last few years in Las Vegas hanging around in the periphery of Tony's circle. On some nights, he'd been surrounded by other young tech millionaire founders and CEOs who came to Sin City for private and exclusive experiences. Though Andy had yet to earn his stripes as a successful tech founder, spending time with his brother had given him a window on such a lifestyle. So shortly after moving back to San Francisco in 2011, Andy started building a company called Lux Delux, an online invitation-only membership club that connected users to high-end experiences in dining, wellness spas, and nightlife in Las Vegas.

Being related to Tony helped in more ways than one. A former Lux Delux employee who joined the company in its early days said the fact that Andy was Tony's brother was a decisive factor in why he decided to join the company. "With that last name, you know, the brother of Tony Hsieh, I felt like he could bring in a lot of resources," the employee recalled. "Maybe Tony might even invest in the company, right?"

In 2012, Lux Delux raised its first significant round of funding. Quite remarkably, Andy put in $3 million of his own money, according to documents. Their father, Richard Hsieh, was the largest outside investor by far, putting in $1.6 million. Their mother, Judy, and Dave each put in around $100,000, with Dave eventually taking on a role at Lux Delux. In fact, every single Hsieh family member was an investor in the company—except for Tony. That said, it is difficult to imagine a scenario where Andy would have had $3 million to invest in Lux Delux unless he had help from Tony.

Other investors included SV Angel, a venture capital firm headed by legendary tech investor Ron Conway; Alex Hsu, the childhood friend of Tony's; and Joe Lonsdale, the future libertarian venture capital investor who would go on to start the data mining behemoth Palantir with billionaires Peter Thiel and Alexander Karp. Joe wrote a roughly $100,000 check to Lux Delux. Asked about the investment a decade later, he wrote, "That was just a small investment and one among over a hundred from that time period—I met him via Tony whom I knew through friends in technology founder circles."

Just as Tony had launched Zappos from his condo in 1000 Van Ness, Lux Delux's product and engineering operations were primarily based out of Andy's San Francisco apartment in the South of Market district, a part of town that had started attracting new tech talent and companies like Airbnb and Zynga. His two-bedroom loft had an open-plan kitchen and dining room, framed by floor-to-ceiling windows overlooking the neighborhood.

But unlike Tony, who likely knew how to code better than all the engineers at Zappos combined, Andy did not bring any software engineering expertise to his work. There was a clear knowledge gap, and some of his employees noticed. One worker recalled arriving at Andy's loft and seeing him frantically scribbling mathematical equations on the windows overlooking the industrial streets of SoMa. Taking a closer look at the figures, the employee realized they were nonsensical formulas and asked Andy what he was doing. "We have an investor coming in," Andy replied. "We need to look like we are a startup."

Andy also enlisted the help of Holly McNamara, whose concierge business had taken off after she left the Delivering Happiness tour, and who had a wide network of contacts in the Las Vegas nightlife scene. She helped Lux Delux get its public relations off the ground, and pitched the company to club promoters, restaurateurs, and other Vegas contacts who could become partners in providing VIP experiences. The company's Facebook page had become a big selling point, given that it had rapidly amassed over 100,000 followers. The data point was promoted in emails to drive partnerships. But shortly after, Andy instructed the company to stop advertising the number of Facebook followers the company had, and Holly wondered if Lux Delux had bought its followers. But Andy was simply following the well-worn path of archetypical tech founder: fake it till you make it. He was finally seizing his opportunity to show the world what *he* could do.

Less than two years after Lux Delux was born, Andy suddenly pivoted the business. Food delivery apps like Postmates and Seamless were becoming popular in San Francisco, and Andy wanted to bring that concept to Vegas. "It wasn't just a partial change but a complete brand identity change," said Jen Louie, who was eventually hired by Andy and given the title of head of strategic partnerships at Lux Delux. Prior to signing on with Lux Delux, she was an independent business development and marketing consultant who had a deep Rolodex in Vegas. Her brother, David Louie, also worked at Lux Delux in a similar capacity and had a close working relationship with Andy. By Jen's recollection, Andy put everything he had into his startup and worked as hard as anyone in the company. Despite her hefty-sounding title, Jen kept her other client work. "Lux Delux was a startup," she said. "So they couldn't pay me enough to be full-time."

In the beginning, Andy appeared to spare no expense for Lux Delux's operations, paying for first-class flights and even private jets for some employees on work trips. But soon after Lux Delux made the pivot to food delivery, Andy asked Jen if she would be willing to work for half her salary. She agreed, attributing it to typical startup woes. A month later, Andy asked her if she would be willing to work for free. She declined and quit shortly after.

Lux Delux never took off, and by the end of 2014, no one seemed to be working for the business. As of 2022 its Facebook page remains active and has more than a million followers. Stock images with general captions alluding to a dreamy and luxurious lifestyle are still posted every few days there and on its Twitter account, which looks more like an account administered by a bot than a real person, and what the business offers today is unclear. Its main tagline, which is imposed on a banner photo of a woman with her back turned to the camera wearing nothing but a bikini bottom, ambiguously states, "Experience Life."

Tony had always made it clear he had no interest in selling shoes. His passion for Zappos came from a desire to build the best customer service experience with a strong company culture that made his employees excited and happy to come to work. When Andy explained his vision for Lux Delux, he painted a rosy picture full of generalities to friends and potential employees—it would be an engineering-driven company, similar to Facebook, and culture would come above all else, he said, parroting lines from *Delivering Happiness*. But oftentimes Andy's employees were left wondering what drove him toward the tech entrepreneur path.

"It felt like he was just repeating things that people said of what a great startup should be," said the former Lux Delux employee. "I never understood why he wanted to build this company. Maybe he just wanted to prove to everyone that he could do it too—maybe not as great as Tony, but at least close to what *the* Tony Hsieh built."

CHAPTER 14

TROUBLE IN PARADISE

Tony's downtown Vegas experiment was now roaring ahead. Dreams were being made, and businesses being built. But soon enough a more troubling reality of building a community emerged, too. It would be one of the youngest members of the community, the recent college graduate Ovik Banerjee, who would reveal its darkest chapter.

Ovik wasn't the most physically affectionate brother—he hated hugs—but he did find ways to connect with his younger brother, Anondo, by discussing and debating their purpose in the world. Their conversations often turned to how they were going to live a meaningful life, how to live alongside their values, and how to be happy. When the opportunity to join the Downtown Project as a Venture for America fellow arose, Ovik felt that he had found a way to answer all of life's biggest questions. He devoured every piece of literature he could find on Tony and his life; he'd read the memoir, and encouraged his family to read it, too. He'd even read the Zappos culture book. In a world where people did a lot of talking, he saw that Tony was doing a lot of doing.

When Ovik's family arrived in Las Vegas to visit him in the summer of 2013, they were, like many who came to downtown Las Vegas, amazed. His mother and father, both immigrants from India, had raised their older son and his younger brother and sister in Hoover, a leafy suburb of Birmingham, Alabama, before moving to nearby Tuscaloosa. In Las Vegas they were put up for free in a luxury high-rise apartment in the Ogden, from where they could view the neighborhood Ovik was living in. They saw that he kept a nice space in the Town Terrace apartments, which was now housing Downtown Project workers, along with his other Venture for America fellows. At Eat one morning, Natalie Young came out to greet Ovik by name, and his parents were glad to see that their son had become a part of a community. Ovik's father, Subhankar, was particularly impressed to hear about how Natalie's restaurant started, and her backstory about straightening her life out in the Strip's kitchens. Business was going so well, she told him, that she was opening a second restaurant in the neighborhood with Tony, this one with a menu focused on fried chicken.

After the meal, Ovik gave his family a tour of the area, starting at the Container Park, which was almost complete and due to open in a few months. Many of the shipping containers had been shifted into position, stacked on top of one another, and would soon be filled with restaurants and bars. In the center would be an elaborate jungle gym, and at the rear, behind a performance stage, would be an old train caboose, which would house a hair salon called Bolt Barber. As they walked by the praying mantis at the entrance, Anondo asked what Ovik thought about the frequent jets of flames it shot from its antennae. Given Ovik's degree in environmental science and his views on global warming, the question made him bristle. "I didn't get to be involved in that decision," he said to Anondo.

In the evening, Ovik took them to the Gold Spike, where they stood in a room that looked like a fun park for adults, filled with foosball, billiards, and ping-pong tables. Kegs of beer were stacked against the wall. Ovik appeared uneasy in this setting; he wasn't a big drinker, and the nonstop-partying side of the Downtown Project didn't appeal to him.

There were a few other things that made him uncomfortable about the Downtown Project, his family later learned. Despite the nice accommodations and pleasant eateries, his first months had been chaotic and directionless; he'd been shifted from project to project, and encouraged to find purpose in the neighborhood on his own. One of his tasks had been to secure building permits for the construction of what would become known as the Learning Village, a series of modular trailers that would house classrooms and meeting spaces on a landscaped lot next to the Container Park. He had no experience obtaining permits but figured he would rely on his intuition, conduct the necessary due diligence, and figure it out.

When he concluded he would need to get a permanent building license, he was instructed by several superiors to get a temporary license instead, as it was simpler to obtain and had fewer restrictions. Even though he knew the Learning Village was being built as a permanent structure, Ovik obliged. The breach of his principles shook him. But his family didn't quite grasp his unease when it came time to leave.

A few months later, when he went home to Tuscaloosa for Thanksgiving, Ovik was visibly distressed. He had been reassigned to work on launching a new project called the 9th Bridge School, a pre-K education facility, and had been tasked by Tony's cousin Connie Yeh to research and help design the curriculum—something he had no training for or business doing, he told his family. But he was most concerned by the prospect of getting fired after he cold-emailed Tony to outline his concerns. Ovik had detailed three major issues with the Downtown Project. There was seemingly no direction or mission, and the core values felt meaningless. There was little communication. And management was not held accountable.

When Tony did respond, he began by telling Ovik that the values and culture of the Downtown Project weren't meant to mirror that of Zappos, and that it took five years to figure out the company's own values and culture. "fred and I are confident about the long-term outcome because we've done this before and know what to expect," Tony wrote in an email.

He then addressed Ovik's complaints point by point, starting with Ovik's concern that the Downtown Project lacked "culture, mission, and core values." Getting the culture right was a priority, Tony wrote, but he countered that it would take time: unlike a company, building culture for a city is a whole other challenge. "At zappos, we can choose who we hire and fire. you can't choose who lives or works downtown, and each business dtp invests in will have a different culture and set of values which dtp needs to somehow integrate with," Tony wrote.

Ovik also said there was poor communication and connectivity within the Downtown Project, and suggested holding monthly meetings to keep the community informed, and serve as a place to air grievances. In response, Tony suggested Ovik take it upon himself to organize meetings if it was something he was passionate about.

And finally, there seemed to be a lack of accountability at employee and manager levels, Ovik wrote, adding that there should be an established line of feedback to ensure that people are meeting their goals. Tony again said this was something that would be addressed over time but added: "i would encourage each employee to just meet regularly with his/her manager to accomplish the above."

When Ovik came back to Tuscaloosa for the winter break, he seemed more at ease. His parents had reassured him that if he did leave the Downtown Project suddenly, they would be there to support him until he figured out his next step. His two-year fellowship with Venture for America would end in the spring anyway, and he was starting to think about returning to school, maybe getting a medical degree like his father. After feeling that he had been forced to compromise his moral compass with the Learning Village permits, one thing he knew was what he didn't want to do with his future: work somewhere that was long on idealism and short on realism. While he was home, Ovik celebrated his twenty-fourth birthday with his family. "Thank you all for the birthday wishes!" he posted on Facebook on December 27. "Looking forward to what my next journey around the sun has in store."

On New Year's Day, he climbed into the car with his parents for the hour-long drive to the airport in Birmingham. He seemed happy. Before getting on the plane, he shot off a tweet: "Vegas friends, anyone want to give a ride to a wayward Indian from the airport at 9pm tonight?" He didn't get any responses, though.

Five days later, on January 6, 2014, Ovik jumped to his death from his apartment balcony.

■ ■ ■

A year before, the body of Jody Sherman, the affable CEO of the e-commerce site Ecomom, who'd arrived in downtown after Tony's tour of the area and subsequent investment, had been found in his car with a self-inflicted gunshot wound to the head. Jody had been seen as an insistently positive member of the community. At forty-eight, he was a little older than the fresh-faced entrepreneurs streaming into the neighborhood, and he had assumed something of a mentor role. His laid-back surfer vibe was a contrast to the typically high-strung demeanor of most founders.

His death had shocked not only the Downtown Project community but also Silicon Valley and Los Angeles, where he'd had a decades-long career as an entrepreneur. Many of his former colleagues and friends posted and wrote about their despair, but they also were forced to consider the fact that not only had he died, but he'd killed himself. Prominent venture capitalist Jason Calacanis wrote at the time that Sherman was remembered for being "relentlessly positive, driven and fun," and that "he was a human router who left an impression."

Calacanis said Jody's death forced him to think about two other entrepreneurs who had died by suicide recently: Aaron Swartz, the twenty-six-year-old co-founder of Reddit, and twenty-two-year-old Ilya Zhitomirskiy, who had founded the social networking site Diaspora. "Perhaps we owe it to these three amazing humans to examine if the pressures of being a founder, the pressure of our community's relentless pursuit of greatness, in some way contributed to their deaths?" Calacanis wrote. "I'm not an expert on suicide, but I am an expert on being a founder. Many of the founders I know have been desperate, depressed and overwhelmed in their careers. For everyone that shared this with me, I'm certain 10 more didn't . . . Is it worth exploring why this happens and if it is, in fact, a trend?"

Over the years such a phenomenon had been explored, but many questions remained. In his 2005 book *The Hypomanic Edge: The Link Between (a Little) Craziness and (a Lot of) Success in America*, John Gartner had explored whether American entrepreneurs share a common condition: hypomania, "a mild form of mania, often found in the relatives of manic depressives. Hypomanics are brimming with infectious energy, irrational confidence, and really big ideas. They think, talk, move, and make decisions quickly. Anyone who slows them down with questions 'just doesn't get it.' Hypomanics are not crazy, but 'normal' is not the first word that comes to mind when describing them. Hypomanics live on the edge, between normal and abnormal." Gartner, a clinical psychologist who taught at Johns Hopkins University Medical School, zeroed in on the tech industry, which had just gone through a boom-and-bust cycle. In a survey of ten internet CEOs, Gartner found that each of them identified with most traits of hypomania: feelings that they were "brilliant, special, chosen, perhaps even destined to change the world"; "channels his energy into the achievement of wildly grand ambitions"; "often works on little sleep"; and "sometimes acts impulsively, with poor judgment, in ways that can have painful consequences." Part of being hypomanic, Gartner stated, was that in addition to euphoric highs and feelings of grandeur came susceptibility to a depressive down cycle that can be magnified under the stresses of leading a company.

A few years after Jody's death, a study was launched at the University of California, Berkeley, led by a professor named Michael Freeman, to study the mental health histories of entrepreneurs. Published in the journal *Small Business Economics* in 2018, Freeman's study found that 72 percent of entrepreneurs acknowledged having either a personal or family history of mental illness. When compared to the general population, Freeman and his team found that 49 percent of entrepreneurs reported having one or more mental health conditions in their lifetime—like ADHD, substance abuse, bipolar disorder, or anxiety—compared to 32 percent of non-entrepreneurs. Depression was specifically high, with entrepreneurs experiencing twice as much as the general population.

While rates of suicide among entrepreneurs have never been adequately measured, there has been growing momentum among some tech leaders to increase dialogue around identifying warning signs. Brad Feld, another venture capitalist, became a shining light for entrepreneurs seeking help after he began speaking openly about his struggle with depression over the years, and highlighted the unique challenges facing those whose identities are often tied to their success. "The intensity of being an entrepreneur, especially when your company is failing, or you are failing at your role, can be overwhelming," he wrote on his blog. "It's ok to fail. It's ok to lose. It's ok to be depressed."

Fear of failure was evidently facing Jody. It was later revealed that his death occurred days before a scheduled company meeting, when he was going to have to inform the board that Ecomom had run out of money, just six months after raising $5 million. The company had been bleeding money thanks to an offer that allowed customers to receive a 50 percent discount every time they purchased from the website, meaning that every time Ecomom sold a product, it actually *lost* money. While it's a strategy employed by some tech companies desperate to build a customer base—before changing the pricing model to a profitable one when enough customers have signed on—it's an extremely risky play. The board only learned that the company was facing bankruptcy after he died, when a recently hired accountant revealed that Jody had asked him to produce several financial forecasts. In the week before his death, after seeing the forecasts, Jody had handed a will to his secretary and made subtly dour comments to the accountant: "If you want to fire me that's ok" and "I'm too old to start over."

In the months after Jody's death, Mark Rowland had been coming and going from Las Vegas as he developed a business plan to launch his mentor service, ROCeteer. He quickly saw that beyond Jody, there were others in the community in need of help, and they had nowhere to turn for it. Many of the entrepreneurs had been handed a $500,000 check to launch their company and then were basically told to run with it.

As more people came to ROCeteer for help, Mark found himself sharing an anecdote about the pressures facing entrepreneurs. Before arriving at the Downtown Project, he was the founder and CEO of StyleTread, the Australian copy of Zappos. Even though he had children of his own, he often compared the growth of his company to fathering a child, and his love of being an entrepreneur was paying off. In 2012, he was on a multicity tour around Australia to talk about StyleTread's success. What his audiences didn't know was that he was also in talks to secure a hefty funding round to keep the company afloat; it was still growing, but its sales alone couldn't sustain the business. A Chinese investor had agreed to provide $10 million, and an Australian firm was willing to give him $7 million, but the fine print was still being negotiated.

The deal was scheduled to close the day before a planned speech in Sydney, and Mark envisioned announcing the deal during the talk. The crowd would respond with raucous applause, he imagined. But as the deadline approached, he received an email: the Chinese firm was backing out. No reason was given. Without the Chinese investor, the Australian firm said it wasn't willing to move ahead either.

It was devastating news: he would have to lay off his seventy employees, and the outward appearance of his image as a successful entrepreneur would evaporate. That and his entire life savings were on the line: without telling his wife, he had used their house as collateral to buy the company's inventory. He would be forced to pull his kids out of private school, and they'd likely have to move. Life as he knew it would end. Driving his car home that night, he contemplated suicide. "God, wouldn't it just be easier if I just ended my life now," he recalled thinking. "Don't have to worry about all this stress, don't have to worry about telling all these people.'"

After twenty seconds of considering the possibility, a rush of faces and memories entered his mind. He had a wife who loved him, two kids who depended on him, and family in England who missed him—human connections. Now his mind was finding ways to reinforce the reasons to stay on earth.

Those few moments in the darkness scared him so much that he vowed never to contemplate suicide again. "When you're potentially gonna lose the company, and potentially going to fire everyone, you get your identity confused with the identity of the company," Mark said. "And then the company's a failure, then you think you're a failure." (As it turned out, Mark secured financing before the deadline and kept the company afloat, selling it a year later.)

Even after Jody's death, the facade of a utopia for entrepreneurs in downtown Las Vegas had remained. But with Ovik's death marking the second suicide in a year, clouds were moving in on the sunshine, rainbows, and open bar tabs. The people who worked, ate, and drank together were now looking for a place to turn to, and found nowhere to go. The Downtown Project acknowledged Ovik's passing in a Facebook post, but no leaders, including Tony, addressed the community with public meetings to process the grief. People could see a doctor at the Downtown Project's medical practice, Turntable Health, who could refer patients to therapists, but they would have to foot the cost on their own.

ROCeteer essentially became a clearing house for people in the community in need, and Mark and his team found themselves hearing the concerns of entrepreneurs and other citizens who felt that they had nowhere to talk about the pressures they were feeling. In extreme cases the ROCeteer staff would pass on information about the suicide helpline and other mental health support services. But ROCeteer could only do so much. Aside from having a life coach on staff, they were not equipped to employ psychotherapists or provide access to therapy services.

Tony's acknowledgment of Ovik's death was limited to a company-wide email to Downtown Project employees, where he announced they would be assessing ways to help the community. "I know it's been a tough couple of weeks for everyone. One of the things that I've learned over the years is that different people grieve and cope in different ways—sometimes we need support, sometimes we need space, and sometimes we need time." Mark, he wrote, had been assigned to lead a group of people to figure out how to "nurture the emotional health of Downtown Project employees, affiliated partners, and the ways in which we support one another." Even though Tony was a difficult person to read at the best of times, Mark felt that Ovik's death had weighed on him. "You could just see it in his face, his body language," Mark said later. "He's a very stoic person . . . it was weighing on him."

With a team of eight others, Mark fielded proposals that ranged from a dedicated crisis hotline to starting a church. One of the initial efforts included taking members of the community on bus trips to the surrounding mountains and valleys for day-long hikes. They then looked at more long-lasting efforts, the most promising of which was brought to the Downtown Project management by a British consultant named Pritpal Tamber, who specialized in advising companies on how to implement healthcare initiatives. Tamber proposed coming into the neighborhood, conducting interviews with some of its members about their access to medical services and their general well-being, and then proposing a "framework" that would underpin the Downtown Project's efforts to improve the mental health of people in the community. However, it was going to cost around $1 million. The Downtown Project deemed it too expensive, and it was abandoned.

Then, four months after Ovik's death, another person died by suicide. Matt Berman, the fifty-year-old founder of Bolt Barber, the hair salon in the Western-style caboose at the back of the Container Park, was found dead at his home. Members of the Downtown Project reeled at the third suicide in sixteen months.

Again, the Downtown Project leadership seemed to be at a loss for what to do. For community members, there was again nowhere to readily seek help, and no public display of grieving. After Matt's suicide, Aimee Groth wrote that she had difficulty processing the loss: "It hardly felt real because no one talked about it. There was no outward mourning the loss of another member of the community."

It turned out that the three suicides were just the tragedies that had bubbled to the surface. As ROCeteer tried to provide support and direct dozens of people to places where they could get help, Mark said that on at least four other occasions he and his colleagues had to intervene and spend time with people who were at high risk of harming themselves.

A few months after Matt's death, Tony was asked by a reporter to comment on the suicides in his community. "Suicides happen anywhere. Look at the stats," Tony said. "It's harder for people who are really good students in school. Then they move into this, where there is no instruction manual, and you have to be MacGyver on your own."

Tony's apathetic response prompted some jaws to drop. Kimberly Knoll, a therapist who specialized in marriage counseling, had been working with some members of the community after Ovik's death. She told a reporter that yes, the pressures of working for startups could trigger dormant, preexisting mental health issues. But in the Downtown Project, "the difference here is the focus on happiness—that's a goal," she said. "If we negate the negative emotions in our lives, it takes us away from happiness and brings around shame. The whole idea of Downtown is grand and wonderful and purposeful, but sometimes the way we're going about it isn't psychologically healthy."

The environment and pressure around happiness, Kimberly said, were unique to Downtown Vegas. "It comes from top down. It comes from Tony, from Zappos," she said to the reporter. "The book is called *Delivering Happiness*."

■ ■ ■

After Ovik's death, Andrew Yang cut ties with the Downtown Project and stopped sending Venture for America fellows. Ovik's father, Subhankar, concluded that Tony had failed in a personal responsibility to maintain the welfare of his eldest son. Tony's absence from any kind of public address further angered him. "With your silence, you've just compounded that failure," Anondo recalled his father saying. Subhankar died four years later, of a heart attack while traveling on an airplane.

What was most painful for Ovik's family was learning that he had written a suicide letter just days after he celebrated his birthday with them. Throughout his life he had struggled with insomnia and was sometimes removed, but no one among his friends or family saw any clear danger that he was at risk of harming himself.

"My brother was an incredibly smart, driven, bright-eyed, bushy-tailed twentysomething-year-old, coming into a place trying to make it better," Anondo said. "I don't blame Tony Hsieh or the Downtown Project. I just blame the broader system that takes advantage of, you know, people who want to try and change the world."

CHAPTER 15

"THE MAYOR OF DOWNTOWN LAS VEGAS"

At some point, people who lived downtown and visiting reporters began affectionately referring to Tony as the "Mayor of Downtown Las Vegas." When Carolyn Goodman, the mayor of Las Vegas, was asked by a reporter for her thoughts on Tony's moniker, she said it made for good PR. "A puff of energy," she said. But for some time, the title had been sharpening the spotlight on Tony's role in the community and raising questions about what exactly he was responsible for. He was, after all, the primary financier of the entire neighborhood, and had the final sign-off when his money was spent. That meant people looked to him for guidance on how to get more of his money. And when people thought about how to envision their neighborhood, it was his philosophies and quotes that people turned to for direction and motivation. With the burden of leadership at his feet, Tony attempted to shrink away from the title by drawing clear distinctions between his social experiment and the actuality of running a city. Much of the confusion, he realized, was of his own doing.

When he and Fred announced the Downtown Project, they did so with enormous emphasis on the word "community." They even invented the metric "return on community" to guide the neighborhood's investments by tracking things like "collisionable hours" (the amount of time people are in public space where serendipitous meetings can occur) and "co-learning" (how much time people spend learning from one another). Tony's philosophy was that a return on community would ultimately lead to more profits if people were being empowered by one another to achieve their dreams.

But in the wake of Ovik's death, a clear fissure had emerged in the veneer of happiness that shone around the Downtown Project, and the community was looking to their mayor for guidance, something Tony was not comfortable with. He now saw that he needed to walk back what it meant to be a part of the Downtown Project. No longer would it be using the metric of return on community. In fact, the word "community" was to be removed from language associated with the Downtown Project. The word was to be replaced by "connectedness." The new "Three C's" of the Downtown Project would be collisions, co-learning, and connectedness.

"In the past, we used the word 'Community' a lot more but we learned that a lot of people misinterpreted or misunderstood our goals," Tony wrote in a post online in February 2014. "There are a lot of people that seem to expect us to address and solve every single problem that exists in a city (for example, homelessness, substance abuse, and mental health). We have to sometimes remind people that we're not the government."

The emphasis on "community" had also created a perception for some that the Downtown Project was a charity or nonprofit. Tony wrote, "We found that when we used the word 'Community,' there were a lot of groups that suddenly expected us to donate money to them or invest in them just because they lived in the community or because it was for a good cause. People would be upset if donating or investing in them did not happen to fit in with our priorities and business goals, and they would refer back to our use of the word 'Community.'"

Tony had also put himself in a seemingly impossible situation: not only was he the default leader of, primary investor in, and visionary behind an entire neighborhood, he was still the CEO of Zappos. He had long stressed that his style of management was purely visionary and that he wouldn't be involved with personnel matters; he had once told a publication, "I view my role more as trying to set up an environment where the personalities, creativity and individuality of all the different employees come out and can shine."

Since 2013, an effort had been underway to roll out a new management structure for the Downtown Project that was meant to eliminate job titles and force people to make up their own roles—kind of like a tribe, Tony would say. Holacracy, as this structure was called, would also further remove Tony from the spotlight, and shift responsibility for the neighborhood away from him. "Tony doesn't really like conflict," said Maggie Hsu, who was assigned to lead the rollout of the management system at the Downtown Project. "Holacracy was this way to diffuse that because he wasn't the bad guy or central decision maker."

The concept of Holacracy was created by Brian Robertson, a software developer who had been trying to reduce management decisions at a company he started. After seeing him at a conference, Tony was immediately struck by how Robertson's management idea could address the issues he was facing: he was drowning in responsibility. During the latter half of 2013, Robertson and his consulting team spent weeks holding seminars with Downtown Project employees to school them on how to give up their titles and, seemingly, their designated responsibilities.

Robertson's rules were governed by the Holacracy Constitution, which he made up, and contained language that was more akin to a scientific study than plain English. That was frustrating for the hundreds of people who had better things to do than decipher its nonsense. When conflicts arose, for example, practitioners were expected to engage in an act called "processing tensions," an act that the Holacracy Constitution defined by the following statement:

A Partner duly filling a Role shall regularly compare the current expression of such Role's Purpose and enactment of its Accountabilities to such Partner's sense of an ideal potential expression of such Purpose and enactment of such Accountabilities to identify gaps between the current reality and such a sensed potential (each such gap a "Tension"). For each tension so identified, such Partner shall attempt to reduce such Tension by identifying and enacting one or more appropriate courses of action given the authorities and other mechanisms available to such Partner under this Constitution.

It was angering for some, eye-rolling for others. Rather than bosses, teams, and divisions, there were now "circles," "links," and "tasks." It sounded confusing, and it was. After endless meetings, the members of the Downtown Project could never quite grasp how to use the system or implement it. Instead it created more friction among the community.

■ ■ ■

As the Holacracy rollout sputtered, some of the Downtown Project's bets were not paying off. A slow-moving exodus had grown into a steady stream of tech companies closing or moving out of Vegas. In addition to the collapse of Ecomom, other companies were either shuttering or leaving Las Vegas for places where they could hire better talent, as efforts in Las Vegas to build a pool of skilled workers paled in comparison to what was being done in other tech hubs. Romotive, which had grown to twenty employees and was widely seen as one of the Downtown Project's most successful investments, left Las Vegas in 2013, merely a year after arriving. A few months after a $5 million funding round led by the venture capital firm Sequoia—spearheaded by none other than Alfred Lin—Romotive announced it was moving to Silicon Valley to be closer to "strategic partners and hiring brilliant senior talent," founder Keller Rinaudo wrote in a community-wide email. "This was a difficult decision for us because Romotive wouldn't be the company we are without the constant support of Downtown Project, Tony, Zach, Fred, and many others." (Years later, Keller pivoted the business to automating logistics with drone delivery and renamed it Zipline. In 2022, Zipline was valued at $2.5 billion and employed 800 people.)

Jen McCabe, an entrepreneur who'd been leading tech investments for the Downtown Project, had been given $10 million to launch a company called Factorli at the start of 2014. It was expected to manufacture small hardware parts with 3D printers in a warehouse the Downtown Project owned. Even before it opened, Factorli had gained so much attention that President Barack Obama highlighted the company during a speech at the White House about innovative American companies. "You've got Jen McCabe," Obama said, "who is setting up a space called Factorli, in Las Vegas, to provide custom, small-scale manufacturing, kind of like a Kinko's or a copy shop, but instead of printing flyers, they're going to be able to print custom parts for American products." But before the warehouse even opened, the company was shut down.

Some of the smaller businesses were faring better, like Natalie's Eat and another restaurant called Vegenation, a vegetarian spot that had opened across the street. A nearby dog park was maintaining steady business. Another restaurant opened by Fred, Nacho Daddy, was a success. Others included Carson Kitchen and La Comida. But it was grueling for other small businesses. Despite claiming that the Container Park received 300,000 visitors in its opening three months, Downtown Project executives saw that the overall neighborhood wasn't getting the foot traffic it had hoped for, and there was a realization that few Zappos employees were venturing far from the campus to mingle in the surrounding neighborhood. Six months after the Container Park opened, Michael Cornthwaite sold his interest in three restaurants he had opened in the center.

With suicides and business failures, cracks were starting to appear in the startup utopia. But none of this was yet apparent in the public narrative about Tony and the Downtown Project. Wide-eyed fascination in the neighborhood continued, and national reporters were still returning to their newsrooms with notepads full of inspiring stories. While on assignment for Re/Code, Nellie Bowles spent three weeks living downtown during the summer of 2014, and on September 29 published the first installment in a planned series of stories: "Downtown Las Vegas Is the Great American Techtopia." In the article, she wrote that "there's an excitement to being in a startup city devoted to startups, a sense of camaraderie." When she asked Tony to explain his phenomenon, he described downtown Las Vegas as "TED meets SXSW meets Burning Man, but as a lifestyle, rather than events . . . and we can scale this to multiple cities."

One person who had been sold on Tony's vision was David Gould, a professor at the University of Iowa who met Tony when he came to speak to Gould's students about unique leadership during his Delivering Happiness bus tour. After the talk, Gould's students had followed Tony all the way back to his bus with more questions. "It was like a real live Pied Piper," Gould said. A few years later, Gould followed Tony, too, leaving his job to come live downtown after Tony said he wanted to push the "boundaries of education" and would fund whatever he wanted to do. While Nellie couldn't figure out exactly what Gould's role was, he told her his title was "Director of Imagination" and that he managed a community space downtown.

One thing Gould mentioned was that he had become bothered by community groups in Las Vegas that were not linked to the Downtown

Project but were pushing for grants and funding. He felt they were taking advantage of Tony's generosity, citing one example of a group of teachers who were seeking funding for a theater. He told Nellie, "The umbrella Tony has in his hand—only so many people can fit under that umbrella."

■ ■ ■

There was a much different story about to break that had not filtered back to Nellie before her article appeared on Re/Code's website. Mike Henry, Downtown Project's director of music booking, had noticed recently that Tony had been in the office frequently, attending meetings with grave-faced leaders like Michael Downs, a local casino executive who had joined the Downtown Project in 2012, which was weird: Tony was almost never in the office. The evening Nellie's story was published, Mike was among a select group of Downtown Project employees who began receiving calls from their managers. Close to midnight, Michael Downs was on the phone. "I imagine you have heard that some changes are going to be made," Downs said. "Your position is not being eliminated. It will be a difficult day for all of us, but you will be fine." Then he hung up. It seemed Mike's suspicions were being confirmed.

That night, Tony texted Michelle D'Attilio, who was back in Milwaukee. Sitting at the kitchen table with her kids, she turned her phone over and read the message. "Some news is gonna come out," he wrote. "It's not going to be great." She called him and they spoke briefly. Though he did not share details with Michelle, she could hear it in his voice. She told him that she wished she was in Vegas right now with him. "It made me realize that he was having a really, really rough night and that he was sad," she later recalled.

Mike's cellphone was pinging with text messages the next morning. When he stepped off the elevator, he ran into his boss, Ashton Allen, who looked like he'd seen a ghost. "Not right now," Ashton muttered as he walked past.

One after the other, employees were instructed to go to an upper level of the building, where six Downtown Project leaders—including Michael Downs and Maggie Hsu—were seated in separate glass offices, each alongside a member of human resources. As the employees sat in front of their respective managers, they were then told they no longer had a job.

Mike and the remaining workers watched the office descend into chaos. Some cried; others looked shell-shocked. Several people huddled in small groups and embraced one another. "It was like a show," Mike recalled. Amid the beanbags, ping-pong tables, and Nerf gun pellets, the shock for some employees turned to white-hot anger. *"This is bullshit!"* one person yelled as they stormed through the office. "Supposed to be about community," wailed another. One person, in a rage, walked over to the wall next to the elevator bank and tore off a large banner pinned to the wall that read, COMMUNITY, COLLISIONS, AND CO-LEARNING.

In total, thirty people lost their jobs out of a staff of one hundred in the Downtown Project's corporate headquarters. In public statements, Tony pointed to the fact that the Downtown Project employed around three hundred people in a community of around eight hundred. But while the number seemed comparatively small, the layoffs became the figurative straw that broke the neighborhood's utopian back.

A day after being quoted singing Tony's praises, David Gould, the "Director of Imagination," wrote an emotional letter announcing he had handed in his resignation before he could be fired. The note, which sounded more like the scrawl of a jilted lover, was published in the *Las Vegas Weekly* and accused Tony and the Downtown Project of "a collage of decadence, greed, and missing leadership."

> *Dear Tony,*
> *We met in the fall of 2010, when your "Delivering Happiness" book tour stopped by my University of Iowa class. I could never have imagined how dramatically that hot August afternoon would change the course of my life. I have retold the story many times of how the students spontaneously followed you out of the classroom that day. Exactly three years later, I left my home, and position at the university, to follow you as well.*

He went on:

> *While some squandered the opportunity to "dent the universe," others never cared about doing so in the first place. There were heroes among us, however, and it is for them that my soul weeps.*

Once local reporters picked up on the story, it was like a balloon filled with happiness had burst. All that was left were sneering onlookers. "'Bloodletting' at Downtown Project with Massive Layoffs," blared the *Las Vegas Weekly*, writing that "Hsieh has washed his hands of Downtown Project recently and has upper management handling the layoffs." Paul Carr, whose coverage of the Downtown Project in NSFWCorp had soured—leading to Tony's refusal to give him more money and forcing him to sell the company to another publication, *Pando Daily*—wrote an article summarizing the comments of his business partner, who said of the layoffs that "bad management and broken promises at the DTP eroded public trust" even as "they were given a pass by 'breathless' reporting in the media." The most scathing piece came from an opinion writer for the *Review-Journal*, who wrote, "The cult of Tony Hsieh developed a crack this past week, and that's a good thing." The columnist, John L. Smith, mocked what he called "Hsieh's true believers," who "bought into his rhetoric like kids waiting in line to sit on Santa's lap." Targeting David Gould, he continued, "What was your first clue, professor? The nebulous business plan? The daily booze-fest? The suspicious suicides of other true believers?" Concluding his piece, Smith's words dripped with condescension: "If losing 30 workers spells the beginning of the end of Hsieh's Downtown Dalai Lama routine, that's a good thing."

A day after publishing her largely positive profile of Tony and the Downtown Project, Nellie Bowles followed up with a series of stories in Re/Code with a rather different tone. She reported that Tony was stepping back from his lead role at the Downtown Project, and quoted an anonymous source who blamed the layoffs on bad hiring practices. "Tony is not always altogether the most wise judge of character. There's a lot of family. There's a lot of drinking buddies. And some poor choices were made," the source said. The *Washington Post* followed up with a piece that suggested Tony's experiment was doomed—"Why Zappos's CEO Couldn't Save Downtown Las Vegas"—while Bloomberg opened its story with "Is Tony Hsieh giving up on Las Vegas?" The online publication *Slate* declared that "if there's a dark side of techtopia—of the arrogant-bordering-on-delusional notion that a multimillion-dollar investment and a happiness manifesto can remake a struggling city—this is it."

After years of reporters coming and going from Tony's social experiment with stories of lives changed and unmatched generosity, he and the Downtown Project were totally unprepared to navigate the media storm, and their rebuttals were drowned out by the slew of negative headlines. In a statement, Tony tried to emphasize the fact he was never the CEO of the Downtown Project, and that his position was the same it had been six months before the layoffs: "an investor, advisor and equivalent of a board member that sets high-level general direction and strategy but is not involved in day-to-day management of people or projects." Unlike a singular business or company, the Downtown Project "is a collection of several hundred businesses and legal entities," each with its own goals and personalities. But his explanations were futile; the Delivering Happiness brand and the utopian messaging around the neighborhood contrasted too starkly against suicides, layoffs, and the realities of managing companies.

Some members of the community tried to boost morale. Mark Rowland and his team at ROCeteer contacted Downtown Project businesses and asked them to submit thank-you notes, which he compiled in a booklet and presented to Tony and Fred. Three dozen businesses responded. "Tony and DTP changed my experience of Las Vegas—and my life!—for the better," Natalie wrote on behalf of Eat. "I probably would have left town two years ago. Instead, I'm a business owner, creating jobs and inspiring positive change in others—just as Tony and DTP did for me."

A group of employees at a company called Launchkey, which provided password-free login software, wrote that the mission of the Downtown Project would prevail. "Changing a city is hard. But so is changing the world," they wrote. "We will all be remembered by the impact we have on the future, not the people we piss off today."

CHAPTER 16

THE ISLAND

There was one other person who stepped in to help Tony, with far greater consequences. Justin Weniger had been around more often since he and Ryan had opened their bars downtown, including Commonwealth. Like the Downtown Cocktail Room, it was inspired by Prohibition-era speakeasies, and had transformed an old, seedy sex shop into a cavernous space for low-key candlelit conversations. Inside, one could find all sorts of trinkets lining the exposed brick walls. Hanging above the twenty-foot-long bar was a magnificent peacock, its plumage fanned out as if it was courting a mate. With a rooftop made for a DJ set, the venue came complete with a secretive speakeasy bar called Laundromat, tucked behind an obscure door.

While Ryan typically ran point on the bars, which they controlled through an entity called Corner Bar Management, and sought new opportunities for Wendoh's media business, Justin had overseen operations and finances for their ventures. More recently, though, Justin been taking a greater interest in the Life Is Beautiful festival and had been leading Wendoh's efforts to help market the event as a media partner. Despite the controversy swirling around the Downtown Project, the festival was still scheduled to launch in a few weeks; Kanye West would be headlining the event.

Tall and tanned with cropped blond hair, Justin was watching the onslaught of bad press when one of his editors at *Vegas Seven* came into his office to let him know they were planning to write a story about the Downtown Project layoffs. "Have you spoken to Tony?" Justin asked.

They hadn't been able to reach him, the editor said. "Well, then it's not a story," Justin replied. Instead Justin suggested he would try to get Tony to agree to an interview, to get the "real story."

Under the headline "Tony Hsieh Speaks" was a glowing two-page Q&A that touted an exclusive interview with Tony. "There are those who want the Downtown Project to fail, and last week, those naysayers were given an unwitting gift," the article stated. "For what it's worth, Hsieh says he isn't worried about the Downtown Project's future."

Opening the feature, the reporter asked, "Why do you think the media has been gunning for the Downtown Project?"

"It's probably a combination of things . . . it could be a branding mistake that causes confusion," Tony replied.

Had all the bad press affected him personally?

"The part that bothered me the most was the misleading headlines, the inaccuracies . . . there was one headline that said I was stepping down from Downtown Project. Similar headlines implied that Downtown Project was falling apart . . . that's not something we ever prepared for."

Tony said he planned to spend hours talking to each person who had been fired, including David Gould. "Stepping back, last week was hard. I got a hundred text messages alone. I have a long list of people to reach out to."

He concluded by acknowledging "we could have done a better job of communicating" but he remained convinced that Downtown Las Vegas had the ingredients to succeed. "I just hope we can do it together."

Much of the news cycle had moved on by the time the article was posted in the second week of October 2014. Tony was preparing to announce the opening of the neighborhood's first grocery. A new boutique hotel would be announced the week after. But after Justin emailed Tony a link to the article, along with an invitation to meet up for a drink, he received a response sometime in the middle of the night: "I really appreciate what you did." It turned out Justin's gesture to commission the article had piqued Tony's interest.

■ ■ ■

A few days before the 2014 Life Is Beautiful festival in October, Rehan got a call from Fred asking him to meet at a wine bar in the Container Park.

While Rehan had maintained his role as the face of the Life Is Beautiful festival in glossy magazine covers and articles, his control over the company had all but been removed after he was replaced as CEO in January by Andrew Donner. Despite the management shift, the festival was expected to lose more money this year, and ticket sales were going to be short. He wasn't sure what was on Fred's agenda, but given the fact he was barely on speaking terms with Andrew and that Fred only weighed in if there was a major development, something felt fateful about the invitation.

As he approached the bar, he saw Fred and Andrew but noticed Tony wasn't there. Surely he would have had to sign off on any major decision. He thought about how his near-daily interactions with Tony had dried up, and he no longer felt like Tony was looking out for him. As his social capital had declined, his rose-tinted view of Tony became jaded. One night a few weeks before the festival, Tony had texted Rehan around 11 p.m. asking him to come meet him at the restaurant Carson Kitchen. When he arrived, Tony was seated with the owner of a local taco shop. He looked up as Rehan approached. The taco shop owner had some ideas about the upcoming festival, he said. Specifically, Rehan should consider ditching Kanye West as its headline act.

The previous year, Kanye had come to downtown ahead of the first festival to tour the grounds and meet with Tony. During a private meeting after the tour, Kanye had asked Tony for his feedback about starting his own shoe company. Tony responded that "we should stick to what we know." A couple of weeks later, Kanye went on a podcast and trashed-talked Zappos. "I got into this giant argument with the head of Zappos that he's trying to tell me what I need to focus on," Kanye said. "Meanwhile, he sells all this shit product to everybody, his whole thing is based off of selling shit product." While Kanye took his idea elsewhere—he partnered with Adidas to launch its Yeezy line of sneakers, creating what would become a $5 billion business (Adidas cut ties with the rapper in October 2022 after he made antisemitic remarks)—he had since come around and agreed to perform at this year's festival.

The taco shop owner explained that because Kanye had disrespected Tony and therefore didn't stand for the values that the Downtown Project and Life Is Beautiful represented, Rehan should publicly announce that Kanye was being thrown off the lineup. Doing that would show Rehan's commitment to the culture and values of the Downtown Project. He could book another headliner, the taco shop owner reasoned, and the announcement would probably create enough publicity that it would sell more tickets. Thinking about how such an announcement would result in Rehan and Life Is Beautiful being blacklisted by all of America's talent agencies, Rehan struggled to swallow his pride, and glanced over at Tony, who didn't look up from his phone. (Rehan ignored the advice, and Kanye headlined the event.)

Now, sitting at the wine bar opposite Fred and Andrew, Rehan listened as Fred told him that they had sold half of the Life Is Beautiful company to Wendoh Media. Justin and Ryan were being brought in as partners for the festival. In exchange, the Downtown Project would be taking a 50 percent stake in Wendoh Media. And the millions of dollars of debt owed by the festival to Tony would be wiped out.

■ ■ ■

Rehan took a few days to process the news. Tony had once asked him what he thought about Justin leading the marketing for Life Is Beautiful full-time, but selling the company hadn't been on the table, nor were Justin's and Ryan's roles as partners. It turned out that after the *Vegas Seven* article, Tony had invited Justin to join him and others, including Fred and Andrew Donner, on a trip to Maui to attend a conference. On the island, Tony probed Justin about his background and was seemingly impressed by his trajectory: from top college football player at UNLV to selling nightclub flyers, publishing magazines, and now operating bars. Justin, Tony said, had all the qualities of MacGyver.

Ryan insisted to Rehan that he had known nothing about the deal until the last minute and that this was something spearheaded by Justin. But, he reasoned, perhaps having Justin involved wouldn't be such a bad thing. Justin and Rehan were around the same age, and Justin was someone Rehan could negotiate with, unlike Andrew. Rehan relaxed a little when Justin reassured him that he could maintain creative control of the event.

But their relationship rapidly soured. Justin confronted Rehan over excessive spending on dinners, clothes, and other entertainment expenses. (Rehan later said Justin never directly confronted him, and said his spending was approved by Fred.) Justin also took issue with the efforts from the

Life Is Beautiful public relations team to get publicity for Rehan, which included a Q&A interview with *Complex* about his personal style and morning routine, a feature sponsored by men's product company Gillette.

Now, instead of jumping on planes for trips to New York or Chicago or Atlanta, Rehan was finding out after the fact that Justin and Ryan were going in his place. By the time the next festival had come and gone in 2015, Rehan was making a last-ditch effort to stay involved. Looking at how much money the festival had lost again, approximately $8.5 million, he proposed bringing in an outside hedge fund to invest and assume the financial burden of future festivals while guaranteeing that it remained downtown. In response, Tony emailed Rehan to say he was meeting with Fred to discuss Life Is Beautiful, but reinforced that he was not involved in the decision-making regarding the festival and that Rehan should instead be seeking approval from Fred. "The only purpose of [Fred] meeting with me (and everyone else) is to get all the different perspectives, *not* for me to greenlight or not greenlight anything."

Rehan pushed for one more meeting with Tony: "Does that mean we can't grab drinks? ;)"

Tony replied, "We definitely can, but it will need to be a little ways out—i just didn't want to delay things on the LIB side as this week is crazy with halloween stuff and amazon visiting us for several days, and i'm out of town next week . . ."

Rehan's reply was his last interaction with Tony: "Cool. Definitely miss hanging out with you man. Let's plan something when you're free."

■ ■ ■

Shortly after, Tony, Fred, Andrew, Justin, and Ryan went on the annual trip to Hawaii. Rehan had asked Fred and Andrew if he could come, but was ultimately denied. When they returned, Andrew Donner invited Rehan to his house, where he informed Rehan that he was being fired. It was Justin's decision, and Tony had signed off on it, Andrew said. Rehan was given $200,000 for his stake in the company—a fraction of the $1 million he had been offered the year before—and signed a document saying he would not speak ill of the festival or its executives.

He left Las Vegas shortly after and moved to New York with his new wife. He remained angry for years, and while he could dismiss Justin as someone he just despised, processing the loss of his relationship with Ryan was much more challenging. At one point Rehan returned to Vegas and ran into Ryan in front of Commonwealth. Standing before Rehan, Ryan maintained that he hadn't known it was going to end the way it did. Rehan could barely hold himself together. "Ryan, there isn't a day that goes by when I don't think about you. I literally think about you every single day," Rehan told him. "And every day, I wish and pray that someone will call me, and tell me that you got hit by a fucking bus."

Like others before him, Rehan felt that Tony had shown him the world and the stars, only to have it all ripped from him in an instant. "It was strangely like a reality show where you could get voted off the island at any given point," Rehan said later. "And in doing so you were very publicly voted off."

As Rehan built a new life in New York, Justin took his place on Tony's island. In the coming years, being voted off was an outcome that Justin would manage to avoid, no matter the cost.

CHAPTER 17

THE TRAILER PARK

Janice Lopez had been watching Tony from afar for years. Ever since they parted ways on the last day of high school, she had often wondered what became of the soft-spoken boy with whom she shared the silence of the theater all those years ago, directing the spotlights onto the stars of their school performances. After Branson, she had faced a decision: either stick with her love of performing arts or pursue her talent for architecture. She chose Hollywood, and after graduating from the University of Southern California, she landed at a boutique talent agency before joining Warner Brothers as a film director's assistant, working on shows like *Friends* and *The Drew Carey Show*. She got married.

As the years wore on, Janice never had to look far to see how her old friend was doing. She read online about Tony selling LinkExchange for millions of dollars to Microsoft, and then saw him on TV, talking about his quirky shoe website. She had been home one day in 2008 when Oprah came on the TV and introduced her next guest: Janice's high school buddy. Jumping up and down at the sight of Tony Skyping into Oprah's studio, Janice couldn't stop laughing. *He totally hacked this shit,* she thought. *He figured out how to not be there, while still being there.*

By the end of 2013, Janice had long since abandoned Hollywood and was working as a real estate agent in Los Angeles. She had also revisited her high school dreams, gone back to college, and launched a career as an interior designer and architect. While she had solidified her professional life, she was now twice divorced, had two kids, and was feeling ready for a change of scenery.

That Christmas, she was in Las Vegas to visit her stepdad with her kids, and was thinking about whom she might know in town to meet up with. Her stepdad had often said that if you reach a standstill in life, ask someone how you can help. Considering her current situation, now seemed like a good time to take his advice.

It was a wild thought, twenty years later and all, but what if she reached out to Tony? She had heard he was building an entire neighborhood or something. She sent him an email—"it's been a hot minute"—and got a reply shortly after saying that he would love to meet, asking her to talk to Mimi about arrangements, and offering to let her stay in one of his crash pads at the Ogden.

As had happened to countless people before her, Janice's life was about to change. Meeting at the Container Park, the two looked at each other for a while. They were both still shy and awkward, but it was like nothing had changed, and Janice felt comfort in seeing him. Tony looked at her seriously and asked what she was up to in life. She told him about her new career as an architect. "How could I be helpful here?" she asked. What she didn't know was that her own skills would serve a crucial part of Tony's next chapter.

■ ■ ■

Once Janice was settled, she learned pretty quickly that she was entering Tony's life at a time when he was searching for his own new direction. As reporters, commentators, and anyone else with an opinion zeroed in on Tony's reputation and legacy, he had begun his retreat. Suddenly the Mayor of Downtown Las Vegas was looking to shed responsibilities and shrink his personal footprint.

Soon after stepping down as leader of the Downtown Project, Tony was told by the building owners of the Ogden that they no longer wanted to lease the units. The landlord was now demanding that Tony either buy the eighty apartments that the Downtown Project was currently leasing—including his personal luxury condo on the twenty-third floor—or vacate the building.

This ultimatum came at an opportune time because Tony no longer wanted to live at the Ogden. Before, he'd welcomed serendipitous moments with strangers in the building. But having an open-door policy no longer served him. Given the media assault in recent months, as well as the legions of followers he had gained in downtown Las Vegas, Tony was feeling exposed. He yearned for privacy.

As Tony and his team brainstormed where he should live next, Janice stood on his twenty-third-floor balcony, looking across Tony's fiefdom of Fremont East. She spotted a row of Airstream trailers glinting in the sunlight, parked in an empty lot about the size of half a city block. They had been purchased by the Downtown Project as part of an ill-thought-out plan to turn them into hotels, and had been sitting idle for more than a year. Her mind started to race. While studying interior architecture at the University of California, Los Angeles, she had gutted and renovated the interior of an Airstream trailer for a project. She walked back inside to where Tony was sitting and typing on his laptop.

"Hey, Tony," she said. Tony continued to type, his eyes locked on the screen. "What if you lived in an Airstream?"

He stopped and looked up.

The idea floated around the room. Tony thought back to the days of his book tour. "When I was on the Delivering Happiness bus, I learned that I didn't need much," he said. "I pretty much had everything I needed on that bus."

Tony sent out a message to his closest friends and confidants: *We're going to do a living experiment for two weeks,* he wrote. *Janice is available . . . tomorrow. Meet her at the Airstream lot, and see if you might be interested in living in an Airstream or tiny house.*

The experiment would last well beyond two weeks. In November 2014, Tony moved into an Airstream trailer permanently, along with about a dozen of his friends, who paid around $950 a month in rent. Janice moved in with her two young children. So did his old girlfriend from the Venture Frog days, Eva Lee, who was in the process of getting a divorce at the time. "The original idea behind it was to basically try to create an urban version of Burning Man where there's just lots of creative stuff going on," Tony later told a journalist. "What I love about it is that the place is literally changing every week."

Within six months, the lot had a name: Airstream Park. The village of trailers and tiny homes on Fremont became Tony's safe haven within downtown Las Vegas. There were live music jam sessions every weekend and a constant stream of art installations that lit up the space. A giant jellyfish was erected at one point. Most nights at the park ended with conversations around campfires, a favorite pastime of Tony's. Eventually, dogs, cats, and chickens settled in the park, as well as a chocolate-brown alpaca named Marley that roamed the grounds. One day Tony took Janice's kids to Zappos for an event and returned with Blizzy, a fluffy white mutt. The dog would be Tony's loyal companion for years to come.

Every Airstream trailer and tiny home opened toward the center of the lot, a common "living room" with AstroTurf carpeting the concrete where people set up camping chairs, tables, and fire pits. To complete the space, a large outdoor screen was set up for movie nights.

Like 1000 Van Ness in San Francisco and the Ogden, in more ways than one Airstream Park became the latest reincarnation of Tony's Harvard dorm room, where everyone he knew and trusted lived within feet of him. Airstream Park, in his mind, was the ultimate utopia of community living.

Even as his net worth crept toward $1 billion, observers pointed out the seeming contradiction in Tony's choice. "With a net worth of $840 million, Tony Hsieh could have a Caribbean island or a palatial estate overlooking an ocean vista all to himself," read one story from the *Washington Post*. "Instead, the Zappos.com chief executive has set down roots in a less exclusive locale: a dusty Las Vegas trailer park."

Reporters seized the opportunity to tour his living quarters. In an interview with the *Las Vegas Weekly* in early 2015, Tony chatted with a reporter in the park's community kitchen, housed in a shipping container. As he tended to a large pot filled with spicy kimchi noodle egg drop soup, he told the reporter, "I have two skills. I'm the world's best iPhone photographer and I'm the best improv soup maker."

In another video segment for ABC News titled "Inside Zappos CEO's Wild, Wonderful Life," Tony gave the reporter a tour, even inviting the camera crew into his small trailer home. In one shot, Tony fed Marley the alpaca a carrot from his mouth. As Marley chomped, Tony's eyes crinkled with laughter. Genuine glee spread across his face.

After a year of turmoil in the Downtown Project, Tony was eager to put forth another image: a simple man of few needs and with a penchant for homemade soups, living among friends and farm animals.

As Tony successfully steered the media coverage, much of it left out other notable components of Airstream Park. Though there were parents and children who lived in the community full-time, the atmosphere was not completely wholesome. Parties happened frequently, alcohol was free-flowing, and recreational drugs were easy to find. "There were people who lived in the village who were sober," said a frequent visitor to the Airstream Park. "But you could also easily go up to anyone there and say, 'Hey, do you have some mushrooms laying around somewhere?'"

It was during this time that Tony met Anthony Taylor. Anthony (not his real name) was working in internet marketing when he was introduced to Tony through a mutual friend at an art show. Tony immediately loved his energy: Anthony Taylor was the quintessential hype guy. Full of excitement and quick to smile, he became the face of the park to many visitors, giving tours and prompting awe among them as he showed them how to live with less—often wearing outfits that looked as if he'd just arrived from Burning Man. At the end of each tour, he'd hand his guests a carrot to feed Marley the alpaca. To his new neighbors at the park he would say it felt like a home, compared to his rough upbringing.

But once the music started and events were in swing, his party boy spirit was complemented by his reputation as the go-to guy for recreational drugs. "A lot of us used to say Tony collected lost souls in a way," said the frequent visitor. "He would bring them into his world, treat them really well, and then they would become fiercely loyal to him. Anthony was one of those people."

Unsurprisingly, he became a polarizing figure within Airstream Park. There were some who saw Anthony as a bad influence on the community. Others sympathized with Anthony's fascination with and devotion to Tony. "People say, 'Oh, he was the Airstream Park drug dealer,'" said the visitor. "Well, if he was, then everyone who lived in the village was. There was not a single person in Tony's close sphere that didn't overlook things that probably should have been thought about."

Either way, it was a lifestyle shared by Tony, Anthony, and many others within the community. Though it was an open secret in downtown Las

Vegas, it was still a part of his identity that Tony preferred to keep away from prying eyes.

Airstream Park gave off an air of radical inclusion—one of the ten guiding principles of Burning Man. But the media coverage never mentioned the six-foot-high concrete wall surrounding the park. There were a few gaps for entry that were guarded by "park rangers," who essentially acted as bouncers for Tony's community. The wall was just tall enough to keep out curious and unwanted eyes, though not so tall as to feel suffocating for its inhabitants. Airstream Park was Tony's world, and he was eager to protect it from anything that might dare invade and disrupt his safe haven.

■ ■ ■

It had been two years since Tony announced Holacracy's roll-out at Zappos, but the company had yet to reach the state of radical self-management he envisioned. In March 2015, he sent a 4,700-word company-wide email. "We've been operating partially under Holacracy and partially under the legacy management hierarchy in parallel for over a year now," Tony started in his note. "Having one foot in one world while having the other foot in the other world has slowed down our transformation towards self-management and self-organization.

"After many conversations and a lot of feedback about where we are today versus our desired state of self-organization, self-management, increased autonomy, and increased efficiency," he continued, "we are going to take a 'rip the bandaid' approach." In other words, employees either had to adopt Holacracy or take a buyout.

Zappos lost 210 out of 1,503 employees over the following months. Some Zapponians had started wondering whether Tony should resign from Zappos. "The brewing employee discontent reflects the paradox at the heart of any company's move to Holacracy," read a *New York Times* story about the debacle. "For all the talk of self-management and consensus building, the decision to go down this path was Mr. Hsieh's alone."

Tony remained defensive about Holacracy to a press that was unwilling to accept it. "The media has kind of portrayed it as 'there's just total chaos,'" he said during an onstage interview with veteran technology reporter Kara Swisher during a conference in early 2016. During the fireside chat, Tony stumbled over his words, appearing even more uncomfortable than he usually was in media interviews. "There actually still is a hierarchy."

"No, I think they portray it as a crazy cult," Swisher responded. The audience laughed.

"A crazy cult, in total chaos," Tony clarified sarcastically.

"Well, that's sort of the definition of a crazy cult," she responded.

The narrative of Tony being the leader of a cult had been building for years. Back when Tony was on his book tour for *Delivering Happiness,* he had appeared on *The Colbert Report* with comedian Stephen Colbert on Comedy Central, during which Colbert—who found it difficult to fathom a company like Zappos, one that only hired employees if they were "a little weird" and could join costume parades and even spend the night in Tony's house in Southern Highlands—asked Tony point-blank, "Is this a cult? Are you Dear Leader father of a cult? Do you have child brides? How far—how much control do you have over these people?" The audience was still laughing then.

People began to throw the word "cult" around more seriously when journalists reported that Tony's friends were required to get tattoos to attend his fortieth-birthday party in December 2013—a small circle, representing a pixel. "It's an intense display of loyalty—getting inked for a boss generally isn't part of corporate culture—and it exemplifies the concerns some Las Vegans have about Hsieh," read a *Las Vegas Sun* report. "Hsieh's grip has reached the point that when online tech publication Gizmodo recently sent a reporter downtown, the author said the entrepreneur's empire 'can feel cultish.'"

From his struggle to upend corporate hierarchy to his devout group of followers, his public image as a zany visionary morphed into a more disquieting figure. "Many believe Hsieh . . . fosters an environment where devotion is rewarded and criticism isn't tolerated," the *Las Vegas Sun* wrote. "Downtown Las Vegas, they say, is becoming Tony's Town, a place where either you follow Hsieh—and line up for a tattoo—or you're deemed in the way."

By the time Tony appeared onstage at the conference with Kara Swisher in 2016, the fissures in Tony's philosophies were starting to appear. And as the public punches started again, this time targeting Holacracy and claiming that he was running a cult, Tony's sanguine exterior started to crack.

■ ■ ■

In Airstream Park, his closest confidants started taking notice. In the fall of 2016, Tony threw a party at Airstream Park for Michelle D'Attilio's birthday. At one point during the night, "Billie Jean" by Michael Jackson blasted through the speakers. As soon as she heard the song, Michelle immediately thought back to her last birthday, when she had been with Tony at a bar with a few girlfriends. When the song came on that night, Tony had hopped out of his chair and started doing the moonwalk. Tony had told Michelle the next day that he used to watch Michael Jackson as a kid and mirror the moonwalk by himself.

So when "Billie Jean" came on at Airstream Park, Michelle urged Tony to do the moonwalk again, in front of all their friends. Tony seemed hesitant, but after some pushing from Michelle and a few others, he did the moonwalk for just a few seconds as partygoers whooped and cheered. He quickly sat back down. Later that night, Tony brought up the moonwalk moment in private.

"Why are you so upset?" Michelle asked.

"Why did you make me do the moonwalk in front of everyone?" he said.

"Because you've done it before and you're so good at it!"

"Listen," Tony said angrily. "I can't just turn it on anytime."

Michelle was confused. *What are we really talking about here?* As she stared at Tony, something about his facial expression made her stop. She looked closer and realized he had tears in his eyes. As she took the moment in, she thought about the recent media coverage as well as Tony's standing at Zappos and the Downtown Project. The pressure was getting to him, she thought.

It was one of the only times she ever saw Tony cry.

CHAPTER 18

THE RIGHT HAND

When Tony had been leaping from one chapter to another—building Zappos, the Amazon acquisition, the *Delivering Happiness* book, the launch of the Downtown Project, Holacracy—there was one man by his side the entire time: Fred Mossler.

Since the early days of Zappos, Fred had been Tony's right-hand man. And when the Downtown Project came along, it was a vision the two men created together. They donned costumes at Zappos all-hands meetings and biked around Burning Man each year. Fred was one of a dwindling number of people who could tell Tony no. He was a giant in the community that they had built. And he had an important role: a check-and-balance for Tony's untethered ambitions and ideas, just as Alfred had been before he returned to Silicon Valley.

But by 2014, Fred was forty-eight, had remarried, and had three children. When Airstream Park was being built, a trailer had been reserved for Fred and his wife, Meghan, whom he had met at Zappos years before. After staying there for a weekend, they decided not to move in. For all the years of unconventionality under Tony's wing, he simply could not stomach moving into a trailer and raising his kids in a pseudo-commune.

As Holacracy continued its troubled rollout at Zappos, Fred supported the effort internally by sending encouraging company-wide emails while listening to employees' gripes with the new system. He appeared in media interviews with Tony to defend the corporate structure. "As I noodle on the press coverage, what no one has mentioned is if *any* company were bold enough to offer their entire employee base a severance the likes of which we did," Fred said during an interview in early 2016. "In reading all the exit interviews and speaking with people leaving, the exodus is less about Holacracy/dissatisfaction and more about the opportunity to pursue other passions or fulfill other goals in life. The fact we can make such an offer and only 18% choose to leave is, I'm guessing, an impressive statistic in the corporate world."

"I completely agree with Fred," Tony said.

But unbeknownst to the wider public, Fred was contemplating his own exit from Zappos. Some Zapponians had started noticing Fred's increasing absence. In the past, when both Fred and Tony were in a meeting, it was not unusual to witness the two debating, with Fred talking Tony down from his outrageous ideas. But Fred, some noticed, had started to disagree less.

"Fred was also at his desk more," said Chris Peake, who reported directly to Fred. "Before, he was never really at his desk. He was usually moving and shaking, just very busy."

A few months after the interview, Fred announced he was leaving Zappos. "I've spent almost seventeen years with Zappos and have seen it grow from a two-bedroom apartment to the amazing company it is today," Fred wrote in a company-wide email. "There are no words that can describe what this company has and what the people in it have meant for me."

He continued, "Tony will remain focused on Zappos, but we'll still be tied at the hip and I still expect to contribute to Zappos as his thought partner. Downtown Las Vegas is where my heart and soul are and where all of my closest friends are. I will always be around and available for collisions downtown."

■ ■ ■

First Alfred and then Fred had served as Tony's life partners, in business and in friendship. Neither of them was afraid to disagree with Tony, and he regarded them as equals. But after Fred's departure, there was no clear successor, and Tony boasted to old acquaintances that his friends kept getting younger and younger. The crowd at Zappos and Airstream Park partied more, disagreed less, and were woefully ill-equipped to become Tony's peers.

Despite surrounding himself with deferential people, Tony still saw value in a right-hand man who challenged him and demanded his respect. When Fred left, Tony started trying to recruit a man named Victor Oviedo, a partner at a New York–based investment firm whose warm eyes and bright smile contrasted with his no-nonsense, Ivy League–bred financier background.

Victor was a partner at SkyBridge Capital, a hedge fund founded by Anthony Scaramucci, the enigmatic Wall Street figure who would later have a tumultuous stint as President Donald Trump's press secretary. Since 2009, SkyBridge had held its annual SALT Conference in Las Vegas, a meeting of the minds where the guests and keynote speakers included billionaires like Michael Bloomberg and Bill Ackman and politicians such as future President Joe Biden and former British prime minister Tony Blair.

In 2017, Victor asked the singer and songwriter Jewel to perform at SALT. Jewel agreed and asked if she could also give a talk on mental health and mindfulness at the conference with her new friend Tony Hsieh. The two had just met on billionaire Richard Branson's Necker Island at another conference, and they had connected on a variety of topics, from Holacracy to mindfulness. Jewel was passionate about mental health, and she told Victor that having Tony at this panel would give it more credibility among the SALT crowd. Victor agreed, and met Tony for the first time at the conference.

Several months later, Jewel invited Victor to a charity event in Las Vegas. Tony, who was also there, threw his usual line at Victor. "The next time you're in town, come stay with me at the Airstream Park," he said to Victor. "My email is Tony@Zappos.com."

"All right, Tony@Zappos.com, next time I'm in town, I'll shoot you an email," Victor said. He thought it was unusual for Tony, a prominent CEO, to invite him to stay with him so soon after meeting. But from their brief interactions, Victor could tell that Tony's life was far from ordinary. A few days later, Victor emailed Tony and told him he already had a trip planned for Vegas later in the month.

Tony wrote back, "Why don't you come to the office for a tour and then come shadow me for a day?"

Soon after, Victor arrived at Zappos and received tours of the company headquarters and the Downtown Project before the guide dropped him off at Airstream Park at the end of the afternoon. He found Tony sitting at a long table with a few other residents, drinking Fernet.

Victor sat down, and the two dove into a conversation about Holacracy at Zappos. Tony told Victor he wanted Holacracy to evolve into a new system called market-based dynamics, in which every team would be run like its own independent business and every employee would have to embrace an entrepreneurial mindset to thrive. The structure was based on Tony's theory that everyone could become a self-starting entrepreneur so long as they were given the tools to succeed. Victor later told confidants that his friendship with Tony began at this precise moment, when he challenged Tony on his new idea.

"What parts of market-based dynamics don't make sense to you?" Tony asked Victor. The others at the table turned to pay attention to the debate.

"This idea you believe in that there is an entrepreneur in everyone," Victor said.

"You don't think anyone could become an entrepreneur?"

"Maybe anyone could be, but not everyone wants to be an entrepreneur, Tony. Some people just want to go to work, and then they want to go home to their friends and family. Or maybe they want to pursue personal hobbies. I just do not agree with the premise of a setting where you force everyone to become an entrepreneur."

Tony stared at him, slowly nodding. He seemed taken aback that Victor was willing to openly debate his theory. Then, Victor looked around the table and saw some of the shocked faces looking back at him. Having spent a lot of time with successful individuals through the SALT Conference, Victor quickly read the room: Tony's intellectual curiosity and his ability to transform ideas into conclusions were elite. But he had surrounded himself with yes-men.

Victor left the trailer park that night wondering if he had gone too far. But the next day Tony again invited Victor to shadow him for the day. Victor sat in on several Zappos meetings, including one in which Tony and his core lieutenants were prepping for a presentation to Amazon's Jeff Wilke, a high-ranking executive who reported directly to Jeff Bezos. Tony asked Victor for his input, despite having no formal role at Zappos. *Is this a test?* Victor thought. *Am I being interviewed right now?*

Tony ended the day by inviting Victor to move to Vegas. "Zero chance," Victor immediately replied.

"How about you come work for me?" Tony asked.

"I have no interest in becoming employee number seven hundred thousand at Amazon," he said.

But they kept talking, and Tony invited Victor on a ski trip to Powder Mountain in Utah with a few of his friends, including Zappos employees and Airstream Park residents. On the ski trip, Victor watched as Tony made soup for the group of twenty people while everyone else played beer pong. Once the soup was served, Tony curled up on a couch in the corner of the living room. People came up to him to chat. When they moved off, Tony would open a book on his lap and read while surrounded by partying chaos.

Victor's excursions with Tony started happening every month, from Zappos meetings in Vegas to Life Is Beautiful festival planning in Hawaii, and even to distilleries in Guadalajara to do research on a potential new tequila branding opportunity with Nacho Daddy. They attended conferences together when Tony was speaking, and met fellow entrepreneurs at their offices to explore various partnerships, from StockX to MIT Labs in Boston.

Then one day, Tony handed Victor forty pages of financial documents. They were a summary of Tony's investments tied to the Downtown Project and the financials for Life Is Beautiful. Tony told Victor he was concerned that he was being ripped off, and he was particularly disappointed with the financial performance and structure of Life Is Beautiful.

Victor went through the documents. "If you are basing the performance solely on financial returns, then your concerns are valid," he said to Tony. But wasn't Tony investing in these ventures to build community? By that metric, Victor said, these businesses are somewhat successful. It appeared that Tony needed Victor to remind him that the community-building aspect of these investments was the ultimate measure of return.

Victor never minced his words around Tony. As a result, Tony kept asking Victor to come work for him at Zappos and the Downtown Project. Tony even recruited others to ask Victor for him. After months of courtship, Victor made his observations clear to Tony. "I would love to do something with you," he said. "But frankly, I think you're wasting your time at Zappos. You've done everything there is for you to do here. When you're ready to jump into your next adventure, I'd be happy to join you as your partner."

Tony struck out with Victor. They remained friends, but Tony still needed a right-hand man in Vegas to deliver on his ideas for Zappos and the Downtown Project. Instead of recruiting from the outside, Tony realized he could find someone within his ranks.

■ ■ ■

"It'd be really fun to just have a ball pit right here," Tony said, pointing to a corner as Tyler Williams followed him around the Zappos campus. Tyler was scribbling down notes as Tony dumped the outputs of his whirring mind onto him. "I would like a slide here that comes from the second floor. It could be great to have music in the plaza, or maybe a dog park."

Tyler had been at Zappos for five years now and had been promoted several times. Internally, he was known as the "Fungineer," a role that served as a clearinghouse for any strange idea that Tony came up with. In one instance, Tony asked Tyler to build a jacket that had built-in portable chargers and other gadgets, similar to the jacket worn by Richard "Data" Wang, a character in the 1985 cult classic *The Goonies*. In another case, Tyler helped build the "instant dance floor" in the Zappos lobby. At the push of a button—which said NEVER PUSH THIS BUTTON—speakers would slide up from the ground, thumping music would blare out, and fog machines would fill the Zappos lobby with smoke, creating the illusion of a dance floor.

In 2016, Tony promoted Tyler to lead Zappos's brand expansion department, giving him a $20 million annual budget. Prior to this, the biggest budget Tyler had managed was around half a million dollars. Tony had also never given the branding role to anyone other than himself.

Tyler, who was a decade younger than Tony, looked up to the Zappos visionary. Like Rehan, who had been swept into Tony's inner circle, Tyler now had a front-row seat to Tony's life as a tech leader and cultural icon. In his new role, Tyler started jetting off with Tony across the world, from music festivals to conferences. When Tony drank a shot of Fernet, Tyler was usually right there with him. When Tony went up onstage to talk about Holacracy, Tyler was sitting in the audience. In many ways, they were polar opposites. Tony was introverted at heart, while Tyler was effusive and loved to entertain. But Tyler was a crutch for Tony in social situations: when Tony wanted to slink into the background, it was Tyler who stepped up to take attention away from him. Tyler was resourceful, and he was usually more or less willing to partake in the festivities. He was now Tony's new right hand.

Being at Tony's side also meant hobnobbing with celebrities like Jewel. The Grammy Award–winning artist had become more involved in Tony's world after the SALT Conference and had recently agreed to build a program at Zappos that could help his employees maintain their mental health. Called Whole Human, it would provide Zapponians with a series of courses on how to achieve optimal emotional and physical health. In their conversations, Jewel and Tony realized their missions and goals were complementary—that fostering Zappos employees' happiness would be key to a successful corporate culture.

But the Zappos definition of employee happiness—an open bar at the office with a philosophy of "work hard, play hard"—was at complete odds with the philosophy that Jewel was trying to introduce. "Happiness is different than excitement," Jewel said. "Excitement and perk-driven culture becomes addictive in nature and creates entitlement." By her definition, in fact, Zappos had it all wrong.

So in the spring of 2018, Jewel organized a mindfulness retreat on the Colorado River in Nevada for about a dozen Zappos employees including Tony and Tyler. While Tony backed out of the trip at the last minute, Tyler and the others showed up with boat gear and coolers full of beer and hard alcohol.

"Hey, guys, that's not the point of this trip," Jewel said. This was to be an alcohol- and substance-free retreat. They chuckled and packed the alcohol back into their cars. For the next few hours, they boated up the Colorado River, stopping by hot springs and cavernous coves. In one of the caves, Jewel sang a capella, her soprano echoing around the red rock chambers. For Tyler, it was one of the most amazing days of his life. He only wished that Tony had been there to experience it.

In fact, Tyler had started to worry about his boss. In the last couple of months, Tyler had started to notice a yellowing in the whites of Tony's eyes—jaundice, he later figured, a symptom of alcoholic hepatitis. Tyler also saw that Tony's hands would tremble during Zappos meetings.

Sometimes during morning meetings, mimosas would appear, and Tony was always a willing participant. Tyler realized that he had never seen a day when Tony was not drinking.

Tyler reached a point in 2018 where he physically could not keep up with his mentor's vices. In the fall, Tyler started experiencing nausea and heartburn. His doctor asked him what his diet looked like, and was shocked to learn how much Fernet-Branca Tyler was drinking. "You are teaching your body not to digest anything, because it's thinking the digestif will do it for you," the doctor told him. The doctor instructed Tyler to make serious life changes.

As Tyler wondered how Tony was stomaching his Fernet habit, he witnessed another, even more troubling encounter. A meeting had been scheduled at the El Cortez between Tony and a man named Ben Jorgensen, a Silicon Valley entrepreneur who had recently raised $30 million for his new blockchain technology company, Constellation Labs.

Ben and Tony had met previously during the early Downtown Project days and had remained friends. There was enough mutual respect between the two men that during a visit to Airstream Park, Tony had once confided in Ben about his frustrations.

"Everybody seems to want something from me," Tony had said.

"I don't want anything from you," Ben said.

"You want my time," Tony said. "It's still something. I'm so tired of it all."

The two ended up going back to his trailer and watching a YouTube video about the perspective of the human eye. There Ben watched as Tony turned off from the world.

Still, Ben had been inspired by Tony's vision and generosity. Many times he had witnessed Tony in conversations gently nudging people toward their purpose.

For the meeting at the El Cortez, Ben had wanted his Constellation co-founders to meet Tony and be inspired. But as the meeting approached, Ben—who had only been working on his startup for eight months and was in the trenches of building it—was forced to reschedule. Tony, who had nearly every waking minute of his life accounted for, made it clear to Tyler in private that he was peeved.

On the day of the rescheduled meeting, Tony showed up at the Parlour Bar at El Cortez with his entourage, Tyler included. As their drinks arrived, Ben discussed his company and his views on the wider crypto community with Tony and his group.

When Ben finished, Tony bored into Ben with a series of questions. "How do you make a business out of crypto? What exactly is the business model?" Tony's tone felt hostile.

As Ben tried to answer, Tony interrupted him. "Well, what is the value of it? How do you even sell that?"

Ben was used to people being skeptical about his cryptocurrency business—it was 2018, after all, when Bitcoin crashed from $20,000 a coin to just over $3,000. But this was the last thing Ben had expected from Tony. He had brought his team to Vegas hoping for what Tony was famous for—encouraging entrepreneurs through productive and inspiring conversation.

"It was a very weird dynamic, and my co-founders eventually started to object to Tony's questions," Ben said later. "They knew how much the meeting meant to me."

As everyone at the table watched the uncomfortable encounter go down, Tyler sat quietly. He had rarely, if ever, seen Tony be so hostile. He wondered whether Tony felt intellectually threatened by Ben, a sign of ego that seemed foreign to the Tony he knew.

The meeting ended on such a sour note that Tyler was compelled to reach out to Ben and apologize. But as he walked away from the El Cortez, he found himself thinking, *Where the hell did that come from?*

CHAPTER 19

GENIE IN A BOTTLE

The small propeller plane was circling high above the playa as Tyler looked out the window. His body felt the hum of the engines as he scanned the view below before him: a sprawling sea of encampments organized in the shape of a horseshoe, a seeming hieroglyphic mirage emerging from the haze of the desert. He felt his adrenaline shoot up, and a smile crinkled across his face. *We're back,* he thought. *Back to Burning Man.*

The annual pilgrimage to Black Rock City—the ephemeral town that exists only one week a year in the name of Burning Man—occurs at the end of every summer. By 2019, Tony and his crew were veterans. To get an invite from Tony was to receive a golden ticket to join his circle of confidants and followers. Tony's camp, which for liability reasons—given open drug use at the camp and the event—was technically called Mimi's camp even though he footed the bill, provided everything a so-called Burner would need to survive and thrive for a week rolling around in the playa dust. Their "Welcome to Burning Man" starter pack included individual trailers with stocked fridges, scarves, dust masks, goggles, and light kits.

Tyler first joined Tony's crew at the festival in 2014. He remembered being told as a child that Burning Man was a gathering of devil-worshiping pagans in the desert, all coming together to burn an idol, procreate, and get weird. But he was no longer that kid, and he was excited to experience the community that had inspired so much of Tony's work in Zappos and downtown Las Vegas.

That first year, Tony never left his side; he wanted to make sure his newest member of the Burning Man crew was having a good time. It was almost as if he wanted to vicariously experience going to Burning Man for the first time again through Tyler. He took videos of Tyler's awed reactions to Black Rock City: tens of thousands of individuals coming together to create a world of kaleidoscopic art and rapture as the sun went down.

He had gone to Burning Man every year since, and they had experienced some wild events. Two years before, on the final night of the festival, Tony had been watching the main ceremony—the burning of the sculpture at the center of Black Rock City—when a man he had just been talking to ran into the fire and died.

Now it was Tony's ninth time at Burning Man and Tyler's sixth. There were first-time Burners in their camp this year, including Tony's parents and his former girlfriend Michelle D'Attilio. For Tony, Burning Man was a place where he could search for inspiration and ideas. Weeks after his first burn on the playa in 2011, he invited four of the founding leaders of Burning Man to Las Vegas to discuss how he could apply the ten principles of Burning Man to Zappos and to the yet undeveloped Downtown Project he planned to build. And through the years, he continued the tradition of taking what he could out of the playa into "the default world"—a term that Burners used in reference to the rest of the year spent away from the festival. Tony purchased a gutted Boeing 747 that acted as a club at Black Rock City for several years, and he intended to bring it to downtown Las Vegas to turn it into an event space.

The theme for Burning Man in 2019 was "Metamorphoses"—a celebration of change and an exploration of uncertainty. But Tony's life had remained unchanged for quite some time, at least by his standards. In 1998, he sold LinkExchange. About a decade later in 2009, he sold Zappos. Now another ten years had passed. He was forty-five years old and Zappos had just celebrated its twentieth anniversary.

Holacracy had failed to take hold, so Tony was now steering the company toward market-based dynamics. The transition was still sluggish at best, and he was pushing his executives to go faster. They pushed back, with long-term veterans like Chris Peake telling Tony they had to go slow in order to educate the thirteen hundred Zapponians on the completely novel corporate structure.

Meanwhile, the Downtown Project was approaching its seventh year, and it was still a money-losing venture. Many of the Downtown Project businesses Tony had invested in had yet to figure out how to be self-sustaining and independent and were still asking him for more funding. Two of his top Downtown Project lieutenants, Fred and Andrew Donner, had taken a step back to focus on their own projects, which made Tony question whether he still had the right group of leaders to steer the project's course. All this made Tony ponder a question he had considered many times before: *What's next?* He was eager to embark on his next chapter.

Members of Tony's Burning Man crew were usually given plastic watches synced to the same time. Phones barely had reception on the playa, so their watches would be the only tool they had to guide meet-up times and points. It was another spectacularly planned year. Around a dozen RVs parked in a circle surrounded a dome tent in the center, where a hanging chandelier illuminated the Persian rugs and accented throw pillows across the ground. Though his parents, Richard and Judy, tried their best to keep up to the pace, they usually turned in early at night-time. Judy took a nap one night on Tony's cloud-nine-themed art car. One night, Tony got Judy, who was wearing a long flowy dress, and Michelle, clad in thigh-high dusty boots and an LED necklace, to dance with each other as a crowd surrounded them. Though Tony knew this would make them uncomfortable, he still pushed them to the front, giggling as he videoed the two women awkwardly dancing together.

Once his parents retired to bed, Tony went off into the night with Tyler. Aside from alcohol and cannabis, of which there was plenty, Tony also sought out psychedelic mushrooms and MDMA to enhance his experience, which he said he used to elicit a different perspective and connection to Black Rock City. "The thing about doing recreational drugs with Tony was everything was always intentional," said a member of his Burning Man crew. "As in, we're going somewhere to see something so we can get inspired and then integrate that thought process into making an environment better for people in the default world."

As they biked through the playa, following the bass lines and neon lights pulsating in the dark, they crossed paths with Shelby Sacco, which is not her real name. She represented a new crop of Burning Man attendees in recent years: techies who came to Black Rock to discover life outside of their screens and algorithms, in the hope of achieving enlightenment.

As the desert's energy throbbed around their chance encounter, Shelby reached into her bag and took out a small container. Inside was a white powder, and she told Tony and Tyler that it was ketamine. Typically used as an animal tranquilizer, ketamine had made an entrance to the rave scene in recent decades, giving users a dissociative high that can distort sights and sounds and make the user feel disconnected from reality—especially when that reality involves physical or mental pain. She explained that ketamine was a nonaddictive drug, there are no hangovers or negative health effects, and under its influence you can only be happy. "Those are two things that Tony always searched for," the Burning Man crew member said. "It was basically described as like the perfect drug."

■ ■ ■

Ketamine was first synthesized in 1956 by chemists at the pharmaceutical firm Parke Davis Company, as a means to replace the surgical anesthetic PCP, which had a tendency to trigger hallucinations and psychotic episodes after surgery. Formerly called CI-581, ketamine was supposed to be a safer alternative, and it went on to become the world's top-selling anesthetic, used by pediatricians and veterinarians. During the 1970s, it was used as an anesthetic in the field for soldiers during the Vietnam War, which sparked the beginning of abuse of the drug when soldiers and veterans became addicted to its hallucinatory and calming effects. But the publication of *Journeys into the Bright World* by Marcia Moore and Howard Alltounian in 1978 offered scientific literature on the potential benefits of the drug, while other advocates like John Lilly, a neuroscientist who later documented his use of the drug in *The Scientist*, helped spread ketamine use across the East Coast social scene in the 1980s and 1990s. The drug moved into raves and clubs, earning the nickname Special K for its trance-inducing qualities on the dance floor. In 1999, ketamine was deemed a Schedule III narcotic by the Drug Enforcement Agency, which meant that unless it was dispensed by a medical practitioner, it would be a crime to sell or intend to sell the drug.

The earliest studies on the effects of ketamine in treating mental disorders started in the 1960s, when a controversial Mexican psychotherapist named Salvador Roquet started using the drug as a form of psychotherapy. Roquet was arrested by Mexican authorities in the mid-1970s due to his use of illegal drugs. "I think the major reason was that conventional psychiatrists were angry at the publicity that Salvador had been receiving," said Stanley Krippner, a psychologist who was a friend of Salvador's and helped facilitate his release from detention.

But a decade later, psychiatrists in the Soviet Union launched their own experiment with ketamine as psychotherapy to treat alcoholism. After ten years of research, Russian doctors Evgeny Krupitsky and A. Y. Grinenko published their findings in the 1990s: "The results of a controlled clinical trial demonstrated a considerable increase in efficacy of the authors' standard alcoholism treatment when supplemented by ketamine psychedelic therapy." The researchers also found that ketamine-assisted psychedelic therapy induced "positive transformation of non-verbalized (mostly unconscious) self-concept and emotional attitudes, to various aspects of self and other people, positive changes in life values and purposes, important insights into the meaning of life and an increase in the level of spiritual development. Most importantly, these psychological changes were shown to favor a sober lifestyle."

In 2000, the drug was tested on patients to treat depression in a study led by Robert M. Berman at Yale University. Seven patients with major depression were given intravenous treatment of ketamine for two days. The researchers found that "subjects with depression evidenced significant improvement in depressive symptoms within 72 hours after ketamine but not placebo infusion."

The research has largely been limited to small sample groups, with a need for more data on longer-term efficacy and safety. But the few that exist show evidence that ketamine, in a supervised setting, could help patients with mood and anxiety disorders. In 2020, psychiatrists at the Karolinska Institutet, a medical research university in Sweden, ran another experiment where thirty patients with "difficult-to-treat depression" were randomly assigned to a ketamine-infusion group or a placebo group. Then in the next phase, those who wanted to could receive ketamine twice for two weeks. "The result was that over 70 percent of those treated with ketamine responded to the drug," the researchers found. Recent studies into the potential therapeutic uses for ketamine have looked into it as a treatment for suicidal ideation, bipolar disorder, post-traumatic stress disorder, and obsessive-compulsive disorder. In addition to anecdotal evidence, word of mouth, and off-label uses, the studies bolstered support for more research into ketamine therapies. But even though ketamine has shown positive signals in research studies to treat mental disorders, professional psychiatrists remain wary of mass-prescribing the drug. "Ketamine has the advantage of being very rapid-acting, but at the same time it is a narcotic-classed drug that can lead to addiction," said Johan Lundberg, one of the authors of a Swedish study on the drug. "So it'll be interesting to examine in future studies if this receptor can be a target for new, effective drugs that don't have the adverse effects of ketamine."

"I think if you put ketamine into an overexcited brain, it will calm it down," said Dr. Karl Jansen, one of the premier researchers in ketamine who has studied the use and abuse of the drug. "If you put ketamine into a calm brain, it will over-excite it. It's probably pro-convulsant in a normal brain, and anticonvulsant in an epileptic brain. It's a very complicated drug."

But it was in California-based tech circles that so-called ketamine clinics—facilities in which licensed doctors administer ketamine in a supervised setting—found an audience in the mid-2010s, around the same time it became clear that entrepreneurs were more susceptible to depression due to the stressors of their jobs. Because the clinics offered the drug for an off-label use, insurance companies would not cover the treatments, so the kinds of patients these clinics attracted were wealthy—from technologists to executives to stay-at-home parents. Those who could afford the treatment would sit back in a reclining chair hooked up to an IV drip as the ketamine triggered hallucinations and other dissociative experiences to help cure mood and anxiety disorders.

The claim that ketamine is nonaddictive has never been supported by any medical research, even though some doctors have made such bold statements. In a 2017 *Los Angeles Magazine* story about the rise of ketamine clinics in the city, Dr. Steven Mandel stated outright that the drug is nonaddictive, "insisting there's no danger of tolerance or addiction."

But abuse of the drug is possible. Ketamine made the crossover from an anesthetic to Special K—the club drug version that can be snorted as a powder instead of being injected. "Recreational users claim that a snort of the stuff (some prefer injection) can make a Daft Punk concert transcendent," read the *Los Angeles Magazine* story.

But snorting the drug in an unsupervised setting is not the same as having a professional administer it with an IV drip. Far from the supervised clinics in California, Tony, Tyler, and their ketamine-espousing friend bent over to snort the white powder as the festival swirled around them. Tyler didn't think much of the drug; it made him feel a little loopy, like he was drunk, but that was the extent of it. And he thought Tony had a similar experience. They said goodbye to Shelby and moved on through the playa.

Unbeknownst to Tyler, a seed had been planted in Tony's head. In recent months, Tony had come to see that his years of alcohol consumption were finally catching up to him, and he had been looking for a healthier alternative. Could ketamine be the answer? Like most ideas that he gravitated toward, its tentacles started to wrap around his mind.

▨ ▧ ▨

About a month later in Las Vegas, the annual Life Is Beautiful festival roared ahead. By now, it had grown to a massive event as part of the international festival circuit, drawing close to two hundred thousand attendees over the course of a three-day weekend. With mind-boggling neon lights and fireworks lighting the downtown Vegas skyline, Tony's vision had again come to fruition: a weekend that his closest friends could come together and enjoy. That year, Tony was most excited to see Billie Eilish, the eighteen-year-old phenom with a propensity to be unapologetically herself. "Tony loved Billie," said Michelle, who attended the festival with her daughter and watched Eilish with Tony. "He just thought she was the coolest."

As the weekend wore on, Tony told Michelle that he had been attending drug-assisted therapies with one of his other girlfriends. He had done a lot of research on psychotherapy, he said, particularly therapies that involve MDMA and psilocybin (the clinical name for the active substance in hallucinogenic mushrooms). Recently psilocybin, in particular, had been getting attention in biotech circles as a legitimate form of treatment for mood and anxiety disorders, but it had yet to pass the clinical trials required to receive approval from the FDA. Like ketamine, a contingent of alternative psychotherapists were using these drugs in an off-label manner. Tony insisted to Michelle that the sessions were mostly for his girlfriend and not for him. But the therapist had been working on Tony, too.

Michelle asked him what they had learned.

"She said there's nothing wrong with me," Tony replied. "Apparently I have it all figured out."

She laughed. *Any therapist who tells a patient, especially one like Tony, that he had it all figured out should have her license revoked*, Michelle thought.

"No, for real," Tony said. "She thinks that the way I think and everything I'm doing is good." And Tony claimed the therapist had said he could not get addicted to drugs because he did not have an addictive personality.

Michelle was hearing a newfound arrogance in Tony's tone. In the years she'd known Tony, her favorite memory of him was when he walked around her in circles at the elevator bank in the Ogden, too nervous to talk. His humility back then had been surprising and endearing. But this new version of Tony that spoke as if he was invincible—she had very little idea where he came from or who he was.

■ ■ ■

A few weeks later, in November, Tony, Tyler, and a few others attended the Summit conference in downtown Los Angeles. It was a four-day gathering of Silicon Valley elite, and Tony had been a regular attendee over the years. The event included talks from Uber CEO Dara Khosrowshahi and SpaceX president Gwynne Shotwell. But of all the technorati in attendance, Tony had only one person he wanted to rendezvous with: Shelby, the woman from Burning Man. He told Tyler he wanted to meet up with her to try ketamine again.

Just as he had researched the science of happiness, how to build a city, and even the art of comedy, Tony had been researching ketamine. He had read several books on the drug, including *The Little Book of Ketamine*, which he later started passing out to his friends. The book doesn't rubber-stamp the drug, but it doesn't indict it either. While researching the drug, Tony read that when under the drug's influence, people can have spiritual and insightful revelations that can provide relief for physical and emotional pain. The most common reason patients want to explore ketamine therapy is to treat depression, but Tony never told his confidants he felt depressed. He framed it more in a spirit of exploration.

And so they met with Shelby again. Over the course of the four-day event, Tony was continuously on ketamine, throughout the day and night. He told those around him that it was triggering his brain in a way that he had never experienced before.

Tyler was right alongside him. He was doing less than Tony—not unusual, given Tony's higher tolerance for substances than most people— but Tyler had also gotten feedback from his wife: "I don't like you on that drug. You're not the same person for three days after you do it."

Tyler also started to notice behaviors in Tony he hadn't seen before. Tony was usually very discreet about his drug use. Discretion was core to Tony's way of living and allowed him to balance the contradictory circles of his life, from corporate boardrooms to festival revelry. But at Summit he was very open about his ketamine use, trying to convince others to do it with him, including the girlfriend he had gone to therapy with. She said no, and later became so concerned about his usage that she ended her relationship with him. Like Michelle, Tyler also started noticing Tony's newfound arrogance.

"I respond to things differently," Tyler heard him say at one point during Summit. "I'm a super genius, and I have complete control. I can do things that others can't. I can download tae kwon do and instantly be a master of it." Tyler realized that Tony was reciting lines and scenarios from *The Matrix*, where Keanu Reeves's character Neo discovers he is living in a simulation and vows to break out of it. There's a famous scene in the film where he "downloads" tae kwon do and kung fu, as if a person could download skills like they would an app on their iPhone. Immediately after the download, Neo becomes a trained fighter.

Tyler was unsure what to make of all this. But after giving it a little thought, he brushed Tony's bizarre claims aside. *He probably just needs to sober up and get some rest,* Tyler thought.

After the conference, Tony immediately wanted more of the drug, and it didn't take long for him to reunite with it again. Around Thanksgiving, Tony toured down the California coast for a series of events and gatherings. It started at Belcampo, a thirty-thousand-acre regenerative and organic farm at the base of Mount Shasta. He came as a guest of the supply chain director, who had heard about Tony's love for Belcampo's famous bone broth. After the farm, he went to Oakland to attend the Soiled Dove, a circus-themed dinner event, as a guest of actor David Arquette. Finally, the trip concluded in South Lake Tahoe for an immersive art event at the MontBleu Hotel. Tyler joined him with Michelle, who had been hired by Tony a few months prior to manage his social media accounts. Shelby was there too.

Only on this trip did Michelle learn that Tony was doing ketamine. She was also told by Tony, Tyler, and Shelby that it was nonaddictive, it was being used in psychotherapy, and it opened up the mind in revolutionary and creative ways. Michelle decided to try it, but she didn't do much, and she finished the trip thinking little of the drug.

A few days later in December, Michelle was in Vegas at the opening of Fergusons, a formerly run-down motel in downtown Vegas that Tony had spent $15 million to convert into a trendy town square. Behind the property, he had built a new and improved Airstream Park, in which he was now living. A series of events had been organized to celebrate the opening of another linchpin of Tony's grand plan for downtown Vegas. His parents, Richard and Judy, had come to support the event. During one performance at the theater room in Zappos headquarters, Michelle took a photograph of Tony as he smiled at the performers onstage.

"This was probably the last time I saw him okay, like in a good space," Michelle later said. "Happy and healthy."

CHAPTER 20

WINTER CAMP

The temperature often hovers above freezing on Las Vegas nights between December and January. The flow of conferences and festivals has typically dissipated by then, and people spend more time making plans to see family than arranging business trips. With the downtime surrounding Christmas and New Year's Eve, Tony had built a weeks-long tradition for his community every year: Winter Camp.

A stream of family-friendly events revolving around Airstream Park, from potsticker-wrapping parties to poetry slams, would keep his circle of friends coming back to his home. Every night, a movie played on the big outdoor screen. It was usually a wholesome time among the Airstream trailers, and now that they had just moved into their new location behind Fergusons, this year was supposed to be special.

But Tony was not himself. His behavior had become so outside the norm that those living with him grew increasingly concerned about it. Tony started telling people that he and Tyler had discovered a new drug called ketamine, prompting many of them to confront Tyler. *Why is Tony so into ketamine?* they would ask. *Why are you encouraging this heavy use of it?*

Tony had secured a large batch of ketamine and was snorting it daily, pressuring those around him to take the drug so they could all be on the same "flow." He invited psychotherapists from a ketamine clinic in Los Angeles to give a talk about the positive effects of the drug. But when they arrived, they only encouraged using the drug in a controlled setting under supervision. In his Airstream trailer, he had a chart that tracked how often he was using the drug, and how much his friends were using it, including Tyler.

Tyler had initially been unperturbed by Tony's ketamine use. But faced with questions and accusations, he started visiting Winter Camp more often to check on Tony. What he witnessed made him realize that something bigger was going on: Tony's world and legacy were now at stake.

Typically, Tony was quiet and reserved. He was often the last to talk and when he did, he was a man of few words. But now he was acting in a manic manner, appearing shirtless and shoeless in the frigid air, pacing around the trailers and tiny homes and ranting about new, strange ideas. He wanted to start a new religion. He claimed he could morph his body into a gazelle and become one with nature and terrain. He was working toward unlocking the escape combination to the universe. If he could break out of this simulation controlled by artificial intelligence, he said to friends, he could become the new controller of the universe and heal everyone from all physical and mental maladies. He started offering everyone massages and would randomly start stretching while walking around Airstream Park. There were moments when his personality went from calm to manic to calm again, as if he were switching it on and off at will. When people asked Tony why he was acting so strangely, he told them it was Method acting.

He also started treating his friends in a way that was alarming and almost cruel. He gave friends "strikes"—like a parental warning issued to a misbehaving child—for interrupting him. He continued to pressure them to do ketamine with him, even when they made it clear that they did not want to. He started putting people on time-out. When his friends told him they were concerned, he offered them half of his net worth if they would sign a pact to never question him.

Tyler started to track Tony's sleep patterns on his Apple Watch—a feature that Tony shared with his close friends—and saw that he was barely sleeping. He also noticed his weight dropping. Tyler made steaks for him, a food that he knew Tony loved, but now they went uneaten.

Tyler was still getting pressured by Tony to do ketamine with him. He would oblige, but he was increasingly worried for his mentor. He wondered if Tony was in a drug-induced psychosis. Tyler started doing his own research, and came across a study in the *Shanghai Archive of Psychiatry* suggesting that about 60 percent of drug-induced psychosis cases can be resolved within a month if the person completely stops taking that drug, 30 percent of cases may persist for one to six months, and about 10 percent can persist for more than six months after drug use ends.

As the reality of the situation began to sink in, Tyler, after some cajoling, got Tony to agree to a pact: they would no longer use ketamine when Winter Camp was over at the end of January.

■ ■ ■

Despite a growing number of concerned friends watching Tony's behavior become more bizarre by the day, those around him still didn't do much to intervene. After all, he was *the* Tony Hsieh. Surely he could handle himself.

For instance, no one seemed too concerned when Tony proposed taking a trip to Maui with a few friends and a baby, to test whether polygamy-style parenting was possible. He had been discussing the concept with close friends for years. "I liked the concepts of the tribes who raised all their children as their own, regardless of whose kids," he once wrote in an email to a friend. "It exists to a smaller extent at Airstream park and I'm pretty confident if you researched you'd find it exists to a greater extent in the US."

The baby boy was Eva's, his ex-girlfriend who was still living at Airstream Park, and Tony was his godfather. Three other friends, including a recent entrant named Don Calder, who oversaw operations of a Burning Man sculpture park in a California ghost town called Nipton, and Jillian Tedrow, a former bartender at Bunkhouse Saloon, came along. Neither Eva nor the baby's father attended.

But some people who had known Tony for a long time felt the change in him more acutely. One night at Fergusons, Mark Guadagnoli, the university professor and former Zappos executive, arrived with his two teenage kids to have dinner with Tony and Michelle. In years past, Mark and Tony would embrace, make note of the fact they missed each other, and then enjoy themselves. But Mark had noticed that this Tony had less time to sit and be present. Tony spoke to Mark and his kids only briefly before disappearing to talk to others. Later, Mark realized that he had been watching his friend spin away like a golf ball. "If you put a little bit of right spin on the ball, it's gonna go straight for a while," he said later. Not until the last moment does the ball lurch away from its straight path.

■ ■ ■

Justin Weniger had also been having a hard time getting in contact with Tony. After what seemed a successful Life Is Beautiful, the festival had again lost money, despite its massive turnout. It was also the last festival Ryan Doherty would be involved with after he and Justin had split their business earlier in the year; Justin had sold his stake in Corner Bar Management, the entity that oversaw their growing portfolio of bars on Fremont Street, in exchange for Ryan's stake in Life Is Beautiful. In other words, Justin bet the farm on the festival.

On Tony's birthday in December, Justin sent him a message wishing him well. He didn't hear back. He did, however, have a meeting scheduled with Millie Chou, the Downtown Project's lawyer. After he arrived at her office, she told Justin he was being removed as CEO, and the festival's director of finance, a man named David Oehm, was replacing him. When Tony did respond days later, he said he had been busy digging himself out of emails and other matters and hadn't had a clue about Justin being removed as CEO. Later that week, Tony agreed to take a break from a poker tournament at Fergusons to meet with Justin.

"Either you knew it and you're a liar," Justin told him, "or you don't know it, and you're stupid. And I know you're not stupid."

Tony looked up at him with a tear in his eye and said something Justin hadn't heard from him before: "I'm sorry."

Two weeks later, Justin met with him at the El Cortez, and found Tony preoccupied by something. Sitting in the bar chain-smoking cigarettes, Tony told him that he was planning a surprise for Ryan Doherty in a few days: "So check this out. I want to turn the laundry room at Fergusons into a spoof of the Laundry Room at Commonwealth." Justin watched as Tony spoke with animation about how he wanted to show his appreciation to Ryan for creating experiences for people with his bars. He was going to blindfold Ryan, give him a vacuum-sealed frozen salmon, pick him up in a roadster from Commonwealth, and then drive him to Fergusons, where a party would be held in the laundry room, complete with chandeliers and furniture like those in the actual Laundry Room bar. *That was my bar and my business six months ago, and I gave it away to do Life Is Beautiful with you,* Justin thought. *Now you're rubbing my nose in it.*

Later, Justin went to the party and watched as Ryan took off his blindfold and put down the fish. Looking bewildered, Ryan walked around before wandering over to Justin. "What the fuck is going on?" he said.

■ ■ ■

Ryan's party was one of several events where Tony raised eyebrows. In January 2020, Michelle came to Vegas to help run social media at the Zappos holiday party. Though Michelle had been largely kept out of the loop regarding Tony's behavior at Winter Camp, she noticed he was unusually elated to see her. Throughout the weekend she woke up every morning to a series of text messages that Tony had sent at odd hours of the night, and she realized he wasn't sleeping. Seeing Tony, it made her think of one of her family members who is bipolar. "There's no other way to put it," she said later. "I've seen manic behavior."

Knowing how drugs and a lack of sleep could take a mental toll on her relative, she decided to raise her concerns to Tony in his trailer at Airstream Park.

"I'm worried about you," Michelle said. "Will you just get some sleep?"

"I'm totally fine," he said. "I will sleep tomorrow."

They went around in circles, talking for an hour. Eventually Michelle started to cry—she could not understand why he refused to sleep. He stared back at her with a blank face and left the trailer.

The next day, Michelle texted Tony to see if he was up. Yes, he wrote back, he had just woken up. Michelle, feeling a sense of relief that he had finally slept, walked over to his trailer to have one more chat before she flew back home to Milwaukee. When she got there, Tony led her to the back of the trailer. They sat on his bed facing the front of the trailer, and he showed her a wall of Post-it notes by the bed. The notes were arranged in a scale, and they were numbered from +3 to -3. Below each number were names of family members and friends.

"You were a plus two until last night," Tony said to her. "Now you're a negative one point five."

Michelle stared at the wall. She noticed that his parents, Richard and Judy, were on the negative scale.

"You were behaving like my parents," he said to her. "You were trying to control me. You were judging me, and I don't want to be judged."

"Okay," she said. She bit her lip to keep the tears from rolling down her face, and walked out of the trailer.

■ ■ ■

Eventually, word of Tony's behavior reached Zappos's top brass. Tyler, now a leader at Zappos who served as a direct conduit to Tony, found himself getting pulled into daily meetings with Zappos leadership. Executives like chief operating officer Kedar Deshpande, chief people officer Hollie Delaney, senior director of culture Christa Foley, and head of internal operations John Bunch were asking for daily updates on Tony's mental and physical state. But despite the alarming reports, they were unwilling to give up on Tony. He was more than just the CEO of Zappos—he *was* Zappos. Further, Kedar, who was effectively second-in-command, had only recently been promoted to the C-suite and was excited about the prospect of working with and learning from Tony.

So the leadership team at Zappos agreed not to alert Amazon to their CEO's current troubles. For decades, Tony had been the fearless leader of Zappos and the Downtown Project. Though he had gotten himself into tough spots before, he had always somehow conquered them. Why was this time any different?

Plus, Tony was still making efforts to keep up appearances. News of a novel and highly infectious virus called COVID-19 had emerged on the other side of the world, threatening to upend the world. Having first appeared in China, it was now showing up in Europe, and governments were being forced to shut down businesses, events, and their economies. Stay-at-home orders were introduced to limit human-to-human interaction. While it was only a matter of time before the virus arrived in the United States, Tony was still sticking to his social events calendar and in the last week of January he had gone to Park City, Utah, to attend the Sundance Film Festival.

But at the start of February, Tony's behavior reached a critical point.

He had been asked to officiate the local wedding of a couple who owned a beloved Thai restaurant downtown. While the bride wore a white qipao (a traditional, formfitting Chinese dress) and the groom wore a suit with a black tie, Tony showed up to the ceremony in a bright orange long-sleeved shirt. Holding a stretching stick covered in Post-it notes as he led the couple through their vows, Tony seemed high, and spoke in a slow and robotic drawl, drawing laughter from many of the wedding guests. Later, some people turned around to see Tony leading a yoga class during the reception.

What seemed funny to the crowd, and which might have been dismissed as "Tony being Tony" in years prior, was yet another alarm bell to his friends who had witnessed him unraveling over the last two months. Almost a dozen people at the wedding called and texted Tyler, who wasn't there, describing Tony's behavior. By this point, Tyler estimated that Tony was doing three to five grams of ketamine a day. Winter Camp was also over by now, and it was clear that Tony had broken the pact they'd made. That night, Tyler went to the trailer park and tried to talk to Tony about his behavior at the wedding. Tony told him that he had not been under the influence of ketamine and that he was simply engaging in Method acting.

"Tyler, you're starting to drain my energy," Tony said to him. "You're constantly coming at me." After their conversation, Tony asked people who had been at the wedding to call Tyler and tell him that they hadn't found his behavior concerning.

By this point, Tyler had started talking to interventionists and researching rehabilitation facilities. He was working with a few others close to Tony, including Ryan Doherty and Mimi Pham, to try to get him to commit to getting help. Tyler also knew he was on thin ice. Tony was worried that his friends were talking about him behind his back—which they were—but he concluded that much of the impetus stemmed from Tyler, and he was becoming increasingly agitated by Tyler's concern.

Taking place beyond the confines of Airstream Park and Fergusons, the wedding had marked a tipping point. Tony's drug use was now an open secret in downtown Las Vegas. And it wasn't just concern for Tony's well-being: he was the central nerve for Zappos, which employed fifteen hundred people and was owned by one of the largest corporations in the world. He was also financing all of the Downtown Project, a city within a city that could crumble if anything happened to him.

Enough was enough. Tony needed to leave Las Vegas and either be immersed in a new environment, away from his access to drugs, or go to a rehab facility. So the night after the wedding, Tyler and one of Tony's former girlfriends entered Tony's trailer and embarked on a heated negotiation with Tony to try to convince him to get out of town, maybe to a place that Tony loved like Park City, Utah. He attended the Sundance Film Festival there every year, he loved to ski, and it was tranquil, far from the sins and impulses of Vegas. He was also in the process of purchasing a house there. "Let's take a group of friends," Tyler pleaded, "and let's just get out of here."

But after a marathon six hours, they were unable to get Tony to commit. At around four o'clock in the morning, Tyler decided to leave the trailer, sensing that Tony had no fight left in him.

Tony remained a scarce presence and barely left his trailer over the next couple of days. Others at Fergusons talked about staging an intervention, but couldn't seem to pin him down.

Among them was Ryan Doherty, who arrived at Fergusons the following evening for a scheduled meeting with Tony. After Ryan waited among the Airstream trailers for hours, Tony never came out to greet him, and he eventually left.

Though the next morning, Ryan returned, and this time walked into Tony's trailer, shutting the door behind him.

Several hours later, the two men emerged and left Fergusons bound for the airport.

CHAPTER 21

FLOW STATE

Tyler stood outside 255 Park Avenue in Utah's Park City and looked up at the house before him through his thick-rimmed glasses. He'd been here many times before. It was right in the heart of Old Town on a street carved into the side of the mountain, as if floating above Park City's saloons and restaurants. Tyler scanned the property—the gray ledger stones framing the wooden garage door, the olive-green weatherboards, its snow-covered roof, and the neighboring houses on either side, one painted in a rich cerulean and the other in farmhouse red. From Main Street, the house was just one of hundreds of vibrant and picturesque ski houses that dotted the mountainside, giving Park City its postcard charm. As he took in the crisp air, Tyler thought back to his last stay here, just a few weeks prior, recalling how he'd felt the last time he was inside this house.

Tony usually rented 255 Park Avenue every year for the Sundance Film Festival, the ten-day affair in Park City at the end of January when Hollywood actors, directors, press, and other industry folk descend on the high-end ski town. Indie film premieres and heavy libations at corporate-sponsored lounges were followed by star-studded afterparties. Beginning in the early 2010s, Silicon Valley became a regular presence at Sundance. Google would host concerts at TAO, a nightclub on Main Street, while Microsoft, still hoping for the success of its search engine, Bing, would take every opportunity to sponsor events and plug its search brand. As Hollywood continued its shift toward digital media, the growing technorati found more and more reasons to bill a trip to the artsy, glitzy event as a corporate outing.

The lodge on Park Avenue was a five-minute walk from the Sundance box office. In years past, Tony would host breakfasts, lunches, and dinners for his friends and guests inside the home. Mimi and Tyler often organized the gatherings, attended by other tech founders and a sprinkle of Hollywood stars. One Los Angeles–based music branding agent who introduced Tony to actor David Arquette and whose clients included hip-hop artists Mary J. Blige and Anderson .Paak said she always made it a point to see Tony at Sundance. "He would rent that home and curate different dinners and conversations," she said. "He wanted to be around that kind of energy and creativity."

Despite Tony's alarming behavior at Winter Camp, attending the film festival had offered what appeared to be a brief return to normalcy in Tony's life just days before he officiated the wedding. That year for Sundance, Zappos partnered with a digital content company called HitRecord, which was co-founded by Joseph Gordon-Levitt, the actor who would go on to play Uber founder Travis Kalanick in a Showtime special called *Super Pumped*, based on the book of the same name by *New York Times* journalist Mike Isaac. Together, they aired ten mini-documentaries at Sundance, each representing one of Zappos's ten core values. Tony spent time with Joseph at the festival, as well as with singer Paula Abdul, whom he had met just a few weeks prior. Paula came to Sundance at Tony's invitation and even stayed on a bunk bed in one of the rooms at Tony's rented lodge. "A trip to Sundance and Zappos all in one week!?" Abdul tweeted. "So fun hanging out with these amazing people that have become my new friends!!"

It might have seemed like any other year, but Tony did not stop doing ketamine for the film festival. Though many who kept company with him were unaware of his increasing habit, he made no effort to hide it in front of Tyler. One night, while the other guests were asleep at the house, Tyler agreed to stay up late with Tony and watch *The Matrix*. Under the drug's influence, Tony insisted that the two of them do ketamine together and reenact scenes from the film between Morpheus and Neo. "I don't want to," Tyler replied.

It was a phrase that Tyler had started saying more in recent weeks as

Tony's requests to do ketamine escalated. Sometimes Tyler would say yes, but as time wore on, he would say no more often than not. It was then usually followed by Tyler telling his boss how he did not like the way Tony behaved on the drug and what his episodes were doing to the wider Airstream community. But Tony always knew exactly what to say to get Tyler to lay off. *I only need to do it for a little longer to figure some things out,* Tony would say, or *I'm dealing with a lot emotionally, and this is the only thing that's helping me.* Tyler would look at his boss and relent.

But at Sundance, the conversation went in a different direction.

"I wish I had a Tyler coin," Tony said one day, staring at Tyler sitting on the couch, "that I could just put into you, and you would do anything that I asked."

Tyler stared back. To think that this might have been Tony's intention all along—that he had been investing all this time and energy into Tyler not because he wanted to mentor him but as a means to groom him into a blind follower—was disturbing. Tyler could barely believe this was the same Tony he had looked up to for so many years.

In the weeks since Sundance, Tony's unraveling had become a public conversation after the wedding in downtown Las Vegas. Inside Tony's Airstream trailer, Ryan Doherty, who had previous experience helping friends with addiction issues, had gotten Tony to commit to finding help by convincing him that if he didn't go to rehab on his own terms, he would lose control of his own narrative if Zappos—or even worse, Amazon—stepped in and forced him to. With Mimi's assistance in making arrangements, he had boarded a private jet with Tony to take him to the facility near Park City. When speaking to friends, Tony had told them that rehab would be like beating a boss in a video game. Tyler didn't know quite what to make of Tony's comparison, but he still felt a tinge of hope.

A week into his stay, Tony called Tyler and asked him to write a list of all the things that he had done in the last few months that seemed concerning. Tony then asked him to come to Park City and present it to him when he was out of rehab. "We can go over the list one by one," Tony said over the phone. It was strange, Tyler thought, but in some ways it was a very Tony kind of ask. It seemed logical and methodical—much the way Tony had always approached and hacked through problems in the past.

While Tyler remained optimistic, Tony stayed in rehab for not quite two weeks before checking himself out of the facility. It had not been enough time, Tyler thought, thinking about the Shanghai Mental Health Center research about how long a person needs to be clean before coming out of a drug-induced psychosis. It simply did not seem like enough time. But it didn't matter what Tyler thought; Tony was already out. A week after Tony's rehab stint had ended, Tyler was now back in Park City, standing in front of 255 Park Avenue, nervously waiting for Tony.

Tony emerged from the house, and they decided to walk to Pink Elephant, a discreet coffee shop on the second floor of a small black building on Main Street. As they walked past snow-covered porches and down the grated steel outdoor stairs that connected the residential streets to the bustling corridor of Old Town, Tyler stole glances at Tony. He seemed normal and calm enough, Tyler thought. Reaching Main Street, they took a quick left and walked inside a multiuse retail space, through a gold-painted door frame and past racks of trendy ski wear, past the buzzing sounds emanating from the clippers at Billy's Barber Shop, then up a flight of stairs that brought them to the coffee bar. Tyler ordered a coffee, black, while Tony opted out of a drink. Once Tyler fetched his cup from the barista, the two settled around a small round table. The coffee shop was noisy and crowded, not uncomfortably, but just enough to mask the strange conversation that was about to unfold.

"So what's on your list?" Tony asked. Tyler pulled the letter out of his pocket and started reading it out loud. He never made eye contact with his mentor as he read. "You said you were becoming Neo from *The Matrix*," Tyler started. "That you were transcending human consciousness. You said you were achieving *Limitless*, unlocking your full brain," referring to the 2011 science fiction movie about a man who takes a drug called NZT-48 that exponentially enhances his intelligence and emotional quotients. The list continued:

You said you could run a three-hour marathon without training.
You said you could grow your height, so that you were seven foot tall.
You said people are molecules.
You said you could download skills, like in *The Matrix*.

You offered a million dollars for somebody to wake you up.

You were telling people, "I'm not mad at you. Because if I were mad at you, it would be like being mad at the dog."

You said you didn't have to pee anymore, that your body could recycle urine.

You said you could manifest things like create water from a spigot.

You said you could solve and cure COVID.

You could solve world peace.

You were interpretative dancing.

You were pretending like you were inside movies.

You started talking like a robot, and started speaking in other made-up languages.

You barely slept.

You forgot things and had no memory.

Reckless, fearless, open drug use, giving everybody a book about ketamine and talking openly about it.

Not enjoying the things you normally like.

The wedding, going from normal to manic.

Putting people on time-out for lowering your energy flow.

Your physical appearance. Weight loss, bruising on your body. Hollow eyes.

Pulled muscles, you were clearly in pain. Blank looks. Stares. No energy.

Tyler slowly looked up. Tony was staring straight at him, giving little away. After a moment of silence, Tony spoke.

"I need to stack all of that as the combination," Tony said, his gaze never leaving Tyler's. "It's all the key to exiting into the next dimension."

Tyler stared back, the same way he had when Tony brought up the idea of a Tyler coin. As he processed what Tony just said, days out of rehab, he came to one simple conclusion: *Tony is still not okay.*

■ ■ ■

Tyler came and went from Park City over the next few weeks, joining a revolving door of friends and family arriving in town to check on Tony. His family—Richard, Judy, Andy, and Dave—were among the first to arrive, and they stayed at a nearby lodge. Tyler, it turned out, was one in a small circle of people who knew Tony had been in rehab. During his time in rehab, Tony was able to use his phone, and he had been sending messages to others, urging them to join him in Park City and stay with him at the rented house in the days after his release. Justin had been flying home from a work trip to Bermuda when he received a text from Tony asking him to come to Park City. Despite Justin's demotion from Life Is Beautiful, he'd heard about Tony's stay in rehab, and decided to go and see him. Suzie Baleson, who had attended events and parties as Tony's plus-one for years and had run into Tony at Sundance just a few weeks before, also accepted an invitation from Tony to join him in Park City. Zappos executives and a younger crowd of friends also got the call-up. Ryan Doherty, however, was not welcome: Tony believed Ryan had duped him into going to rehab under false pretenses, and deemed him persona non grata.

Tony indicated that he intended to stay in the town for the foreseeable months, a decision cemented by his purchase of a new ski lodge at 1422 Empire Avenue, a chalet sunk into a sloping neighborhood a half mile from Main Street. He'd first inquired about the property when he'd been in town for Sundance, and after a month of negotiating, he took over the building.

Across the street from a parking lot at the bottom of Park City mountain, where skiers and snowboarders trudged awkwardly toward the chairlifts, the five-bedroom property was impressive. Hardwood beams as thick as trees emerged from cemented blocks of river rock, holding up the eaves that framed the front of the home. Thanks to two pines that stood on either side of the short driveway, and neighboring homes that looked like they were designed by the same architect, the property was barely noticeable to passersby.

The unassuming exterior belied a grandiosity within. At the center of the house was a timber staircase that spiraled up three floors like a drill bit. Walls and ceilings had exposed framing, giving the feel of a wealthy man's log cabin, and the hardwood floors were covered in immaculate rugs. In the mornings, Tony could wake up in the master bedroom to a vivid panorama of the famed mountain through two red-framed doors that opened onto a balcony hanging over the garage.

He first invited Suzie and Justin to stay at the lodge with him, along with an assistant, Juliet. Justin had most of his wealth tied up in the Life Is Beautiful festival, and now, with all live events canceled for the foreseeable future, it was entirely unclear whether the festival would survive. The cancellation of live events had also impacted a large chunk of Suzie's prospective income. Her company, Wellth Collective, had been planning to organize events at SXSW—which was now canceled—and many of her clients were cutting back on marketing expenditures. Aside from seeing their friend, being in proximity to a man as wealthy as Tony would have been a comforting notion as they stared down the uncertainty of the pandemic.

At first, they implemented a regimented program around Tony, reasoning that if he was in recovery, then his environment should revolve around health, wellness, and productivity. The space became a co-working and living area where Tony could receive his guests and work on sporadic projects. Suzie ordered workout equipment and a Peloton exercise bike to turn one room into a gym, while Justin started organizing hikes through the mountains.

Over the coming months, however, those who entered Tony's orbit found themselves in situations that prior to Tony going to rehab would have been considered "normal." But now the shots of Fernet, hours-long trips on psychedelic mushrooms, and spending his money at his request on dinners, accommodations, real estate, and private jets all came across differently.

He often seemed coherent during walks at dawn through the mountains and during dinners at the lodge. His obsession with devouring books also had not abated and on most mornings he and Justin would allocate an hour to reading followed by discussion. This would then lead to Tony writing his conclusions on Post-it notes and slapping them on walls around the house, creating a dizzying visual scene of his thoughts. But it was hard to ignore that his outlandish ideas, once seen as the musings of a contrarian thinker, could now be interpreted as symptoms of psychosis.

Along with Tyler, several other members of the Zappos leadership had been making trips to Park City. Tony hadn't been out of rehab for long, and his future at the company was increasingly unclear. Over barbecues and meetings in the lodge's vast interior to discuss work matters, company leaders like Kedar Deshpande and John Bunch, the latter leading the rollout of Zappos's market-based dynamics program, listened as Tony dictated new ways to run the company.

It was difficult to ignore that Tony's behaviors were a significant departure from his typical demeanor during discussions with leadership. Normally he would sit quietly in a corner and type on his laptop, occasionally speaking up to offer a thought, or sometimes not speaking at all. Now he was commanding a room for thirty minutes at a time without letting others talk, and directing the Zappos leaders to execute wildly irrational ideas.

For years, he had been fixated on the concept of flow states, a widely held belief in Silicon Valley and upper corporate circles that individuals can improve their output and well-being by striving to be "in the zone." One text he frequently invoked was *Stealing Fire*, a bestselling book that outlined a road map for achieving a state of positive psychology. One of the authors, Steven Kotler, had previously written another bestselling book, *The Rise of Superman*, which studied the neuroscience behind the peak performance of action sports athletes. With *Stealing Fire*, he and co-author Jamie Wheal expanded that research to conclude that seemingly any discipline could achieve an "optimal state of consciousness where we feel our best and perform our best." After consulting and studying the methods of CEOs, Navy SEALs, and scientists, they argued that when this state is achieved, motivations like self-awareness and time fall away as mental and physical performance takes hold. It's easy to imagine a jazz player reaching this state every time they pick up an instrument, for example, but harder to picture an academic being in the zone for weeks at a time to finish their dissertation. Its teachings didn't veer too far from the Challenge Point Framework that Mark Guadagnoli had espoused all those years ago at the steakhouse in Henderson with Fred, Alfred, and Tony, describing how giving people a task of optimal difficulty can help them learn faster.

While he talked about how he was trying to achieve his own flow state, Tony told the executives that the concept should be scaled up from individuals to the entire Zappos workforce. Under other circumstances the idea could have been seen as just another one of Tony's edgy, if sometimes weird, ideas to manage his company. After all, these executives were working for a company that had a corporate culture unlike any other company of its scale, where employees had tripped on psychedelic drugs with the CEO at Burning Man, visited his home at his trailer park, and led wild parades through the company offices.

To achieve company-wide flow state, Tony proposed, they should entirely do away with organizational calendars and instead introduce a new way of managing schedules: if everyone was in the same flow state, they would just know where to be, and when to join meetings. More than once he said that if all the employees were in the same flow state, then he could show them his superpowers.

As he pushed the patience of Zappos leaders, he developed an obsessive focus on testing the boundaries of his own mental and physical strength. Over the years at conferences, Tony had met Wim "the Ice Man" Hof, the Dutch athlete known for his ability to expose his body to conditions of extreme cold, and had been somewhat intrigued by his achievements. Hof first gained renown for swimming a record fifty-seven meters under an ice sheet, then went on to set numerous Guinness World Records for feats like running the fastest barefoot half-marathon across ice and spending the longest time in direct contact with ice (more than two hours). In an ultimate show of his ability, he once climbed 24,500 feet up Mount Everest wearing only shorts (he aborted the ultimate mission to the peak due to a foot injury).

Using a combination of yoga, meditation, cold exposure, and breathing techniques, Hof had been able to defy what were commonly thought of as the limits of the human body. Dutch scientists had studied Hof's practices and found that, in short, he had developed a heightened control of his body's stress hormones. He had gained a following of people trying to emulate his practices and launched an eponymous patented regimen that employed his disciples to teach others how to test the limits of their bodies. As it turned out, one of these disciples worked in Utah, so Tony hired him to spend time at the lodge, training him and his friends on how to implement Hof's methods into his own daily regimen. Tony started doing away with shoes on hikes through the surrounding mountains. One day, he, Justin, and Tyler sat next to one another in gigantic ice buckets on the rear deck after a lengthy meditation and breathing exercises. Tony and Justin would go on jogs through the town wearing only T-shirts, even as snow fell around them in below-freezing temperatures.

Hof's teachings planted a seed within Tony to study the much broader field of biohacking. The concept had become popular recently in Silicon Valley, where prominent tech leaders like Twitter CEO Jack Dorsey had begun to talk about their embrace of it. In addition to cold exposure therapy and enhanced breathing techniques, Dorsey had spoken about eating only one meal a day and fasting completely on weekends as a way to improve his tolerance of stress and optimize other aspects of his health. Others had invoked biohacking as the logic behind various experiments aimed to increase longevity. Dave Asprey, the self-described "father of biohacking" who founded the Silicon Valley supplement startup Bulletproof Nutrition, underwent an operation where a doctor harvested stem cells from his bone marrow and then injected them back into his body in the hope that it would enable him to live to 180 years old. And in the far nether regions of biohacking are people who call themselves "grinders," those who implant computer chips under their skin in experiments to wire the brain directly to a digital output. While such efforts sound radical to most people, they have become widely accepted, even adopted, as ways to further the realm of productivity and individual betterment within Silicon Valley, a place where its leaders consistently pioneer what was previously thought unimaginable. Living longer, for example, is something that Larry Ellison, Jeff Bezos, and Peter Thiel have each spent millions of dollars on researching. But as his fixation on biohacking and flow states deepened, Tony was venturing closer to a dark rabbit hole from which he might not escape.

His friends in Park City tried to find comfort in reverting to their old habits, despite his changing behavior and ever-grander visions. Some clinked shots of Fernet with him. For some Zappos executives, the longstanding bizarre corporate culture seemed to be re-creating itself on a smaller scale in Park City. Brandon Hollis, Zappos's chief legal counsel, was often around, either manning the barbecue or downing drinks with his boss. Tyler and Tony would embark on so-called hero's journeys, where they would take a handful of hallucinogenic mushrooms and trip for half a day while remaining motionless—something they had done many times before. Despite Tyler's concern for Tony, there were parts of their friendship that he appeared unable to let go of.

By April, another element was added to Tony's vortex of people: a crew of younger friends who were there to party and have fun.

■ ■ ■

At 3:22 p.m. on the last Saturday of May, President Donald Trump and Vice President Mike Pence watched from a viewing pad in Cape Canaveral, Florida, as a rocketship lifted off, en route to space. Made by SpaceX, Elon Musk's aerospace manufacturer, the flight was historic, marking the first privately owned spaceship to carry astronauts into space and heralding a new era in spaceflight. It also was the first time astronauts had eschewed NASA's Airstream-built Astrovan to shuttle them to the launch pad since spaceflight began in 1961. Instead, they climbed into Musk-owned Tesla SUVs while listening to AC/DC.

On a television screen within 1422 Empire Avenue in Park City, Tony was also watching as the rocket passed through the stratosphere. Tony had often talked about Elon Musk. Elon's pronouncements about a multiverse and the concept that we are all living in a simulation were things that Tony believed in, and for that reason he saw Elon as an equal. Tony had long harbored Elon's belief, shared by many people who build artificial intelligence technology, that humans exist in multiple dimensions and our current experience is no more than a simulation. Just as with religion, only faith binds its believers, but the notion has recently taken on new dimensions, so to speak, with Facebook's introduction of a "metaverse," where one can interact with others in a virtual world.

Tony believed Elon Musk was a person of a caliber shared by Jeff Bezos and Steve Jobs, a group that he saw himself as a part of. Surrounding him in the lodge were Zappos employees who he deemed had failed to execute on ideas, like implementing a company-wide flow. Not only were they not doing as he demanded; they were becoming a frequent presence in his home. He'd been especially incensed by the presence in his house of Brandon Hollis, who in his role as general counsel of Zappos had been reporting back to executives what he'd been seeing. Brandon had also relaxed into the comfort of Tony's home and had been staying there without asking Tony if he minded. (Brandon later disputed this, stating that Tony "expressly" invited him and provided "continued permission" for him to stay at 1422 Empire.) At one point a guest of his came to stay for several weeks, and then another guest Brandon had invited came to stay.

As Tony stared at the television screen, a tap was dripping in his mind. Then the faucet broke.

"I've been doing it all wrong," he said, standing up in the middle of the room. He picked up his laptop, sat at a nearby table, and began bashing the keyboard. It looked as if he was hardwired into the computer itself.

For as long as he could remember, he'd been trying to empower others. What he really needed to do, he told those in the room, was to operate at his own full mental capacity. Just as Elon was sending astronauts into space, Tony's intellect and drive could come up with a cure for COVID-19. He would usher in world peace. No goal would be too grand. All he needed was to reach the flow state.

"We have to go faster," he said, not looking away from the screen.

He paused momentarily to scribble messages on Post-it notes, which he stuck on the wall. The words "flow state" appeared among arrows and other markings. Those standing around him exchanged glances.

Tony wanted people who could execute his vision, whatever that may be. "I need the message to get out to people that I'm willing to pay top dollar."

■ ■ ■

There was a lot happening when Tyler walked into the house that afternoon. He could see that a new array of Post-it notes now covered the wall behind where Tony was sitting, and people were quietly muttering to one another. One person said something about Tony having a revelation. Taking in the scene of the living room, Brandon approached Tyler with a baffled look on his face. Brandon told him that Tony had set him and another person an objective: to get everyone in the same flow state. If they could achieve the task, then he would pay him $100,000. Brandon acquiesced to Tony's insistence, though he told Tyler he had at least negotiated the figure down to $10,000.

Tyler suggested they rent a pontoon boat at Deer Creek Reservoir, about twenty miles south of Park City. If everyone was chatting, eating, drinking, and swimming together, Tyler reasoned, then perhaps Tony would see that everyone was in a synchronized flow state.

A short time later, the two Zappos executives and Tony joined half a dozen others, including Suzie and Justin, in a black Sprinter van parked in front of Tony's chalet. One of Tony's on-again off-again girlfriends, Ali Bevilacqua, was there, too. With Tyler behind the wheel as the Sprinter wound its way south, everyone seemed excited for the day ahead. Tony had a serene look on his face.

As the only person in the group who knew how to drive a boat, Tyler volunteered to be captain for the day. The passengers were giddy as the boat, stocked with drinks, food, and blankets, put-putted away from the shore.

Almost as soon as the land began to recede behind them, the calm was interrupted by a disturbing storm in the form of Tony. As the sun crested high above the lake, Tyler looked over from the boat's controls to see something change in Tony's demeanor, as if a switch had been flicked. Tony had a Sharpie in his hand and was scribbling what appeared to be Egyptian hieroglyphs on his arms and torso. Others turned their heads to steal a glance at him before averting their eyes. The more furiously he dragged the marker over his body, the more he began muttering to himself. He flinched and tightened his jaw, and some heard him spitting the words "flow state."

He stood up and stalked to the rear of the boat, where he sat in the shade of the upper deck. As the boat idled in the middle of the lake, Tony's flinching became more violent.

Someone jumped into the lake, making a splash.

"You are interrupting my flow state," Tony yelled. "I need to be in a flow state."

He lurched up, snatched a blanket, and climbed up to the upper deck. Everyone watched in silence as he curled up in a fetal position and pulled the blanket over him. His mumbling continued, sometimes breaking out into incoherent shouts. The words "flow state" kept coming.

Tyler steered the pontoon boat back to shore. The fun was over. Everyone was mostly silent on the journey home, and once they reached the chalet, a quiet fell over the house. Ali was sobbing to herself. Others looked ashen-faced. Tony, they believed, seemed to have found more ketamine.

Tyler trudged up the winding staircase to Tony's bedroom. Until they'd set out on the boat that afternoon, Tyler had been hopeful Tony might be changing for the better. Now it was clear that Tony had found his kryptonite, and Tyler's hope was replaced with dread. As he reached the top of the stairs, he looked up to see Tony standing in the doorway.

Before Tyler could say anything, Tony said, "Hey, I just want you to know. I was acting."

Tyler stared back at him.

"I had tasked Brandon to get everyone in flow, and I was trying to be a hindrance," Tony said.

Tyler looked back at him with quiet disappointment. Tony sensed it.

"Can you tell everybody in the house that that's what I was doing?" Tony said.

Before Tyler turned to go back downstairs, Tony said something that made Tyler feel defeated.

"If you don't question me again," Tony said, "I'll give you half my net worth."

CHAPTER 22

THE GORDIAN KNOT

"Let's go for a walk," Tony said. "I've got a surprise."

It was a morning in early June in the midst of the COVID-19 pandemic, and Justin was standing in the living room of the lodge. Tony's episode on the boat had made clear to the group that he was far from okay. Justin, Tyler, and others had concluded that Tony may have acquired more ketamine during a visit from Anthony in the days before they went out on the lake, and they had each taken turns demanding that Anthony not provide Tony with drugs. While Tyler had left for Vegas to put some space between him and Tony, Justin had reached an agreement with Tony and scrawled the terms of a new "contract" on a piece of paper, stipulating that Tony would not do any chemical drugs for thirty days—specifically ketamine—and that if he planned to do mushrooms, he would have to notify Justin ahead of time. The penalty would be a loss of friendship, and Tony would need to donate to a charity.

Justin walked out the front door, following Tony as he took a left, heading south down Empire Avenue. "Pop quiz," Tony said, turning to him. "Do you remember the year Zappos was founded?"

They took another left down a side street, and Justin thought for a moment. There was a woman who worked behind the front desk in the lobby of Zappos's Las Vegas headquarters who was a huge Prince fan. Under the company's market-based dynamics program, which encouraged employees to start their own ventures within the company, she had launched her own bar in the lobby called the 1999 Bar—in honor both of Prince's famous song and of the year that Zappos was founded.

They took another left down a street that ran parallel to Empire Avenue. "It was 1999," Justin replied.

They walked for another minute, and then Tony stopped in front of a towering three-story house clad with navy and brown timbers, built on a river-rock foundation. It looked more suited for a corporate retreat than a weekend getaway with friends. Justin figured you could throw a stone over the property's back fence and hit the lodge they had just walked from.

"Go type it into that door right there," Tony said, pointing to a keypad on the front door.

Bewildered, Justin walked over to the door and pressed in the code. The door clicked open.

"Well," Tony said, gesturing, "let's go in, then."

Tony had grown tired of the constant stream of people coming and going from his lodge at 1422 Empire, so he'd decided to rent this mansion around the block as a way to reclaim his privacy. His thinking, he told Justin, was that he could get people like Brandon Hollis out of his home, while employing other friends, like Jillian, who'd managed one of his now-shuttered Las Vegas bars, to run the property. It also fit in with his plans to create a new community in Park City. Artists, entrepreneurs, and others could come to see him and pitch him on ideas of how they were going to build something, just as previous entrepreneurs and guests had done while staying at Tony's apartments in the Ogden.

Complete with a Jacuzzi, indoor gym, billiards room, elevator, and sauna, the ten-bedroom, ten-bathroom mansion was listed on rental websites like Expedia and Vrbo as the "Epic Lodge." Tony had struck an agreement with the owner to lease the property on a month-to-month basis, with an option to perhaps buy it.

"I want you to make this the Life Is Beautiful house," Tony said, walking through the home. He had been coming up with all sorts of ideas for Life Is Beautiful since the pandemic had canceled the festival. Justin's proximity to Tony also meant that his role remained central to Life Is Beautiful, and Tony had been discussing some ideas with him for how he could lead it forward.

A few weeks before, they had hiked up Park City mountain and reached the backside of the slope, where Tony had first spotted what he believed was a natural amphitheater in the mountainside. Turning to Justin, Tony had proposed they launch a COVID-friendly festival, where everyone could socially distance outside. Tony would give Justin $100 million to pull it off. Justin had ignored the proposal, and he was now shooting down this idea. Most of the festival's employees had been furloughed; immediately occupying a multimillion-dollar house named after the festival would make for terrible optics.

After some wrangling, Tony proposed the property be called the "Welcome House," and that it would serve as base camp for the dozens of people that Tony was inviting into town to help him create his new community. The contradiction between Tony's need for privacy and his instinct to invite anyone who'd come and stay on his dime wasn't lost on Justin. But, Justin figured, if Tony could make it thirty days without another drug-induced psychotic break and was surrounded by people looking to innovate, then perhaps they could build from there.

■ ■ ■

On the morning of June 27, Steve Maroney, a man who went by his nickname Steve-O, and who had been a driver for Tony for years, steered his coach into Park City. Along with Tyler and a half dozen others, including Ava Zech, the daughter of a Zappos executive whom Tony had dedicated his memoir to when she was just eleven years old, Steve-O had driven overnight from Vegas, and was stopping in Utah to pick up Tony and Justin before heading north to Montana for the annual July 4 trip. In years past, the Montana trip was one of the highlights of the year. The group would stay at a lodge on the eastern bank of Flathead Lake, facing the Blacktail Mountains. Aside from daily barbecues and hikes, the group would typically work remotely during the day and Tony would feverishly respond to emails. Then, when the clock struck 5 p.m., happy hour would commence, and the libations would come out.

This year was different from others, however. Not only because of pandemic-imposed hurdles, but because it was unclear whether Tony would slip again.

The jury was still out on whether Tony was making his way back to reality. He'd spent the past few weeks focused on business ideas and had shown some determination to get back on track. He'd stuck to his commitment to Justin and appeared to have stayed away from drugs. He was still devouring books, and he had resolved his privacy issue: Brandon Hollis and others had now settled into bedrooms in the Welcome House.

Word had also spread far and wide that Tony was looking to do deals and was spending his money again, like in the early days of the Downtown Project in Las Vegas. More people arrived in town at his invitation, as well as on his promises of vast sums of money and a mandate only to build *something*. Tony had been leading the ever-growing group hiking through Park City's mountains each morning. To manage the influx of guests arriving at the Welcome House, Suzie struck an agreement with Tony to use her company, Wellth Collective, to manage the operations of the house— organizing transportation, events, and accommodations—for a fee.

People from all eras of Tony's life were arriving by the busload with business ideas. One new arrival was asked to build a 3D printing lab at the Welcome House. Another group of people pitched an idea for cashing in on the COVID-19-driven boom in demand for personal protective equipment.

One apparent deal had consumed him: a virtual reality company that had agreements with commercial landlords to set up demonstrations in malls. While the pandemic had forced malls across the country to close, putting the virtual reality company at risk of bankruptcy, something obscure got Tony's attention. As he described it to Justin, the company had exclusive rights to stream Disney-owned content in live settings—a clause that Tony proclaimed would return a billion-dollar payoff once people returned to malls. He was determined to raise funding for the company and save it, but a deadline to invest was looming in the week before July 4, and so he asked Justin to help him close it. In Tony's mind, he was the one who could identify million-dollar ideas that could become billion-dollar companies, and he was going to pay whatever people asked.

Despite cautious optimism about Tony's condition, Tyler had been somewhat reticent about reentering Tony's Park City orbit. Since he'd been back in Vegas, he had been receiving calls from several people who had seen Tony in Park City. Tony had been talking maniacally at points, they told Tyler, returning to his goals of ensuring world peace and curing COVID-19. Tony had conducted some meetings while in his underwear.

Other times he talked about how he had psychic abilities and had learned how to levitate.

After stepping off the bus, Tyler walked into the Welcome House for the first time and saw faces he didn't know. His concerns were confirmed when he learned about one woman staying at the Welcome House. She was a Zappos employee who worked in the tech department and had arrived in town at Tony's invitation. After meeting Tony for the first time, he had offered to give her $10 million to start a new business with undefined goals. She barely knew him, and had expressed her discomfort to a friend when Tony had asked her if she would join him on the July 4 trip to Montana as a plus-one.

Tyler found Tony and interrupted a one-on-one meeting he was having. Tony was visibly enraged, but Tyler calmly said the Zappos employee wouldn't be joining them in Park City, nor did she want to accept his multimillion-dollar offer.

■ ■ ■

The Montana trip seemed destined to be a failure before it even started. For one, there seemed to be something off with Tony. As the group prepared to leave Park City, he had walked onto the bus wearing nothing but pajama pants and holding only a box of crayons. As the bus wound out of Park City, he emerged from his bedroom at the rear of the bus and called for everyone's attention. There would be a change of plans: he and Justin would spend only twelve hours in Montana, using each hour to complete an activity they would typically do during the week-long trip. One hour for jumping in the lake. One hour to do the mouse race. One hour at Burger Shack, and so on. Then he and Justin would take the bus back to Park City that night and work on the virtual reality deal for the rest of the week.

The bus was quiet for a moment, and then Ava spoke up. "That's a bummer," she said. "We don't go to Montana just to go to Montana. We go to Montana because that's the time that we get to spend with you when you're not working."

Tony's expression flickered, and his eyes drifted around the cabin coldly. "Well, I'm paying for everyone to be here. You should all be more grateful." He looked at Ava's boyfriend and noted aloud that he was on the trip, all expenses paid. His eyes then fell on Tyler. "Tyler, you never pay attention," he said. Tyler sat in silence as Tony assigned him a percentage rating for his supposed attention span. Tony then berated Tyler for having poor bus etiquette and leaving his shoes on the bunk. After hurling more insults, Tony retired to his bedroom. Justin followed him.

■ ■ ■

The bus was rolling through the Montana plains when an alarm woke Tyler soon after dawn. During his rant, Tony had told Tyler he would pay him $1 million to wake him up at 8 a.m., giving him enough time to prepare before their 10 a.m. arrival at the lodge. After climbing out of his bunk, Tyler walked to Tony's bedroom and saw that the room was a mess, but Tony wasn't there. In the bathroom, past Tony's bed, Tyler could hear the shower running. *He's up already,* Tyler figured. He knocked on the bathroom door, but no one responded.

Tyler went to the front of the bus and chatted with Steve-O as the bus pushed north. Twenty minutes later, he went and knocked on the bathroom door again. Still no answer. *This is a really long shower,* thought Tyler. He knocked a half dozen times over the next hour and a half without response.

It was almost ten o'clock when the bus reached the lodge and swung into the parking lot. Tyler went to check on Tony once more, but this time he saw water seeping from under the bathroom door. He knocked furiously and called out until he was jolted by a response.

"*Get Justin,*" Tony screamed from behind the door. "*Everyone else get the fuck off the bus.*"

Tyler sighed deeply. He walked to Justin's bunk and shook him awake. "Good luck, man," Tyler said.

Once everyone had filed off the bus and headed to check into the lodge, Justin crouched outside the bathroom. The floor was wet. "What's going on?" he said through the door.

"Justin, is that you?" Tony replied.

"Yeah."

"Are you alone?"

"Yeah."

Justin could hear the shower still running. Before they'd gone to bed last night, he and Tony had chatted briefly in Tony's bedroom. Tony had even told a few jokes, and he was under the impression Tony had cooled off since railing against his guests.

Justin looked around Tony's bedroom. It was a mess. His eyes fell to the bed, where he saw a crumpled gold foil wrapper. He'd seen them before, back at the Empire Avenue house in Park City: they were used to store magic-mushroom-infused chocolates. Then he saw a second wrapper, and a third. He counted five in total. A single mushroom chocolate could typically induce a hallucinogenic trip for hours, even an entire day. Whatever Tony was experiencing now would be beyond what any mind could sustain.

Justin walked back to the bathroom door, and was hit by the smell of shit. The shower had stopped running. "The water, I need the water, I need the water," Tony yelled. The bus's tank, it seemed, was empty. Justin stepped off the bus and tried to think. The gray water would begin backing up through the shower drain and flood the bus with sewage if they refilled the tank before draining the gray water tank first. And dumping the gray water in the lodge's parking lot wasn't an option.

Back on the bus, Justin told Tony through the bathroom door that the shower would have to stay off. "You had one job," Tony roared. "Are you bringing a commitment? Everyone breaks commitments, everyone breaks commitments. We had a contract, we had a contract that you were going to fix the water."

"Tony, you need to stop this," Justin growled back.

"Just get the fuck off my bus," Tony screamed. "You're useless."

Justin tried to calm him down. Eventually silence fell between the two men.

"Justin," Tony said finally, his voice muffled by the door. "Do you trust me?"

"Yeah, I trust you, Tony."

"Do you trust me unconditionally?"

"No, I don't trust anyone unconditionally. But I trust you generally; we can agree on that."

"I need you to trust me unconditionally."

"I can't trust you unconditionally unless I know what you're gonna ask me."

There was a long pause before Tony spoke in a lowered voice. "I'm going to solve corona. I'm going to solve COVID right now. I almost have it figured out." He paused again. "I just need more mushrooms."

"I'm absolutely not doing that," Justin replied.

"I will give you a million dollars right now."

"Tony, there's no amount of money in the world—"

"I'll give you $10 million right now."

"Tony, there's no amount of money in the world—"

"I'll give you half of my net worth," Tony said. "We're going to be partners in everything that I do going forward. And if you trust me, I promise you this is going to work out, and we're going to solve corona, we're going to solve COVID, we're gonna create world peace, and we're gonna change the world together. You just have to trust me."

Justin found himself with few levers left to pull, if any. How long would he have to stay with Tony until his trip ended? And how long would it be until Tony was capable of a rational conversation? On the other hand, if he left the bus, Tony might find a way to get more drugs to Montana.

As Justin considered his options in silence, Tony's voice came through the door once more. "Fine. I'll find somebody else that will."

■ ■ ■

It had been a long day for those at the lakeside lodge. Tyler, drained of patience, decided not to venture onto the bus. But he knew there was something he had to do. On the phone to the Zappos leadership team, he informed them that something needed to be done about Tony: the events of the past day proved he wasn't going to get better. Tyler didn't know what action needed to be taken, but the ball was now in corporate's lap.

Some people had stepped onto the bus and tried reasoning with Tony, only to walk off in tears or leave shaken at his condition. During the day, Tony came to believe that he was in an active shooter simulation and started trashing the bus. Perhaps most distressing, Tony at one point asked his friends to join in a suicide pact with him. Dying, he told them, was the best way to transcend human consciousness, and the only way to hack the "AI simulation" was to burn the bus with them all inside.

Ava, who had started the trip excited to spend time with Tony, left the bus looking visibly distraught. When she walked past Justin, who sat under a nearby tree most of the day, she wouldn't say what had been discussed. She only offered that "Tony wants to damn you to a multidimensional hell."

Justin had kept an eye on the bus throughout the day to make sure Tony didn't leave. If Tony was seen in public in this state, the secret would be out, and the world would know the happiness guru of Zappos was in a really bad place; he could picture the headlines. Tony never tried to leave the vehicle, but instead made it clear that Justin was no longer in his circle of trust. Toward the end of the day, he told Justin there would be a private jet leaving in the early hours of the next morning to fly him back to Salt Lake City. Tony would be taking the bus back to Park City. This actually didn't seem like a bad idea, Justin thought. Perhaps Tony would calm down without Justin around, and rest for a few hours on the ride back. Then, once they were back in Park City, they could discuss what had happened.

Unbeknownst to Justin, Tony had been sending messages far and wide from inside the bus. Later that evening, two chartered jets arrived at a nearby airport. Anthony Taylor had arrived in one; Ali Bevilacqua was in the other. It seemed Tony was willing his wishes into being.

■ ■ ■

The next morning, twenty-four hours after they'd arrived, Tyler and the rest of the Montana group decided that they'd stay there until they could find their own way back to Park City. Before leaving on the bus the night before, Tony had agreed to share his location in a group message chat with members of the Montana trip, allowing them to follow his movements.

Tony seemed to be coming down from his trip, Steve-O reported to Tyler that morning, but he was still in the process of calming down. They were due to arrive back in Park City later that afternoon, Steve-O told him. Justin would already be there by then and could meet Tony when he arrived.

But though the plan seemed straightforward, Tony managed to derail it. At one point, Tyler got wind that Tony had been texting people asking them to join a scavenger hunt, the specifics of which he couldn't figure out. Tyler checked Tony's location and realized the pulsing blue dot on his phone screen hadn't moved for a while. It appeared to be in Salt Lake

City. The only person they knew who lived there was a friend of Anthony Taylor's. Tyler connected the dots. "Please don't give Tony ketamine," Tyler wrote in a text to Anthony. "I know I can't match whatever Tony is offering, but I'll give you everything I have in this life."

Anthony didn't respond. Tony wasn't responding to texts either. Tyler wrote to him: "How come you're not texting me? Did you stop trusting me?"

Tony's reply came soon enough. In the group chat, he sent a screenshot of Tyler's text to Anthony. He followed up with a large block of text accusing Tyler of going behind his back. Then, in rapid-fire instructions, Tony demanded that Brandon Hollis, the Zappos general counsel, write up a contract guaranteeing the transfer of Tyler's assets to Anthony.

Tyler sent a text to the group chat, addressed to Tony: "We are all your friends and love you but the last couple days you've attacked each and every one of us for no reason. Elissa and I paid to be here to connect and spend time with you. We love you. No matter how much you push us away or attack us, we love you. No matter what you say we love you. Wish you were here to spend an amazing week with us." It was the last time Tyler ever communicated with Tony.

■ ■ ■

Justin had arrived back in Park City by now, and spent much of the day trying to figure out his next move. Tony had made it twenty-eight days into his agreement to abstain from drugs. But he'd broken his commitment and was now seemingly at the point of no return. Either Justin had to commit to getting Tony medical help—an effort that had failed before—or it was time for him to go back to Vegas and move on.

That evening, Justin was on his way home after meeting Suzie for dinner at a restaurant in town when he received a call shortly before midnight. It was Juliet, one of Tony's assistants. She was at the house at 1422 Empire, and Tony had just arrived at the home. He was acting manic, she said. He was rearranging furniture and other objects, placing candles everywhere, and talking desperately to himself. She was there with Ali, and they were each in separate rooms upstairs.

Justin headed to the house. It was quiet when he arrived. He found Ali and Juliet downstairs. They seemed tense. Tony had calmed down, they told him, but was now upstairs in his room. Justin told them he was going to stay nearby at the Welcome House. *If anything happens, call me.* He'd leave his phone on loud.

■ ■ ■

Around 4 a.m., Justin was woken by rapid knocking on his bedroom door. It was Suzie. She had received a frantic stream of messages from Ali and Juliet and had come to the Welcome House to wake him up. He checked his phone and saw that he'd missed more than twenty calls, and dozens of texts. *Tony is breaking things in the house, he's writing messages on the walls,* came the urgent messages from Ali and Juliet. *He's talking to himself about multiple dimensions.*

Justin ran into the street but stopped short before he reached the house. Tony's bedroom upstairs had a balcony that overlooked Empire Avenue. If he saw Justin approaching the house, he might be startled, and, depending on his state of mind, it couldn't be ruled out that he might harm himself. Justin walked around the property before reaching the front entrance. He pushed open the door, and time slowed down as he came to terms with the nightmare he was witnessing.

He could see candles flickering from within the darkened house, revealing streams of water cascading down the grand staircase at the center of the home. Smashed glass and plates were strewn across the floor. Candles were everywhere. On the walls were messages scribbled by a furious hand with a thick black marker. Names of friends. Incoherent text and Post-it notes across every wall. Then Justin noticed one message on the front door: "This is Tony's house. He gets what he wants."

Walking around the exterior of the home and looking through the windows, Justin tried to process the scene. Tony appeared to have flooded a bathroom upstairs after trashing the house. It occurred to Justin that if a live wire were to come into contact with the flowing water, the house could go up in flames.

Justin met Ali and Juliet at the back door and they left the property. He returned to the Welcome House around the corner and dialed a number for mental health services in Park City, before the operator patched him through to 911. He stressed that he wanted to remain anonymous and was calling on behalf of his friend, who was a "high-profile" person and who appeared to be having a psychotic break and was at risk of hurting himself.

Several police cars arrived within minutes, and Justin went out to the street to meet them a few houses down. An ambulance arrived seconds later, followed by firefighters. The police found Tony sitting on his back porch. Despite the devastation around him, his expression was serene.

■ ■ ■

For the second night in a row, Justin and Suzie met for dinner in town and tried to piece things together.

After Tony was taken to Park City Hospital, Justin had called Mimi because she managed Tony's medical records and personal information. He also called Richard Hsieh and recounted what had occurred over the past twenty-four hours. Considering the destruction done to the property, and the perceived risk that Tony could have harmed himself, or others, Justin felt sure Tony would be held at the hospital for at least a few days, until a psychiatric evaluation could be completed. That would then provide an opening to potentially coax Tony back into a rehab facility.

Justin and Suzie hadn't been allowed to join him in the hospital because they weren't family, so they had remained at the Empire Avenue house throughout the day. Mimi had hired professional cleaners to help restore the building, and a flood damage service arrived, cut holes in the wall, and used heaters to blow hot air into the walls to dry them out. They scrubbed the walls to wash away the black marker, and all of the Post-it notes were removed. Furniture was reorganized. And garbage bag after garbage bag was filled with broken glass and plates.

At one point Justin had gone into Tony's en suite bathroom and found a glass bottle, like an old-fashioned milk bottle, tipped over on the floor beside the toilet. The bottle was about a third full of what appeared to be vitamin capsules. By the brown substance within them, he assumed they were mushrooms. A handful of the capsules were scattered across the floor. It was impossible to tell if the bottle had been full or where it had come from, but as he looked around the house, Justin could only wonder.

At the restaurant, Suzie ordered a margarita. After the events of the past forty-eight hours, they decided, perhaps Tony had finally hit rock bottom. The only feasible outcome, they thought, was that Tony would be committed to a psychiatric facility or rehab, and then the slow road to recovery would begin.

Their conversation was interrupted by Suzie's phone ringing. It was an unknown Utah number. Odd, she thought, considering it was late. She held the phone to her ear, and Justin watched her face drain of blood. She looked up and mouthed: "It's Tony."

The hospital was releasing him.

"What do you mean?" Suzie said into the phone.

Justin called the police officer who had taken Tony from the house the night before. *Why is Tony being released?* The police have no power to stop Tony from leaving the hospital, the officer told him; all they could do was pass on their recommendation to the medical staff.

A short time later, Justin and Suzie pulled into the emergency room entrance and saw a figure huddled on the curb. Tony was wrapped in a purple puffer jacket and wearing gray sweats. He looked up, his eyes glazed and hollow.

CHAPTER 23

STICKY NOTES

The sun was beating down on Park City when David Hill cracked his first beer of the day. He and his friend Tyler Davis had just sat down on the front porch after a morning hiking the surrounding mountains and were using the moment to relax before a night of July 4 celebrations. A small garden separated the blue miner's cottage from the sidewalk, and from where they were sitting, they could look up and down the street toward the hills at each end of Park Avenue.

"Happy Fourth of July!" they called out to a group of people walking by, lifting their drinks.

It was a marvelous day. The skies were clear, and the sound of one of their favorite bands, the reggae funk group Iration, was playing from a speaker on the porch. The two men had known each other since they were kids, and trips like this were among the few times they could catch up. Tyler lived in Florida and worked at a real estate company, while David worked at a recruiting firm in Dallas.

"Happy Fourth!" they hollered with big grins at two men walking by.

After the pandemic closure of the spring, Park City had reopened its restaurants in June and had become a hot spot for those in need of the outdoors. Tyler and David had rented the cottage via Airbnb for the long weekend; it was the first time they'd been able to get away with friends since the pandemic had started.

As the reggae played, Tyler stared after the two men who'd just walked past, and noticed one of them wasn't wearing shoes—an odd sight in a ritzy town where financial advisors and tech workers in polo shirts and vests line the sidewalks. He exchanged a glance with David as they realized the two men had turned around and were now walking back toward them. One man was taller and looked to be about fifty, with long gray-streaked hair that dangled over his shoulders, giving him the look of an older "hippie guy," Tyler recalled. The other man, without the shoes, looked more disheveled as he came closer. With a cigarette hanging out of his mouth, he was wearing a tattered maroon button-down shirt. His blue jeans scuffed along the ground.

"What are you guys up to?" the shoeless man said, looking at them with glassy eyes. On the porch, Tyler and David tensed slightly and mumbled something about relaxing and drinking beers.

"How long are you guys staying here?" the man asked. They told him they had been renting the house from Airbnb and planned to leave the next day.

"Why don't you stay for an extra week?" he said. "I'll pay for the Airbnb."

What is going on here? Tyler thought. These two strange men, standing in front of them chain-smoking cigarettes, were now proposing they cover the cost of the Airbnb so they could stay another week?

The shoeless man looked at David. "What do you do?" he said. David was cautiously interested to see where this was going and told him he worked in recruiting.

The man became more animated. "I'm actually trying to recruit people to move to Park City," he said. "Would you be willing to start recruiting for me?"

"Well, we focus on, like, sales recruiting, specifically software and medical device sales," David said.

"What's your placement fee?" the man responded.

"On average, $10,000."

The man said he would pay double that for every person that David could recruit to come to Park City.

After some more back-and-forth, David gave the man his phone number, and then wrote the man's contact information on a piece of paper, but threw it away. "I legitimately thought he was homeless," David recalled. "I didn't think that the deal was serious at all."

Had David followed up, he would have joined a burgeoning group of people about to make fortunes off a seemingly unwell man.

■ ■ ■

Three weeks later, Tony was walking through a cavernous living room, his footsteps echoing on hardwood floors. As the real estate agent guided him and his friends past a river-rock wall, he looked through floor-to-ceiling windows toward an expansive balcony that overlooked a blue-green lake. In the distance, the mountains framed the horizon. Tony turned to the real estate agent. "I'll double your commission if you let me smoke a cigarette right now."

The sprawling ranch at 2636 Aspen Springs Drive would be the first of almost a dozen properties Tony would buy nearby, but it was by far the most impressive. Sunk into the base of Iron Mountain in a small, exclusive neighborhood about three miles north of Park City's town center, the property fell away from the street, obscured by paper birch and pine. Driving past, one could fail to notice the mansion's exterior. The nine-bedroom home spread across two floors and a loft space; several rooms had fireplaces. Below the balcony was an enclosed gym and indoor pool, and somewhere within the rabbit warren of rooms was a theater, cellars, and multiple bars. Outside, the lake lapped softly on a small sandy beach, and farther down the hill a two-story carriage house complete with its own horse corral had been converted into a guest residence with a panoramic view of a rolling meadow all the way to the four-lane state highway a quarter mile away.

The $15 million Tony put up for the house was but a fraction of his spending in recent weeks, and he was only getting started. Ever since his release from the hospital, Tony had become convinced that he was building a whole new world in Park City. He was fixated on building his community—an ecosystem, as he called it. He was putting out the call far and wide for people to join him: to friends in Las Vegas, former girlfriends, people he'd spoken to at conferences, people he'd met at Burning Man— seemingly everyone he knew. He told people that he wanted to build a new community here in this swanky mountain town, home to the rich and famous. Like Las Vegas, only better.

What that meant, exactly, wasn't clear to anyone who accepted his invitation. But Tony was making them an offer that made it easy to put aside any doubts. They could come and stay in one of his mansions, most often rent-free, all expenses paid. Food would be catered. They would be hired as "project managers" and be given free rein to invent their own roles and find their purpose. In return they'd earn more money than they ever had before. If they could show Tony a tax return, he would double their best salary. Only one other primary condition came with some of these life-changing contracts, often written on neon-colored Post-it notes: those who arrived had to "be happy."

Adding to the stream of people who had been coming and going from Park City in previous months, dozens more arrived to see what the buzz was about. Friends and former confidants at Zappos and the Downtown Project arrived in town, including Janice Lopez, John Bunch, and Jamie Naughton, his chief of staff and head of corporate communications at Zappos. So did Don Calder, the man who'd joined Tony in Hawaii for the baby experiment during Winter Camp. Rachael Brown, his former girlfriend, moved into the ranch, and Blizzy, Tony's beloved fluffy white mutt, was brought along, too.

In addition to handling social media accounts, Michelle D'Attilio was hired to create websites for various projects that Tony and Suzie were building. The day after he purchased the ranch, Tony led Michelle around the grand estate. He was wearing sweatpants, but no shirt or shoes. Michelle had heard about what happened in Montana and the destruction at 1422 Empire, and she was now visiting every other week to check on him. She hadn't brought up his meltdown, reasoning that she might have more sway over him if she worked behind the scenes to support him, rather than question his behavior and risk joining Tyler on the time-out list.

During one visit earlier in the month, she had noticed how dirty Tony's feet were. Michelle snapped a photo of them and sent it to a friend who had been with Tony. "Has he washed his feet?" she texted her friend. "What's going on?"

As Tony and Michelle walked the property, they stopped at the front porch and sat on the ground with their backs to the main door. As they had countless times before, they sat in silence taking in the pristine air and summer heat.

At last Tony turned to Michelle. "I'm thinking of retiring from Zappos," he said. "What do you think?"

By now, Zappos executives were more than aware of Tony's troubles. It was unclear to Michelle whether this thought had come to Tony of his own volition or if he was starting to get pressure from the company to take a step back. Michelle looked at her friend. She noticed his face was unwashed and gaunt. He seemed sober but exhausted. She could sense the weight on his shoulders.

"Do whatever is going to make you happy," she said. "You've done so much already for so many people. It's okay for you to step back and take care of yourself."

Tony stared back at her. The silence hung for a moment longer before someone approached them, breaking their moment of solitude.

■ ■ ■

To accommodate the swelling number of people arriving in Park City, the ranch served as the nerve center of Tony's new world. A stream of tour buses and Sprinter vans shuttled people to and from Las Vegas, cluttering the quiet residential street in front of the property. Tony hired a chef from Las Vegas to run the kitchen and build out the equivalent of a restaurant operation; with a $10,000-per-day budget, caviar was on the menu one day, king crab legs another. Beyond the bedrooms in the main building and the extra rooms in the carriage house, Tony ordered Airstream trailers and tiny homes to be parked in the horse corral, allowing for more people to stay on-site. Tony ended up spending more than $50 million on seventeen houses and vacant lots in the Park City region to accommodate his followers.

New arrivals, whether they'd known Tony for months or years, found themselves entering a community where there existed a clear hierarchy of people, each wrestling for power, influence, and Tony's attention. At the top of the pyramid, Mimi and Suzie established themselves as competing factions seeking to serve as gatekeepers to the community. Mimi spent most of her time away from Park City but beamed into Tony's bedroom during daily video conference calls and secured the role of managing logistics at the ranch: ordering food, paying bills, and monitoring who was leaving and arriving. Tony also assigned Mimi to be the final sign-off on most business ideas, ventures, or other major purchases. Outside of the ranch, most logistical issues were claimed by Suzie and her employees at Wellth Collective, who served as the primary travel agent for people arriving in Park City, coordinating where they would stay, what flights they were booking, and how they were getting to and from the airport.

Others seemed to have less defined roles. After hearing Tony's plan to build a new community in Park City, Victoria Recano, the TV reporter Tony had first met in San Francisco twenty years before, arrived with her husband and children in July, moving into one of the properties with a mandate, among other things, to produce videos for Tony to watch. Among the first projects Tony assigned her was to produce a video about herself, a forty-five-minute compilation of her news clips and family videos spliced together. Soon after, Tony told her he wanted a documentary on the history of the Swahili people, the millennia-old civilization from the coastal areas of East Africa near Tanzania. "Defining the Swahili people isn't easy," Victoria's raspy newswoman voice declared over images of men in robes standing by ragged tents in the desert. "It all depends on who you ask, where you ask it, and when. It's very tricky."

Millions of dollars were being promised every week, for salaries, for projects, and for investments, and Tony hired a team of court reporters—people typically employed to transcribe legal proceedings—to stay at the ranch and document his conversations. Mark Evensvold, who for years had managed the Nacho Daddy restaurant in Las Vegas, which Tony part-owned with Fred Mossler, came to Park City, and on the lakefront one afternoon in August, Mark and Tony discussed the terms of Mark's purpose in Park City, while a court reporter typed nearby, recording their words. Mark's roles would involve overseeing several bars at the ranch—the bar next to Tony's bedroom, another one next to the pool, and the upstairs kitchen bar—to make sure they were always stocked and in service. If Tony wanted to go to sleep, Mark would have to tell people to leave. In addition, he could also embark on other projects that interested him. Maybe he could build a koi pond or construct a treehouse? "You just work on whatever you feel like," Tony said. "There's no real schedule."

On a Post-it note, in a barely legible scribble, Mark wrote down the terms of the deal they'd just discussed. Tony asked him to read it aloud. "I will arrive on-site here as of September 20, 2020, responsible for bars, help with security and project management. Salary is $450K a year," Mark said. As a sign-on bonus, Mark went on, Tony would transfer most of his 25 percent stake in Nacho Daddy to Mark.

Tony leaned over and signed his name on the note.

CHAPTER 24

OLD FRIENDS AND NEW

The Hsieh family had already come and gone by the time Tony bought the ranch. After Tony's episode at 1422 Empire Avenue and subsequent stay in the hospital, Richard had arrived in Park City with Judy, Dave, and Andy. Despite their arrival, Tony spent little time with them, and asked friends to ensure that he would never be left alone with them.

In the moments Tony did spend with his family, he left them struggling to connect with their boy. At one point Tony told them that he planned to start a new family business. The purpose of the endeavor was unclear, but it was the responsibility of each of his family members to come up with a plan to raise money in a few weeks. He never followed up. During another moment with Judy, he said he would be open with her if she would act like his friend. If she acted like a family member, then he would hide information from her. When she told him that he needed to see a therapist, he said he would, but only if for every minute he was in therapy she would be in an ice bath. When she pressed the therapy point once more, mentioning his issues with attention, Tony left the house in a rage.

When it came time for the family to depart, Andy thought twice about leaving. Despite their distance over the years, seeing a swirl of new people he had never met before made him want to stay in Park City and keep an eye on his brother. Ten days later he returned and quickly realized that he'd entered an ecosystem where people were competing for Tony's money, pitching projects that didn't make sense, and living in houses they would never be able to afford otherwise. And there was a rule that ominously dictated many behaviors in the Park City enclave: never tell Tony you were concerned about his behavior. To do so meant risking excommunication, along with Tyler and Ryan Doherty.

One solution Andy came up with was to bring in people he could trust to identify bad actors. As it happened, Andy knew that his brother had been wanting for a while to work with their longtime friend Tony Lee. Lee had spearheaded Wells Fargo's loans to Zappos in 2003 when it was close to bankruptcy. Since then, Lee had worked at a number of smaller banks before settling in Texas to manage the finances of the Bass family, the oil dynasty that was worth more than $5 billion. He and Andy had remained close friends over the years; Andy had asked Lee to be the best man at his wedding before it was canceled. Now, at a time when his brother's spending was spinning out of control, Andy figured they could benefit from a professional financial manager to conduct some due diligence.

Lee was reluctant to entertain the idea of uprooting his life in Texas and to leave a comfortable job to join the mania of Tony's world, but he agreed to a meeting. During a dinner in late July at a restaurant on Main Street, Tony told him that he was turning Park City into a community similar to the one he had built in downtown Las Vegas, but better. Lee's role would involve overseeing all finances in the Park City ventures. As he had done with others, Tony offered to pay double Lee's current salary, which meant he would be earning $1.5 million a year. Sensing Lee's hesitancy, Tony turned to one of the people at the dinner, Ryan Fitzpatrick, and suggested that if he could convince Lee to stay, he'd receive a 10 percent commission, or $150,000.

After dinner, Andy pulled Lee aside. Coming to Park City made sense for multiple reasons, he said. Andy and Lee could finally work together after trying to figure out a way for years. Second, Andy said, with Lee overseeing the finances, he could also help weed out people who were taking advantage of his brother.

■ ■ ■

Andy's request came with a sense of urgency, as money was streaming from Tony's accounts. If people had concerns about taking money from a man drifting further from reality, few seemed to consider the Faustian bargain they were entering—an oversight that took vivid form when Tony found another destructive fascination.

In the weeks after his release from the hospital, Tony returned to the idea of biohacking as a way to increase his own personal output, and became convinced that inhaling nitrous oxide was a way to heighten his blood oxygen levels and eliminate the need for sleep. Better known as laughing gas for its use at dental offices, nitrous oxide is commercially available as an everyday kitchen item: the cartridges used in cream whipping machines, known as Whip-Its. The shiny silver canisters are about two inches in length and slot into Whip-It machines. While it's illegal to inhale the gas, it has found popularity with teenagers who can't legally buy alcohol and among festival revelers seeking a cheap, quick high. Inhaling the gas induces an immediate high, making one feel relaxed and sometimes giggly for a minute or two.

But the brain can only handle so much nitrous oxide before it begins to dissociate and lose connection with reality. Excessive use can lead to brain damage, and some teenagers have died from chemical asphyxiation; the actress Demi Moore passed out with seizures and was sent to a hospital after a night of inhaling Whip-Its. Between cigarettes, Tony was inhaling from the Whip-It canister like he was drinking water from a bottle. As he sat in bed at the ranch, the floor around him was covered by hundreds of Whip-It cartridges. By one estimate, Tony was using more than fifty a day. "You could hear his dog coming because it would jingle jingle through the things," one person who was at the ranch daily recalled.

Tony found comrades to indulge his newest addiction. Among them was Don Calder, who had been pitching Tony on potentially buying the town of Nipton and all of its sculptures as a Burning Man–style fun park. When their canisters ran empty, they were replenished from a pallet of Whip-It cartridges like those used to stock department stores, which Tony kept in the garage.

Tony's near-constant stream of nitrous oxide prompted strange behavior. One time Tony stepped on glass, cut his foot, and walked around the ranch leaving streaks of blood on the floor—a trail, Tony said, that would make it easy to find him. On another occasion, he tried starving himself of food and water to eliminate the need to use the bathroom. His physical appearance changed, and his weight fell below one hundred pounds, leaving his frame looking skeletal. His head seemed to bulge above his body, while his slender limbs moved with fatigue.

At one point paranoia took hold, and Tony was convinced one morning that Tyler was in Park City, trying to stage an intervention. The scare prompted him to hire a legion of black-clothed security guards to form a human perimeter around the ranch. Visitors who came to see Tony encountered guards in different wings of the property, as if they were entering a fortified estate.

Tony then became fixated on finding ways to justify his nitrous oxide habit, and dispatched those around him to find out more about it. Victoria produced another video at his request, this one titled "The Nitrous Oxide Advantage," a montage of psychedelic images and videos cut between sound bites from supposed experts answering questions Victoria had crowdsourced from people at the ranch. "Nitrous oxide has control over the brain in ways no other drug does," Victoria's voice-over said. "It is at our lowest level of brain wave activity. Any lower and we are brain dead."

Not unlike what he'd done during his fascination with ketamine, Tony called for research on whether nitrous oxide was something that could change lives; maybe it could become another legal high like marijuana. He found a willing volunteer in a man named Nadeem Nathoo, the co-founder of an organization called the Knowledge Society, who was also seen inhaling nitrous alongside Tony. Nadeem had met Tony after a conference one night in Las Vegas. His organization offered training programs to high-achieving teenagers interested in entrepreneurship and seeking internships at places like Microsoft and IBM. Nadeem had arrived in Park City after receiving a text from Tony, and at Tony's insistence Nadeem invited three alumni of the Knowledge Society program to join them as well. Almost as soon as they arrived, the fresh-faced twentysomethings were asked to produce a research paper on the health benefits of nitrous oxide.

Tony dipped in and out of megalomania. One morning he preached to Michelle about achieving world peace. Given that he was paying her to oversee his social media accounts, he posited how they could be used for such a goal. Before going down the rabbit hole, Michelle said, they needed to define what world peace meant. For Michelle, it meant a world with peaceful resolutions to conflict. Tony's definition was both more simplistic and reductive: for him, world peace meant a world without any conflict. "He wanted to create this playground where everyone would be happy," she said later.

Everyone in Park City understood that the best time to speak with Tony was at dawn—it was when he was at his most lucid. Justin and Suzie, who had both remained in Park City but were staying in other houses, would often join Tony on the lakefront beach as he cooked breakfast and was more clear-eyed. There they would discuss business affairs—from property acquisitions to contracts with new entrants—before Tony's mental state declined throughout the day.

Tony raised eyebrows by leading group hikes through the mountains without shoes on while inhaling from his nitrous cartridge. While he was initially seen at mealtimes and held meetings in various rooms at the ranch to discuss the stream of projects being pitched to him, he gradually started spending more time in his bedroom, and would hold court while sitting in bed, surrounded by nitrous oxide cartridges. "His room looked like a homeless shelter," Andy said later. "There was feces on the ground. Plants in his toilets. Broken glass, broken plates all over the ground. Rotten food under the bed. Rotten food on the walls . . . it was disgusting."

■ ■ ■

People were finding new ways to spend his money, as Tony seemed willing to spend himself broke. On multiple occasions he said he wanted to shed any attachment to the world he'd created in Las Vegas. There were too many broken commitments there. And rather than his community coming together for him, they'd forced him into rehab instead. No more Zappos. No more shoes. No more Downtown Project. No more people asking for money to build a community he no longer cared about.

One way to achieve this, Tony declared, was that he would sell his entire real estate portfolio in Las Vegas. Despite having paid in excess of $200 million for the properties downtown, he wanted them gone, no matter the price. To execute the plan, he turned to the two people who'd been meeting him every morning on the beach. On a Post-it note stuck to his bedroom wall, he delegated the task to Justin and Suzie. The first person to bring him back a deal would earn a 10 percent commission.

Such agreements were encouraged by a nonsensical incentive scheme Tony had come up with, called 10X. It started when Tony declared that for his new community to be more effective than his Las Vegas experiment, it must reconsider how output was achieved and measured. Therefore, he told people, everything would need to be achieved in multiples of ten: ten times faster, ten times bigger, ten times *more*. Initially, the first iteration of 10X launched with a noble goal: to help the town of Park City reopen amid the pandemic. Suzie had been in charge of spearheading the effort with her company, Wellth Collective. With the help of a recently hired assistant named Elizabeth Pezzello, who in turn had brought her fiancé, Brett Gorman, to Park City to work for Suzie, the three approached restaurants downtown and secured agreements to book them out on Sundays, guaranteeing thousands of dollars for revenue-starved businesses. The plan was to walk around downtown and sell $10 memberships to people, granting them an all-you-can-eat-and-drink pass to any of the restaurants; participants were given T-shirts and merchandise with a 10X logo. It might have sounded charitable, given that the venture made no financial sense, but the state of Utah took issue with running an open bar tab on an entire town and shut the program down after its second week.

But the philosophy of 10X remained, and morphed into something else. In addition to the double-your-best-salary deals, Tony vowed that anyone who spent his money would be entitled to a 10 percent commission on the amount they spent. If someone booked out a restaurant and spent $1,000 on the tab, for example, they would earn $100. If they recruited someone to live in Park City, they'd be entitled to a 10 percent commission on that person's annual salary. And if someone could source a real estate deal and spent $1 million on the property, that person would be entitled to $100,000. Starting with smaller tasks around the ranch and expanding all the way to Tony's entire Las Vegas real estate portfolio, commissions were being doled out on a daily basis.

■ ■ ■

Tony Lee had by now assumed the role of financial overseer and had a front-row seat as money left his old friend's bank accounts. Unlike the mundane stock performance charts Lee had been overseeing for the Bass family, he was now staring at receipts for investments in gold and real estate properties, hot air balloons, and proposals for helicopter tour companies.

Lee could also see those vying for Tony's money beginning to fight for it—a development often motivated by the 10X incentive program. For many of the big-ticket items, Mimi and Suzie were attempting to establish themselves as the source of deals, to prove to Tony that they were deserving of a commission. This manifested in strange ways. One day, Suzie's top assistants, Elizabeth and Brett, who were employed by Wellth Collective, announced that they had been hired to cater solely to Tony. As part of the swap, they would now be paid through an LLC that Mimi controlled, and Elizabeth and Brett would be getting a pay raise: each would be earning hundreds of thousands of dollars.

For years, Mimi had been paid a flat $9,000-a-month salary from Tony, in addition to travel expenses. But after Tony's Park City chapter began, Mimi negotiated a pay raise and was now earning a $30,000-per-month base salary—a sum that soon became dwarfed by the money she was scooping up in 10X commissions.

In total, through an LLC she controlled, Mimi sent invoices for what amounted to more than $20 million. In one case, Mimi "managed" a contractor who was being paid $83,333.33 a month for "assistance and management of various projects"—earning her $8,333 every time the contractor was paid by Tony. When Tony bought a fleet of buses and asked that Mimi arrange for them to be retrofitted at a cost of $3.7 million, she took 10 percent of the fee. Then there was the $7 million acquisition of the Big Moose Yacht Club, an event space on prime real estate at the foot of Park City's ski lifts, which entitled Mimi to a $700,000 commission.

In a twisted way, Tony's incentive structure was working the way he envisioned it; people were vying to execute his every whim. When he had an idea to launch a film studio that produced documentaries, Mimi took up the proposition. On a sticky note, she and Tony wrote up the terms of a contract to set up an LLC with $10 million to fund documentary film projects produced by an existing studio called XTR. The LLC would be controlled by Tony, Mimi, and her boyfriend, Roberto Grande, a former lawyer and aspiring film producer. As part of the agreement, Mimi and her boyfriend were entitled to 55 percent of the profit from the venture, despite not putting in their own money. And in line with 10X, Roberto would be entitled to a $1 million commission for setting up the LLC. Mimi then charged Tony another 10 percent fee on the cost of hiring the lawyers to arrange the $1 million commission payment to Roberto.

It might have seemed excessive, but two months later, Roberto told XTR that Tony had approved another $7.5 million for the venture. It's unclear if the money was wired, but soon afterward, the attorneys who had written up the terms for the $1 million commission payment to Roberto amended the contract to state he was now owed $1.75 million.

Mimi's efforts often came into conflict with those of Suzie, and at one point she introduced a "Suzie penalty," which Tony agreed to: for every day Suzie was on one of Tony's properties, Mimi would fine him $30,000. While it seemed outrageous, Tony racked up $1.83 million in fees under the scheme and received an invoice from Mimi's boyfriend. Tony ended up paying $420,000.

But Suzie gained ground in other ways and successfully convinced Tony to commit to one-on-one time, which gave rise to other opportunities. After her restaurant program on Main Street was abandoned, Tony told her she had a $1 million weekly budget to throw events around Park City every Sunday, a figure Suzie claimed she never spent in its entirety. Then, in addition to trying to broker a deal to sell Tony's real estate portfolio, she worked with Tony to launch a project known as the Magic Castle, a $5 million proposal to turn an event space in town into a co-working facility. Like Peter Pan's Neverland, every new project or idea could sound enchanting.

Another person Mimi seemed to be constantly feuding with over the 10X commissions was Andy. Since Tony had met Paula Abdul earlier in the year, he had wanted to convince her to come to town and do some shows; because tours had been canceled as a result of the pandemic, she had spare time. So Tony proposed that Paula do 180 shows at a local event venue known as Yellowstone for a $9 million contract. Whoever could close the deal would get the $900,000 commission. Andy claimed that he had arranged it, while Mimi argued that in fact she was entitled to it, but nothing ever came of the proposal. In another dispute, Andy and Mimi lobbied Tony regarding who they thought was entitled to a 10 percent commission on the $15 million ranch he was now living in.

Andy tried to rally support among others to pursue deals with Tony's money. At one point, he urged Janice to try and convince Tony to invest $10 million in an entity that would own a tequila company. He brought it up to her on at least five other occasions, eventually suggesting she ask for $50 million for the venture. But Janice refused, and it went nowhere.

Lee, for his part, initially seemed to encourage Andy's pursuit of Tony's commission payments. After Tony had dangled the 10 percent commission in front of Ryan Fitzpatrick at their initial dinner in July, Andy encouraged Tony Lee to make it clear to his brother that it was he who was entitled to the commission, if he ended up taking the job.

"You are welcomed [*sic*] to go broker a deal for me," Lee wrote in a text to Andy. "Go talk to him."

"Yeah I'll talk to him," Andy replied. "Tell him I'm your broker."

Lee seemed enthused. "You have to earn your commission now and make it happen. :)) hope tony pays you."

"I'll make it happen with Tony! And you make it happen with him that I'm your broker :)," Andy replied.

"The higher my number whether 1.4 or 1.5 [million dollars] you will get a bigger commission. Go fight for me now. :))"

"Win win!" Andy wrote back. "Mainly excited for you to be here and we can hang out together."

Lee later claimed he wasn't aware how ill Tony was until after he decided to take on the role. After he started working, he soon soured on Andy and came to believe that he was seeking to exploit his sick brother, rather than protect him. At one point, Lee claimed that Andy asked him to divert as much as $100 million to an account he controlled, to put aside for Tony's "retirement," which he refused to do; a claim Andy later denied.

As for Andy's efforts to secure a 10 percent commission on Lee's salary, worth hundreds of thousands of dollars, those fell by the wayside when Tony himself refused the proposal.

It didn't seem to matter though, as Andy had already negotiated his own salary contract with his brother—one valued at $1 million a year.

CHAPTER 25

WHO WILL SAVE YOUR SOUL?

The chaos spiraling within Tony's community was finally about to spill into public view, but for just a moment. On a Sunday evening in August, as the sun began its descent behind Iron Mountain, a group of residents were huddled at the top of the driveway of 2636 Aspen Springs Drive. As they waited to enter the ranch, there was an element of cautious curiosity; mention of the address had raised eyebrows among the neighbors for weeks.

Among those gathered was Bill Ciraco, a former Wall Street trader who had reached the edge of burnout before moving into the neighborhood with his wife and teenage daughter a few weeks before. At first he'd been enamored of the area, a cluster of ski chalets and palatial winter lodges strung along a one-mile loop of road that ascends and descends the base of Iron Mountain, granting a panorama of the valley below. Bill's real estate agent had told him the neighborhood had an active homeowners association, made up primarily of year-round residents who looked out for one another (in part through the security cameras that peered out from under the eaves) and knew when something was amiss. An unknown car with out-of-state plates parked in the street for too long could prompt alarm and even a 911 call. And unless an invite was issued by one of Aspen Springs's wealthy residents, strangers had no business being there. It was like a gated community but without the gate, Bill had been told.

But after the disturbances of the past few weeks, he was wondering whether he'd made a huge mistake. Two weeks after moving in with his wife and teenage daughter, Bill learned that a supposed billionaire had paid $15 million for the ranch at the bottom of the loop, one of the neighborhood's most extravagant properties. While he'd initially been buoyed by the idea that the sale could raise home prices in an area he'd just moved into, his excitement turned to concern when he'd seen a group of security guards flanking the property—hardly the image of a safe neighborhood. A deluge of vehicles had started coming and going from the property, too. As many as twenty-five cars lined the street outside the home at one point, and then even tour buses began arriving at the property. Finally, what felt like nonstop nights of parties had prompted 911 calls from neighbors.

Now, gathered at the problem house, some nodded in agreement that the recent events had been a great concern to their tranquil community. An olive branch had arrived the day before, in the form of an email to the homeowners association inviting the neighbors for a night of cocktails and entertainment at the ranch. The message also revealed that their new neighbor was Tony Hsieh, the CEO of Zappos, a company that Amazon had bought for over $1 billion. Outside of a small group of people, no one even knew Tony was here. Perhaps tonight the neighbors would have an opportunity to quiz Mr. Hsieh on what business he had being in Aspen Springs.

Bill made his way down the driveway with the neighbors, where they were asked to stand in front of the garage to wait for a COVID-19 test. A man wearing a denim jacket weaved through the group; a red bandana was tied around his neck. With a grin, he introduced himself as Anthony.

"I'm Tony's guy," Anthony said. He raised a fistful of bandanas and motioned for Bill to take one and tie it around his wrist. "It's so Tony knows who his guests are versus his employees." As he took a bandana, it took a moment for Bill to register where he had met guys that reminded him of Anthony. On Wall Street, the best traders didn't have to work for Morgan Stanley to get the best clients. With charisma and million-dollar smiles, they just had to raise hype by spending more on strippers and cocaine.

Standing on the deck, Bill took a glass of wine from a server and observed the scene around him. A few dozen people dressed like hipsters stood around, chatting. Most looked to be in their late twenties or early thirties. Someone passed by and mentioned that Tony was so happy to host all the neighbors. Bill thought it was weird that Tony was being spoken for. Where was he? Bill's mind drifted to one of those celebrity cocktail parties he'd attended at the Mondrian in West Hollywood. Everyone was smiling and looked pleased to be at a fancy party. They were there on the host's dime, but no one really even knew the host.

The small talk was interrupted by a woman who stood in front of the fireplace holding a microphone. "We have a special guest here tonight," she said, prompting a murmur. "Jewel is here to perform." Cocktails at a supposed billionaire's home were one thing. But a private show with a Grammy-winning artist was pretty cool, Bill thought; he was a longtime fan and the proud owner of Jewel's first album.

Jewel emerged from the far side of the room, wearing a pink tie-dyed flight suit that faded to purple down the leg. Two lengths of blond hair fell below a cream cowboy hat and swung over her chest as she moved in front of the microphone, holding a guitar. Introducing herself, she told her audience about her life story, growing up in Alaska, overcoming great hardship, experiencing homelessness in California, and being a victim of abuse. She now led a charity that helped youth get back on their feet in underserved communities.

Then she began to sing. More than a dozen candles shimmered on the table in front of her as she swayed and dipped with her guitar. The living room was shrouded in dusk by the time she sang her final ballad, "Who Will Save Your Soul." She reached a crescendo, then descended into the final chorus:

. . . And who will save your soul?
If you won't save your own?

The room was silent for a moment before those gathered broke into raucous applause. Everyone marveled at what they'd seen. Whatever the disturbance of the past few weeks, the neighbors agreed there seemed to be a sincere effort to make peace with them.

Only they couldn't thank their host. Tony was still nowhere to be seen. Bill was grinning when a woman approached him and the neighbors, identifiable by their red bandanas. "We are moving on to the dinner section of the night," she said. "So we're going to have to ask you to leave." Bill's wonderment vanished like a wisp of smoke.

■ ■ ■

People outside of Tony's inner circle had been trying to reach him for weeks. While the neighbors didn't know it, they were part of a growing group of people to whom Tony Hsieh remained unseen. As stories of outrageous spending, drug use, and neighborhood uproar filtered beyond the properties in Park City, those in Las Vegas began to discuss what to do about Tony. The lives of thousands of people—employees at Zappos, the Downtown Project business owners, residents of the community he had built in Las Vegas—were vastly impacted by the whims of a man who was descending into madness. These concerns had become even more urgent when word got back to the Downtown Project executives that Tony intended to sell his entire Las Vegas real estate portfolio, doing away with the Downtown Project, Fergusons, and everything else he owned there.

On multiple occasions Michael Downs, the Downtown Project executive, and Jen Taler, who lived at Fergusons and oversaw operations there, had arrived in Park City to try to find out what Tony's intentions were for both institutions. After learning that Tony was trying to sell his entire real estate portfolio, both left incensed, not knowing what was next. Without more money from Tony, their world in Las Vegas would likely collapse.

Since leaving in June, Tyler had shared what occurred on the bus to Montana with some people in Las Vegas and at Zappos, and momentum grew to send an interventionist to Park City to, effectively, retrieve Tony. With the help of Tony's parents, Tyler arranged for an interventionist named Elisa Hallerman, who specialized in celebrity cases, to go to Park City in early August. In order to get her onto the property, Tyler needed to convince someone who was on the ground at the ranch to add Elisa's name to an approval list for the security guards.

Tyler called Michelle just before midnight on August 4. "We have to get Tony healthy," Tyler said to her.

Michelle was exasperated. Not only had Tyler become persona non grata by this point, but there was now a narrative in Park City that Tyler had a savior complex. There were also other rumors—rumors that Tony believed—that Tyler was going to come onto the property and kidnap

Tony in order to get him into rehab. Tony's paranoia was also being fueled by whispers that his parents were preparing to set up a conservatorship, a court order that allows guardians to make decisions for individuals deemed incapacitated or incapable of managing their own affairs.

"Tyler, I get it," Michelle said. "We're working on it. But your involvement right now is causing more issues. You are creating more paranoia, and we are trying to get him help. Just let us do this."

The next morning, Michelle received a text message from Justin—he had found a doctor that he believed could help Tony. He wanted Michelle to walk the doctor onto the property that day at 11:30 a.m. With the intent of appeasing Tyler, Michelle texted him to let him know that there was a doctor coming to the ranch. But Tyler had other plans, and once he heard from Michelle, he notified the interventionist. Fifteen minutes before Justin's doctor was scheduled to arrive, Hallerman showed up at the ranch in a car with two other men—plainclothes police officers—and asked the security team for Michelle. When she came out, Hallerman introduced herself and asked Michelle to join her in the car.

"We have extremely powerful people that have hired me," Hallerman said to Michelle inside the car. "This is a Michael Jackson situation, do you understand? You would be liable if he dies."

As Hallerman bore into her, Michelle saw the doctor Justin had sent walking up the hill. She immediately jumped out of the car and took him onto the property in hopes of finding Tony. Before they could, however, the security team—unaware of any scheduled medical visits, and operating under strict instructions to keep strangers out—pulled Michelle and the doctor into two separate rooms and interrogated them.

While Michelle and the doctor were being questioned, Hallerman demanded that Tony come outside to see her and the two police officers for a welfare check—typically an in-person visit from law enforcement officers responding to a request from a friend or family member concerned about a person's mental or physical health. Standing at the top of the driveway, Tony talked with her and passed the welfare check. "He could snap in and out of anything," Michelle later said.

At the end of their discussion, Tony asked the officers who had requested the welfare check. "Your parents," they responded. Even though the family had been involved in organizing the intervention, it was untrue that they had asked for the welfare check—it was technically Tyler who had done so. But Tony made it clear to those at the ranch that his parents were now excommunicated. People within the house were similarly irritated by the unsolicited intervention attempt, and Tyler stopped receiving updates from Suzie, Justin, and Michelle.

■ ■ ■

Other friends began making individual efforts with more desperation. From Las Vegas, Tony's old friend Mark Guadagnoli had on multiple occasions tried to reach him on his phone to schedule a visit. Instead he received responses from Elizabeth Pezzello, who was now managing most of Tony's communications, telling him that Tony was either out of town or unavailable. She didn't know when he'd be free.

A few days after the failed intervention, Mark decided to call the Park City police and request that they do a welfare check. On the phone to a clerk, Mark provided his details, gave the address of Tony's ranch, and expressed that he was concerned for his friend's safety. The clerk said they'd send a car out to the address. Thirty minutes later Mark received a call from a Park City police officer who wanted to know who he was, why he wanted the welfare check conducted, the nature of his relationship with Tony, and how long he'd known Tony. Mark answered the questions, adding that he'd known Tony for "less than twenty years." The officer sounded more annoyed than willing to help, but agreed to call Mark once a wellness check had been done.

Hours went by without a response, and Mark decided to call the police station again and leave a message with the clerk. The officer phoned back two hours later and told him that no, he hadn't conducted the welfare check or gone to the house. Instead, he knew people at the house, and they'd told him everything was okay. "I don't understand why you wouldn't have just gone to the house yourself," Mark said. The officer told him, "That's not the way we do it. I already knew these people, and I trust them."

It so happened that Fred Mossler and his wife, Meghan, were also in Park City that day. It was the second time they'd come to check on Tony. Seeing the state Tony was in, this time had been harder than before. After talking with him on the beach, they resolved that he was very ill. When it came time for them to leave, Suzie offered to walk them to their car. As they neared the car, Suzie turned to them and asked that upon their return to Vegas they please urge people to stop calling in welfare checks. That morning alone, she'd learned of a welfare check request that had been put in from a friend who had known Tony for "less than twenty years."

■ ■ ■

Ultimately, it was Jewel who, with her star power, could glide past the guards and Tony's followers to capture his attention long enough to hold a mirror up to him. Eager to move past the disturbances of the past week, Tony had been anticipating her arrival and was excited to show her around his compound and the world he was building there.

When she received the invitation, Jewel was at first reluctant to go. Over text message, Janice Lopez had told her that Tony recently bought a large property, and wanted to host her; it would be a COVID-friendly environment. If she was willing, Tony would send a coach or private plane, Janice told her.

Jewel had spent the pandemic at her home in Telluride, Colorado, a town tucked away in the San Juan mountain range, known for its world-class skiing and unpretentious airs. She spent those months taking long hikes and watching her son canoe across the lake by her home. The last thing she wanted was to leave her bubble of tranquility. But something about the text worried her.

Unsure of what to do, she asked her friend and business partner Ryan Wolfington what he thought.

"What's your gut telling you?" Ryan asked.

"I'm worried about Tony," she said. "But I feel like it's the right thing to do."

Before they left, Ryan called Tyler, whom he had come to know over the years from the work that Jewel did with Zappos, to ask if there was anything they should know before their visit to Park City.

"It's not gonna be what you think," Tyler said. "You're gonna have to be really prepared for what you walk into."

With that in mind, Jewel, Ryan, and Aphrah Brokaw, who oversaw operations of Jewel's holding company, flew to Park City. Arriving at the ranch, the first thing Jewel was struck by was the contingent of security guards meeting them. It was so unlike the last time they'd seen Tony at his trailer park in Las Vegas, where he'd been there to greet them. Looking toward the compound, they were soon greeted by a group of Tony's assistants. "It's so good to have you here," a member of the welcoming party said to Jewel and her team, grinning at them.

At the ranch, they were told that Tony was going through a creative stage and was in the process of finding himself. He'd been supporting the community and individuals; through 10X he'd been trying to motivate people to build businesses to change the world.

Tony was waiting for Jewel by the spa, they said. While Jewel went to find him, Ryan and Aphrah were given a tour of the property. When they walked through the house, they noticed a dozen people sitting around seemingly doing nothing; those were court reporters who transcribed conversations around the ranch, they were told. Everyone they encountered seemed to have forced grins pasted across their faces, as if they were welcoming arrivals for a tour around Willy Wonka's chocolate factory. "Tony's a genius," said one person. "Tony's doing really great things," said another.

Hundreds of candles lit the rooms throughout the home, and melted wax covered the floor and window sills. As their tour continued, they noticed that water was gushing from the sinks and showers, even though no one was using them. The sound of running water, they were told, was intended to emulate the sounds of nature, specifically the ambiance of the Amazon jungle. Standing outside an exterior window looking into Tony's bedroom on the ground floor, they were shown a ten-foot surfboard covered in AstroTurf that balanced on the window sill, serving as a ramp to enter his room. Inside, the room was trashed; the floor was covered in discarded Whip-It canisters.

It was hard to ignore how the opulence of the home contrasted with the filth that filled it. Food scraps and dirt littered the floor, along with discarded clothes and misplaced furniture. They were particularly disturbed to see hand-sized clusters of trash covered in candle wax. A closer look revealed that the wax-covered substance was dog feces.

Outside, Jewel found Tony sitting next to the pond in the area known as the spa. Walking toward the beach, Jewel saw that the spa was a ditch dug into the side of the bank, shielded by a tattered rag hanging on a clothesline. Tony was meditating, seated on one of two chairs positioned next to a table. A large bowl filled with discarded Whip-It canisters sat on the table; hundreds of canisters and dozens of cigarette butts lay on the sand.

Greeting Jewel, Tony looked around and explained that he often bathed here. The pond itself was where they washed many of the dishes and kitchen utensils, to reinforce a natural way of living. The sight of Tony's gaunt face was disorienting and became only more so when he began to explain what he was working on. The secret to everything he was doing in Park City, he told Jewel, was world peace. He showed Jewel a Post-it note covered with a scribble of numbers and markings, which he said was an algorithm he'd written to enable him to "scale world peace" within six months.

■ ■ ■

Reconvening at the carriage house, where they were expecting to stay, Jewel discussed next steps with her team.

"As the president of Jewel Inc., it is my obligation to tell you that you being here could compromise you," Ryan said. "There's obviously something untoward going on here. There's clear drug use. This could become a liability."

Jewel looked up at Ryan and sighed. They would stay to help Tony, she told him.

Looking around at the house—the filth, the drugs, the sycophants—they became convinced that Tony was going to die if he stayed on this path. They concluded that there seemed to be no one in Tony's current orbit aware of his fate—or, if they were aware, then they were willingly enabling his demise and being paid for it.

Ryan went back to the main house of the ranch with Aphrah, in an attempt to get a better handle on the environment. As they walked to the kitchen on the second floor, Elizabeth greeted them both, and she and Aphrah exchanged phone numbers. Elizabeth then introduced them to Suzie, who told them she owned a wellness business and threw events with Deepak Chopra. Others joined the conversation.

At one point, someone told Ryan and Aphrah that if they wanted Tony to donate to Jewel's nonprofit, Inspiring Children Foundation, all they needed to do was write a dollar amount on a Post-it. Anything less than

$2 million was okay, but anything over would have to go through Tony's lawyers, they were told.

Like a bribe, Jewel thought, when Ryan told her about the offer.

The next night, Tony, Jewel, and a few others gathered in the theater for a screening of one of Tony's favorite films, the 1941 Frank Sinatra classic *Las Vegas Nights*. Seated on a lounge, Jewel told Tony about a manuscript she was working on, and mentioned that she had thought about addiction as a topic for the book. In between sips from his Whip-It canister, Tony immediately became agitated. He said that drugs were both mind- and heart-opening.

"I'm not worried about me, because I can see through it," he said. "I'm the 1 percent of people that can use these substances, and they become good. They become a skill." He went on, "It becomes a value add to my life. But most people, they don't know how to do that, and we're gonna teach people how to do that."

Jewel was unmoved. If Tony wanted her to be someone who would agree with him, she told him, she wouldn't.

"That's why I've gotten rid of anybody who comes into my ecosystem and talks about these things in a way that isn't aligned with what we're doing," he said. "Because, you know, people have always doubted what I'm doing."

He'll get rid of anyone who doesn't support his drug use, she thought.

She resolved that she needed to send a message to Tony and everyone who was living in his Park City world: Tony was going to die, and those around him were being put on notice. Jewel had planned to stay for as long as a week, and before arriving, she'd agreed to do a performance for Tony's guests. But now the purpose of their stay took on a new meaning. Jewel and her assistants spent their days and evenings speaking with the other guests at the ranch to determine whom they could trust and who was there simply to take from a sick man. As she created the set list for the performance, she thought about how her lyrics now took on a heavier meaning.

Before walking into the living room to perform her set, Jewel and her team were told that the neighbors had been invited to attend the performance. Later, they learned the neighbors had been calling the police and complaining about the disturbance to their community; the security guards, parade of vehicles, and parties had been a rude shock. Jewel's presence was supposed to legitimize what was happening here to the outside world, her team concluded.

For a brief moment, Tony emerged from his bedroom to see Jewel sing, only to retreat again before the neighbors noticed him.

■ ■ ■

At one point during her stay, Jewel walked out to the front of the ranch to see Tony greeting a group of men. They had arrived in a truck, on the bed of which was fastened a giant octopus sculpture about the size of a sedan. Tony had seen the beast once before at Burning Man and been enamored by its appearance. It had since been on display in Nipton, and Don had arranged for Tony to bring it to the ranch. It was missing two of its tentacles now, but it was just as impressive as he'd remembered. As Jewel watched them unload the sculpture, she heard that one of the men had COVID-19 but had decided to come anyway, so she demanded he stay away from Tony.

Her team tried to intervene and influence in other ways, and Ryan tried speaking with Andy. The conversations were shallow and brief. But on the night of her performance, Ryan approached Andy, and told him of their concerns about Tony's well-being. He explained to him their background in helping folks with mental health problems. After listening quietly, Andy asked, "Can we talk about this privately tomorrow?"

The next morning, the day that Jewel was scheduled to leave Park City, her team invited Andy to come speak with her at the carriage house for privacy. Andy arrived with one demand: "I can't have anybody knowing that we are talking about this. I can't get kicked out of here because I am the only one looking out for Tony, and anytime somebody tries to do something, the people around him really bad-mouth them, Tony gets paranoid, and then kicks them out of his life."

As the conversation progressed, Jewel and Ryan laid out to Andy their observations and their concerns. They said they believed Tony was in a drug-induced psychosis. It was reaching a critical juncture, and it was time for doctors to come in to assess Tony. But their main message to Andy was simple: Tony was going to die very soon if no one stepped in.

For a few moments Andy looked silently at Jewel and Ryan. Finally he said, "I don't know what to do. I need your help. Can you help me get professionals or get somebody or do something? Someone tried to get doctors here," he said, referring to the failed intervention attempt by Elisa Hallerman. "Tony has banned my parents—I'm not even allowed to talk to them. If they find out I'm talking to my parents, Tony won't have anything to do with me."

They ended the conversation with Andy agreeing to keep them updated on Tony's condition as they started efforts to get Tony professional help. As Jewel and her team left the ranch, they stopped at the top of the driveway, where there was a huddle of security guards at the entry gate. "Who's in charge?" Jewel asked. One of the guards stepped forward. "Do you know what your oath is?" she continued. "Your oath as a security or a police officer is to honor and protect, do no harm. To help people, to protect people from doing harm to themselves and others.

"There's people taking advantage of Tony in there. There's dangerous behavior. He's not being protected. He's being taken advantage of. And I'm putting you on notice that someone's going to die in there. He's gonna light that house on fire."

She held the guard's gaze. "If anything happens to my friend Tony Hsieh, I'm gonna hold you 100 percent accountable."

■ ■ ■

By Labor Day weekend, barely a night had gone by when music hadn't been pounding across the pond, cars weren't lining the street, and shouts weren't echoing through the neighborhood. The night of cocktails and Jewel's performance had done little to stop residents like Bill Ciraco from calling the police with noise complaints. Some nights people were gathered on the ranch's beach watching movies on an outdoor screen, surrounded by hundreds of candles and tiki torches. On other nights, neighbors had been horrified to see giant flames spitting above the trees from what they later discovered were hot air balloon baskets.

On the night of September 8, police were called to the house shortly after 11 p.m., after yet another neighbor said that "music was blasting" from the property. When the police arrived, the music had been shut off, but the lead officer, Leslie Welker, insisted that this time they needed to speak with Tony Hsieh in person. She had been at the house multiple times now, and the noise complaints hadn't been stopped by only talking with the security guards.

The owner of the security company, Shawn Kane, approached Welker and said that Tony was sleeping and unavailable. Welker looked over her shoulder and noted the fact that most of the lights were on in the house, and inside she could see a "large" group of people. "It appeared that Kane and his employees were trying to stop us from going down to the house and trying to make contact with Hsieh," Welker wrote in her police report later.

Sensing that they were being had, Welker and her partner walked past the guards and down the sloping driveway toward the front door of the home. Through the windows on either side of the door, they could see people milling about. After half an hour, Shawn came to the door, this time with two men who identified themselves as Don and Andy. They told Welker that they were in charge of the house, in addition to Tony, who wasn't available. They complained that neighbors had been harassing them; they had only been singing karaoke. Don provided his contact information when Welker asked. Andy refused to offer more than his first name.

As the officers went back out into the darkness, they walked by the giant octopus, lying like a sentry to the dark world Tony had built.

CHAPTER 26

ON THE EDGE OF THE ETHER-WORLD

A decade before, Tony Hsieh had been on the cusp of national celebrity, a newly certified tech tycoon with a grand ambition to create his own world in Las Vegas, a world where the opportunity to be happy was core to its existence. He had just traveled the country with his *Delivering Happiness* memoir in hand, offering a template for how people, companies, and the world could be happy. Fans were introduced through his recollections to an intensely curious child wunderkind who built a life that thrived on human connection. He spoke of experiences that had shaped him, and how they informed his decisions. Toward the end of his book, Tony urged his readers to reflect by asking two questions: What is your goal in life? And why?

Tony had often recounted that one of his first memories as a child was of catching fireflies in a jar. During a Zappos all-hands meeting one year, Tony took to the stage with the motivational speaker Simon Sinek, a former advertising executive who had sold books on how to influence human behavior, among other things, and had a hugely successful run on the TED Talk circuit. Tony's first memory was significant, Sinek told the audience, because every person's worldview is a product of the experiences they had when they were young. Tony "sees everybody as a firefly," Sinek said, sitting next to Tony on an oversized box, their legs dangling beneath them. "He sees the entire world as people with bright lights. He doesn't distinguish who are the bright ones and who are the dim ones; everybody has a bright light and everybody is out there doing their thing.

"If you put them in a container," Sinek went on, "where all of their brightness comes together, you create a flashlight. You can actually light a path for somebody else. And I firmly believe that when you are at your best, that is what you are doing with Zappos."

The message could hardly be limited to Zappos, and in his bestselling book *Start with Why*, Sinek writes that inspiration is one of two ways to influence human behavior. It takes time and hard work, but in the end it is more likely to result in loyalty, love, and a shared vision. The ecosystem Tony had built in Las Vegas had begun as a self-contained community of strivers and doers, bound by the goal of seeking and achieving happiness. Just by asking near-strangers a simple question—"If you could do anything in the world, what would you do?"—Tony had inspired hundreds of people to chase their dreams, building businesses and experiences overnight, and changing lives along the way. Time and again, Tony had used his money to inspire others, from Natalie Young's first restaurant to Rehan Choudhry's vision of Life Is Beautiful. In essence, Tony had been doing the same thing since he was a child: finding lights, collecting them, and then inspiring them to illuminate a path forward for others.

Inspiration can be futile, though, and somewhere along the way in Tony's sprawling Las Vegas community, his ability to inspire fell to the inevitability of human conflict, leaving those in his village desperate for his validation. It was something he was often unable to give, and with few requests other than for more money, the singular goal of happiness gave way to a sense that it wasn't happiness everyone was chasing after all. Perhaps it was security. At one point, it seemed, Tony had stopped searching for happiness, too.

The other way to influence others, Sinek writes, is manipulation. And while Tony's ability to inspire was a feature of him at his best, by the time he arrived in Park City, his dreams had been reimagined by a mind decaying by the day, and he'd created a new world whose citizens were often motivated by greed. A world of extravagant homes far from his trailer park, filled with people who hated one another but said yes to him, knowing that more fortunes were on the way. Rather than pushing people to chase their dreams, Tony had used his wealth to goad compliance.

There were efforts to curb his behavior by some who stayed to help, sure. Efforts to bring in doctors and therapists, and to deny his most outlandish financial escapades, which would have rendered him broke.

But toward the end, his mother, his father, Fred, and Alfred—people who had said no over the years, no matter the cost—were all gone. Like wealthy geniuses afflicted by drug addiction before him, Tony Hsieh was on an island of his own making, one where his delusions had replaced his reality. There was no happiness or inspiration here in Park City, only money.

Perhaps it was the fear of being voted off Tony's island that kept people close to him. Maybe they were motivated by a will to help him, or a desire to take money from him, or both. But as days turned into months of living alongside this version of Tony, there could be no illusions about what those in Park City were a part of. And the music didn't stop. It got louder, even as the sounds of his former life faded.

In late August, Tony bought a convoy of tour buses for a cross-country voyage. He came up with the idea that buses were the transportation of the future, and he believed he could get people like Elon Musk to invest in a bus convoy venture. All on Tony's dime, the purpose of the trip was to drive Rachael Brown to New London, Connecticut, where she'd just purchased a home.

But the timing of the trip coincided with another important task. Tony was aware that he was supposed to sign documents to confirm his resignation from Zappos. Suzie, who was not going on the tour, initially asked Michelle to deliver the documents to Tony. But Michelle was only going on part of the bus tour, so she was never sent the documents. Instead, Elizabeth Pezzello was tasked with delivering them to Tony.

A few days later, on Monday, August 24, 2020, the company announced that Tony was stepping down from Zappos. The company's chief operating officer, Kedar Deshpande, released a clinical-sounding statement: "We want to thank Tony for his 20 years of work on behalf of Zappos customers, and we wish him well in his retirement." Immediately after the announcement, Michelle's phone rang. It was Andy on the line, and he needed her to track all the news stories that were being written about Tony's retirement. It appeared that the timing of the announcement had taken Tony by surprise.

It had also deeply upset him, and it remained unclear to many of his friends whether he had actually signed the documents or if Zappos, recognizing an impossibly deteriorating situation, had made the executive decision to remove him.

Tony resolved only to keep moving in the same direction. One week in September, Justin told him that he only had $12 million to his name—a false figure meant to encourage him to rein in his spending. Soon after, with a hefty supply of nitrous canisters in tow, Tony took a dozen people on a private jet to Alaska to meet with Brock Pierce, the former child-actor-turned-crypto-billionaire who was running an independent campaign for U.S. president. During a talk at the Anchorage hotel where they were staying, Brock detailed his journey through spirituality, touched on the multiverse, and discussed with Tony whether the Illuminati were real. When Brock was finished, Tony told those gathered that he was giving each of them $1 million to pursue their own spiritual journeys—it seemed to be fate he'd brought twelve people with him, he told them. Justin would be responsible for distributing the funds. (Justin didn't follow up, and Tony didn't ask about it again.)

Finally there was an excursion five hours south of Park City to a sprawling compound near St. George, Utah, called Holmstead Ranch Resort, which was for sale. Arriving on a tour bus, the group marveled at the size of the property and its numerous cabins, which came complete with an idyllic lake and an amphitheater. Tony envisioned turning it into his own theme park or event space, something like his very own Disneyland. While Suzie negotiated the sale price with the owner, Tony told Justin that he could use the property to launch events linked to Life Is Beautiful, and talked with Andy and Don about hosting a Rufus Du Sol concert there.

But the excursions and events served as little more than distractions from the fact that Tony was on a wretched path, and it was becoming impossible for those orbiting around him to ignore that they were part of his journey. A week after Jewel left Tony's world, a letter had arrived at the ranch, penned by the musician. Standing in his fiefdom, Tony had called together a group of people to view the letter, including Rachael Brown and Michelle, and asked someone to read it out loud.

Hi Tony,
It was great seeing you.
I feel compelled to write:
I am going to be blunt.

I need to tell you that I don't think you are well and in your right mind. I think you are taking too many drugs that cause you to disassociate.

Your intelligence is formidable, but I see you creating rationalizations that are ludicrous and medically unsound, and the people you are surrounding yourself with are either ignorant or willing to be complicit in you killing yourself.

Your body cannot take not sleeping. And the amount of N_2O you are doing is not natural. You will not hack sleep and you will not outsmart nature.

Your goal of creating a new country is amazing, but you are not in a state to execute it.

When you look around and realize that every single person around you is on your payroll, then you are in trouble. You are in trouble, Tony. I cherish you & can't in good conscience not speak up. Anyone who sees you would be worried. It is not healthy or sane.

If the world could see how you are living, they would not see you as a tech visionary, they would see you as a drug addicted man who is a cliché. And that's not how you should go down or be known. Please don't be like the stereotype of a billionaire who surrounds himself with yes-men and goes from eccentric to madness—but never sees the line that is crossed because he won't listen to anyone that loves him.

Maybe people are too polite or need too much money from you to tell you that the only harm to you right now is yourself. Please get sober. Prove that it is your brilliance that can pull off the impossible, and not the drugs. If you can only create and be brilliant when you are high, then it is not you anyway. It's the plant speaking through you and anyone can be that. And I believe you are more than that.

Your talent is for human connection. For creating culture for humans to thrive in. Not velocity. Everyone has their talent, don't throw yours away because you are comparing yourself to someone else . . . you can't connect when you are dissociating or high. You cannot connect to anyone. You are rambling and not making sense, but you think you are. I need to be clear. You sound like a crazy person when you are talking and no one seems to be telling you. It's because you are also very smart. And they are used to you being eccentric. What you are saying isn't smart. It's mental. The brilliance for creating connection is killed by the fantasy world you are living in. You can't even connect with me or anyone who comes to the house. It's sad. I find it incredibly sad and I don't think this is your time to die.

You made some sort of promise to humanity when you were young, to solve complex problems and create connection. You did that but now you have lost your way. The wolf is lost out on the edges of the ether-worlds. You can not help the pack from where you are. No one worth their salt will take you seriously right now.

Please get grounded. If you want to save this planet, come back to earth and get to work in a way that will make a difference.

I say this with love, and as possibly the only person in your circle who is not on your pay roll.

I am here to help in any way I can.

J

Tony asked Michelle to post a photo of the letter on his social media accounts. Fighting back tears, she said no. But for weeks, the letter was affixed to a window overlooking the pond, for all to see.

CHAPTER 27

BLIZZY

"We're going to Hawaii!" Elizabeth Pezzello exclaimed.

Alongside her fiancé, Brett Gorman, she was standing in front of a screen clicking through a PowerPoint presentation. A few others stood around the garden outside Tony's bedroom window. As one slide shifted to the next, Elizabeth and Brett showed a beautiful mansion on Maui, proposing a long weekend trip before Thanksgiving. As they scrolled through the slides, options for different-sized Gulfstream jets appeared on the screen, along with corresponding pricing options.

Since Tony had taken them on as assistants, Elizabeth and Brett had become somewhat of a power couple in Park City. Many in Park City had bristled at how the pair had worked their way into Tony's inner orbit. But they controlled much of Tony's outgoing communication and served as gatekeepers to those who met with him. They had assumed the master bedroom of the ranch and had hired a legion of their own assistants to help them complete a list of seemingly nonsensical tasks, including arranging for their own dog to be cleaned and producing a daily newsletter called *Blizzy Ranch Daily News*. Often at night, they would go into town for expensive dinners. They had also found mutual benefit in aligning themselves with Andy, counseling him as he feuded with Suzie and Mimi.

Considering the trips of the past few months, their Hawaii idea might not have seemed too far-fetched. But Tony was particularly unstable. Just days before, he had been taken to the hospital after complaining that he thought his blood had turned to metal. It would have been the best opportunity yet to get Tony admitted had he not grown impatient while waiting to be processed in the ER and demanded that his friends, including Andy, Don, Janice, and Justin, return him to the ranch.

A small glimmer of hope had arrived when Don convinced Tony to start taking nicotinamide adenine dinucleotide, or NAD, a brain supplement that can help improve cognitive function. A nurse had been at the ranch administering the supplement to Tony via an IV drip for several hours a day, and some people had remarked that Tony seemed more clear-eyed after the sessions. Miraculously, he had stopped doing nitrous oxide as a result, and elements of his old self had begun to shine through in conversation; he was lucid and laughing. Carting him away again on a private jet would only disrupt whatever limited will Tony might have had to continue taking the supplement.

As Elizabeth and Brett scrolled through dollar sign after dollar sign on the PowerPoint presentation, some people looked on in disgust.

■ ■ ■

But Elizabeth and Brett got their way: Hawaii would be one of several stops on another whirlwind tour. Along with Tony, an assistant, Andy, Rachael Brown, a musician named Daniel Park, the NAD nurse with her IV drip in tow, and Tony's dog, Blizzy, they returned to Connecticut at the start of November to hang out at Rachael's house in New London for a couple of days.

Janice Lopez was among those who had stayed behind at the ranch to try to clean up the place and get things in order. Before the group left, she had hugged Andy, feeling comforted that Tony would be in good hands if his brother was by his side. He promised to stay in contact.

Only a few days went by before the group's plans changed. The national election had come and gone, with Joe Biden defeating Donald Trump, and Brock Pierce was looking to celebrate his birthday and the end of his campaign, and to meet with friends who had supported him. While the group had intended to stay in Connecticut, they decided to make a trip to San Juan, Puerto Rico, to attend Brock's birthday party.

They were en route to the airport when Janice, back in Utah, received a call. It was a FaceTime from Andy. He was holding the phone as Tony's face appeared on the screen. Tony was leaning against the wall of the coach, holding a Whip-It canister.

"Did you get my text?" Tony asked.

She hadn't seen it, but smiled as her screen lit up: "R2D2 needs C3PO."

"Come to Puerto Rico," he said.

"I can't," she replied, "I have the kids."

Tony pushed. Could she trust Don to look after them?

"I promised them more time, T, so they're here to hold down the fort," she said.

Tony paused for a moment, then looked around, as if digging for a memory.

"We've known each other a long time," he said, thinking of the Branson School and those moments of silence in the theater. "Remember when we used to just hang in the rafters?"

Aside from the fact that he was holding a Whip-It canister, something was off, Janice thought. Tony only ever became nostalgic when they were alone.

Tony's demeanor became serious. "Who do you trust?"

"What are you talking about?" she said.

"Like who do you trust around here in this ecosystem?"

Janice looked at Don, and Andy through the phone, and chuckled. "Well, I trust these two yahoos," she said. "And I trust you."

Tony looked into the camera as his voice fell to a whisper. "Don't trust anyone."

Then, in a murmur, he repeated it again. "Don't trust anyone."

■ ■ ■

Janice received infrequent updates from Tony's entourage from then on, and her worry only grew deeper when others told her that Tony was trashing the hotel room, and that he'd locked himself in the bathroom with Blizzy.

The next morning she received another call, this one more disturbing. It was from a woman named Karla Ballard, a tech entrepreneur who had run alongside Brock as his vice presidential pick. She was in San Juan and had just gotten off a FaceTime call with Tony. He had called in distress from his hotel room, and now Karla was panicked.

"What's going on with Blizzy?" Karla said.

"You do realize I'm not there?" Janice said. "I didn't go to Puerto Rico."

"Yeah, but I can't get hold of anyone else," Karla said.

Tony had been frantic, Karla recounted, telling her that Blizzy was not well. *The dog is sick,* he had said. Judging by his agitation, Karla thought Blizzy could be dying, but Tony wasn't offering more details, nor would he show her the dog. When she suggested calling a veterinarian to the hotel room, Tony said no. He was adamant. Then the call ended.

"Is he okay?" Janice asked of Blizzy. "Is he alive? Is he dead?"

"He's alive," Karla said. "But not well."

Though not for long. Soon after, when the others finally arrived in Tony's hotel room, Blizzy's body was saturated with water and bloated. The dog was dead.

■ ■ ■

The group flew back to Connecticut, bringing the animal's body in a cooler. In the backyard of Rachael's home, they held a small ceremony as Blizzy was buried in a hole dug in the ground.

Tony was inconsolable, and for the next few days he seemed lost in a stupor, inhaling from his Whip-It flask constantly. Like before, he rearranged furniture in the home, lit dozens of candles, and left a trail of nitrous oxide canisters in his wake, much to Rachael's chagrin.

After midnight on November 16, a fire alarm shrieked through the home, sending an automatic signal to the local firehouse. A crew of firefighters arrived, but left the property after being told it was a false alarm.

Twenty minutes after the crew left, however, another fire alarm summoned them back to the home, and this time the firefighters insisted on being let in. While the man who answered the door protested their entry, inside they found a room hazed in smoke, melted plastic on the stove, and some cardboard that was hot to the touch. They put the burned items in a sink and soaked them while the smoke dissipated, and then left again.

By the next evening, before they were due to embark on Elizabeth and Brett's proposed Hawaiian getaway, Rachael had had enough and ordered Tony to leave her home. It was approaching midnight, and the flight to Maui was due to leave in a few hours. He could have slept at a nearby hotel, or even in one of the vehicles on standby. But as they yelled at each other, Tony marched outside into the freezing air and stood on the beach at the rear of Rachael's home. She technically didn't own the beach, he told her, so she couldn't stop him from spending the night there. Andy and Brett came outside to mediate, and then Tony pointed to a shed attached to the side of the house. He would sleep there, he pronounced.

Just as they had done time and again before, those around Tony relented.

CHAPTER 28

THANKSGIVING

Vernon Skau had reason to hope that Tony would survive that evening. Arriving at the house minutes after Tony had been taken away by paramedics, New London's fire marshal checked in with Tom Curcio, the fire chief. There had been a fire in the shed, Curcio told him.

Walking around the scene, Skau spoke to the other fire investigators, who told him that the paramedics had been able to resuscitate Tony in the back of the ambulance. At the hospital, the machines had detected a pulse. Tony was still alive, and despite the fire, he'd made it out with barely a scratch; there were no serious burns on his body aside from superficial tissue damage on his shoulder.

Skau, who has a round, welcoming face that betrays a no-nonsense approach to his work, set about interviewing those at the scene to figure out what had happened. In his twenty years as a firefighter with the New London Fire Department, he had learned that to get the most accurate record of what happened, witnesses had to be separated and interviewed immediately. While he spoke with Rachael Brown, police and firefighters jotted down details provided by the others, who were interviewed in vehicles parked in front of the home.

A picture quickly emerged. After the argument with Rachael, Tony had gone to the shed to wait until it was time to leave for the flight to Hawaii. It was freezing outside, and Tony had tried to stay warm, first by covering himself with a blanket and then by lighting pieces of paper and a Ziploc bag on fire. Surveillance footage from a camera affixed to the top of the shed showed Brett and an assistant frequently checking on him. Then, at one point, the assistant had dragged in a propane space heater to try to warm the space.

But a glaring question remained: What was Tony doing when the fire started? At 3:15 a.m., the surveillance footage showed that Tony had pushed open the shed door and dragged the propane heater outside, only to bring it back into the shed a few moments later. At this time, something was overheating in the shed, and a trail of smoke and small embers could be seen drifting out. Then, inexplicably, after Tony pulled the door shut behind him, the sound of a deadbolt latching shut could be heard.

A few minutes later, Andy had approached the shed and knocked, telling Tony it was time to leave for the flight, evidently unaware of the danger his brother was in. *Come back in five minutes,* Tony had told him. Two minutes later, the carbon monoxide alarm started shrieking, a loud hissing sound could be heard, and smoke was billowing from the shed. As Elizabeth called 911 and fire crews were dispatched to the property, Andy, Brett, and the assistant had tried breaking down the locked door, without success. From within the shed, they could hear a loud hissing noise.

Vernon's early hypothesis was that a tragic accident had occurred. He considered the role of the propane space heater. Given its proximity to the source of the fire, and the abundance of black soot nearby, it seemed evident that the tank had become overheated by coming into contact with some sort of heat source, and then forced the relief valve to open—as it is designed to do under pressure, and likely the source of the loud hissing sound—releasing propane gas that came into contact with an open flame within the shed.

But it was unclear if the heater itself had been the source of heat that triggered the tank to release gas. Perhaps the heater had come into contact with some sort of combustible, like paper or other storage items in the shed, and then ignited. Though this theory seemed somewhat unlikely: when Tony had brought the heater outside, the surveillance footage appeared to show that the heater was not working at the time.

Another theory, that burning cigarettes or the marijuana pipe lying on the ground could have ignited one of the objects scattered across the floor, like the blanket, also seemed unlikely. Skau knew that cigarettes rarely start fires and can take anywhere between twenty-two minutes and five hours to ignite another object, by which point they are likely burned out anyway.

The presence of candles in the shed could also have started the fire, providing a naked flame to ignite a combustible. Several candles were lying around the area where the fire had started, and earlier in the night, one of the candles had been burning the blanket when the assistant asked Tony to extinguish it before it caught fire.

However, a gray basket on the other side of the shed, away from where the fire started, presented a final potential explanation, one more troubling. Inside it were pieces of burned paper, which appeared to be Post-it notes. Closer to the source of the fire, a Ziploc bag also held pieces of burned paper. It would be impossible to determine Tony's reason for lighting the pieces of paper, but their presence suggested he might have either recklessly or intentionally started the fire. There also was no clear explanation for why the shed door had locked once Tony closed it for the last time.

Once the fire started, if the release of propane gas hadn't rendered Tony unresponsive, the cluster of Fernet bottles, Whip-It canisters, and a marijuana pipe indicated he'd been heavily inebriated as the flames engulfed the shed.

The only person who could provide answers was Tony. A few hours after arriving at Lawrence Memorial Hospital in New London, he'd been airlifted by helicopter sixty miles west down the Connecticut coast to Bridgeport Hospital, to the state's burn center, where he'd been transferred to an intensive care unit.

Once he arrived back at the firehouse the following afternoon, Vernon called the hospital, and requested an update on Tony's condition. The response was limited: critical but stable condition.

What wasn't clear to Vernon, or to anyone outside the hospital, was the extent of any internal damage Tony had sustained. The first effects of smoke inhalation come within seconds, bringing an onset of nausea and loss of vision. Once carbon monoxide fills the lungs, it attaches to red blood cells, starving the body's organs of oxygen. Death can occur within minutes, and even if the victim survives, the effects of carbon monoxide poisoning all but guarantee brain damage.

Every day, once at the start of his shift, and once at the end, Vernon called the hospital for an update. The response was always the same: critical but stable. With each call, Vernon reported Tony's status back to Tom Curcio. With a short crop of brown hair and a bushy mustache that makes him immediately identifiable around town as the fire chief, Tom was vaguely aware of Tony Hsieh: his wife was a loyal Zappos customer and had been buying shoes from the website for years. She later bought him a copy of *Delivering Happiness*. "I couldn't put the book down," Tom recalled. "It just seemed like wherever he jumped to, wherever he went, he took an interest in that town or city, and he did a lot for it."

As Tony's days in the hospital wore on, it became clearer that if he was going to make it out alive, he likely wouldn't emerge the same person, and Vernon was beginning to sense that he might never learn how the fire started.

The morning after Thanksgiving was the start of Tony's ninth day in the hospital. Outside of his family and some of his friends, the world had no idea that Tony Hsieh had been in a coma for over a week. Vernon, who'd spent the previous day surrounded by his children and grandchildren, called the burn unit in Bridgeport from his home. The reply from the hospital staffer was different this time: "He's just passed."

CHAPTER 29

THE AFTERMATH

The day after Thanksgiving, Michelle was relaxing in her living room in Milwaukee with her boyfriend and daughter when the phone rang. It was Jamie Naughton, Tony's longtime confidant from Zappos. Michelle was anticipating good news, as she had been hearing the same report as Vernon Skau: critical but stable. In the days before, a message had been sent out to friends, stating that Tony's vitals were improving.

But the call didn't go as Michelle expected. "He—he died," Jamie said.

Michelle froze. Unable to process what she was hearing, she emotionally shut down. "He died," Michelle repeated out loud. Her daughter looked at her and burst into tears.

She had little time to process the news. A few hours later, she received a call from a woman named Puoy Premsrirut who had been working as Tony's attorney for the last few months. She was with Tony's family. "We'd like for you to write the post to tell the world," Puoy said. The next day, a message was posted on Tony's social media pages at 9:30 a.m.:

Today we are saddened to share the news of Tony's passing. We can only imagine what he would say if he were here to announce this to you all, but we envision his message would resonate that: Energy cannot be created or destroyed. Energy is the ability to bring about change. Tony has given energy to so many people. For those who knew him well, you

*knew of his childlike wonder; his love for experiences and relationships
over material things.*

Let us all feel Tony's energy and use it to deliver happiness.

The outpouring of grief was immediate. From President Bill Clinton to Ivanka Trump, thousands of people took to social media to share memories, photos, and videos of a man who was universally admired. Jeff Bezos was among the peers, employees, and complete strangers who came together in a mass of voices on Twitter, Instagram, and Facebook, each reciting stories of lives changed by Tony's vision and generosity—cementing a legacy of humanity rarely left behind by business leaders.

"I treasure every conversation I ever had with Tony Hsieh," Clinton wrote. "He was fascinating, brilliant, and inspiring, and his unwavering efforts to spread happiness—and enthusiasm for mentoring young entrepreneurs—touched countless lives for the better." Ivanka Trump posted a collage of photos taken with Tony over the years. One photo was the image of them standing in front of the White House, taken years before Ivanka became the First Daughter. In another photo, Jared Kushner and Jen Taler are standing with Ivanka and Tony on a casino floor, laughing while eating hot dogs. "Celebrating the life while mourning the loss of my dear friend Tony Hsieh," she wrote. "Tony was a deeply original thinker always challenging me to reject conformity & follow my heart. Tony was driven by the mission of delivering happiness & brought joy to all who knew him. Rest In Peace Tony."

In Jeff Bezos's tribute to Tony on social media, the Amazon founder wrote, "The world lost you way too soon. Your curiosity, vision, and relentless focus on customers leave an indelible mark. You will be missed by so many, Tony. Rest In Peace."

Many of the public figures who wrote tributes to Tony had little to no knowledge of what the last twelve months of his life had been like. One person who did was Jewel, who posted a twelve-minute video elegy to Tony in the days after his passing. "I sat here for a long time before I pushed Record, trying to figure out what to say," she started slowly. "I've seen a lot of posts which are beautiful but I haven't really been able to bring myself to post." The singer paused and looked down at the guitar on her lap. "The brain can't comprehend why you can't just call that person anymore. The heart can't understand why you can't just hug that person anymore," she said quietly, fighting back tears.

She then recounted how she'd first met Tony on Necker Island, and the conversations they'd had over the years. "I remember he asked me what was my definition of success," she said. "I can't remember what my answer was. But I remember his—his answer was the willingness to lose it all.

"He really brought a lot of love and joy into the world. His idea of collision points—again, mimicking nature, it was quantum. That molecular level of these atoms colliding and creating new things and that's what he was creating with the Downtown Project. How cool was that?

"We were very lucky to have known Tony," she continued. "And I'm sad and sorry that he's gone. I'm sure his cosmic spirit is floating around here so I would like to sing."

She then turned to her guitar and started to sing "Over the Rainbow."

Tears were streaming down her cheeks as she sang, "When all the world is a hopeless jumble and the raindrops tumble all around, heaven opens a magic lane."

■ ■ ■

In downtown Las Vegas, emotions ran high. What started as sorrow and despair rapidly morphed into shock and anger, as more and more stories of Tony's physical and mental decline over the last twelve months came into view. There was also an underlying fear of what would happen to the entire community now that Tony was dead, especially when it emerged that he had died without a will. Tony had picked up so many bills, millions of dollars every year, for so many ventures in Las Vegas since the birth of the Downtown Project.

Tony hadn't ended up selling his real estate portfolio while he was alive, but instead had agreed to another deal Justin had brought him in his final months. In the weeks before his death, Tony had instead closed on a deal to pay Andrew Donner's company $65 million to buy the Zappos headquarters. Perhaps a final protest to the company he had spent two decades building, only to be unceremoniously farewelled.

Now residents of his neighborhood wondered if Richard and Andy, who had been named co-administrators of Tony's estate by Clark County

District Court, would sell the estate's property portfolio to the next oppor-
tunistic developer, turning downtown Las Vegas into another swampland
of high-rise luxury hotels and loud casinos. Zapponians, meanwhile,
feared for their company's future. Would Zappos, the company that was
so crucial to Tony's legacy, get hacked into parts and disappear into Amazon's corporate crypt?

For those outside of Las Vegas, it was hard to come to terms with Tony's
passing without an explanation for his death. How did a seemingly healthy
and massively successful forty-six-year-old tech visionary die so suddenly?
Some wondered if he'd had a terminal illness that he had kept secret. One
rumor was that Tony had been kidnapped by the mob for ransom and
his death was the result of the kidnapping gone wrong. Without answers,
people had started to fill in the gaps with outlandish theories and musings.

The reality was worse. Many who knew Tony but had lost touch with
him in recent years echoed a similar sentiment when they heard about the
events of his last year: "I wish I had been there to help him."

What became clear was that the community Tony had built from the
ground up had failed to come together in his time of need. Despite the
various efforts to get Tony help, they were not coordinated and were ultimately futile. It was partly Tony's own doing—his paranoia had spread
and bred feelings of mistrust among the entire group. Michelle admitted
that, at Tony's request, she had ignored Tyler's calls for periods of time
when she was in Park City, having bought into the idea that Tyler had
gone too far. "It was like groupthink," Michelle recalled, pointing to the
psychological phenomenon common in cults that drives people to desire
conformity within a group. "It was the only explanation."

■ ■ ■

There had also been vast sums of money on the line, which blinded some
in Park City to the fact that Tony was slowly killing himself. Just how
much money came into view shortly after his death.

Alongside her boyfriend, Roberto Grande, Mimi filed the first lawsuit
in February, three months after the fatal fire, in Clark County Superior
Court. "Mimi Pham had been Tony Hsieh's assistant, right hand person,
and friend for the seventeen years preceding his death," her initial filing
read. The complaint stated that the two were so close that Tony had used

Mimi's cellphone as his own, that he had put cable and utility bills in her name, and that they shared the same address on their driver's licenses. "Unlike the relationship that existed between Tony Hsieh and Mimi Pham, neither Richard Hsieh nor Andrew Hsieh had a close personal relationship with Tony Hsieh, even though they are blood relatives. In fact, although Andrew Hsieh moved to Park City, Utah, to live with Tony Hsieh in the calendar year 2020, that is not an indication of a familial bond as he was offered $1,000,000 annual salary in exchange for said move."

Mimi sued the estate and the Hsieh family for $130 million. She hired high-profile Vegas lawyers David Chesnoff and Richard Schonfeld, whose previous clients included Paris Hilton, Bruno Mars, and Robert Durst. In Mimi's creditor's claims to the estate, she stated she was owed $9 million as part of the fees related to managing Park City properties and the documentary film company venture. She sued for anticipated profit from the film company, claiming she was entitled to $75 million. Finally, she and Roberto said they were owed an additional $25 million for "interference with the contract and the prospective economic advantage."

The next week, Puoy Premsrirut filed court documents stating she was owed $360,000 in legal fees. Two months later, in April, Tony Lee sued the estate and the Hsieh family for $7 million for breach of contract, claiming he was promised an annual $1.5 million salary for five years. "At no time during Tony Hsieh's life did Andy Hsieh or Richard Hsieh ever challenge or question the validity of the Guaranteed Contract," Lee said. He also questioned the intentions of Tony's younger brother in his lawsuit, labeling Andy as an enabler of Tony's drug and alcohol use. "It was Andy that arranged the purchase of thousands of canisters of nitrous oxide at an alarming rate for Tony Hsieh's continued use when others who cared for Mr. Hsieh refused to do so," read Lee's complaint. Lee claimed that Andy "plied Tony Hsieh with alcohol" and attempted to divert millions of dollars from Tony's account to his own.

Mark Evensvold, who had shown up in Park City with no mandate but to make up a role, sued the estate next, for $12.5 million, two months after Tony Lee's lawsuit. "A man who supposedly had business dealings with the late tech mogul . . . leaves more than one question unanswered," read a local Las Vegas news report about the case. The complaint included a transcript of the conversation with Tony, typed by the court reporter, and a copy of the contract scrawled on the Post-it note as evidence of a legitimate agreement.

Several months later, both Suzie Baleson and Justin Weniger filed claims against the Hsieh estate for alleged money owed. Justin filed his creditor's claim "out of an abundance of caution," the filing claimed. Justin said he was "justly due and owned" a 27.7 percent equity interest in Life Is Beautiful.

Suzie and her company, Wellth Collective, sued the Hsieh family for $8.7 million for work that she did for Tony in Park City. Her lawsuit also included a copy of the Post-it note that detailed the Magic Castle project, which Suzie said was supposed to receive $5 million from Tony. It also added that when Tony agreed to his contracts with Suzie, he "had clarity in what he had asked" her to do.

By the end of Tony's chapter in Park City, it later emerged, the balance on his line of credit was more than $250 million.

■ ■ ■

In the months after Tony's death, the family largely kept quiet. Only one statement, from Richard, was released shortly after Tony's passing: "We are so deeply grateful for the outpouring of love and respect shown in the wake of Tony's passing. There is no human that did not fall in love with Tony's humanity, which is why so many have been left heartbroken."

But with the family's silence, a vacuum formed, and the debates and rumors around Andy's role in Park City slowly came to a boil of confusion and outrage. The lawsuits from Mimi and Tony Lee painted Andy as a Judas-like character who took advantage of his older brother on his darkest days and kept him sick by fueling him with a never-ending supply of drugs and alcohol. Revelations of the $1 million annual salary and images posted to social media of him attending film premieres and walking the red carpet with Elizabeth and Brett to celebrate the release of projects by XTR reinforced to some onlookers an image of a man reaping riches from his deceased brother.

What that narrative disregarded, however, was that for the last months of Tony's life, Andy was secretly in constant contact with Jewel and Ryan Wolfington. The communications were clandestine because Andy feared that Tony would throw him out of his inner circle, as he had done with his mom, dad, and Tyler. The singer arranged a consultation for Andy with Dr. Blaise Aguirre, a child and adolescent psychiatrist whose patients included highly suicidal individuals, so that Andy could better handle Tony's deteriorating state. With Dr. Aguirre's advice, the plan was for Andy to somehow facilitate a hospital visit for Tony, which could then set into motion the family's plans to put Tony under a conservatorship and get him into a recovery facility. But every state has its own laborious process for setting up a conservatorship, and given Tony's constantly changing whereabouts, it made the plan—which would have required a doctor to declare Tony unfit to handle his own affairs, as well as a judge to confirm the ruling—difficult to execute. At one point, the family had doctors and attorneys in Nevada, Utah, and Connecticut on standby. But in the end, the effort was futile.

Some viewed Andy as the ultimate grifter who helped lead his brother to his death. Others saw Andy as an unwilling participant, forced to play by the twisted rules in Park City in order to stay close to his brother and not be excommunicated. Many wondered whether the events of the last twelve months would lead to a fissure in the Hsieh family, most notably between Richard and Andy, who were now co-administering Tony's legacy.

They got part of the answer in the fall of 2021, nearly eight months after Tony's passing, when the Hsiehs filed a scorched-earth response to Mimi's and Tony Lee's lawsuits. The family hired Vivian Thoreen, a high-powered attorney based in Los Angeles whose clients included Jamie Spears, the father of pop icon Britney Spears. The legal team asked some of Tony's closest confidants—from Tyler to Suzie—to sit for hours-long depositions and recount the events of 2020. In a court filing, the family issued blanket denials of nearly every allegation that Mimi made against Andy. The family accused Mimi, her boyfriend, Roberto, and Tony Lee of having "coordinated, influenced, and directed Tony's activities in and around Park City, and deliberately profited from their insider status and Tony's vulnerability."

The family laid bare Tony's struggles and demons well before 2020. "Despite his professional successes, Tony struggled with significant social anxiety," the family wrote in the filing. "Tony's mind moved at an incredible speed and Tony described using alcohol as a social lubricant to alleviate his social anxiety and to allow him to better communicate and make deeper connections to the people around him." The family revealed that Tony had prescriptions for Adderall (to treat attention deficit hyperactivity disorder), Xanax (to treat anxiety and panic disorders), and Ambien (to treat insomnia). The Hsiehs also stated that Tony suffered from depression.

According to the family, ketamine was Tony's attempt to find a healthier alternative to his alcohol and prescription medication consumption. But "it immediately caused Tony to suffer from disorganized delusions and delusions of grandeur. While Tony was known as a man with elaborate ideas, those same ideas while Tony was under the influence of Ketamine were delusional and destructive. Among other effects, the delusions caused Tony to believe he needed to consume more Ketamine in order to solve the problems existing within the delusion."

Charting the events from Tony's ketamine usage at the Summit conference in Los Angeles through Park City in great detail, the court filing documented how mentally debilitated Tony had become and that anyone who had engaged with him in business in the months after were taking advantage of a sick man who needed help. "While Tony had always been an unconventional thinker and risk taker, there had always been a method and principles guiding Tony's professional endeavors," the family's response read. "While using Ketamine, Tony was unable to exercise reasonable diligence and judgment and was vulnerable to those trying to take advantage of him."

Or as another friend of Tony's put it, "The king had no clothes and the sycophants wouldn't say a fucking word."

■ ■ ■

It is indisputable that Tony had been surrounded by people who took advantage of his generosity—and his ego—during his last year in Park City. This dynamic, however, was sometimes countered by good intentions and actions, even from those who made business deals with him, from Justin and Suzie's health regimen to Mimi's role in helping to get Tony into rehab. Andy had slipped vitamins and protein supplements into Tony's food. Amid the attempts to get Tony help, what emerged in the hundreds of hours of interviews we conducted with people who witnessed Tony's descent was that there were no heroes or villains. Some well-meaning actors gave in to the temptations of greed, while supposed bad actors had complicated histories that gave their roles context.

Mimi and her boyfriend eventually dropped their lawsuit against the Hsiehs, a year after Tony's death. In a victory for the family, Mimi also agreed to pay the Hsieh estate $750,000 to settle all claims. Tony Lee's lawsuit and a number of other creditor claims remain ongoing.

Two months after Suzie filed her claim against the Hsieh estate, she launched a venture capital firm called Wellth Ventures, "committed to building a healthier, more sustainable and more connected world" with another partner. Per a press release, billionaire Richard Branson has "made a financial commitment to support Wellth Ventures' activities." The same release also states that Suzie "worked in real estate and accounting as a partner in a $350 million Las Vegas–based development fund," but made no mention of Tony Hsieh or the Downtown Project.

Justin, as it turned out, had been successful in negotiating a deal for Life Is Beautiful during his year in Park City, and in February 2022 *Rolling Stone* announced it had acquired a majority stake in the festival. "The combination of *Rolling Stone*, with our scale of over 60 million readers, and our ability as a journalistic outfit, to combine that skillset with an unbelievable live event that attracts 180,000 people a year—that's new territory and really, really compelling," CEO Gus Wenner said. But by then, Justin had been paid for his equity and parted ways with the festival.

Elizabeth and Brett got married in Park City, in a ceremony attended by Richard, Judy, and Andy. After moving to Florida, Elizabeth started a wellness company selling NAD therapies.

Kedar Deshpande, who was appointed chief executive of Zappos after Tony, served only a year at the helm before leaving for another role. In the summer of 2022, the fears of Zappos employees were realized, and under its new CEO, Scott Schaefer, a stream of longtime executives were let go from the company.

Tyler remained, maintaining his role of director of brand experience at the company. He is creating an archive of Tony-related assets to present to the Hsieh family from Zappos.

Michelle continued to do media work for the Hsieh family, including the launch of the Tony Hsieh Award, which recognizes individuals who have achieved "significant advancement and bold innovation." Collaborators on this include TED Talks, Alfred Lin, and Fred Mossler. In 2016, years after Tony texted her the message, "This too shall pass," Michelle had the phrase tattooed on her back in Tibetan. After Tony's death, she added "12.12" above the existing tattoo—for Tony's birthday.

Fred, his wife, Meghan, and their children still live in downtown Las Vegas. After Fred left Zappos, the couple started a new company, Ross and Snow, which sells authentic Italian leather shoes. In 2022, after Justin left Life Is Beautiful, Fred accepted an invitation from Richard and Andy to join the board of the festival.

As for Andy, perhaps no person has remained a more polarizing figure in the remnants of Tony's community. But beyond the debate swirling around his motivations in Park City, there remained a seemingly unanswered question: Why did Andy film his brother as he lay dying on the stretcher?

In hindsight, some considered his actions as documenting the event, however tragic, to gather evidence for the conservatorship he and the family were preparing. Perhaps he just hadn't realized that his brother was actually dying.

There was another reading of his actions, however. In the months leading up to Tony's end in Connecticut, Andy had been frequently filming his brother and telling those around them that it would be good content for a documentary he was thinking of putting together about his brother's life—even while he was being stretchered into an ambulance without a pulse.

Just as Tony was the only person who knew how the fire started, only Andy could explain why he pulled out his phone while emergency crews worked on his brother. He has declined to talk to reporters, maintaining his silence.

In July 2022, nearly two years after Tony's death, Richard notified the court that Andy was no longer a co-administrator of Tony's estate.

■ ■ ■

In his memoir, Tony wrote that if you ask why enough times in life, the ultimate answer is always happiness. But not until the final pages, in the first passage of his epilogue, does Tony offer a clue to his own reason, a question he answers with more questions.

As a guiding principle in life for anything I do, I try to ask myself, *What would happen if everyone in the world acted in the same way? What would the world look like? What would the net effect be on the overall happiness in the world?*

Tony considered himself a builder—of companies, experiences, and communities. With these building blocks, he thought, he could build his way to happiness—that this ephemeral state of mind was an end output that could be achieved with only a source code.

In the end, he kept acquiring and building until eventually, he had everything in the world—and it still wasn't enough.

Herein lies the tragedy of this story. Because for all those whose lives he touched—from Canady Hall A in Harvard to those who followed him for two decades at Zappos, and all the strangers in between—they could agree on one thing: Tony Hsieh was more than enough.

■ ■ ■

Walking through Aspen Springs in the months after his death, one could see a reminder that Tony once lived here. Down the sloping driveway of his sprawling ranch was a large sculpture, seven feet tall and thirty feet long. A psychedelic array of royal blue tiles flowed seamlessly into orange, a mosaic that wrapped around a half dozen concrete tentacles—two were missing. The remaining limbs were contorted in a menacing position, as if they were about to whip forward.

Looming behind them was an enormous bulbous head, burrowed into the dirt, as if hiding in the sand of the ocean floor, waiting to seize its prey. Two black eyes the size of hands peered forward, keeping watch on the front door of the estate.

The octopus had arrived that afternoon in August 2020 as the swirl of chaos at the ranch reached a crescendo. Tony had wanted art scattered through his property to re-create an element of Burning Man in Park City, just as he had done in Las Vegas. But unlike other sculptures at the property, the octopus was poised in the brush, center stage. It was the first thing Tony would see when he entered the property and when he left it.

It remained there, like a sentry, as Tony spent his final months spiraling toward his fatal end. It was there as his contingent of followers grew. As tens of millions of dollars drained from his bank accounts. As the memory of all that he had achieved in life faded amid his isolation from family and friends, old and dear. As he became a gaunt shadow of his former self, his genius obscured by drug addiction and breaks with reality. The octopus lay there, waiting.

Many years before, when Tony was a boy, he had sat down in front of a typewriter to write a poem. Embodied within a child's drawing that depicts a vividly soulless creature with hollow eyes and grasping tentacles, his words recount a nightmare in which he is running down the street he grew up on, Coast Oak Way. He is running from a slimy, smiling octopus that is chasing him—why, he doesn't know.

I run down the street, passing a court.
The Octopus is getting even closer.

He tries to climb a brown wooden wall, but he keeps slipping. No one is around to help him. The octopus is advancing. He is being chased farther from home.

I run around the corner up Canyon Oak.

Then the monster of Tony's mind arrives.

The Octopus grabs me
And then there's darkness.

I am now wide awake.

EPILOGUE

Fred Mossler was the first to arrive at the Parlour Bar on a sweltering September afternoon. As his wife, Meghan, stepped inside next to him, his eyes scanned the black lounge chairs and booths. Tucked within the rabbit warren of the El Cortez's gaming room floor, the bar rang with the dings and chimes of the slot machines. Effervescent air pushed through the vents above, suppressing the tobacco smoke that trailed through the room.

With a pair of sunglasses resting atop his graying hair, he wore a royal blue and white checkered button-down shirt that hung loosely from his shoulders. A soft familiarity washed over his face as he walked farther into the space, glancing for a moment at a booth in the far corner.

There was nothing visibly remarkable about the sunken leather seat. But Fred held countless memories of sitting there, next to Tony, hunched over their laptops. On two round knee-high tables, shots of Fernet would be placed between the keyboards and notepads, and they'd down the alcohol amid discussion of their next idea or their next deal. A revolving cast of dreamers and doers would join them, for advice or to pitch them new business. A smoke trail would float up from an American Spirit between Tony's fingers, a dreamlike glow forming around his stoic expression.

Now on the wall was a plaque above the leather booth in which Tony once sat. *Tony's Corner,* it read.

Dedicated to a true visionary and champion of Downtown Las Vegas, Tony Hsieh.

This corner of the Parlour Bar was a favorite meeting spot for Tony and his Zappos and Downtown Project teams for many years.

The power outlet below was installed to help power their smart devices as big ideas were hatched and big deals were made.

Fred looked up as two other people walked through the rows of black-jack tables and entered the bar. He greeted a Zappos employee with an enthusiastic handshake, and they spoke quietly as other figures began appearing in the space.

Justin Weniger walked in, wearing a black T-shirt emblazoned with the Life Is Beautiful logo. He looked around while greeting the party. It was the first day of the 2021 Life Is Beautiful music festival, and Justin's three-day event was scheduled to start in half an hour. In years past, Tony had traditionally hosted a kickoff brunch for his friends at the trailer park. But this time, Justin had organized the gathering to toast Tony's memory before the festival started.

On this afternoon, thousands of people would descend on Tony's neighborhood to fill the empty parking lots, its restaurants, and its streets, while a kaleidoscope of laser beams and lights would draw them further into the labyrinth of the world Tony built. Before international stars like Megan Thee Stallion, Glass Animals, and Tame Impala would lead the revelers to move in unison, just as Tony had with the other ravers all those years ago in the San Francisco warehouse, the horizon would swallow the sunlight as the night summoned the neons to light the desert valley.

As far as the eye would allow, from the downtown that Tony had built all the way to the corporate casinos to the south, the lights would speckle the panorama like stars. Though Tony wouldn't be there to see his creation come to life this night, the lights of Las Vegas would shine a little brighter than they ever had before.

Fred stood up and walked over to the bar to join a Zappos employee. A dozen people had showed up to the toast.

"Let's make this year the best festival ever," one person sitting at the table said.

"Obviously this year is going to be different," added another.

Fred returned to the booth, carrying glasses of Fernet. "Here's a little shot for our friend," he said. He leaned over, then placed the glass where Tony used to sit.

ACKNOWLEDGMENTS

This book is the product of hundreds of conversations with people who knew Tony intimately through each chapter of his life. Without them, we would not have been able to share Tony's story in such depth, nor been able to capture why it matters to each of us. For their support and trust, we are deeply grateful to them for allowing us to tell the story of their dear friend.

We want to thank Randall Lane, our editor at *Forbes*, who urged us to pursue our first story about Tony in December 2020, and whose encouragement, guidance, and prose got us through two days, and one long night, to ensure that we delivered "Tony Hsieh's American Tragedy." That effort was supported by leaders within *Forbes*'s editorial team, including Luisa Kroll, Kerry Dolan, Michael Noer, Alex Konrad, and Jessica Bohrer, and highlighted the magazine's ability to support its reporters in pursuing and delivering high-caliber journalism and storytelling.

Henry Holt & Co. have been remarkable partners, and we count our lucky stars that it was Sarah Crichton who found us. It was her unwavering belief in the story of Tony Hsieh, and in us, that ensured that this book was written. Our stellar editors, Serena Jones and Anita Sheih, showed incredible attention to detail, asking questions, pointing out narrative holes, and suggesting changes that breathed life into our manuscript. Additionally, we want to thank Michael Cantwell for providing a thorough legal review, and Majd Al Waheidi for doing a fantastic job fact-checking our book; we are thankful for their diligence.

Our agent, Ethan Bassoff, with Ross Yoon, also took a chance on a pair of first-time book authors. Over two years, Ethan listened to our complaints, insecurities, and ideas, and provided nothing more than wisdom, advice, and comfort as we stumbled along this journey. From proposal to prologue, Ethan shepherded us through, and for that we are immensely grateful. We also want to thank Howard Yoon for his role in helping us reframe parts of the manuscript.

From Angel: To my two sisters, Christine and Carmen—for without their wisdom and encouragement, I would be nowhere close to where I find myself today. To Mom and Dad, thank you for all that you have sacrificed. To Gorjan Hrustanovic, for putting up with me all these years. In truth, you've been my best friend ever since we met, even if neither of us can agree on when that was.

To Kerry Dolan, Keren Blankfeld, Duy Linh Tu, and Marie Beaudette, thank you for taking a chance on me. I owe my sanity and levity to my girlfriends in San Francisco and Los Angeles—thank you for saving me from a humorless, self-serious reality.

To my coauthor David, thank you for the last two years, from your encouragement to your pasta Bolognese to your pretty awful jokes. There'd be none of this without you.

From David: I have too many people to thank from both sides of the Pacific, but I'd like to make sure Meg Kissinger and Kevin McKenna know how grateful I am for their mentorship and friendship. I'm equally grateful for my editors at *Forbes*, Jeff Taylor, John Paczkowski, and Katharine Schwab. To Inti Pacheco, Grace Ashford, Majlie de Puy Kamp, Jacqueline Williams, and Kristin Schwab: thank you for supporting me in more ways than one.

There are few words available to describe how incredible it has been to work on this book with Angel. In addition to being a killer reporter, her empathy can be seen throughout this manuscript. Reporting, debating, and writing alongside her for the past couple of years has been an experience I will treasure.

My deepest gratitude is reserved for my family, who have kept me afloat with their love, and continue to inspire me. Each day I'm grateful for Michael, who always listens, and for Kate, whose wisdom knows few bounds. For Dad, my first reader for so many years, and for Mum, who never stops asking questions, and taught me to do the same.

A NOTE ON SOURCES

The Hsieh family did not respond to our requests for interviews, nor did they respond to extensive fact-checking questions. The family has been involved in litigation for much of the past two years. Vivian Lee Thoreen and Stephanie Berardino, their attorneys, did not respond to our repeated requests for interviews or for comment.

A few months into our writing process, the Hsieh family began to respond to the lawsuits with surprising candor, laying bare Tony's struggles to the world. We interpreted these documents as the Hsieh family's way of presenting their side of the story to the public. We incorporated information from their court filings in our book to the extent possible, in addition to reviewing thousands of pages of court documents filed by other parties, as well as police and fire reports; all have been cited in the endnotes.

We interviewed more than 150 people for this book. Some spoke to us for dozens of hours, recounting both joyful and painful memories. They shared videos and photographs, digging up digital photographs from long-lost cloud drives or yearbooks in dusty garage boxes. Many of them worked for Tony, Zappos, or the Downtown Project; were classmates of Tony's from elementary school to Harvard; or have known the Hsieh family socially. Some of our sources only spoke to us on the condition of anonymity. On-the-record sources are cited in the endnotes.

Relying on individual recollections can give rise to errors due to the fickleness of memory. To counter this, we re-interviewed a number of sources regularly over the course of a year and a half to reconcile their accounts with those of others and to ensure accuracy. All quoted dialogue in the manuscript has been drawn either from recollections of people who were present for those conversations, from audio or video recordings, or from written records.

The manuscript was independently fact-checked by Majd Al Waheidi, who knew the identity of each source, checked each quotation, and accessed all of our reporting and research materials—from legal documents to interview recordings.

In the first half of 2021, we spent more than a month reporting from downtown Las Vegas, where we stayed at the Ogden and immersed ourselves in the neighborhood that Tony built. We later returned to attend Life Is Beautiful in September 2021. We also traveled to Park City, UT, New London, CT, New York City, and the San Francisco Bay Area. We consulted the University of Illinois Archives, which had an extensive library of accounts and details of Taiwanese and Chinese student life and culture at the institution starting from the early 1900s. We were lucky to connect with Salvatore de Sando, a trained archivist who was no longer working with the university at the time, but still pointed us in the right direction and helped us with our research.

For Tony's earlier years, we drew information—including inner dialogue and thoughts—from his book, *Delivering Happiness*. We cross-referenced his account of events with some of his close friends, peers, and employees and sometimes found discrepancies between those accounts. We made note of these discrepancies in the manuscript.

In addition to our sources, we drew on research from other journalists, including the *Wall Street Journal* reporters Kirsten Grind and Katherine Sayre, whose book *Happy at Any Cost: The Revolutionary Vision and Fatal Quest of Zappos CEO Tony Hsieh* provided an account of Tony's life, and Aimee Groth, whose reporting in various publications and her book *The Kingdom of Happiness: Inside Tony Hsieh's Zapponian Utopia* provided a first-person account of Tony's Downtown Project.

Most notably, we were able to piece together parts of Tony's downtown Las Vegas world from articles published by the *Las Vegas Review Journal* and *Las Vegas Sun*—reporting that underscored the necessity and importance of local journalism.

For the events of the last year and a half of Tony's life, we relied largely on legal filings and on the accounts of people who were there, and we appreciate just how gracious they were with us. They continued to cooperate, even when we asked them to recount painful memories from 2020. This book would be without depth had they not entrusted us to deliver a narrative that is both honest and cautionary. We thank them for their trust.

NOTES

Prologue

xiv **Elizabeth was one of them:** Multiple anonymous sources.

xiv **outside the shed door:** Details of the fire, including the hours leading up to it, were documented in incident reports, videos, and photos provided by the New London Police and Fire Departments as part of their investigation into the cause of the accident.

xiv **lighting a Ziploc bag on fire:** New London Fire and Police Department documents.

xv **Elizabeth dialed 911:** Recording of 911 call released by New London Police Department.

xvi **they found him lying faceup:** Incident reports provided by New London Fire and Police Departments.

xvii **Bezos said at the time:** "Video from Jeff Bezos About Amazon and Zappos," YouTube, posted by 07272009july, July 22, 2009, https://www.youtube.com/watch?v=-hxX_Q5CnaA.

xvii **during talks with Oprah:** TV interview, *The Oprah Winfrey Show*, episode "Millionaire Moguls," October 23, 2008.

xvii **and Barbara Walters:** "The Mastermind of 'Delivering Happiness,'" YouTube, posted by ABC News, August 3, 2012, https://www.youtube.com/watch?v=p4OBZFVwu1s&t=5s.

xvii *New York Times* **bestseller:** "We're #1 on The New York Times Bestseller List!," Delivering Happiness website, retrieved July 31, 2022, https://blog.deliveringhappiness.com/blog/were-1-on-the-new-york-times-bestseller-list.

xvii **toured the late-night TV shows:** TV interview on *The Colbert Report*, August 1, 2011, https://www.cc.com/video/mqbxt0/the-colbert-report-tony-hsieh.

xvii **shared the stage with Bill Clinton:** "Local Laboratories: Tony Hsieh," YouTube, posted by Clinton Global Initiative, July 2, 2014, https://www.youtube.com/watch?v=OHqslKiU4yY.

xvii **Ashton Kutcher:** "Delivering Happiness with Ashton Kutcher and Demi Moore—Part One," YouTube, posted by Delivering Happiness, March 21, 2011, https://www.youtube.com/watch?v=z-K0r5821Kw.

xvii **Richard Branson:** Branson, Richard, "Tony Hsieh Remembered," Virgin company

website, November 30, 2020, https://www.virgin.com/branson-family/richard
-branson-blog/tony-hsieh-remembered.

xvii **Jewel:** Instagram post, December 1, 2020, https://www.instagram.com/p/CIQ
_i8bnZIu/?hl=en.

xvii **Maggie Hsu:** Interview with Maggie Hsu, February 10, 2021.

xviii **"a young Buddha":** Schoenmann, Joe, "What's Behind Tony Hsieh's Unrelenting Drive
to Remake Downtown Las Vegas?," *Las Vegas Sun*, April 20, 2012, https://lasvegassun
.com/news/2012/apr/20/behind-tony-hsiehs-passion-remake-downtown-las-veg/.

xviii **photo taken at Microsoft's headquarters:** Rich, Motoko, "Why Is This Man Smiling?," *New York Times*, April 8, 2011, https://www.nytimes.com/2011/04/10/fashion
/10HSEIH.html.

xviii **who is eating a hot dog:** Ivanka Trump, @IvankaTrump, "Celebrating the life while
mourning the loss," Twitter, November 28, 2020, 11:13 a.m., https://twitter.com
/ivankatrump/status/1332719265900879872.

xviii **built a trailer park . . . a pet alpaca, and his dog:** "Inside Zappos CEO's Wild, Wonderful Life," YouTube, posted by ABC News, August 12, 2015, https://www.youtube
.com/watch?v=3S9J0IGmRPo.

xix **introduced to ketamine:** Some details of the events of 2020 are documented in a court
filing from the Hsieh family in response to various lawsuits. Other sources are either
noted in the narrative or in other footnotes in following chapters. See Baby Monster
LLC v. PCVI LLC, Richard Hsieh and Andrew Hsieh, A-21-828090-C, Eighth Judicial
District Court, Nevada, August 23, 2021, PCVI LLC's Answer to Second Amended
Complaint, Counterclaim, Third Party Complaint and Demand for Jury Trial (n.d.).

xx **were optimistic:** Interview with Vernon Skau and Tom Curcio, February 20, 2021.

xx **sent a whoosh of ignited gas:** New London Police and Fire Departments documents.

xx **turned off his life support:** New London Police and Fire Departments documents.

xx **Bill Clinton:** Bill Clinton, @BillClinton, "I treasure every conversation," Twitter, November 30, 2020, 8:08 p.m., https://twitter.com/billclinton/status/1333578663380520961.

xx **Ivanka Trump:** Ivanka Trump, @IvankaTrump, "Celebrating the life while mourning
the loss," Twitter, November 28, 2020, 11:13 a.m., https://twitter.com/ivankatrump
/status/1332719265900879872.

xxi **the first article:** Au-Yeung, Angel, and Jeans, David, "Tony Hsieh's American Tragedy: The Self-Destructive Last Months of the Zappos Visionary," *Forbes*, December 4,
2020, https://www.forbes.com/sites/angelauyeung/2020/12/04/tony-hsiehs-american
-tragedy-the-self-destructive-last-months-of-the-zappos-visionary/.

xxiv **started filming:** Video footage provided by New London Police and Fire Departments;
multiple anonymous sources.

Chapter 1: The Golden Child

1 **"To me . . . money meant that later on in life":** Hsieh, Tony, *Delivering Happiness: A
Path to Profits, Passion, and Purpose* (Grand Central Publishing, 2012), 10.

2 **As one historian put it:** Olson, Emily. "Remembering Silicon Valley's Trailblazing 'Trou-
blemakers'" TheSixFifty, December 7, 2017, https://www.thesixfifty.com/remembering
-silicon-valleys-trailblazing-troublemakers-3968/.

3 **In one issue from 1984:** Sklarewitz, Norman, "Tim Knight: The Computer Opened a
Window," *Boys' Life* 74, no. 9 (September 1984): 96.

3 **"I learned":** Hsieh, *Delivering Happiness*, 14.

5 **Richard earned his PhD:** De Sando, Salvator, "Illini Everywhere: Taiwanese Illini, Since

1922," Student Life and Culture Archives, University of Illinois at Urbana-Champaign, February 28, 2018, https://archives.library.illinois.edu/slc/taiwanese-illini/.

5 **to get her PhD in psychology:** Hsieh, Judy S., "The Cognitive Effects of Chinese Language Training in a Sample of Chinese-American Children," PhD diss., California School of Professional Psychology at Berkeley/Alameda, 1991.

6 **recognized Taiwan:** Office of the Historian, U.S. Department of State, "The Taiwan Straits Crises: 1954–55 and 1958," https://history.state.gov/milestones/1953–1960 /taiwan-strait-crises.

6 **Ang Lee:** National Taiwan University of Arts, "NTUA Hall of Fame, Alumni," 2006, https://portal2.ntua.edu.tw/enntua/4_102.htm.

6 **co-founder of Garmin:** Garmin company website, https://www.garmin.com/en-US /company/leadership/executive/min-kao/.

6 **dating back to the early 1900s:** De Sando, "Illini Everywhere."

6 **in the same field:** De Sando, "Illini Everywhere."

6 **for social work:** De Sando, "Illini Everywhere."

7 **He became a member:** De Sando, "Illini Everywhere."

7 **his research received funding:** Hsieh, Richard Chuan-Kang, "Molecular Thermodynamics and High Pressure Kinetics of Polar Reactions in Solutions," PhD diss., University of Illinois, 1991, 183.

7 **catching fireflies in jars:** "Simon Sinek Talks Culture with Zappos CEO Tony Hsieh," YouTube, posted by Simon Sinek, August 1, 2019, https://www.youtube.com/watch?v =uqUx4BJ1ENY.

7 **where the family moved:** Hsieh, *Delivering Happiness*, 7.

8 **Among the expectations outlined for him:** Hsieh, *Delivering Happiness*, 7.

Chapter 2: Wide Awake

10 **Confederate states:** Brenner, Keri, "Marin's Dixie School District Officially Changes Name," *Mercury News*, July 10, 2019, https://www.mercurynews.com/2019/07/10 /dixie-changes-name-to-miller-creek-elementary-school-district/.

10 **"Tony H.":** Conversation with David Padover, June 2021.

10 **"Somehow my parents managed to find":** Hsieh, Tony, *Delivering Happiness: A Path to Profits, Passion, and Purpose* (Grand Central Publishing, 2012), 7.

11 **The Three Investigators:** On-background conversation with a childhood friend, February 2021.

12 **The yearbook page:** Source material from a childhood friend, 1985 Dixie Elementary School yearbook, 47.

15 **"enclave within an enclave":** Dougherty, Conor, "California Prep School Shaken by Arrests of Headmaster and Woman, 21, on Drug Charges," *New York Times*, October 7, 2014, https://www.nytimes.com/2014/10/08/us/branson-prep-school-shaken-by -arrest-of-headmaster-thomas-price-with-a-woman-21-on-drug-charges.html.

15 **$50,000-a-year-tuition:** "Affording Branson," Branson school website, https://www .branson.org/admissions/affording-branson, accessed August 25, 2022.

15 **in the county:** "History Watch: Lagunitas Country Club Built on Site of 'Pink Saloon,'" *Marin Independent Journal*, July 19, 2018, https://www.marinij.com/2015 /07/13/history-watch-lagunitas-country-club-built-on-site-of-pink-saloon/.

15 **$220,000:** Data USA of Deloitte, Datawheel and Cesar Hidalgo of MIT Media Lab,https: //datausa.io/profile/geo/ross-ca/#:~:text=In%202019%2C%20Ross%2C%20CA%20 had,%2C%20a%20%E2%88%9210.2%25%20decrease, accessed December 5, 2022.

15 **$2 million:** Data USA of Deloitte, Datawheel and Cesar Hidalgo of MIT Media Lab.https: //datausa.io/profile/geo/ross-ca/#:~:text=In%202019%2C%20Ross%2C%20CA%20 had,%2C%20a%20%E2%88%9210.2%25%20decrease, accessed December 5, 2022.

15 **admitted to Branson:** On-background conversation with childhood friend, February 2021.

16 **plotting which Grateful Dead shows:** On-background conversation with former Branson teacher, June 2021.

16 **"I remember thinking that the first day":** Hsieh, *Delivering Happiness*, 15.

17 **phone sex operator:** Hsieh, *Delivering Happiness*, 16.

18 **"A++++++++++++":** Hsieh, *Delivering Happiness*, 19.

18 **"excellence in classroom achievement and other pursuits":** 1990 and 1991 Branson School yearbook, provided by anonymous source.

18 **reads the caption:** Branson School yearbook, provided by anonymous source.

19 **"I walked away":** Hsieh, *Delivering Happiness*, 20.

20 **yearbook page:** Branson School yearbook, provided by anonymous source.

Chapter 3: The Bet

23 **by the other colleges:** Hsieh, Tony, *Delivering Happiness: A Path to Profits, Passion, and Purpose* (Grand Central Publishing, 2012), 19.

23 **eight U.S. presidents:** "Obama Joins List of Seven Presidents with Harvard Degrees," *Harvard Gazette*, November 6, 2008, https://news.harvard.edu/gazette/story/2008/11 /obama-joins-list-of-seven-presidents-with-harvard-degrees/.

23 **over a hundred Olympians:** "Olympians," Harvard University, May 5, 2020, https: //gocrimson.com/sports/2020/5/5/information-history-olympians.

23 **"yielded the most":** Hsieh, *Delivering Happiness*, 8.

24 **rarely be the case:** Private conversation during a virtual memorial service among some of Tony's Harvard-era friends, December 2020.

24 **"There was a core group":** Hsieh, *Delivering Happiness*, 24.

24 **In one candid photograph:** Provided by anonymous source.

25 **leaving open Tuesdays and Thursdays:** Hsieh, *Delivering Happiness*, 19.

25 **for sixteen hours straight:** Hsieh, *Delivering Happiness*, 24.

25 **scanned copy:** Provided by anonymous source.

26 **"The bad news":** Hsieh, *Delivering Happiness*, 25.

26 **harvard.general message board:** Wong, Brant K., "Senior Forms 'Bible' Study Group on 'Net," *Harvard Crimson*, May 12, 1995, https://www.thecrimson.com/article/1995 /5/12/senior-forms-bible-study-group-on/.

27 **"Programmers Win Contest":** Imes, Ann M., "Programmers Win Contest," *Harvard Crimson*, February 1993, https://www.thecrimson.com/article/1993/2/20 /programmers-win-contest-pa-harvard-team/.

27 **named Larry Page and Sergey Brin:** Board of Trustees page on The Exploratorium website, https://www.exploratorium.edu/about/board-of-trustees/craig-silverstein, accessed October 23, 2022.

28 **"NYU blended seamlessly into the urban jungle of Manhattan":** "Helping Revitalize a City | Hsieh, Tony," YouTube, posted by Long Now Foundation, May 1, 2020, https://www.youtube.com/watch?v=aQ0wo-pczoI.

31 **weddings and other catered events:** Hsieh, *Delivering Happiness*, 26.

31 **for the federal government:** Hsieh, *Delivering Happiness*, 26.

31 **code name "Secret":** Hsieh, *Delivering Happiness*, 26.

33 A photograph taken on that day: Provided by anonymous source.

34 "To me, it seemed like a win-win": Hsieh, *Delivering Happiness*, 51.

Chapter 4: LinkExchange

35 "I felt that I'd succeeded": Hsieh, Tony, *Delivering Happiness: A Path to Profits, Passion, and Purpose* (Grand Central Publishing, 2012), 30.

35 "The Year Everything Changed": McCracken, Harry, "1995: The Year Everything Changed," *Fast Company*, December 2015, https://www.fastcompany.com/3053055 /1995-the-year-everything-changed.

36 the website domain Yahoo.com: Wolfe, Jennifer C., and Chasser, Anne H., *Brand Rewired: Connecting Branding, Creativity, and Intellectual Property Strategy* (Wiley, 2010), 145.

36 started an email distribution list: Craig Newmark Philanthropies website, https: //craignewmarkphilanthropies.org/about-us/craig-newmark-bio/, accessed August 25, 2021.

36 Match.com: Kushner, David, "Recruiting Women to Online Dating Was a Challenge," *The Atlantic*, April 2019, https://www.theatlantic.com/technology/archive/2019/04 /how-matchcom-digitized-dating/586603/.

36 in Seattle: Stone, Brad, *The Everything Store: Jeff Bezos and the Age of Amazon* (Little, Brown, 2013), 28.

36 continues to prohibit: McPhate, Mike, "California Today: Silicon Valley's Secret Sauce," *New York Times*, May 19, 2017, https://www.nytimes.com/2017/05/19/us /california-today-silicon-valley.html.

42 I can't believe this is real: Hsieh, *Delivering Happiness*, 46.

42 Kate O'Brien's: From interview with Kevin Ascher, May 2021.

42 "Where Wuppies Gather": Angwin, Julia, "Where Wuppies Gather: DrinkExchange Draws Hundreds Every Month," *San Francisco Chronicle*, September 6, 1997, https: //www.sfgate.com/business/article/Where-Wuppies-Gather-DrinkExchange-draws -2808693.php.

43 impromptu trip to Yosemite: Conversation during a virtual memorial service among some of Tony's Harvard-era friends, December 2020.

45 August 1998: "Russia Rebounds," International Monetary Fund, September 9, 2003, https://www.imf.org/external/pubs/nft/2003/russia/.

45 "At the time, I didn't think": Hsieh, *Delivering Happiness*, 47.

46 "the evil empire": Interview with Steve Valenzuela, former chief financial officer at LinkExchange, May 2021.

46 "Without getting into too much detail": Hsieh, *Delivering Happiness*, 50.

47 "Well, I guess the deal closed": Hsieh, *Delivering Happiness*, 50.

Chapter 5: Raving

49 "The steady wordless electronic beats": Hsieh, Tony, *Delivering Happiness: A Path to Profits, Passion, and Purpose* (Grand Central Publishing, 2012), 79.

50 "They not only created Internet communities": Buck, Stephanie, "During the First San Francisco Dot-Com Boom, Techies and Ravers Got Together to Save the World," *Quartz*, August 2017, https://qz.com/1045840/during-the-first-san-francisco-dot -com-boom-techies-and-ravers-got-together-to-save-the-world/.

50 One reveler recounted: Durbin, Samantha, "Acid, Dance, Unity: What Happened to the '90s Bay Area Rave Scene?," The Bold Italic, June 2019, https://thebolditalic

.com/acid-dance-unity-what-happened-to-the-90s-bay-area-rave-scene -50a5320b7001.

50 **National Drug Intelligence Center:** "Other Dangerous Drugs," National Drug Intelligence Center, California Northern and Eastern Districts Drug Threat Assessment, January 2001, https://www.justice.gov/archive/ndic/pubs/653/odd.htm.

50 **"optimal conditions":** "Five Things to Know About MDMA-Assisted Psychotherapy for PTSD," Mount Sinai Physician's Channel, https://physicians.mountsinai .org/news/five-things-to-know-about-mdma-assisted-psychotherapy-for -ptsd#:~:text=%E2%80%9CPeople%20taking%20MDMA%20report%20 feelings,of%20difficult%20or%20traumatic%20material.%E2%80%9D, accessed October 23, 2022.

51 **deflect reporters' questions:** Hochman, David, "Playboy Interview: Tony Hsieh," *Playboy*, April 16, 2014.

51 **"At raves, it was part":** Hsieh, *Delivering Happiness*, 80.

51 **after her pet frog:** Private conversation during a virtual memorial service among some of Tony's Harvard-era friends, December 2020.

52 **Cisco Chinese Chicken Salad:** Dean, Katie, "Not Just Food, It's Fancy Food," *Wired*, January 22, 2003, https://www.wired.com/2003/01/not-just-food-its-fancy-food/.

52 **"We could create our own adult version":** Hsieh, *Delivering Happiness*, 56.

55 **"Dot-Com Party Madness":** Cave, Damien, "Dot-Com Party Madness," *Salon*, April 25, 2000, https://www.salon.com/2000/04/25/party_5/.

55 **"The company had 200 customers":** Adler, Carlyle, "The Fresh Prince of Software," CNN, March 1, 2003, https://money.cnn.com/magazines/fsb/fsb_archive/2003/03/01 /338759/index.htm.

55 **"It's simply become part of the way":** Cave, "Dot-Com Party Madness."

56 **Alfred and Sanjay often skipped the Club BIO nights":** Anonymous source, February 2021.

57 **There's a photo of the just-married couple:** Provided by an anonymous source.

57 **In one photograph for the *San Francisco Chronicle*:** Sinton, Peter, "Incubators Coddle Web Startups," *San Francisco Chronicle*, December 8, 1999, https://www.sfgate .com/business/article/Incubators-Coddle-Web-Startups-2891370.php.

58 **AskJeeves, . . . Entango, NeoPlanet, and Fusion:** Tom, Allison, "Venture Frogs: Startups Haven't Croaked," CNN, July 6, 2001, http://www.cnn.com/2001/CAREER/trends /07/06/venture.frogs/.

58 **$7.5 million to a company called eCompanies:** Loftus, Peter, "ECompanies Pays $7.5 Million for Domain Name 'Business.com,'" *Wall Street Journal*, November 30, 1999, https://www.wsj.com/articles/SB943997934427207890#:~:text=ECompanies%2C%20 a%20Santa%20Monica%2C%20Calif,Internet%20domain%20name%20to%20date.

58 **Bank of America paid $3 million:** "BofA Paid Big Bucks for Domain," *Wired*, February 8, 2000.

58 **a bid for $823,456:** "Drugs.com: The $823,000 Name," CBS News, August 16, 1999, https://www.cbsnews.com/news/drugscom-the-823000-name/.

58 **Alex Hsu's cellphone number:** Anonymous source, July 2021.

58 **Tony's immediate thought:** Hsieh, *Delivering Happiness*, 57.

Chapter 6: The Shoe Guy

61 **A few days later, in June 1999:** Email from anonymous source.

61 **Tony said he should put an extra "p" in it:** Hsieh, Tony, *Delivering Happiness: A Path to Profits, Passion, and Purpose* (Grand Central Publishing, 2012), 33.

62 over turkey sandwiches and chicken noodle soup: Hsieh, *Delivering Happiness*, 56.

62 "Nick and Fred were exactly the type": Hsieh, *Delivering Happiness*, 34.

62 They invested $500,000 in seed capital: Eng, Dinah, "Nick Swinmurn: Zappos' Silent Founder," *Fortune*, September 5, 2012, https://fortune.com/2012/09/05/nick -swinmurn-zappos-silent-founder/.

63 a $68.3 million exit: Lin, Alfred, "My Final Letter to Tony Hsieh," *Forbes*, December 1, 2020, https://www.forbes.com/sites/alexkonrad/2020/12/01/my-final-letter-to-tony -hsieh-by-alfred-lin/?sh=533275f1239b.

63 Zappos was days away from running out of cash: Hsieh, *Delivering Happiness*, 72.

63 "I have my birthday party this weekend": Hsieh, *Delivering Happiness*, 73.

64 "Isn't this amazing?": Hsieh, *Delivering Happiness*, 84.

65 the stock market cratered: Tymkiw, Catherine, "Bleak Friday on Wall Street," CNN Money, April 14, 2000, https://money.cnn.com/2000/04/14/markets/markets _newyork/.

65 "Our decision to focus": Dean, Katie, "Drugs.com Kicks Domain Habit," *Wired*, June 1, 2001.

65 "Right now, because we are unprofitable": Hsieh, *Delivering Happiness*, 100.

66 "The situation was dire": Hsieh, *Delivering Happiness*, 103.

67 cost about $2 million: Hsieh, *Delivering Happiness*, 107.

67 "Where are we going to get the money?": Hsieh, *Delivering Happiness*, 108.

67 "What would make Zappos better?": Interview with Fred Mossler, December 3, 2020.

67 pour $6 million: Eng, "Nick Swinmurn."

67 tripled to $8.6 million: Hsieh, *Delivering Happiness*, 109.

68 20 percent of their inventory: Hsieh, *Delivering Happiness*, 111.

69 "Zappos was saved": Hsieh, *Delivering Happiness*, 116.

69 "As your friend and financial adviser": Hsieh, *Delivering Happiness*, 120.

70 nearly quadrupled its revenue to $32 million: Hsieh, *Delivering Happiness*, 124.

70 the company ended with $70 million in gross sales: Hsieh, *Delivering Happiness*, 132.

71 deliberating between various cities: Hsieh, *Delivering Happiness*, 134.

71 Seventy employees agreed to make the move: Hsieh, *Delivering Happiness*, 135.

Chapter 7: The Trifecta

72 go over and introduce himself: Interview with Mark Guadagnoli, April 6, 2021.

73 tenured kinesiology professor at the University of Nevada, Las Vegas: Mark Guadag- noli online biography, https://www.unlv.edu/people/mark-guadagnoli, accessed October 23, 2022.

73 He explained: Interview with Mark Guadagnoli, April 6, 2021.

73 Challenge Point Framework: Guadagnoli, Mark A., and Lee, Timothy, D., "Chal- lenge Point: A Framework for Conceptualizing the Effects of Various Practice Condi- tions in Motor Learning," *Journal of Motor Behavior* 36, no. 2 (2004): 212–24.

73 St. Louis Rams: "Pfeiffer Kicks Way into Rams Camp," UNLV press release, July 26, 2004, https://unlvrebels.com/news/2004/7/26/Pieffer_Kicks_Way_Into_Rams _Camp.

74 cited his research: List of citations on PubMed, https://pubmed.ncbi.nlm.nih.gov /?linkname=pubmed_pubmed_citedin&from_uid=15130871.

74 Tony was listening with intense curiosity: Interview with Mark Guadagnoli, April 6, 2021.

75 **"We don't know; we'd like for you to tell us":** Interview with Mark Guadagnoli, April 10, 2021.

75 **three-day "camps":** "Zappos Insights Training Events," https://www.zapposinsights .com/training, retrieved July 30, 2022.

76 **making $800 million a quarter:** eBay SEC filing 10K, 2004 Annual Report, February 28, 2005, https://d18rn0p25nwr6d.cloudfront.net/CIK-0001065088/647583bb -4282-488d-9bcd-c334e206c1ae.pdf.

76 **acquired the payment processing company PayPal for $1.5 billion:** SEC filing, July 8, 2002, https://www.sec.gov/Archives/edgar/data/1103415/000091205702026650 /a2084015zex-99_1.htm.

76 **bought Rent.com:** Mangalindan, Mylene, "Ebay Purchases Web Site Rent.com for $415 Million," *Wall Street Journal,* December 17, 2004, https://www.wsj.com/articles /SB110324713823002980.

76 **25 percent stake in Craigslist:** Richtel, Matt, "Ebay Buys 25% Stake in Craigslist, an Online Bulletin Board," *New York Times,* August 14, 2004, https://www.nytimes .com/2004/08/14/business/ebay-buys-25-stake-in-craigslist-an-online-bulletin -board.html.

76 **no longer books but electronic gadgets:** "Amazon.com Electronics Sales Surpass Books Sales for the First Time," Amazon press release, November 30, 2004, https://press.aboutamazon.com/news-releases/news-release-details/amazoncom -electronics-sales-surpass-books-sales-first-time.

77 **$70 million in sales:** Hsieh, Tony, "How I Did It: Zappos's CEO on Going to Extremes for Customers," *Harvard Business Review,* July–August 2010.

77 **in a conference room at a DoubleTree hotel:** Stone, Brad, *The Everything Store: Jeff Bezos and the Age of Amazon* (Little, Brown, 2013), 203.

77 **"I realized that to Amazon":** Hsieh, Tony, "Why I Sold Zappos," *Inc.,* June 1, 2010, https://www.inc.com/magazine/20100601/why-i-sold-zapposs.html.

77 **Zappos's company policies:** Hsieh, Tony, *Delivering Happiness: A Path to Profits, Passion, and Purpose* (Grand Central Publishing, 2012), 156.

77 **five closest pizza shops:** Hsieh, *Delivering Happiness,* 146.

78 **"Read this by Wednesday":** Interview with Chris Peake, March 24, 2021.

79 **$1 billion in revenue by 2010:** Hsieh, *Delivering Happiness,* 120.

82 **"achieving their goal in life, whatever it was":** Hsieh, *Delivering Happiness,* 131.

83 **"Whether it's the happiness that customers feel":** Hsieh, *Delivering Happiness,* 229.

83 **Zappos employees were milling about:** Interview with Mark Guadagnoli, April 10, 2021.

84 **"Here's the frequency of the top ten words":** Interview with Mark Guadagnoli, April 10, 2021.

84 **Under images of shoes and notices of promotions:** Endless.com website front page, October 5, 2007, https://web.archive.org/web/20071005045713/http://www.endless .com/, retrieved April 29, 2021.

85 **$100 million in sales in a single month:** Hsieh, "Why I Sold Zappos."

85 **convey a straightforward message:** Carlson, Nicholas, "Layoffs at Zappos, According to Employee Tweets, CEO Blog," Business Insider, November 6, 2008.

85 **laying off 8 percent of its workforce:** Hsieh, *Delivering Happiness,* 193.

86 **facing a dwindling number of bad options:** Hsieh, *Delivering Happiness,* 207.

86 **Jeff interrupted:** Hsieh, "Why I Sold Zappos."

87 **have twenty-five times more impact there:** Interview with Fred Mossler, December 3, 2020.

87 **On July 22, Tony sent an email to his employees:** Hsieh, *Delivering Happiness*, 219.

88 **at a value of $1.2 billion:** Hsieh, *Delivering Happiness*, 220.

88 **"Most people came dressed as either brides or grooms":** "AWESOME ZAPPOS VEGAS PARTY!!!," YouTube, posted by Zappos.com, January 19, 2010, https://www.youtube.com/watch?v=hJrxTR4z2b0.

88 **"Tony didn't mind throwing a thousand plates":** Interview with Chris Peake, May 6, 2021.

88 **"You're in such great hands":** "Video from Jeff Bezos About Amazon and Zappos," YouTube, posted by 07272009july, July 22, 2009, https://www.youtube.com/watch?v=-hxX_Q5CnaA.

Chapter 8: Delivering Happiness

89 **gliding around a kitchen island on a scooter:** Interview with Holly McNamara, March 6, 2021.

90 **Northern California's Lake Tahoe:** Lim, Jenn, "First There Was a Book . . . ," Delivering Happiness website, 2011, https://blog.deliveringhappiness.com/blog/first-there-was-a-book.

90 **Excedrin, an over-the-counter migraine medicine:** Hochman, David, "Playboy Interview: Tony Hsieh," *Playboy*, April 16, 2014.

91 **peppering her with questions:** Interview with Holly McNamara, March 2021.

92 **"never around":** Interview with Holly McNamara, March 2021.

92 **her apartment in Los Angeles one weekend:** Interview with Holly McNamara, March 2021.

92 **shoe conference in 2005:** Interview with Mimi Pham, May 13, 2021.

93 **She had previously had a brush with the law after a drug-related incident:** Grind, Kirsten, and Sayre, Katherine, *Happy at Any Cost: The Revolutionary Vision and Fatal Quest of Zappos CEO Tony Hsieh* (Simon & Schuster, 2022), 426.

93 **Joey Vanas:** Interview with Joey Vanas, May 2021.

93 **"Just ask her to clean it up":** Interview with Holly McNamara, March 2021.

94 **"She was telling him something":** Interview with Patricia McHale, March 2021.

94 **"I'm outside South by Southwest":** "Tony Hsieh Delivering Happiness Book & Bus Tour," YouTube, posted by Techco Media, March 16, 2010, https://www.youtube.com/watch?v=rM4IaM2Qsww.

94 **During one flight:** Interview with Holly McNamara, March 2021.

95 **sponsors at the launch parties:** "Delivering Happiness, Book Launch Event Recap: April–June 2010," PowerPoint presentation, June 23, 2010, sent by anonymous source.

95 **a guest judge on *The Apprentice*:** Norman, Jean Reid, "Zappos CEO Appears on 'Celebrity Apprentice,'" *Las Vegas Sun*, March 9, 2009, https://lasvegassun.com/news/2009/mar/09/zappos-ceo-appears-celebrity-apprentice/.

95 **Ivanka and Tony had been photographed:** Snyder, Gabriel, "Do You Trust These People to Save the Economy," Gawker, March 6, 2009, https://www.gawker.com/5165880/do-you-trust-these-people-to-save-the-economy.

95 **Tony provided an editorial review:** "Women Who Work," Penguin Random House website, https://www.penguinrandomhouse.com/books/544570/women-who-work-by-ivanka-trump/9781524734411, retrieved July 31, 2022.

95 **his new publicist, Christine Peake:** Interview with Christine Peake, March 10, 2021.

96 **"Do you think he's going to find this funny?":** Interview with Holly McNamara, March 2021.

96 top of the *New York Times* bestseller list: "We're #1 on The New York Times Best-seller List!," Delivering Happiness website, https://blog.deliveringhappiness.com/blog/were-1-on-the-new-york-times-bestseller-list, accessed October 23, 2022.

97 a three-month, twenty-three-city bus tour: Interview with Holly McNamara, Match 6, 2010.

97 purchased a tour bus from the Dave Matthews Band: Lim, Jenn, *Beyond Happiness: How Authentic Leaders Prioritize Purpose and People for Growth and Impact* (Grand Central Publishing, 2021), 2.

98 "Project Specialist Supreme": Delivering Happiness website, April 2011, https://web.archive.org/web/20110314092020/http://www.deliveringhappiness.com:80/contact/.

98 did not actually travel with the bus for the majority of the tour: Interview with Joey Vanas, May 2021.

99 "Little Miss Sunshine": Delivering Happiness website, April 2011, https://web.archive.org/web/20110314092020/http://www.deliveringhappiness.com:80/contact/.

99 Holly went to speak with Tony: Interview with Holly McNamara, March 2021.

100 In tears, Holly called Patricia: Interview with Patricia McHale, March 23, 2021.

100 "It's human nature to want to help people": Email provided by anonymous source.

101 he sent an email, reminding those on the bus tour: Email provided by anonymous source.

101 Holly brought up the battle against Mimi: Interview with Holly McNamara, March 6, 2021.

101 The bus crew had filmed a rap music video: "Happy Wrap—Take One," YouTube, posted by DeliveringHappiness, September 20, 2010, https://www.youtube.com/watch?v=NtiIXo9Id-s.

102 Tony used ResultSource: Bercovici, Jeff, "Here's How You Buy Your Way onto the New York Times Bestsellers List," *Forbes*, February 22, 2013.

103 One day, Mimi called Patricia: Interview with Patricia McHale, March 23, 2021.

103 However, Holly recalled: Interview with Holly McNamara, March 10, 2021.

Chapter 9: The New Project

105 "When you have the little Z's": "From 2010: Zappos CEO Tony Hsieh," YouTube, posted by CBS Sunday Morning, November 28, 2020, https://www.youtube.com/watch?v=wSHG3EU1EZ4.

106 full-body Spider-Man suit: "The Mastermind of 'Delivering Happiness,'" You-Tube, posted by ABC News, August 3, 2012, https://www.youtube.com/watch?v=p4OBZFVwu1s&t=5s.

106 race down a miniature track: "The Mastermind of 'Delivering Happiness.'"

106 Donald J. Pliner slip-ons: Rich, Motoko, "Why Is This Man Smiling?," *New York Times*, April 8, 2011, https://www.nytimes.com/2011/04/10/fashion/10HSEIH.html.

106 "At times, Mr. Hsieh came across as an alien": Rich, "Why Is This Man Smiling?"

107 A year after the sale Alfred departed: Arrington, Michael, "Alfred Lin to Leave Zappos, Join Sequoia Capital," TechCrunch, April 9, 2010, https://techcrunch.com/2010/04/09/alfred-lin-leaves-zappos-joins-sequoia-capital/.

107 he joined the board of Airbnb: TechCrunch, "Airbnb's Brian Chesky on How He Met Board Member Alfred Lin," September 27, 2013, https://techcrunch.com/video/airbnbs-brian-chesky-on-how-he-met-board-member-alfred-lin/.

108 Cities "spur innovation": Silver, Diana, "Up, Up, Up," *New York Times*, February 11, 2011, https://www.nytimes.com/2011/02/13/books/review/Silver-t.html.

109 **would take over the old City Hall building:** Schoenmann, Joe, "Zappos Views Las Vegas City Hall as Perfect Fit for New Headquarters," *Las Vegas Sun*, November 29, 2010, https://lasvegassun.com/news/2010/nov/29/zapposcom-moving-green-valley-las -vegas-city-hall/.

109 **closed on the acquisition of the property in the summer of 2012:** Toplikar, Dave, "Las Vegas City Council Approves Final Deal Bringing Zappos Downtown," *Las Vegas Sun*, February 1, 2012, https://lasvegassun.com/news/2012/feb/01/las-vegas-city-council -approves-final-deal-bringin/.

110 **"We need one of those":** "Zappos and Downtown Project: Tony Hsieh," YouTube, posted by Wisdom 2.0, March 3, 2014, https://www.youtube.com/watch?v=1kaAV bf-17w.

110 **he also found the campuses incredibly insular:** "Zappos and Downtown Project: Tony Hsieh."

110 **"The more we thought about it":** "Tony Hsei The City as a Startup–H264 MOV 1280x720 GBG Water 1800," YouTube, posted by GreenBiz, March 15, 2017, https: //www.youtube.com/watch?v=lkQVPx5kAxc.

110 **apply with a video cover letter:** "Zappos Is a Weird Company—and It's Happy That Way," YouTube, March 2, 2017, posted by PBS NewsHour, https://www.youtube.com /watch?v=5mknIg_Abfw&t=237s.

111 **became a Zappos legend:** Garfinkel, Perry, "Engineering Happiness at Zappos," *New York Times*, August 4, 2017, https://www.nytimes.com/2017/08/04/business /engineering-happiness-at-zappos.html.

111 **He started at the call center:** Garfinkel, "Engineering Happiness at Zappos."

111 **he made a centaur costume:** Bell, Jennie, "True Stories of How Tony Hsieh Taught His Zappos Team the Meaning of 'Wow,'" *Footwear News*, December 21, 2020, https: //footwearnews.com/2020/business/retail/tony-hsieh-zappos-employee-stories -1203085519/.

111 **"What are you doing tonight?":** Bell, "True Stories."

111 **A red double-decker, a school bus:** Bell, "True Stories."

112 **finally moving the Zappos headquarters:** Toplikar, "Las Vegas City Council Approves Final Deal."

112 **either conference rooms or a speakeasy:** Lazar, Shira, "What Happens in Vegas Stays in Vegas, Unless You're Tony Hsieh," *Entrepreneur*, March 12, 2013, https://www .entrepreneur.com/article/226056.

112 **"the city as a startup":** "Zappos and Downtown Project: Tony Hsieh."

112 **The $350 million would be distributed across four categories:** "Zappos and Downtown Project: Tony Hsieh"; Semuels, Alana, "$350 Million Might Not Be Enough to Save Las Vegas," *The Atlantic*, March 2, 2015, https://www.theatlantic.com/business /archive/2015/03/350-million-might-not-be-enough-to-save-las-vegas/386213/.

112 **$50 million to invest in tech startups:** Downtown Project company website, https: //dtplv.com/portfolio_page/technology-startups/, accessed October 23, 2022.

113 **Underpinning the Downtown Project were three central goals:** "Zappos and Downtown Project: Tony Hsieh."

113 **return on community (ROC):** "Zappos and Downtown Project: Tony Hsieh."

113 **return on luck (ROL):** "Zappos and Downtown Project: Tony Hsieh."

113 **"This is part of the reason":** "Tony Hsei: The City as a Startup," https://www.youtube .com/watch?v=lkQVPx5kAxc.

114 **"Some speculate it's ego":** Schoenmann, Joe, "What's Behind Tony Hsieh's Unrelenting Drive to Remake Downtown Las Vegas?" *Las Vegas Sun*, April 20, 2012, https://

lasvegassun.com/news/2012/apr/20/behind-tony-hsiehs-passion-remake-downtown-las-veg/.

Chapter 10: The Desert Tech Utopia

115 **Natalie's life changed:** Interview with Natalie Young, March 8, 2021.

117 **Michael slid into the booth and sat next to her:** Interview with Natalie Young, March 8, 2021.

119 **the Gold Spike casino, which advertised:** Bohler, Peter, "How Zappos' CEO Turned Las Vegas Into a Startup Fantasyland," *Wired*, January 21, 2014.

119 **gang members had once robbed the place at gunpoint:** "21 Las Vegas Gang Members Indicted on Federal Racketeering, Murder, Drug and Firearm Charges," press release, United States Attorney's Office, Nevada, August 14, 2003, https://www.justice.gov/archive/usao/nv/news/2003/08142003b.html.

119 **a woman was shot by her husband in the parking lot:** Choate, Alan, "Woman in Critical Condition After Downtown Shooting," *Las Vegas Review-Journal*, November 17, 2008.

119 **patrons could stand on its roof:** Travel Nevada, "Atomic Liquors," https://travelnevada.com/bars/atomic-liquors/, retrieved July 31, 2022.

120 **"Downtown is a happening scene":** Video of interview with 702.tv, *Las Vegas Weekly*, provided by James Woodbridge.

120 **he co-founded the Neon Reverb festival:** Interview with James Woodbridge, April 9, 2021.

120 **"Can we build a ski slope right here?":** Toplikar, David, "Goodman: Zappos Move a 'Watershed Moment' for Downtown Las Vegas," *Las Vegas Sun*, December 1, 2010.

121 **poor sales following the Great Recession:** Green, Steve, "Buyers Sue for Deposit Money on Downtown Condos," *Las Vegas Sun*, July 1, 2009, https://lasvegassun.com/news/2009/jul/01/buyers-sue-deposits-back-downtown-luxury-condos/.

121 **when Tony moved there in May 2011:** Corbett, Sara, "How Zappos' CEO Turned Las Vegas Into a Startup Fantasyland," *Wired*, January 21, 2014, https://www.wired.com/2014/01/zappos-tony-hsieh-las-vegas/.

122 **When the Downtown Project was announced in January 2012:** Downtown Project 2019 pitch deck, provided by anonymous source.

122 **portfolio of almost a thousand apartments:** Snel, Alan, "Downtown Project Breaks Through with Apartment Building," *Las Vegas Review-Journal*, April 18, 2015, https://www.reviewjournal.com/local/local-nevada/downtown-project-breaks-through-with-apartment-building/.

122 **Tony convinced the organization:** Pratt, Timothy, "What Happens in Brooklyn Moves to Vegas," *New York Times Magazine*, October 19, 2012, https://www.nytimes.com/2012/10/21/magazine/what-happens-in-brooklyn-moves-to-vegas.html.

123 **She submitted her proposal seven times:** Interview with Natalie Young, March 8, 2021.

123 **The loan would be interest-free:** Interview with Natalie Young, March 8, 2021.

124 **Standing on the corner of Seventh Street and East Carson:** Interview with Natalie Young, March 8, 2021.

124 **Ideas ranged from an outdoor chess board:** Image provided by anonymous source.

125 **Tony asked Carr what he wanted to do:** Carr, Paul Bradley, "Tony," *Paul Bradley Carr* (blog), November 29, 2020, https://paulbradleycarr.com/2020/11/29/tony/.

125 **Tony would end up investing around half a million dollars:** Lacy, Sarah, "NSFW Corp. Raises Mid-Six Figure Seed Deal (Our Incredibly Biased Report)," Pando, July 4, 2012.

125 **Mark Rowland, a British retail executive:** Interview with Mark Rowland, March 22, 2021.

126 **Keller Rinaudo, a recent Harvard graduate:** Harvard University, "In a First, Scientists Develop Tiny Implantable Biocomputers," ScienceDaily, May 22, 2007, www.sciencedaily.com/releases/2007/05/070521140917.htm.

126 **Rinaudo was given $500,000:** Schoenmann, Joe, "Joe Downtown: Is Romotive's Departure a Sign of the Future?," *Las Vegas Weekly*, March 20, 2013, https://lasvegasweekly.com/column/joe-downtown/2013/mar/20/joe-downtown-vegastechfunds-romotive-silicon-valle/.

126 **Keller said he chose downtown Las Vegas:** Corbett, "How Zappos' CEO."

126 **"Downtown basically sells itself":** Pratt, "What Happens in Brooklyn."

126 **"Even though there's plenty of parking":** "Tony Hsieh Talks Downtown Las Vegas, Zappos, and More at Samsung SXSW 2013," YouTube, posted by What's Trending, March 10, 2013, https://www.youtube.com/watch?v=Iwm9gL9IkH4.

127 **"They'd be talking passionately":** Interview with Mike Henry, April 20, 2021.

127 **Tony struck an agreement:** Venture for America, "Venture for America December Newsletter," December 14, 2012, https://ventureforamerica.org/2012/12/venture-for-america-december-newsletter/.

127 **Ovik had studied environmental science and biology:** University of North Carolina at Chapel Hill, "Water Institute Community Mourns Passing of Former Student Banerjee," January 14, 2014, https://sph.unc.edu/sph-news/water-institute-community-mourns-passing-of-former-staff-member-banerjee/.

127 **"The path will not be easy. Urban revitalization":** "You're Moving to Vegas?," *Polis* (blog), July 19, 2012, https://www.thepolisblog.org/2012/07/youre-moving-to-vegas.html.

128 **"Tony asked them to submit anything":** Spillman, Benjamin, "Burning Man Culture Spreads in Downtown Las Vegas," *Las Vegas Review-Journal*, September 24, 2012, https://www.reviewjournal.com/entertainment/arts-culture/burning-man-culture-spreads-in-downtown-las-vegas/.

128 **"It is not about, 'Let's try to make'":** Spillman, "Burning Man Culture Spreads."

128 **the Oasis Motel:** Snel, Alan, "Downtown Project Unveils Boutique Hotel Oasis," *Las Vegas Review-Journal*, October 21, 2014.

128 **purchased an abandoned convenience store:** Kirk, Mimi, "The Rise of Adaptive Reuse in Las Vegas," *Architect Magazine*, May 1, 2019.

Chapter 11: Life Is Beautiful

130 **When the Cosmopolitan opened in December 2010:** The Cosmopolitan of Las Vegas, "The Cosmopolitan of Las Vegas Opens Its Doors," press release, December 17, 2010, https://www.prnewswire.com/news-releases/the-cosmopolitan-of-las-vegas-opens-its-doors-112093394.html.

130 **In its first eighteen months, dozens of headliners:** Interview with Rehan Choudhry, March 4, 2021.

130 **His life in Vegas:** Interview with Rehan Choudhry, February 18, 2021.

131 **Rehan had first met Ryan:** Interview with Rehan Choudhry, March 4, 2021.

131 **"I was very new to the city":** Interview with Rehan Choudhry, March 4, 2021.

131 **stammered his way through a thirty-second elevator pitch:** Interview with Rehan Choudhry, June 21, 2021.

131 **It reminded Rehan:** Interview with Rehan Choudhry, February 18, 2021.

132 **the festival would lose around $600,000 in its first year:** Life Is Beautiful pitch deck, provided by an anonymous source.

132 **When they arrived, Fred informed him:** Interview with Rehan Choudhry, February 18, 2021.

133 **During one press interview:** Patterson, Spencer, "Chatting with the Man Behind Planned Downtown Festival Life Is Beautiful," *Las Vegas Weekly*, November 13, 2021, https://lasvegasweekly.com/as-we-see-it/2012/nov/13/chatting-man-behind-planned -downtown-festival-life/.

134 **Another slighted Neon Reverb musician:** Interview with anonymous source.

134 **"We drank the Kool-Aid":** Interview with Rehan Choudhry, December 9, 2020.

135 **Aimee had been a senior editor:** Groth, Aimee, *The Kingdom of Happiness: Inside Tony Hsieh's Zapponian Utopia* (Simon & Schuster, 2017), 19.

135 **Later at a Manhattan nightclub:** Groth, *The Kingdom of Happiness*, 73.

135 **Tony had recently expanded his Delivering Happiness brand:** Delivering Happiness website, https://www.deliveringhappiness.com/about.

135 **In one video interview:** "Drinking Vodka with Tony Hsieh (Zappos) and Jenn Lim (Delivering Happiness)," YouTube, posted by mediatechsocial, May 17, 2012, https: //www.youtube.com/watch?v=qBUfRf_VkmA (no longer available).

136 **Jon Greenman . . . came to see Tony:** Interview with Jon Greenman, February 22, 2021.

136 **On the first visit:** Interview with Ying Liu, May 10, 2021.

136 **On her second visit:** Interview with Ying Liu, May 10, 2021.

137 **Visitors like Ivanka Trump:** Ivanka Trump, @IvankaTrump, "Tony would want us to celebrate his life," Twitter, November 28, 2020, https://twitter.com/IvankaTrump /status/1332748999883976711?s=20&t=Xay0_RegJzR46iM3qUgeRg.

138 **"At some point along the way, I stopped getting hangovers":** Interview with Rehan Choudhry, February 18, 2021.

139 **Andrew offered Rehan $1 million:** Interview with Rehan Choudhry, December 9, 2020.

139 **On October 26, around thirty thousand people:** Patterson, Spencer, "Time of Our Life: Downtown's Life Is Beautiful Exceeds All Expectations," *Las Vegas Weekly*, October 31, 2013, https://lasvegasweekly.com/ae/music/2013/oct/31/life-is-beautiful -festival-exceeds-expectations/#/0.

139 **"Tony was really excited":** Interview with Joey Vanas, May 26, 2021.

140 **On the second and final day of the festival, strong winds:** Patterson, "Time of Our Life."

Chapter 12: The Darwinian Perspective

141 **At thirty-nine, with two teenage kids:** Interview with Michelle D'Attilio, April 2, 2021.

142 **"more affordable and less exclusive than TED Conferences":** McKinney, Sarah, "Amanda Slavin: The Creative Catalyst Behind CatalystCreativ," *Forbes*, March 19, 2014, https://www.forbes.com/sites/sarahmckinney/2014/03/19/amanda-slavin-the -creative-catalyst-behind-catalystcreativ/?sh=6fbbd5aa72ae.

143 **One of Tony's favorite books:** Hochman, David, "Playboy Interview: Tony Hsieh," *Playboy*, April 16, 2014.

143 **that ultimately convinced her to move to the downtown neighborhood:** Groth, Aimee, *The Kingdom of Happiness: Inside Tony Hsieh's Zapponian Utopia* (Simon & Schuster, 2017), 73.

143 In an interview with *Playboy*: Hochman, "Playboy Interview."
145 the company's famous quarterly all-hands meetings: Boley, Michael, "Meet the Women Who've Changed Zappos History," Zappos, March 5, 2019, https://www.zappos.com/about/stories/womens-history-zappos.
145 "When you are his plus-one to something": Interview with Suzie Baleson, July 29, 2021.
146 "He barely answered": Interview with Antonia Dodge, April 23, 2021.
148 "Come to Hawaii with me": Interview with Michelle D'Attilio, April 2, 2021.
151 he would tell people she was his ex-girlfriend: Interview with Michelle D'Attilio, June 9, 2021.

Chapter 13: Andy

152 passed the roles down to his brothers: Hsieh, Tony, *Delivering Happiness: A Path to Profits, Passion, and Purpose* (Grand Central Publishing, 2012), 14.
153 Dave was soft-spoken and awkward: Interview with Jen Louie, April 20, 2021.
153 industrial engineering program at Stanford University in 1994: Andrew Hsieh, LinkedIn page, https://www.linkedin.com/in/andrewhsi3h/, accessed October 23, 2022.
153 Dave, meanwhile, went with Richard and Judy to Hong Kong: Hsieh, *Delivering Happiness*, 14.
153 Andy took part in Rush Week: Interview with anonymous source.
154 As one Lambda Phi Epsilon alum put it: Interview with anonymous source.
154 When Andy's turn came: Interview with anonymous source.
154 Andy graduated from Stanford in 1999: Andrew Hsieh, LinkedIn page.
154 specialty food marketing company: Andrew Hsieh, LinkedIn page.
154 one of Tony's units in 1000 Van Ness: Interview with James Henrikson, March 7, 2021.
154 "Tony's batcave": Interview with James Henrikson, March 7, 2021.
155 "If there was a problem with Andy": Interview with Chris Peake, April 10, 2021.
155 he had been assigned to work with Mark Guadagnoli: Interview with Mark Guadagnoli, November 16, 2021.
156 young tech millionaire founders and CEOs who came to Sin City: Interview with Jen Louie, April 20, 2021.
157 "according to documents": Funding documents provided by anonymous source.
157 "That was just a small investment": Email from Joe Lonsdale, March 14, 2021.
157 Andy's San Francisco apartment: 601 4th Street, Unit 213, San Francisco, CA 94107, per funding documents.
157 companies like Airbnb and Zynga: Cutler, Kim-Mai, "Watch Tech's Takeover of San Francisco's Office Space in This Visualization," TechCrunch, February 25, 2015, https://techcrunch.com/2015/02/25/tech-office-space/?ncid=rss.
157 One worker recalled arriving: Interview with anonymous source.
158 first-class flights and even private jets: Grind, Kirsten, and Sayre, Katherine, *Happy at Any Cost: The Revolutionary Vision and Fatal Quest of Zappos CEO Tony Hsieh* (Simon & Schuster, 2022), 147.
158 its Facebook page: https://www.facebook.com/LuxDelux/, accessed February 1, 2022.

Chapter 14: Trouble in Paradise

160 he hated hugs: Interview with Anondo Banerjee, March 12, 2021.
161 At Eat one morning: Interview with Anondo Banerjee, March 12, 2021.

161 **"I didn't get to be involved in that decision":** Interview with Anondo Banerjee, June 24, 2021.

161 **things that made him uncomfortable about the Downtown Project:** Interview with Anondo Banerjee, March 12, 2021.

161 **One of his tasks:** Bowles, Nellie, "The Downtown Project Suicides: Can the Pursuit of Happiness Kill You?," Vox, October 1, 2014, https://www.vox.com/2014/10/1/11631452/the-downtown-project-suicides-can-the-pursuit-of-happiness-kill-you.

162 **"fred and I are confident":** Groth, Aimee, *The Kingdom of Happiness: Inside Tony Hsieh's Zapponian Utopia* (Simon & Schuster, 2017), 152.

163 **When Ovik came back to Tuscaloosa:** Interview with Anondo Banerjee, June 24, 2021.

163 **the body of Jody Sherman:** Chang, Andrea, "After Jody Sherman Death, Tech Community Seeks Dialogue on Suicide," *Los Angeles Times,* February 1, 2013.

164 **Prominent venture capitalist Jason Calacanis wrote:** Calacanis, Jason, "Do We Need to Talk About Suicide?," Pando Daily, January 31, 2013, retrieved August 1, 2022, http://web.archive.org/web/20130204052814/https://pandodaily.com/2013/01/31/do-we-need-to-talk-about-suicide/.

165 **Freeman's study found that 72 percent of entrepreneurs:** Freeman, Michael A., "The prevalence and co-occurrence of psychiatric conditions among entrepreneurs and their families," *Small Business Economics* 53 (2019): 323–42, https://link.springer.com/article/10.1007/s11187-018-0059-8.

165 **"The intensity of being an entrepreneur":** Feld, Brad, "Founder Suicides," October 2, 2014, https://feld.com/archives/2014/10/founder-suicides/.

165 **It was later revealed:** Shontell, Alyson, "The Story of a Failed Startup and a Founder Driven to Suicide," Business Insider, April 4, 2013, https://www.businessinsider.com/jody-sherman-ecomom-2013-4.

166 **In the week before his death, after seeing the forecasts:** Shontell, Alyson, "A Grave Financial Error Sank a Startup and Contributed to its Founder's Suicide," Business Insider, April 24, 2013, https://www.businessinsider.com/jody-sherman-ecomom-and-a-grave-financial-error-2013-4.

166 **In 2012, he was on a multicity tour around Australia:** Interview with Mark Rowland, March 23, 2021.

167 **"God, wouldn't it just be easier":** Interview with Mark Rowland, March 23, 2021.

167 **"When you're potentially gonna lose":** Interview with Mark Rowland, March 23, 2021.

167 **Tony's acknowledgment of Ovik's death:** Email provided by anonymous source.

168 **Tamber proposed:** Email shared by anonymous source.

168 **Matt Berman, the fifty-year-old founder:** Schoenmann, Joe, "Joe Downtown: Tragedy, Secrets and the Tough Side of Downtown Development," *Las Vegas Weekly,* June 4, 2014, https://lasvegasweekly.com/column/joe-downtown/2014/jun/04/joe-downtown-tragedy-secrets-and-tough-side-downto/.

168 **After Matt's suicide, Aimee Groth wrote:** Groth, Aimee, *The Kingdom of Happiness: Inside Tony Hsieh's Zapponian Utopia* (Simon & Schuster, 2017), 191.

169 **"Suicides happen anywhere":** Bowles, "The Downtown Project Suicides."

169 **"the difference here is the focus on happiness":** Bowles, "The Downtown Project Suicides."

169 **Andrew Yang cut ties with Tony:** Groth, *The Kingdom of Happiness,* 157.

169 **"With your silence, you've just compounded that failure":** Interview with Anondo Banerjee, March 12, 2021.

169 **What was most painful for Ovik's family:** Interview with Anondo Banerjee, March 12, 2021.

170 **"My brother was an incredibly smart"**: Interview with Anondo Banerjee, March 12, 2021.

Chapter 15: "The Mayor of Downtown Las Vegas"

171 **"Mayor of Downtown Las Vegas"**: Walker, Alissa, "Meeting Tony Hsieh, the Mayor of Downtown Las Vegas," Gizmodo, January 14, 2014, https://gizmodo.com/meeting-tony-hsieh-the-mayor-of-downtown-las-vegas-1500530600.

171 **"A puff of energy"**: Bowles, Nellie, "Downtown Las Vegas Is the Great American Techtopia," Vox, September 29, 2014.

172 **"In the past, we used the word 'Community'"**: "Downtown Project: Collisions, Co-Learning, Connectness," Evernote, February 7, 2014, https://www.evernote.com/shard/s16/client/snv?noteGuid=66aed622-6730-4009-86b0-2d2ffe7ea26f&noteKey=0fca9f01d630275220b4caea45a4bb41&sn=https%3A%2F%2Fwww.evernote.com%2Fshard%2Fs16%2Fsh%2F66aed622-6730-4009-86b0-2d2ffe7ea26f%2F0fca9f01d630275220b4caea45a4bb41&title=Downtown%2BProject%253A%2BCollisions%252C%2BCo-Learning%252C%2BConnectness.

172 **"I view my role more as trying to set up"**: "Zappos Milestone: Q&A with Tony Hsieh," *Footwear News*, May 4, 2009.

173 **"Tony doesn't really like conflict"**: Interview with Maggie Hsu, February 21, 2021.

173 **"A Partner duly filling a Role"**: Quoted in Groth, Aimee, "The Story of the Man Who's Flattening the World of Corporate Hierarchies," Business Insider, January 16, 2014, https://qz.com/167145/the-story-of-holacracys-founder-began-when-he-started-coding-at-age-6/.

174 **"strategic partners and hiring brilliant senior talent"**: Lacy, Sara, "More Bad News for Vegas Tech Fund: Star Company Romotive Is Moving to the Bay Area," Pando.com, March 15, 2013, https://web.archive.org/web/20140213154736/http://pando.com/2013/03/15/more-bad-news-for-vegas-tech-fund-star-company-romotive-is-moving-to-the-bay-area/, retrieved August 2, 2022.

174 **Jen McCabe . . . had been given $10 million**: Bowles, Nellie, "Factorli, an Early Casualty of the Las Vegas Downtown Project," Vox, September 30, 2014.

174 **"You've got Jen McCabe," Obama said**: Obama White House Archives, "Remarks by the President at the White House Maker Faire," June 18, 2014, https://obamawhitehouse.archives.gov/the-press-office/2014/06/18/remarks-president-white-house-maker-faire.

175 **the Container Park received three hundred thousand visitors**: Morrison, Jane Anne, "Las Vegas Council Favors Allowing Minors at Container Park," *Las Vegas Review-Journal*, February 19, 2014.

175 **Michael Cornthwaite sold his interest in three restaurants**: Shoenmann, Joe, "Joe Downtown: Group Lauds Container Park as It Pulls Plug on 3 Shops There," *Las Vegas Sun,* April 1, 2014.

176 **Close to midnight, Michael Downs was on the phone**: Interview with Mike Henry, April 27, 2021.

177 **"It was like a show"**: Interview with Mike Henry, April 27, 2021.

177 **In total, thirty people lost their jobs**: Snel, Alan, "Downtown Project Lays Off 30 Workers; Hsieh Role Unchanged," *Las Vegas Review-Journal*, September 30, 2014.

179 **In a statement, Tony tried to emphasize**: Bowles, Nellie, "Tony Hsieh Answers Some of Our Questions About the Future of Las Vegas's Downtown Project," Vox, October 2, 2014.

179 **compiled in a booklet**: Provided by Mark Rowland.

Chapter 16: The Island

180 **"Have you spoken to Tony?":** Interview with anonymous source.

181 **he received a response sometime in the middle of the night:** Interview with anonymous source.

181 **Rehan got a call from Fred:** Interview with Rehan Choudhry, December 9, 2020.

182 **Tony had texted Rehan:** Interview with Rehan Choudhry, February 18, 2021.

182 **Kanye went on a podcast:** Ellis, Bret Easton, "B.E.E.-KANYE PART 1-11/18/2013," Podcast One, November 18, 2013.

182 **"I got into this giant argument":** Chan, Jennifer, "Kanye West Slams Zappos CEO: 'He Sells All This S—t Product to Everybody,'" E! News, November 19, 2013, http://www.eonline.com/news/482850/kanye-west-slams-zappos-ceo-he-sells-all-this-shit-product-to-everybody.

183 **Tony probed Justin about his background:** Interview with anonymous source.

183 **Justin confronted Rehan over excessive spending:** Interview with anonymous source.

184 **In response, Tony emailed Rehan:** Email provided by Rehan Choudhry.

184 **Rehan was given $200,000 for his stake:** Provided by anonymous source.

Chapter 17: The Trailer Park

188 **Tony sent out a message:** Interview with anonymous source.

188 **$950 a month in rent:** "Inside Zappos CEO's Wild, Wonderful Life," YouTube, posted by ABC News, August 12, 2015, https://www.youtube.com/watch?v=3S9J0IgmRPo.

189 **conversations around campfires, a favorite pastime of Tony's:** Interview with anonymous source.

189 **a chocolate-brown alpaca named Marley:** "Inside Zappos CEO's Wild, Wonderful Life."

189 **a common "living room":** Video interview with Shira Lazar, *Adventures in Curiosity*, "Inside Ferguson's Downtown Project Las Vegas With Tony Hsieh," February 14, 2019.

189 **"With a net worth of $840 million":** Holley, Peter, "Why This CEO Is Worth Almost $1 Billion but Lives in a Trailer Park," *Washington Post*, July 21, 2015, https://www.washingtonpost.com/news/the-switch/wp/2015/07/21/why-a-ceo-worth-840-million-lives-in-a-trailer-park-with-his-pet-alpaca/.

189 **Tony chatted with a reporter:** Totten, Kristy, "Living Small: At Downtown's Airstream Park, Home Is Where the Experiment Is," *Las Vegas Weekly*, February 5, 2015, https://lasvegasweekly.com/news/2015/feb/05/airstream-park-experiment-living-small-hsieh-downt/#/0.

190 **Anthony . . . was working in internet marketing:** Interview with anonymous source.

190 **"not a single person in Tony's close sphere":** Interview with anonymous source.

191 **Airstream Park gave off an air of radical inclusion:** "What Is Burning Man? The 10 Principles of Burning Man," Burning Man website, https://burningman.org/about/10-principles/, accessed October 23, 2022.

191 **4,700-word company-wide email:** Groth, Aimee, "Internal Memo: Zappos Is Offering Severance to Employees Who Aren't All In on Holacracy," *Quartz*, March 26, 2015, https://qz.com/370616/internal-memo-zappos-is-offering-severance-to-employees-who-arent-all-in-with-holacracy/.

191 **Zappos lost 210 out of 1,503 employees:** Usufzy, Pashtana, "200 Accept Buyouts at

Zappos After Management Changes," *Las Vegas Sun*, May 5, 2015, https://lasvegassun
.com/news/2015/may/05/200-accept-buyouts-zappos-after-companys-managemen/.

191 **"The brewing employee discontent"**: Gelles, David, "At Zappos, Pushing Shoes
and a Vision," *New York Times*, July 17, 2015, https://www.nytimes.com/2015/07/19
/business/at-zappos-selling-shoes-and-a-vision.html.

191 **"The media has kind of portrayed it"**: "Tony Hsieh Explains Why He Sold Zappos
and What He Thinks of Amazon (Full Interview)," YouTube, posted by Recode, May
24, 2016, https://www.youtube.com/watch?v=69WEofQd1DM&t=54s.

192 **"It's an intense display of loyalty"**: Komenda, Ed, "Is Tony Hsieh Downtown Las
Vegas' Savior or Conqueror?," *Las Vegas Sun*, February 23, 2014, https://lasvegassun
.com/news/2014/feb/23/tony-hsieh-downtown-las-vegas-savior-or-conqueror/.

192 **"'can feel cultish'"**: Walker, Alissa, "Zappos Isn't a Cult? All Tony Hsieh's Friends Got
Matching Tattoos," Gizmodo, February 24, 2014, https://gizmodo.com/zappos-isnt-a
-cult-all-tony-hsiehs-friends-got-match-1529721696.

193 **The pressure was getting to him, she thought:** Interview with Michelle D'Attilio,
April 15, 2021.

Chapter 18: The Right Hand

194 **"As I noodle on the press coverage"**: Ferenstein, Greg, "Exclusive: Zappos CEO
Responds to Reports of Employee Departures After Radical Management Experiment," Medium, January 19, 2016, https://medium.com/@ferenstein/exclusive-zappos
-ceo-responds-to-reports-of-mass-employee-departures-after-radical-management
-3f6c51a71928.

195 **"I completely agree with Fred"**: Ferenstein, "Exclusive."

195 **A few months after the interview:** Reingold, Jennifer, "Another Zappos Leader
Departs," *Fortune*, April 13, 2016, https://fortune.com/2016/04/13/another-zappos
-leader-departs/.

196 **Ivy League–bred financier background:** "Leadership," Stagelight Group, https:
//www.stagelightgroup.com/leadership, accessed September 1, 2022.

196 **tumultuous stint:** Tracy, Abigail, "West Wing Chaos: Scaramucci Abruptly Fired
as White House Communications Director," *Vanity Fair*, July 31, 2017, https://www
.vanityfair.com/news/2017/07/the-mooch-cut-loose-scaramucci-fired-as-white
-house-communications-director.

196 **SALT Conference:** "SALT Conference Returns to Las Vegas May 7–10, 2019 Targeting
Growth," press release, SALT conference, November 1, 2018, https://www.prnewswire
.com/news-releases/salt-conference-returns-to-las-vegas-may-7–10–2019-targeting
-growth-300741703.html.

196 **In 2017, Victor asked the singer and songwriter:** Interview with anonymous source.

196 **Necker Island:** Instagram post, December 1, 2020, https://www.instagram.com/p
/CIQ_i8bnZIu/?hl=en.

196 **"All right, Tony@Zappos.com":** Interview with anonymous source.

199 **"It'd be really fun to just have a ball pit":** Interview with anonymous source.

199 **"Fungineer":** Garfinkel, Perry, "Engineering Happiness at Zappos," *New York
Times*, August 4, 2017, https://www.nytimes.com/2017/08/04/business/engineering
-happiness-at-zappos.html.

200 **Called Whole Human:** Jarvey, Natalie, "CES: Jewel Launches Platform to Bring
Mindfulness to the Workplace," *Hollywood Reporter*, January 9, 2018, https://www
.hollywoodreporter.com/news/general-news/ces-jewel-launches-platform-bring
-mindfulness-workplace-1073163/.

200 **Jewel organized a mindfulness retreat:** Interview with anonymous source.
201 **Tyler reached a point in 2018:** Interview with anonymous source.
201 **Ben and Tony had met:** Interview with Ben Jorgensen, October 22, 2021.

Chapter 19: Genie in a Bottle

203 *We're back,* **he thought:** Interview with anonymous source.
203 **Tony's camp, which for liability reasons:** Interview with anonymous source.
204 **he invited four of the founding leaders:** Burning Man Project, "Tony Hsieh's Legacy Reminds Us All of the Importance of Community," December 10, 2020, https://journal.burningman.org/2020/12/news/global-news/tony-hsieh-legacy/.
204 **Tony purchased a gutted Boeing 747:** Johnson, Shea, "Zappos Will Use Burning Man 747 Jet for Downtown Project," *Las Vegas Review-Journal*, February 17, 2020, https://www.reviewjournal.com/news/politics-and-government/las-vegas/zappos-will-use-burning-man-747-jet-for-downtown-project-1959430/.
204 **"Metamorphoses":** "2019 Art Theme: Metamorphoses," Burning Man website, https://burningman.org/about/history/brc-history/event-archives/2019-event-archive/2019-art-theme-metamorphoses/.
204 **market-based dynamics:** Peake, Chris, "First Steps for Learning and Engaging," Zappos, May 5, 2019, https://hatch.apps.zappos.com/evolve/first-steps-for-learning-and-engaging.
205 **Members of Tony's Burning Man crew:** Interview with anonymous source.
205 **Judy took a nap . . . cloud-nine-themed art car:** Interview with Michelle D'Attilio, June 9, 2021.
205 **Though Tony knew this would make them uncomfortable:** Interview with Michelle D'Attilio, June 9, 2021.
206 **Parke Davis Company:** Li, Linda, and Vlisides, Phillip E., "Ketamine: 50 Years of Modulating the Mind," *Frontiers in Human Neuroscience*, November 15, 2016, https://www.ncbi.nlm.nih.gov/pmc/articles/PMC5126726/.
206 **replace the surgical anesthetic PCP:** Chun, Rene, "Inside the Los Angeles Clinic That Uses Ketamine to Treat Depression," *Los Angeles Magazine*, June 19, 2017, https://www.lamag.com/longform/the-ketamine-club/.
206 **During the 1970s, it was used:** Domino, Edward F., and Warner, David S., "Taming the Ketamine Tiger," *Anesthesiology* 113 (2010): 678–84, https://pubs.asahq.org/anesthesiology/article/113/3/678/10426/Taming-the-Ketamine-Tiger.
206 **offered scientific literature:** "History of Ketamine in Psychiatric Medicine," Avesta Ketamine Wellness, https://www.avestaketaminewellness.com/blog/history-of-ketamine-in-psychiatric-medicine.
206 **in the 1980s and 1990s:** "History of Ketamine in Psychiatric Medicine."
206 **Special K:** "Ketamine," Drug Enforcement Administration, September 2019, https://www.deadiversion.usdoj.gov/drug_chem_info/ketamine.pdf.
206 **Schedule III narcotic:** "Schedules of Controlled Substances: Placement of Ketamine into Schedule III," Drug Enforcement Administration, https://www.deadiversion.usdoj.gov/fed_regs/rules/1999/fr0713.htm.
207 **Salvador Roquet:** Witt, Emily, "Ketamine Therapy Is Going Mainstream. Are We Ready?," *New Yorker*, December 29, 2021.
207 **due to his use of illegal drugs:** Correspondence with Stanley Krippner, PhD.
207 **Evgeny Krupitsky and A. Y. Grinenko:** Krupitsky, E. M., and Grinenko, A. Y., "Ketamine Psychedelic Therapy (KPT): A Review of the Results of Ten Years of Research," *Journal of Psychoactive Drugs* 29, no. 2 (1997).

207 **In 2000, the drug was tested:** Berman, Robert, Cappiello, Angela, et al., "Antidepressant Effects of Ketamine in Depressed Patients," *Biological Psychiatry* 47 (2000): 351–54, https://www.amg-ketamine.com/wp-content/uploads/2021/06/6-Antidepressant.pdf.

207 **"difficult-to-treat depression":** Tiger, Mikael, "A Randomized Placebo-Controlled PET Study of Ketamine's Effect on Serotonin1B Receptor Binding in Patients with SSRI-Resistant Depression," *Translational Psychiatry* (2020): art. 159, https://www.nature.com/articles/s41398-020-0844-4.

208 **"I think if you put ketamine":** "A Brief Chat with Dr. Karl Jansen," Scotto, http://scotto.org/listing.php?id=178, accessed October 23, 2022.

209 **Could ketamine be the answer?:** Baby Monster LLC v. PCVI LLC, Richard Hsieh and Andrew Hsieh, A-21--828090-C, Eighth Judicial District Court, Nevada, August 23, 2021, PCVI LLC's Answer to Second Amended Complaint, Counterclaim, Third Party Complaint and Demand for Jury Trial (n.d.).

209 **two hundred thousand attendees:** Kim, Kyndell, "Thousands Expected for 'Life Is Beautiful' Music Festival in Las Vegas," KTNV, September 20, 2019, https://news3lv.com/news/local/thousands-expected-for-life-is-beautiful-music-festival-in-las-vegas.

Chapter 20: Winter Camp

214 **What he witnessed:** Interview with anonymous source.

214 **But now he was acting in a manic manner:** Baby Monster LLC v. PCVI LLC, Richard Hsieh and Andrew Hsieh, A-21-828090-C, Eighth Judicial District Court, Nevada, August 23, 2021, PCVI LLC's Answer to Second Amended Complaint, Counterclaim, Third Party Complaint and Demand for Jury Trial (n.d.).

214 **sleep patterns on his Apple Watch:** Interview with anonymous source.

215 **came across a study:** Deng, Xianhua, "Long-term Follow-up of Patients Treated for Psychotic Symptoms That Persist After Stopping Illicit Drug Use," *Shanghai Archives of Psychiatry* 24, no. 5 (2012): 271–78, https://www.ncbi.nlm.nih.gov/pmc/articles/PMC4198875/.

215 **"I liked the concepts of the tribes":** Provided by anonymous source.

216 **"If you put a little bit of right spin":** Interview with Mark Guadagnoli, April 10, 2021.

216 **Justin sent him a message:** Interview with anonymous source.

216 **"Either you knew it and you're a liar":** Interview with anonymous source.

217 **Looking bewildered, Ryan walked around:** Interview with anonymous source.

217 **"There's no other way to put it":** Interview with Michelle D'Attilio, June 15, 2021.

217 **"I'm worried about you":** Interview with Michelle D'Attilio, June 15, 2021.

218 **asking for daily updates:** Interview with anonymous source.

218 **agreed not to alert Amazon:** Interview with anonymous source.

219 **Holding a stretching stick covered in Post-it notes:** Video provided by anonymous source.

219 **increasingly agitated by Tyler's concern:** Baby Monster LLC v. PCVI LLC, Richard Hsieh and Andrew Hsieh, A-21-828090-C, Eighth Judicial District Court, Nevada, August 23, 2021, PCVI LLC's Answer to Second Amended Complaint, Counterclaim, Third Party Complaint and Demand for Jury Trial (n.d.).

Chapter 21: Flow State

221 **Silicon Valley became a regular presence at Sundance:** Wu, Tim, "Silicon Valley Takes on Hollywood—at Sundance," *Slate*, January 23, 2012, https://slate.com/culture/2012/01/silicon-valley-at-the-sundance-film-festival-tech-companies-taking-on-hollywood.html.

221 Google would host concerts: "Civil Wars to Headline Google Music Series at Sundance," *Rolling Stone*, January 13, 2012.

221 Bing: Wu, "Silicon Valley Takes on Hollywood."

222 a digital content company called HitRecord: "HITRECORD Returns to Sundance Film Festival 2020 to Celebrate Its Vibrant Community with Live Projects, in Collaboration with Zappos," press release, December 19, 2019, https://www.prnewswire.com/news-releases/hitrecord-returns-to-sundance-film-festival-2020-to-celebrate-its-vibrant-community-with-live-projects-in-collaboration-with-zappos-300977684.html.

222 Zappos's ten core values: "Announcing HITRECORD x Zappos at the Sundance Film Festival," HitRecord, December 19, 2019, https://hitrecord.org/records/4099581.

222 even stayed on a bunk bed: Interview with Victoria Recano, April 19, 2021.

222 Abdul tweeted: Paula Abdul, @PaulaAbdul, "A trip to Sundance and @Zappos all in one week," Twitter, January 30, 2020, https://twitter.com/paulaabdul/status/1223068569694605312.

223 "I wish I had a Tyler coin": Interview with anonymous source.

223 asked him to write a list of all the things: Baby Monster LLC v. PCVI LLC, Richard Hsieh and Andrew Hsieh, A-21-828090-C, Eighth Judicial District Court, Nevada, August 23, 2021, PCVI LLC's Answer to Second Amended Complaint, Counterclaim, Third Party Complaint and Demand for Jury Trial (n.d.).

224 The list continued: Reference to this list is cited in Baby Monster LLC v. PCVI LLC, Richard Hsieh and Andrew Hsieh, A-21-828090-C, Eighth Judicial District Court Nevada, August 23, 2021, PCVI LLC's Answer to Second Amended Complaint, Counterclaim, Third Party Complaint and Demand for Jury Trial (n.d.)

226 Tony was able to use his phone: Baby Monster LLC v. PCVI LLC, Richard Hsieh and Andrew Hsieh, A-21-828090-C, Eighth Judicial District Court, Nevada, August 23, 2021, PCVI LLC's Answer to Second Amended Complaint, Counterclaim, Third Party Complaint and Demand for Jury Trial (n.d.).

226 The unassuming exterior belied a grandiosity within: Zillow listing, 1422 Empire Avenue, Park City, https://www.zillow.com/homedetails/1422-Empire-Ave-Park-City-UT-84060/89095788_zpid/, accessed October 23, 2022.

227 At first, they implemented a regimented program around Tony: Interviews with anonymous sources.

227 Over barbecues and meetings: Interviews with anonymous sources.

229 fifty-seven meters under an ice sheet: Weeks, Jonny, "A Cold-Water Cure? My Weekend with the 'Ice Man,'" *The Guardian*, May 8, 2019.

229 fastest barefoot half-marathon across ice: Guinness World Records website, https://www.guinnessworldrecords.com/world-records/fastest-half-marathon-barefoot-on-icesnow, retrieved August 2, 2022.

229 Mount Everest wearing only shorts: Odell, Michael, "He Swims in Ice and Climbs Everest. Meet Tough Guy Wim Hof," *The Times* (London), March 7, 2017.

230 180 years old: Kelly, Guy, "Meet the Man Who Plans to Live to 180 (and Has Spent $2 Million Trying)," *The Telegraph*, January 22, 2021, https://www.telegraph.co.uk/men/thinking-man/meet-man-plans-live-180-has-spent-2million-trying/.

230 Tyler and Tony would embark on so-called hero's journeys: Interviews with anonymous sources.

231 At 3:22 p.m. on the last Saturday of May: Luscombe, Richard, and Sample, Ian, "SpaceX Successfully Launches Nasa Astronauts into Orbit," *The Guardian*, May 30, 2020.

231 presence in his house of Brandon Hollis: Interviews with multiple anonymous sources.

232 **"We have to go faster":** Interview with anonymous source.

232 **Brandon approached Tyler:** Interview with anonymous source.

233 **Others turned their heads to steal a glance at him:** Interviews with multiple anonymous sources.

Chapter 22: The Gordian Knot

235 **"Pop quiz," Tony said, turning to him:** Interview with anonymous source.

236 **Expedia:** Expedia listing, https://www.expedia.com/Park-City-Hotels-Massive -10-Bed-10-Bath-Luxury-Mountain-Home-In-Old-Town.h54112819.Hotel -Information, retrieved August 3, 2022.

236 **Vrbo:** Vrbo listing, https://www.vrbo.com/1997020, retrieved August 3, 2022.

237 **Steve-O . . . steered his bus into Park City:** Interviews with anonymous sources.

238 **for a fee:** Interviews with anonymous sources.

238 **a virtual reality company:** Interviews with anonymous sources.

239 **Tyler found Tony:** Interview with anonymous source.

239 **destined to be a failure before it even started:** Baby Monster LLC v. PCVI LLC, Richard Hsieh and Andrew Hsieh, A-21-828090-C, Eighth Judicial District Court, Nevada, August 23, 2021, PCVI LLC's Answer to Second Amended Complaint, Counterclaim, Third Party Complaint and Demand for Jury Trial (n.d.).

239 **nothing but pajama pants and holding only a box of crayons:** Baby Monster LLC v. PCVI LLC, Richard Hsieh and Andrew Hsieh, A-21-828090-C, Eighth Judicial District Court, Nevada, August 23, 2021, PCVI LLC's Answer to Second Amended Complaint, Counterclaim, Third Party Complaint and Demand for Jury Trial (n.d.).

239 **he and Justin would spend only twelve hours in Montana:** Interview with anonymous source.

240 **The bus was rolling through the Montana plains:** Interviews with multiple anonymous sources.

241 **Justin walked back to the bathroom door:** Interview with anonymous source.

242 **and tried reasoning with Tony:** Interviews with multiple anonymous sources.

242 **active shooter simulation . . . suicide pact:** Baby Monster LLC v. PCVI LLC, Richard Hsieh and Andrew Hsieh, A-21-828090-C, Eighth Judicial District Court, Nevada, August 23, 2021, PCVI LLC's Answer to Second Amended Complaint, Counterclaim, Third Party Complaint and Demand for Jury Trial (n.d.).

245 **Around 4 a.m., Justin was woken by rapid knocking on his bedroom door:** Interview with anonymous source.

Chapter 23: Sticky Notes

248 **"Happy Fourth of July!" they called out to a group:** Interview with Tyler Davis and David Hill, December 15, 2020.

250 **Tony turned to the real estate agent:** Interviews with multiple anonymous sources.

250 **The sprawling ranch:** Zillow listing, 2636 Aspen Springs Drive, Park City, UT, https://www.zillow.com/homedetails/2636-Aspen-Springs-Dr-Park-City-UT-84060 /68846639_zpid/, retrieved August 3, 2022.

252 **Zappos executives were more than aware of Tony's troubles:** Interview with anonymous source.

252 **pressure from the company to take a step back:** Baby Monster LLC v. PCVI LLC, Richard Hsieh and Andrew Hsieh, A-21-828090-C, Eighth Judicial District Court, Nevada, August 23, 2021, PCVI LLC's Answer to Second Amended Complaint, Counterclaim, Third Party Complaint and Demand for Jury Trial (n.d.).

253 **Among the first projects Tony assigned her:** Video provided by anonymous source.

253 **Mark and Tony discussed the terms:** Mark Evensvold, Creditor's Claim, In the Matter of the Estate of Anthony Hsieh, filed June 1, 2021, Clark County District Court, Case No. P-20–105105-E.

Chapter 24: Old Friends and New

255 **The Hsieh family had already come and gone:** Baby Monster LLC v. PCVI LLC, Richard Hsieh and Andrew Hsieh, A-21-828090-C, Eighth Judicial District Court, Nevada, August 23, 2021, PCVI LLC's Answer to Second Amended Complaint, Counterclaim, Third Party Complaint and Demand for Jury Trial (n.d.).

255 **At one point Tony told them:** Grind, Kirsten, and Sayre, Katherine, *Happy at Any Cost: The Revolutionary Vision and Fatal Quest of Zappos CEO Tony Hsieh* (Simon & Schuster, 2022), 212.

255 **Ten days later he returned:** Baby Monster LLC v. PCVI LLC, Richard Hsieh and Andrew Hsieh, A-21-828090-C, Eighth Judicial District Court, Nevada, August 23, 2021, PCVI LLC's Answer to Second Amended Complaint, Counterclaim, Third Party Complaint and Demand for Jury Trial (n.d.).

256 **longtime friend Tony Lee:** Tony Lee and his company, Pelagic LLC, filed a lawsuit after Tony's death, detailing his account of events in 2020. See Pelagic LLC v. PCVI LLC, Richard Hsieh and Andrew Hsieh, First Amended Complaint, Eighth Judicial District Court, Nevada, A-21-833547-C.

257 **became convinced that inhaling nitrous oxide:** Baby Monster LLC v. PCVI LLC, Richard Hsieh and Andrew Hsieh, A-21-828090-C, Eighth Judicial District Court Nevada, August 23, 2021, PCVI LLC's Answer to Second Amended Complaint, Counterclaim, Third Party Complaint and Demand for Jury Trial (n.d.).

257 **the actress Demi Moore passed out:** TMZ, "Demi Moore Health Crisis . . . Inhaling Nitrous Oxide," January 26, 2012, https://www.tmz.com/2012/01/25/demi-moore -whip-its-nitrous-oxide-seizure/#.TyFWacVSRvY.

257 **hundreds of Whip-It cartridges:** Baby Monster LLC v. PCVI LLC, Richard Hsieh and Andrew Hsieh, A-21-828090-C, Eighth Judicial District Court, Nevada, August 23, 2021, PCVI LLC's Answer to Second Amended Complaint, Counterclaim, Third Party Complaint and Demand for Jury Trial (n.d.).

257 **Tony found willing comrades like Don Calder:** Interviews with multiple anonymous sources.

258 **Victoria produced another video:** Video provided by anonymous source.

258 **Nadeem had arrived in Park City:** Interviews with anonymous sources.

259 **Andy said later:** Pelagic LLC v. PCVI LLC, Richard Hsieh and Andrew Hsieh, Creditor Pelagic's Motion For Order Nunc Pro Tunc Concerning Order Granting Ex Parte Application To Accept Resignation Of Co-Administrator, Eighth Judicial District Court, Nevada, P-20-105105-E. Transcripts of Andy's depositions were part of the exhibits in this court filing.

259 **he wanted them gone:** Interviews with multiple anonymous sources.

260 **Initially, the first iteration of 10X:** Interviews with anonymous sources.

261 **Elizabeth and Brett would be getting a pay raise:** Interviews with multiple anonymous sources.

261 **she took 10 percent of the fee:** See Baby Monster LLC v. PCVI LLC, Richard Hsieh and Andrew Hsieh, A-21-828090-C, Eighth Judicial District Court, Nevada, August 23, 2021, PCVI LLC's Answer to Second Amended Complaint, Counterclaim, Third Party Complaint and Demand for Jury Trial (n.d.).

261 **set up an LLC with $10 million:** See Mr. Taken LLC v. Pickled Entertainment v. Jennifer "Mimi" Pham, Roberto Grande and Baby Monster LLC, A-21–829006-B, Eighth Judicial District Court, Nevada, Pickled Entertainment's Answer, Affirmative Defenses, Counterclaims, Third Party Claims and Demand for Jury Trial, May 25, 2021, 20.

263 **Lee wrote in a text to Andy:** Pelagic LLC v. PCVI LLC, Richard Hsieh and Andrew Hsieh, Creditor Pelagic's Motion For Order Nunc Pro Tunc Concerning Order Granting Ex Parte Application To Accept Resignation Of Co-Administrator, Eighth Judicial District Court, Nevada, P-20-105105-E. Text messages were part of the exhibits in this court filing.

Chapter 25: Who Will Save Your Soul?

264 **a group of residents were huddled:** Interview with Bill Ciraco, March 27, 2021.

266 **Jewel emerged from the far side of the room:** Video provided by anonymous source.

267 **Michael Downs . . . and Jen Taler . . . had arrived:** Interviews with anonymous sources.

267 **Tyler was going to . . . kidnap Tony:** Interview with Michelle D'Attilio, July 1, 2021.

268 **once he heard from Michelle, he notified the interventionist:** Baby Monster LLC v. PCVI LLC, Richard Hsieh and Andrew Hsieh, A-21-828090-C, Eighth Judicial District Court, Nevada, August 23, 2021, PCVI LLC's Answer to Second Amended Complaint, Counterclaim, Third Party Complaint and Demand for Jury Trial (n.d.).

268 **Tony talked with her and passed the welfare check:** Baby Monster LLC v. PCVI LLC, Richard Hsieh and Andrew Hsieh, A-21-828090-C, Eighth Judicial District Court Nevada, August 23, 2021, PCVI LLC's Answer to Second Amended Complaint, Counterclaim, Third Party Complaint and Demand for Jury Trial (n.d.).

269 **Mark decided to call the Park City police:** Interview with Mark Guadagnoli, April 15, 2021.

270 **Suzie turned to them:** Interviews with anonymous sources.

270 **When she received the invitation:** Interview with a member of Jewel's team, April 2021.

271 **The sound of running water, they were told:** Interviews with anonymous sources.

275 **On the night of September 8, police were called to the house:** Police report provided by Park City Police Department under Government Records Access and Management Act, Utah.

Chapter 26: On the Edge of the Ether-World

277 **one of his first memories as a child:** "Simon Sinek Talks Culture with Zappos CEO Tony Hsieh," YouTube, posted by Simon Sinek, August 1, 2019, https://www.youtube.com/watch?v=uqUx4BJ1ENY.

279 **Tony bought a convoy of tour buses:** Interviews with multiple anonymous sources.

279 **the company announced that Tony was stepping down from Zappos:** Schulz, Bailey, and Velotta, Richard N., "Zappos CEO Tony Hsieh, Champion of Downtown Las Vegas, Retires," *Las Vegas Review-Journal*, August 24, 2020, https://www.reviewjournal.com/business/zappos-ceo-tony-hsieh-champion-of-downtown-las-vegas-retires-2102935/.

279 **Michelle's phone rang:** Interview with Michelle D'Attilio, September 10, 2021.

279 **It had also deeply upset him:** Baby Monster LLC v. PCVI LLC, Richard Hsieh and Andrew Hsieh, A-21-828090-C, Eighth Judicial District Court, Nevada, August 23, 2021, PCVI LLC's Answer to Second Amended Complaint, Counterclaim, Third Party Complaint and Demand for Jury Trial (n.d.).

280 **One week in September, Justin told him:** Interview with anonymous source.
280 **Finally there was an excursion:** Interview with multiple anonymous sources.
280 **letter . . . penned by Jewel:** Provided by anonymous source.

Chapter 27: Blizzy
283 **"We're going to Hawaii!":** Interviews with multiple anonymous sources.
283 **somewhat of a power couple:** Interviews with multiple anonymous sources.
283 **producing a daily newsletter:** Provided by anonymous source.
283 **he had been taken to the hospital:** Interviews with multiple anonymous sources.
284 **A nurse had been at the ranch:** Interviews with multiple anonymous sources.
284 **Janice, back in Utah, received a call:** Interview with multiple anonymous sources.
285 **had just gotten off a FaceTime call with Tony:** Interview with Karla Ballard, October 24, 2021.
286 **in a cooler:** Interviews with multiple anonymous sources.
286 **A crew of firefighters arrived:** Incident report provided by New London Fire Department.
287 **She technically didn't own the beach, he told her:** Incident report provided by New London Police Department.

Chapter 28: Thanksgiving
288 **Vernon Skau had reason to hope:** Interview with Vernon Skau, February 20, 2021.
288 **A picture quickly emerged:** "Origin and Cause" incident report provided by New London Fire Department.
291 **Tom was vaguely aware of Tony Hsieh:** Interview with Tom Curcio, February 20, 2021.

Chapter 29: The Aftermath
292 **The day after Thanksgiving:** Interview with Michelle D'Attilio, November 8, 2021.
292 **"We'd like for you to write the post to tell the world":** Interview with Michelle D'Attilio, November 8, 2021.
293 **Bill Clinton:** Bill Clinton, @BillClinton, "I treasure every conversation," Twitter, November 30, 2020, 8:08 p.m., https://twitter.com/billclinton/status/1333578663380520961.
293 **Ivanka Trump:** Ivanka Trump, @IvankaTrump, "Celebrating the life while mourning the loss," Twitter, November 28, 2020, 11:13 a.m., https://twitter.com/ivankatrump/status/1332719265900879872.
293 **Jeff Bezos:** Instagram post, November 28, 2020, https://www.instagram.com/p/CIJYUQhHzLq/.
293 **twelve-minute video elegy:** Instagram post, December 1, 2020, https://www.instagram.com/p/CIQ_i8bnZIu/?hl=en.
295 **Mimi filed the first lawsuit in February:** Mimi's company is called Baby Monster LLC. See Baby Monster LLC v. PCVI LLC, Richard Hsieh and Andrew Hsieh, Complaint and Demand for Jury Trial, A-21-828090-C, Eighth District Court, Nevada.
296 **Paris Hilton:** Toplikar, Dave, "Paris Hilton Pleads Guilty in Las Vegas Drug Arrest," *Las Vegas Sun*, September 20, 2010, https://lasvegassun.com/news/2010/sep/20/paris-hilton-plead-guilty-vegas-drug-arrest/.
296 **Bruno Mars:** Ritter, Ken, "Bruno Mars Gets Date for Las Vegas Cocaine Plea Deal," *Las Vegas Sun*, February 4, 2011, https://lasvegassun.com/news/2011/feb/04/us-bruno-mars-vegas-arrest/.

296 **Robert Durst:** Bagli, Charles V., "After a 14-Month Delay, Robert Durst's Murder Trial Returns to Court," *New York Times*, May 17, 2021.

296 **The next week, Puoy Premsrirut filed:** Ferrara, David, "Attorney Seeks $360K in Legal Fees from Tony Hsieh's Estate," *Las Vegas Review-Journal*, February 16, 2021, https://www.reviewjournal.com/crime/courts/attorney-seeks-360k-in-legal-fees -from-tony-hsiehs-estate-2282089/.

296 **Two months later, in April, Tony Lee:** Pelagic LLC v. PCVI LLC, Richard Hsieh and Andrew Hsieh, First Amended Complaint, Eighth Judicial District Court, Nevada, A-21–833547-C.

297 **both Suzie Baleson and Justin Weniger:** Charns, David, "I-Team: Company Seeks Millions from Tony Hsieh's Estate, Some for 'Magic Castle' Project, Included Traveling Magicians," 8 News Now, November 22, 2021, https://www.8newsnow.com /investigators/i-team-special-reports/i-team-company-seeks-millions-from-tony-hsiehs -estate-for-magic-castle-project-included-traveling-magicians/; Newburg, Katelyn, "Life Is Beautiful CEO Withdraws Creditors Claim in Tony Hsieh Case," *Las Vegas Review-Journal*, January 28, 2022, https://www.reviewjournal.com/crime/courts/life -is-beautiful-ceo-withdraws-creditors-claim-in-tony-hsieh-case-2520681/.

297 **Only one statement:** Au-Yeung, Angel, and Jeans, David, "Tony Hsieh's American Tragedy: The Self-Destructive Last Months of the Zappos Visionary," *Forbes*, December 4, 2020, https://www.forbes.com/sites/angelauyeung/2020/12/04/tony-hsiehs-american -tragedy-the-self-destructive-last-months-of-the-zappos-visionary/.

297 **Andy was secretly in constant contact:** Interview with a member of Jewel's team, April 2021.

298 **doctors and attorneys . . . on standby:** Interview with a member of Jewel's team, April 2021.

298 **scorched-earth response:** Baby Monster LLC v. PCVI LLC, Richard Hsieh and Andrew Hsieh, A-21-828090-C, Eighth Judicial District Court, Nevada, August 23, 2021, PCVI LLC's Answer to Second Amended Complaint, Counterclaim, Third Party Complaint and Demand for Jury Trial (n.d.).

301 **Richard notified the court:** In the Matter of the Estate of Anthony Hsieh, Eighth Judicial District Court, Nevada, P-20-0105105-E.

303 **a poem:** Provided by anonymous source.

IMAGE CREDITS

Fig. 11 Portrait of Tony Hsieh with his book, *Delivering Happiness*. Bloomberg/Getty Images

Fig. 12 Tony Hsieh with Senator Harry Reid and President Barack Obama at a fundraising event in July 2010, courtesy of an anonymous source.

Fig. 13 Tony Hsieh judging Halloween contest, 2013. Ethan Miller/Getty Images

Fig. 14 Tony Hsieh and Mimi Pham, 2014. Michael Kovac/Getty Images

Fig. 15 Tony Hsieh and Michelle D'Attilio, courtesy of Michelle D'Attilio.

Fig. 16 Tony Hsieh at Bigfork, Montana, 2017, courtesy of an anonymous source.

Fig. 17 Tony Hsieh with Justin Weniger, Ryan Doherty, and Tyler Williams, courtesy of an anonymous source.

Fig. 18 Tony Hsieh with Fred Mossler and others at Zappos event. Denise Truscello/Getty Images

Fig. 19 Tony Hsieh cooking at Park City home, 2020, courtesy of an anonymous source.

Fig. 20 Andy Hsieh with Brett Gorman and Elizabeth Pezzello at 2021 Tribeca Film Festival. Noam Galai/Getty Images

Fig. 21 Photo of burned-out shed at 500 Pequot Avenue, New London, Connecticut, November 2020. Courtesy of New London Fire Department.

Fig. 22 Photo of backyard of 500 Pequot Avenue, New London, Connecticut, November 2020. Courtesy of New London Fire Department.

Fig. 23 Memorial of Tony Hsieh at Fremont Street Experience, December 2020. Bryan Steffy/Getty Images

INDEX

ABOUT THE AUTHORS

Angel Au-Yeung is a reporter for the *Wall Street Journal* and a former staff writer for *Forbes*. She was born in Hong Kong and grew up in California, the youngest of three sisters. She attended UC San Diego for undergrad as a cognitive neuroscience major and Columbia University for her graduate degree in journalism.

David Jeans is an investigative reporter for *Forbes*, where he covers the tech industry. He holds a master's degree from Columbia Journalism School and has reported for the *New York Times*, the Associated Press, and other publications. He grew up in Melbourne, Australia, and lives in New York City.